MERLIN
THROUGH
THE AGES

Merlin, the enchanter (Louis Rhead, 1923)

MERLIN THROUGH THE AGES

*A Chronological Anthology
and Source Book*

EDITED, TRANSLATED AND COMPILED BY
R. J. STEWART AND JOHN MATTHEWS

FOREWORD BY
DAVID SPANGLER

BLANDFORD

A BLANDFORD BOOK
First published in the UK 1995 by
Blandford
A Cassell Imprint
Cassell plc, Wellington House
125 Strand, London WC2R 0BB

Distributed in the United States by
Sterling Publishing Co., Inc.,
387 Park Avenue South, New York,
NY 10016-8810

Distributed in Australia by
Capricorn Link (Australia) Pty Ltd,
2/13 Carrington Road, Castle Hill,
NSW 2154

**A Cataloguing-in-Publication Data entry
for this title is available from the British
Library**

ISBN 0-7137-2468-4 (hardback)
      0-7137-2466-8 (paperback)

Typeset by Bookworm Typesetting, Manchester
Printed and bound in Finland by Werner Söderström Oy

CONTENTS

DEDICATION

To my own Merlin Emrys, with love.

J. M.

To the memory of Alan Barrett, who designed the production of *The Birth of Merlin*
for Theatre Clwyd in 1989.

R. J. S.

This prophecy Merlin shall make, for I live before his time.

William Shakespeare, *King Lear* Act 3, Scene 2

ACKNOWLEDGEMENTS

Thanks to Caitlín as ever for helping with last-minute things and for her translation of
the *Poem of the Lore* by Villemarque. To Ari Berk, bibliophile extraordinaire, for references to manuscripts in the Ashmolean Collection. To the folk at Leopard Press for
photocopying. To Eva Wilson for permission to reproduce the decorative motifs. To all
and any copyright holders (every effort has been made to contact everyone in this category; if we have failed to do so this will be corrected in any future editions in response
to their contacting us). To Blandford Press for permission to reprint some of the essays
from *The Book of Merlin* and *Merlin and Women*.

J. M. and R. J. S.

PREFACE
THE FIGURE OF MERLIN THROUGH THE AGES

ACCORDING TO THE Medieval French *Story of Merlin*, the last person to hear the voice of the great magician was Sir Gawain. At the time, he was in some difficulty himself, having been turned into a dwarf. Yet he still remembered to carry home to Arthur the last words of the mage:

> *Never shall no man speak with me after you, therefore it is for nothing that any man should try to seek me out.*

This last call, the 'Cri de Merlin' as it is called in some texts, still echoes in our ears, just as the figure of Merlin himself continues to exert a profound fascination on the Western world. Dozens of books, plays and films have appeared in recent years, which have kept the focus of attention on this remarkable being – a figure who combines the roles of wise man, seer, prophet and shaman, and whose story is one of the great native epics of Britain.

That Merlin is a British or at least a Celtic figure is important. While the Arthurian legends of which he is such an important part betray the extensive influence of French and Germanic storytellers, the story of Merlin, in its purest form, draws entirely upon native British traditions and beliefs. Despite efforts to trace his origins back to Atlantis, he remains essentially a Celtic figure, whose characteristics are traceable to specific themes within Celtic tradition.

Having stated this much, we should also mention the deep mythic and cultural connections between Merlin and the primal Apollo, both originating in the tribal prophetic traditions shared by the Celts and their cousins the ancient Greeks. The Greeks themselves had a tradition (quoted by Diodorus Siculus) that Apollo came to them from the land of the Hyperboreans, and this is discussed later in the book in 'Merlin, King Bladud and the Wheel of Life' by R. J. Stewart and in 'Mabon, the Celtic Divine Child' by Caitlín Matthews in Part 6. In the primal stream of tradition that holds the deepest lore of Merlin and Apollo, both beings are concerned with the light within the land, the sun at midnight, the Underworld. In later formal religion, Apollo becomes the deity of an arisen sun, while the medieval Merlin, whose texts hold many traces of classical Greek mythology and astrology, becomes a druidic figure, holding together many strands of wisdom teaching through the prophecies and tales associated with his name.

Merlin indeed represents a very ancient strand of wildness within human nature. He grows out of the tradition of the wild man who was seen, by medieval writers, as akin to 'natural man', a being somehow poised between the states of wildness and civilization, belonging perhaps to a lost golden age. This is especially poignant when we consider that Merlin himself strove to recreate that golden time, a perfect earthly kingdom over which Arthur, his protégé, would rule, guided by the mage's wisdom, protected by his magic, steered through the shoals of life on his way to winning the greatest of goals – the Quest for the Grail.

But these things were not to be, given the nature of humanity. The kingdom fell because the vessels – including Arthur himself – were too weak to contain the glories of the Grail. The great vision of the Round Table, built by Merlin himself – 'Round, in the likeness of the world' – where all men would meet as equals, fell away, broken by the internecine quarrels of the knights, the illicit love of Lancelot and Guinevere (strength and beauty personified), wracked by the bitterness of Arthur's son, Mordred, begotten of his own half-sister. Small wonder if Merlin chose to flee from this failure of his dream and to withdraw into his 'Esplumoir', the observatory built for him by his sister, and there to live out his days – perhaps into and beyond our own time – in study of the patterns within the heavens: a far more productive study than that of human frailty.

It is this atmosphere of possible glory crossed by impending doom which gives the Arthurian cycle its peculiar power to enthral us to this day. We know the torments and suffering of these human people as well as we know ourselves. Merlin, a principle mover in all of this, is bound to capture our attention, concentrating, as he does, so many of the themes of the great cycle in his person.

In our own time Merlin continues to re-emerge in a variety of disguises. He can be recognized in the character of Obi Wan Kenobi in George Lucas's *Star Wars* trilogy, in the figure of Dr Who in the popular TV series (indeed, in one of the last episodes to be transmitted, 'Battlefield' by Marc Platt in 1991, this is very clearly hinted at) and again in the powerful character of Gandalf from J.R.R. Tolkien's *Lord of the Rings*.

The most interesting thing about all of these appearances – as in the character of Merlin summed up in so many of the modern versions of the story discussed below in 'Merlin in Modern Fiction and Cinema' (Part 6) – is the underlying consistency of the characterization. Despite all the years which have elapsed since Merlin first walked the stage of literature and tradition, his personality has changed very little. He is still, to this day, a wise and generally beneficent being, whose actions and purpose, while seldom wholly revealed, suggest an ongoing influence in the affairs of the human race.

This is not primarily a scholarly collection, but one which sets out to give an overview of the truly vast literature of Merlin for the general reader. Thus, in the case of old and sometimes difficult texts, we have adopted the approach of either giving brief excerpts from the text or (as in the case of the prolix Auchinleck manuscript *Arthour and Merlin*) an extended abridgement. However, we have tried, wherever possible, to give details of reliable modern editions of the full texts, where these exist, to enable the interested reader to follow up on the material we have included here.

Many other texts relating to Merlin exist which, for reasons of space or because they were outside our brief, have been omitted. In particular there are versions of the stories in Old French, Italian and German which remain untranslated, and we must await the labours of various scholars before these can be brought into the area of the more general readership they deserve.

Indeed, it is an astonishing fact that as yet no full translation of the great *Vulgate Cycle* of Arthurian tales exists – though parts have appeared over the last 20 years. This work alone adds more to our understanding of Merlin's complex role in the Matter of Britain. Hopefully it will not be long before this great work is available to English readers in general.

Meanwhile, we offer this selection of texts, essays, poems and plays about Merlin to all those who love the myths and legends of Britain, and to all who have experienced, in whatever way, the power of Merlin for themselves.

R. J. STEWART, Bath
JOHN MATTHEWS, Oxford

FOREWORD

THE ONCE AND FUTURE MERLIN
by David Spangler

WHEN I WAS eight years old, my father gave me a book called *The Adventures of King Arthur and the Knights of the Round Table*. Like many young boys before me, I thrilled to the stories of Arthur and his knights, and spent many happy hours dreaming of being a knight myself, rescuing damsels and fulfilling quests. However the character that most seized my imagination was not a king or a warrior. It was the enigmatic figure of Merlin.

Excalibur, the Fellowship of the Round Table, Camelot: these were all parts of Arthur's story; they defined him as the unknown boy who became the king and sought to build a new model of civilization. But Merlin, to me, was outside all this; he was more than simply a part of Arthur's story. He seemed to belong to a different story, one that was older, larger and somehow more real. Merlin's story intersected that of Arthur, but neither began nor ended with it. Beyond Camelot, I was sure, there was another Merlin.

This is a book about that other Merlin. Perhaps it would be more accurate to say the other Merlins, since in these pages you will encounter many different images of this mysterious character. From shaman to sorcerer, from wild man to wizard, from adept to artificial intelligence advising a spaceship-riding Arthur of the far future, Merlin is shaped and reshaped to fit many stories. He is the once and future magician.

The magician is a particularly powerful archetype for our Western civilization. As the man of power who controls through will and knowledge the mysterious and primal forces of creation, he is the one who learns, the one who shapes, the one who is master. As such, he has been a paradigmatic figure for our civilization, a model or guide of what we should become and what, since the Enlightenment, we *have* become, though through science, technology and industry, rather than spells and conjurations.

Yet, when the magician is seen primarily as a person of power and the goal primarily one of control, an imbalance results. Something is missing. This, too, we see in our modern Western civilization. We have achieved capabilities of shaping nature that would be magical to our ancestors, yet we are paying a terrible price in the form of environmental and social degradation. We have fulfilled the dream of being the adept, but the dream is becoming a nightmare.

Perhaps this is where we need to look at the image of the magician more closely to see what we have missed. Merlin used his magic to help guide Arthur in creating a new kind of civilization, but though Merlin was powerful, the core of Camelot was based on right, not might, and on service rather than dominion.

I have three little figures that stand on my desk. Two of them suggest to me the transformation that needs to take place in our image of the magician, and by extension in our images of the nature and use of power. The first of these is a toy figure of Mickey Mouse in his role as the sorcerer's apprentice from the film *Fantasia*. He is a colourful figure in a red robe, a conical blue magician's hat perched jauntily on his head between his ears, one hand thrust back, the other, holding a wand, thrust forward in a gesture of control. He is in the process of controlling the powerful forces of the storm, the waves of the sea and the orbits of stars. He stands alone on the high mountain peak, the master of all he surveys, or so it seems. Yet, if we remember the story, this power is only a dream, and the apprentice awakes to find himself at the mercy of the forces he has conjured up and can no longer control.

To me Mickey in this role symbolizes the old image of the magician, the one our civilization has often taken to heart without fully understanding the consequences.

The other figure is that of Yoda, the alien Jedi Master of the Force from the *Star Wars* trilogy of films. He also is a magician-like figure of great power, yet his capabilities come not from dominion over anything but from integration with the presence of life itself. The Force is a field or emanation from all living beings; it is perhaps the life – the soul – of the universe itself. You cannot wield it without becoming one with it, so a Jedi Master is not separate from the forces he controls. Whereas the sorcerer's apprentice stands alone in awesome isolation upon the mountain peak, Yoda lives in simplicity in the midst of a swamp, surrounded by, and at one with, the green and juicy forces of life itself. He is more Zen monk or mystic than magical adept, yet all the universe is an open book to him and his power is as great as any wizard's.

Yoda represents an adept whose power comes through integration and attunement rather than through domination. In this, he resonates with the earlier images of the Merlin who is a servant of the land and at one with the forces of nature. If Merlin's beginnings lie with some legendary nature demigod, then, perhaps, as the circle closes back upon itself, that is where the future of Merlin – and of the image of the magician – lies as well: the adept who is at one with the world and whose power comes from that oneness. This is Merlin as Jedi Master: Merlin Yoda, one with the Force.

The third figure I have on my desk is even more interesting when thinking about the nature of Merlin. This is a small pewter statue of Merlin holding the infant Arthur in his hands, while about his feet curls a dragon who is holding the magician's staff. To one side stands a pedestal with an open book upon it. The expression of love and pride on the old wizard's face as he looks down at the baby in his arms would do justice to any father. Here is Merlin, surrounded by the symbols of his awesome power – his staff, the dragon, the book of mysterious knowledge – yet being vulnerable and human at the same time.

This is Merlin the Guardian, Merlin the Custodian, Merlin the Nourisher. This, for me, is the essence of Merlin. He is not one who acquires and wields power for its own sake, but one who uses whatever power or resources are available to bring something new into being, and to guard and nourish it until it is able to take its rightful place in the scheme of things, whether it is a baby, an idea or a civilization. He is power in service to unfoldment and evolution, power in service to new vision and new possibilities.

In this guise, Merlin is to me an archetype not only of a magician but of what it means to be human. If figures like Merlin have such power in our collective imaginations, it is because we intuitively know that we are all potential magicians. We all have the capability of shaping our world and we do so in innumerable ways. Yet, it is not the power to shape alone that is sufficient. We also need – and we also possess – the power to love and to be at one with that which we shape, and to allow it to shape us as well in a relationship of mutual growth and emergence. It is this very human quality which I believe Merlin embodies. He is not only the image of the powerful magician. He is the archetype of ourselves when we are most fully and nobly human.

The Merlin I first met as a child, Arthur's wizard, is a compelling figure. We do not do him justice, though, when we limit him to the image of a medieval wizard with pointy hat and magic spells. In seeking for and finding the much broader range – the larger story – which he inhabits, we can begin to find the true Merlin, the larger Merlin. In so doing, we may begin to have deeper and larger insights into ourselves.

The value of the work which John Matthews and R.J. Stewart have done over the years in their scholarship on Merlin has been to rescue this figure from simply being the wizard of Camelot, and to uncover his larger dimensions, and, by extension, our larger dimensions as well. This book summarizes that work in a magnificent manner. It is a tribute to the magician who has so haunted our imaginations for centuries; the once and future Merlin.

Part 1

THE EARLIEST MERLIN MATERIAL

INTRODUCTION

THE EARLIEST WRITTEN references to Merlin come from the bardic literature of the Celts and from the life of the Celtic Saint Kentigern. Both refer to the figure of a wild man living alone in the woods, driven mad by his witnessing of a battle in which his friends and kinfolk were slain. In the *Life* of Kentigern we hear of the madman Lailoken who is brought back to sanity through the actions of the saint. In a handful of poems attributed to Merlin himself (here called Myrddin; for a translation of these poems see below), there appears a fragmentary story in which, once again, the subject appears to be living alone in the woods, half mad and half inspired, occasionally attended by his half-sister Gwenddydd.

None of this material was written down before the Middle Ages, so it is difficult to say with any certainty how old the stories are. It was, of course, the pseudo-historian Geoffrey of Monmouth who, *c*.1134, made the Latinized 'Merlinus' into a household name by compiling the *Prophecies*, from which we have quoted extensively in Part 2 of this collection. When, in 1138, Geoffrey published his *Historia Regum Britanniae*, he included the prophecies again, and added a version of the story of the wondrous child Merlin, probably taken from the earlier writings of the ninth-century monk Nennius. This rapidly became one of the most famous and popular books of its time, something, indeed, of a medieval 'best seller', and the name and character of Merlin were forever after inseparably connected with those of Arthur and his Knights, whose deeds Geoffrey also chronicled.

The earlier figure of Myrddin Wyllt (the Wild) was soon immortalized by Geoffrey in his *Vita Merlini* (see Part 2), in which the story of the king driven mad by the sight of the death of his friends and family is repeated and elaborated. His sources for this story were almost certainly founded on earlier Welsh legends and traditions relating to the figure of the wild man of the woods – or, as he is termed in Irish tradition, the *gelt*. A description of this character, from the thirteenth-century Norse *Speculum Regale* describes him in such a way that a comparison with the materials gathered below leaves little doubt as to the similarities:

> It happens that when two hosts meet and are arrayed in battle-array, and when the battle-cry is raised on both sides, that…men run wild and lose their wits…And then they run into a wood away from other men and live there like wild beasts, and shun the meeting of men like wild beasts. And it is said of these men that when they have lived in the woods in that condition for twenty years then feathers grow on their bodies as on birds, whereby their bodies are protected against frost and cold.

It is this Merlin, rather than the more familiar medieval magician, who is represented in the material gathered below. It presents a very different figure, but one in whom we can none the less recognize the seeds of the character he was to become. We are told by various sources that the druids were composed of three orders or classes, *bards, vates* and *druids*. The druids were judges, with authority that was more than local or tribal. The bards were the preservers of knowledge, genealogy, poetry and the overall inheritance of culture and tradition. Vates, however, were prophets or seers, who wandered freely from place to place, were given respect and were treated with some caution. They were wild and mad, possessed by the power of prophecy or by the deity. The primal Merlin is, therefore, associated with this class of seers.

Interestingly, Geoffrey of Monmouth clearly describes Merlin (in the *Vita Merlini*) as a madman and a wild man, but he later describes him as a judge of princes, in other words a druid. At the close of the *Vita*, the aged (and finally sane) Merlin refuses to judge or advise princes who have come to him, preferring to retire to spiritual contemplation. It seems likely that Geoffrey has in mind the tradition that one became a druid only after having been a bard or a prophet. The bardship in the *Vita* is embodied by Taliesin, who hands on the wisdom tradition to the mad Merlin as part of his cure.

The earliest Merlin is both child and young man, driven mad by grief, suffering and the prophetic powers. It seems likely that *Myr*, meaning sea, or *Myrddin* meaning sea-man, is a title for a class of wild seers, rather than one historical person. Our modern English word mirth is derived from Icelandic and Old English, and Merlin is associated with mad laughter. The connection is loose, but poetically suggestive.

MERLIN THE ENCHANTER
AND MERLIN THE BARD
by W. D. Nash

W.D. NASH is best remembered for his important early study of Celtic materials in *Taliesin, or the Bards and Druids of Britain*, published in 1858. In the essay included here, which was printed along with Henry Wheatley's edition of the *English Prose Merlin* (see below), he turns his attention to the figures of Myrddin Wyllt and Myrddin Sylvestris, plotting a course through the complex pattern of their mutually overlapping development. In so doing he raises a number of questions concerning the identity of Merlin and the way in which his story spread and developed. Though his scholarship is dated and occasionally superseded by more recent work, this essay is still one of the best we have discovered on the origins and development of the diverse materials which gave us the figure of Merlin as we now know him.

In the Arthurian romance, the figure of Merlin the prophet and enchanter stands out as distinctly as that of Arthur the warrior and king. To the necromantic skill and wise counsels of Merlin, Arthur owes his birth, his crown, and his victories. The one represents the intellect, the other the force of the world depicted in these poems. If the origin of the British Arthur has given rise to an interminable discussion, the origin and native soil of the legend of Merlin are involved in equal obscurity. In the Welsh legendary history no name is so famous as that of Merlin, with one exception perhaps, that of Taliesin. The name of Merlin especially was assigned to the numerous spurious prophecies which were produced with a political object in the fourteenth and fifteenth century. But it is more than doubtful that the traditions in which the legends have been founded are of Welsh origin, meaning by Wales the country west of the Severn.

The legend of Merlin, such as it appears in all the mediæval romances, including the present one, has reached its full phase of development, through a set of intermediate changes, of which however we are unable to trace the progress, except at that point where it is presented to us in the form preserved in Geoffrey of Monmouth. The earliest notice of the marvellous boy, born of a virgin without the intervention of an earthly father, whose generation is ascribed to an incubus or spirit of the air, is found in the 'Historia Britonum', attributed to Nennius, written probably as early as the eighth century. According to this earliest authority, the prophetic child was called Ambrosius; the name of Merlin was then unknown, at least is not recorded. 'Rex autem adolescenti ait; quod nomen tibi est? Ille respondit, Ambrosius vocor.' Here a copyist or the original writer has added by way of commentary, for it clearly forms no part of the answer, 'quost brythannice embres guletic'; 'which is in the British tongue Emrys Guletic', i.e. King Ambrosius. The name Emrys is certainly a Welsh corruption of the Roman name Ambrosius and has no etymological basis in the Welsh language. The name Ambrosius was at the date of the 'Historia' a well-known appellation, and is expressly given by the earlier Gildas as the name of the Roman-British leader, 'Ambrosius Aurelianus, a modest man who of all the Roman nation was then alone in the confusion of this troubled period by chance left alive', and under whom the Britons took up arms and made head successfully against the Saxon invaders. Some strange confusion of the legends caused the author of the 'Historia' to identify the boy 'born without a father' with the Roman-British Ambrosius. 'Rursumque rex; de qua progenie ortus es? Qui respondit; Unus ex consulibus Romanorum pater meus est.' So Gildas had related to Ambrosius Aurelianus that 'his parents, for their merit, had been adorned with the purple.' The boy, moreover, is no longer the prophet or magician, but the king, for Vortigern at once yields up to him that city on the summit of the mountain Heremus in the province of Guenet (Snowdon in North Wales), and all the provinces of the western part of Britain. Farther on we find that Ambrosius 'qui fuit rex magnus inter reges Britanniæ', bestowed two provinces, Built and Guorthegirnaim on Pascent, the younger son of Vortigern.

It would seem also that the real birth and parentage of Aurelius Ambrosius, the king, were actually unknown, and however strange it may appear that in matters of so much importance and interest for the history of the times, the truth should have been unknown at so early a date after the occurrence of these events, and at a time when Britain possessed monastic establishments and writers not devoid of learning according to the learning of the times, it is certain that the utmost confusion and obscurity prevail as well as to the personages as to the events of this troubled period. Vortimer, the son of Vortigern, Aurelius Ambrosius, and Uther Pendragon represent in some respects one and the same person. Two traditions respecting the origin of Ambrosius and Arthur were current. The one given in the Amorican book latinized by Geoffrey of Monmouth represented them as of Armorican descent, but traced their lineage to that Conan Meriadoc, a chief of Britain west of the Severn, who had accompanied Maximus to Gaul to aid him in his struggle for the imperial crown, and had with his host of Britons been settled by Maximus in the Armorican provinces. The other legend, to which I am inclined to attribute a greater amount of historical truth, connects the two brothers who are fabled to have expelled the Saxon robbers from the British soil and in the person of their successor ruled over the whole western Roman empire, directly with Maximus himself. Certain it is that there are two Celtic – we may perhaps say two Cymric – localities in which the legends of Arthur and Merlin have been deeply implanted and to this day remain living traditions cherished by the peasantry of these two countries, and that neither of these is Wales or Britain west of the Severn. It is in Brittany and in the old Cumbrian kingdom south of the Firth of Forth, that the legends of Arthur and Merlin have taken root and flourished. Geoffrey of Monmouth represents Merlin as living in the country of the Gewisseans 'at the fountain of Galabes, which he frequently resorted to'. In Brittany his resort was the forest of Broceliande, in which was also a fountain of mysterious virtue. In the Vita Merlini, the Caledonian Merlin is described as seated, after his calamity, by the side of a fountain of healing waters.

> Fons erat in summo cujusdam vertice montis
> Undique praecinctus corulis densisque frucetis
> Illic Merlinus consederat; inde per omnes
> Spectabat silvas cursusque locosque ferarum.

The original locality of the traditions which have furnished the groundwork of these world-renowned romances is probably the Cumbrian region taken in its widest extent from the Firths of Forth and Clyde southward and westward along the borders of the Northumbrian kingdom, in which the famous exploits of the British Cymric struggle with the Northumbrian Angles became the theme of a native minstrelsy, transplanted into Brittany by the refugees from the Saxon conquest, and moulded into the romances with which we have been made acquainted, by the Norman trouvères.

M. de la Villemarqué, who has so zealously and successfully explored the legendary antiquities of Armorica, endeavours to connect the Breton name of the enchanter, *Marzin*, with a name belonging to the classical mythology, that of Marsus, a son of Circe, from whom were fabled to be descended a remarkable race or clan who were all reputed magicians, and especially serpent charmers, and mediciners. The name Marsus and Marsi became in the first centuries of the Christian æra a generic term for the serpent charmers or wizards. According to M. de la Villemarqué the name Marddin signified among the Welsh that which Marsus signified among the Romans; and more particularly a diviner or wizard sprung from the intercourse of a fairy or familiar spirit with a Christian virgin. In Breton the word *Marz*, derived from the ancient Marsus, signifies 'a wonder', 'a prodigy'; hence the enchanter or prophet is called Marddin or Marzin, 'a wonderful man'. These ingenious speculations do not appear to rest on any probable ground or to be supported by anything more durable than conjectural interpretations of mediæval Welsh fictions. M. Villemarqué's explanation also assumes that the names Merlin of Geoffrey of Monmouth and the romancers, and Merddin of the Welsh Genealogies, the Triads and the Breton ballads, are identical, and farther that

**King Vortigern and the youthful Merlin (Miranda Grey,
from *The Book of Merlin*)**

Merddin or Marzin is the original form out of which the name Merlin has been derived. It is more probable, however, that the Breton Marzin is simply the Welsh Merddin, and that the name was brought into Armorica along with the legends which had already confounded the Ambrosian Merlin with the Cumbrian bard to whom the prophetic character of the mythic 'son of the Nun' had already been attributed.

The most salient points in the original legend of the Vortigernian Merlin or Ambrosius, as given in 'Nennius', are the opinion of the Magi of the king that the blood of a human victim was required to render stable the foundations of the building whose walls fell to the ground as often as erected, and the supernatural knowledge possessed by the child intended for the victim. This knowledge the legend appears intended to intimate, was the consequence of the parentage of the child born of the commerce of an incubus with a nun, as learnedly expounded by the chief magician Maugantius, quoted 'Apuleius in his book concerning the Demon of Socrates'.[1] Mr. Herbert, in his notes to the Irish 'Nennius', has shown that the practice of auspicating the foundations of cities, temples, or other solemn structures, by human sacrifice was not unknown in the East. But it is very remarkable to find in the legend of St. Oran of Iona, in the land of the Celtic Picts, a statement of a similar practice at the foundation of a Christian church in the sixth century of the Christian era. 'By the working of evil spirits the walls of the church, then being built by St. Columba, fell down as soon as they were built up. After some consultation it was pronounced, that they never could be permanent till a human victim was buried alive. Oran, a companion of the saint, generously offered himself and was interred accordingly. At the end of three days St. Columba had the curiosity to take a farewell look at his old friend, and caused the earth to be removed. To the surprise of all

---

1. Geoffrey of Monmouth, Book VI., ch. 18.

beholders Oran stood up and began to reveal the secrets of his prison-house, and particularly declared that all that was said of hell was a mere joke. This dangerous impiety so shocked St. Columba that, with great policy, he instantly ordered the earth to be flung in again. Poor Oran was overwhelmed, and an end for ever put to his prating. His grave is near the door of the chapel of St. Oran, distinguished only by a plain red stone.'[2] Whether the statement be true or not, it is evident that both here and in the Vortigernian legend it is founded on a well-known and widely-spread tradition which is evidence of the actual existence of such a custom both in Britain and Ireland. St. Columba and Oran or Odhran were both Scots from the neighbouring island, though the locality of the legend is the country of the Cruithne or Picts.

The two curious ballads which have been, with others, published by M. de la Villemarqué,[3] depict Merlin as he has always existed in the minds of the Breton peasantry, and as he is certainly intended to be in the original legend, a magician possessed by supernatural powers, if not given to diabolic arts. The Welsh legends, on the other hand, ignore the magic and represent the enchanter as a pious Christian. The monstrous fable of the conversion of King Lucius to Christianity in the first century, and during the full dominion of the Romans in Britain, of his correspondence with Pope Eleutherius and his establishment of a Christian hierarchy in Britain, having once been accepted by the monkish writers of Welsh descent, it became necessary that all persons renowned in legend or tradition subsequently to the first century should be represented as Christians and saints. We find accordingly that Merlin Ambrosius or, as the Welsh call him, Merddin Emrys, is represented in the Triads as one of the three chief Christian bards of the Isle of Britain, the other two being the celebrated Taliesin, and that other Merlin of whom we shall presently have to speak, Merddin ab Madawg Morvran. According to other Welsh authorities he was not only the bard, but the chaplain of Aurelius Ambrosius, a skilful mathematician, and the architect who constructed the 'Gwaith Emrys', or work of Ambrosius, 'called by the English Stonehenge', on Salisbury plain.

This fiction that Merlin, the enchanter, was a historical person, a Christian clergyman, and the bard of the king Aurelius Ambrosius, has been adopted by M. de la Villemarqué, who has here certainly not displayed his usual sagacity, but has allowed himself to be led astray by the supposed authority of the Welsh Triads, to which indeed he, in common with most of the continental writers on this subject, attributes an antiquity and importance which by no means belongs to them. 'Ambrosius', he says, 'commenced by being the bard of Ambrosius Aurelianus, whose name he adopted. At first he filled, in the service of this king, a post similar to that filled by the poets in the service of the chiefs of the Celtic clans; but in advancing life, he resembled more the ancient British Bards or Druids. We may even assert that if any one in the British isle has represented in Christian times the *vates* of the olden time, if any one has enjoyed their privileges, known their secrets, preserved their traditions, led their mysterious life – if any one can give an idea of these enthusiasts, at once pontiffs, sages, prophets, astrologers, magicians, poets and national musicians, it is incontestably the bard of Ambrosius Aurelianus.'[4] M. de la Villemarqué in these observations attributes to Merlin a historical character, for which there appears to be no foundation whatever, and we ought, I think, to look upon the figure of the great enchanter as a pure work of fiction woven in with the historical threads which belong to the epoch of the Saxon wars in Britain.

2. Pennant's Second Tour in Scotland, cited in Herbert's Nennius, Appendix, p. xxv.
3. Barzaz Breiz.
4. Myrddhin, p. 32.

It is evident that in the original legend, as it existed in the eighth or ninth centuries, the wonderful child who afterwards developed into Merlin was identical with Aurelius Ambrosius, the conqueror of Vortigern. The name *Merlin*, afterwards applied, is an epithet derived from the supposed birth of the child, the offspring of a nun, Mableian, Mac-leian, Mab-merchleian, a name which took the Latinized forms of Merlinus, Mellinus, Merclinus. This in fact appears to be the epithet given to Myrddin Emrys in the very ancient stanza of *Englynion y Bedeu*, or 'Verses of the Graves', which is printed – [5]

> Bed An ap llian ymnewais
> Vynyd lluagor llew Emreis
> Prif ddewin merdin Emreis

translated by Mr. Stephens – [6]

> The grave of the son of the Nun,
> The companion of the lion of Emrys,
> The chief diviner Merdin Emrys is
> in Newys mountain.

The text of the stanza ought to be corrected to 'un mab llian, the only son of the Nun.' At what time the character of prophet and magician originally belonging to Merlin Ambrosius, the contemporary of Vortigern Aurelius Ambrosius and Arthur, was ascribed to that other Merlin called Silvestris or Caledonius, and by the Welsh Merddin Wyllt, it is difficult to decide, further than that it was in the interval between the compilation of the 'History of Nennius' and that translated by Geoffrey of Monmouth.

It appears to be historically certain, that about the date of the sixth century, there lived a personage who under this name of Merddin, or as it is written in the oldest Welsh form Myrtin, acquired celebrity as a bard, if not as one gifted with supernatural powers. According to the Welsh genealogies, he belonged to the same northern clan which furnished nearly all the heroes and personages of Welsh romance, with the exception of Arthur himself and his immediate ancestors, who are represented as of southern Armorican descent. So far from being of unknown or mysterious birth, the pedigree of Merddin Caledonius is as well ascertained as that of any other British celebrity. He was the son of Madog Morvryn, descended in the sixth or seventh generation from the chief of the great clan known to us by the probably corrupt name of Coel Godebog, and a kinsman of the undoubtedly historical chieftain and warrior Urien Rheged. The event which appears to have rendered him celebrated, and to have been the source of his fame as a prophet, was the circumstance of his having become insane, and consequently an object of superstitious veneration, after the disastrous battle of Arderydd, fought between the Cumbrian chief Rhydderch Hael, and another Cymric regulus Gwenddolen, the son of Ceidio. That some Cymric legend of this battle was current as late as the twelfth century, is evident from the Latin poem founded upon it, which under the title of *Vita Merlini* is attributed to Geoffrey himself. In this poem the confusion which had already begun as to the persons of the two Merlins is manifest. The Welsh had converted the name of the Roman *Mari-dunum* 'Sea-town', into *Caermyrdin*, having altogether lost the original signification of the name. By a very ordinary etymological process this Caermyrdin was derived by the monkish historical

---

5. Myvyr. Arch. i. 65.
6. Literature of the Kymry, p. 241.

writer from the name of Myrdin, the bard and diviner, *Caer-myrdin*, 'the city of Myrdin'. Hence it was to this place that the origin of the child born without a father, 'Mab-leian', the son of the Nun, was referred, and hence also the Caledonian or Cumbrian Myrdin was represented as a regulus or King of Demetia in South Wales, the country in which Caer-myrddin was situated.

> Clarus habebatur Merlinus in orbe Britannus
> Rex erat et vates, Demetarumque superbis
> Jura dabat populis, ducibusque futura canebat.

Merddin, the son of Morvran of Northern Britain, certainly had no connexion with Caer-myrddin (Caermarthen in South Wales), but, like all other British celebrities of the northern Cymric kingdom, he has been located by the Welsh writers in Britain west of the Severn.

Some authors, and among others Mr. Stephens,[7] whose opinions on these subjects are always entitled to respect, seem to have thought that the Emrys or Merddin Emrys of Vortigern and Merddin the son of Morvryn must be taken to have been one and the same person, and that the latter is the one whose character formed the nucleus from which the other was developed. It seems to me, on the contrary, that so far from the Caledonian Merlin having been either identical with, or the prototype of, the Vortigernian Merlin, the romantic fictions which belong to the latter has been ascribed to the Caledonian Merddin, probably for no better reason than the supposed similarity or identity of the names of the two. According to the old chronicler Ranulph Higden, in the fourteenth century, the Caledonian Merlin was buried at Bardsey, the island of the Welsh saints, in North Wales. The Ambrosian or Vortigernian Merlin, however, so far from having a known burial place, still lives in an enchanted sleep, to wake again when the time comes for the re-appearance of Arthur and his knights, to do battle once more for the crown of Britain. ...

[A] point in which the two Merlins are clearly distinguished is the association with the Caledonian Merlin of a twin sister, called in the Latin 'Vita Merlini' Ganieda, in the Welsh poems by the genuine Cymric name of Gwendydd, 'the dawn' or Aurora.

We may have noticed that the author of the 'Polychronicon' was acquainted with a different tradition of the cause of the insanity of the Caledonian Merlin from that contained in the Latin 'Vita Merlini'. In the former the event is attributed to the appearance of a phantom or monster in the air, in the latter to the grief experienced by the bard at witnessing the slaughter of his kinsmen in the fratricidal strife in which he was himself engaged, and which he had assisted to provoke. Among those who fell in the battle of Ardeydd were his friend and patron Gwenddolen, and the son of his sister Gwendydd. These unfortunate transactions are frequently alluded to in the Welsh poems attributed to the Caledonian Merlin.

In the romance now published, the personal history of Merlin, and the story of his betrayal by the fairy Vivienne, are the same as those ordinarily found in these romances. Another and a different reason for the disappearance of the magician is, however, given in the Welsh Triads, which commemorates the circumstance under the title of 'The Three Losses by Disappearance of the Island of Britain'. 1. Gavran, son of Acddan, with his men, who went to sea in search of the Green Islands of the Floods, and nothing more was heard of them. 2. Merddin, the bard of Ambrosius, with his nine scientific bards (*culveirdd*), who went to sea in the house of glass, and there have been

---

7. Literature of the Kymry, p. 209.

no tidings whither they went. 3. Madawg, son of Owain Gwynedd, who, accompanied by three hundred men, went to sea in ten ships, and it is not known to what place they went. The story of the ship of glass was no doubt borrowed by the compiler of the Triads from some of the mediæval romances of the thirteenth century, such as that which attributes a somewhat similar voyage to Alexander, and to which there is a distinct allusion in a fragment preserved in the Myvyrian Archaeology, entitled 'Anrhyfeddodau Alexander'.[8]

The legend of Merlin's having been enclosed in a vault, or according to M. de la Villemarqué in an enchanted bower, by his false paramour, is however the more widely spread, though the locality attributed to the event naturally varies. According to some versions of the story the forest of Broceliande in Brittany, according to others Cornwall, was the scene of the triumph of woman's wit over the sage's wisdom.

> Meruelous Merling is wasted away
> With a wicked woman woe might shee be,
> For shee hath closed him in a craige
> On Cornwel coast.[9]

This tradition of an enchanter enchained in bonds of perpetual sleep may not impossibly be of far more ancient date than is commonly imagined; and perhaps in many of the fragmentary legends preserved in the Welsh language there are the remains of sagas dating from Roman or even ante-Roman times. A very curious British tradition has been preserved by Plutarch, which may perhaps lie at the root of the perpetual slumber of the renowned British enchanter. It is as follows: – 'A little time before Callistratus celebrated the Pythian games, two holy men from the opposite parts of the habitable earth came to us at Delphi – Demetrius the grammarian from Britain, returning home to Tarsus, and Cleombrotus the Lacedæmonian. But Demetrius said that there are many desert islands scattered around Britain, some of which have the name of being the islands of genii and heroes; that he had been sent by the emperor, for the sake of describing and viewing them, to that which lay nearest to the desert isles, and which had but few inhabitants; all of whom were esteemed by the Britons sacred and inviolable. Very soon after his arrival there was great turbulence in the air, and many portentous storms; the winds became tempestuous, and fiery whirlwinds rushed forth. When these ceased, the islanders said that the departure of some one of the superior genii had taken place. For as a light when burning, say they, has nothing disagreeable, but when extinguished is offensive to many; so likewise lofty spirits afford an illumination benignant and mild, but their extinction and destruction, frequently, as at the present moment excite winds and storms, and often infect the atmosphere with pestilential evils. Moreover, that there was one island there wherein Saturn was confined by Briareus in sleep; for that sleep had been devised for his bonds; and that around him were many genii as his companions and attendants.'

The expression which Plutarch reports as having been used by Demetrius the grammarian, 'that sleep had been devised for his bonds', may be reasonably supposed to have been repeated by that traveller from statements made to him by the natives of the islands which he had visited. The tradition has never I believe been before noticed in connexion with this subject, and though it may be only a casual coincidence, the expression above referred to certainly exactly describes the device attributed to the nymph who devised sleep for the bonds of the great enchanter of the Cymric people.

8. See the text and translation in my 'Taliesin', p. 253.
9. Collection of Ancient Scottish Prophecies. Edinb. 1833.

THE POEMS OF MERLIN

translated by John Matthews

THE FIGURES OF Merlin and Taliesin have much in common. Both are the product of mysterious births, both possess prophetic and bardic abilities, and both are connected to the Arthurian court, Merlin as Arthur's adviser, Taliesin as his bard. Their prophecies also have many points of similarity. They appear to be largely made up of compilations based on much earlier genuine prophetic material, to which later generations have added stanzas in the style of the original bards. If these are successfully isolated and removed from the extant texts, we are left with a good idea of the originals.

The prophecies of Merlin are contained chiefly in dialogues either between himself and Taliesin, or himself and his sister, Gwenddydd, who was herself recognized as a prophet. Apart from these there is a poem (or possibly poems) addressed by Merlin to a pig and to a particular apple tree beneath which he was accustomed to take shelter. All are set during a period of inspired madness, during which time Merlin lived as a wild man in the wilderness and was visited by various people in search of widsom.

The prophecies are, for the most part, of a general kind, referring to political events, battles and so forth – and to known events and people. These are identifiable as separate from the underlying matter of the poems, which deal with the story of Myrddin's madness, and of the period he spent in the wilderness attended by a pig (a creature sacred to the Celts) and remembering the terrible battle in which he lost his reason. He thinks also of his sister Gwenddydd, who has deserted him because he (apparently) killed her son, and of his enemies, who seek his destruction. Interspersed with these are prophecies of events which took place long after – probably in the eighth or ninth centuries, when heroes like Cynan and Cadwaladyr had replaced Arthur as the expected deliverer of the Cymry.

That some of the material relating to Myrddin has been suppressed is beyond question, so that we have little or no chance of establishing a full text of the remaining Myrddin poems. At one time these may have formed verse interludes of a longer prose account of Myrddin's life – such a one as evidently formed the basis of Geoffrey of Monmouth's Latin poem *Vita Merlini* (see pages 52–61) which tells the story in full and makes use of the above poem as well as others which belonged to the ancient sage of Myrddin.

In the *Oianau* (Greetings) several verses are omitted here, as being later additions made after the coming of the Normans. As it is, verses five to seven almost certainly belong in this category, though references to the Franks (Normans) may well have been inserted within the individual verses for those to the Saesons, Picts or Scoti. Much of the poem still clearly refers to the story of Myrddin Wyllt as it appears in the *Vita Merlini* – and to Myrddin's long sojourn in the wilderness, 'snow to my knees, ice in my beard'. The rest is a pitiless catalogue of battle and death: the final image, of the two bridges, somehow suggesting bridges of human bodies, which can almost never be sufficient until the end of time – a bleak prospect, as one might expect from the isolated spirit of Myrddin.

In the poem which follows, which is a dialogue between Taliesin and Merlin, the differences between these two major bardic figures becomes clear. The poet who wrote this piece, whoever he may have been, clearly recognized the individuality of his characters. The prophecies are again of a general kind, with several interpolated references to medieval events.

The reiterated sevens, the stark images of war and battle, bear the weight of truth. The two great bards strike sparks from each other as their *awen* lifts them into the realm where they can see what has been and what will be.

A Fugitive Poem of Merlin in his Grave and *The Dialogue of Myrddin and his Sister Gwenddydd*, which follow again the underlying theme of the poet's dark life, underpin the prophetic content. In the latter poem, the initital two lines of Gwenddydd's questioning make reference to her brother's actual life. It is possible that the end of the poem, which shows some evidence of Christian doctoring, may once have formed part of a separate elegy on the death of Merlin written in the voice of his sister. Certainly much of the imagery is powerful and unforgettable in its stark simplicity.

The poems have been translated before, notably by W.F. Skene in the nineteenth centruty and more recently by Peter Goodman. The former are far from satisfactory both in language or in an understanding of the meaning contained within the poems. In the versions of Myrddin's surviving poems which are given here in new translations by John Matthews, an attempt has been made to provide diplomatic versions in which the obvious interpolations have been edited out, giving an idea of the quality of the original poems. Such omissions are indicated by the presence of ellipses [...] in the text.

AFFALANNAU (Appletrees)

I

Sweet appletree, your branches delight me,
Luxuriantly budding, my pride and joy!
I will prophesy before the lord of Macreu,
That on Wednesday, in the valley of Machawy
Blood will flow.
Lloegyr's blades will shine.
But hear, O litle pig! on Thursday
The Cymry will rejoice
In their defence of Cyminawd,
Furiously cutting and thrusting.
The Saesons will be slaughtered by our ashen
    spears,
And their heads used as footballs.
I prophesy the unvarnished truth –
The rising of a child in the secluded South.

II

Sweet and luxuriant appletree,
Great its branches, beautiful its form!
I predict a battle that fills me with fear.
At Pengwern, men drink mead,
But around Cyminawd is a deadly hewing
By a chieftain from Eryri – til only hatred
    remains.

III

Sweet, yellow appletree,
Growing in Tal Ardd,
I predict a battle at Prydyn,
In defence of frontiers.
Seven ships will come
Across a wide lake,
Seven hundred men come to conquer.
Of those who come, only seven will return
According to my prophecy.

IV

Sweet appletree of luxuriant growth!
I used to find food at its foot,
When, because of a maid,
I slept alone in the woods of Celyddon,
Shield on shoulder, sword on thigh.
Hear, O little pig! listen to my words,
As sweet as birds that sing on Monday –
When the sovereigns come across the sea,
Blessed by the Cymry, because of their
    strength.

V

Sweet appletree in the glade,
Trodden is the earth around its base.
The men of Rhydderch see me not,
Gwendyyd no longer loves nor greets me.
I am hated by Rhydderch's strongest scion.
I have despoiled both his son and daughter:
Death visits them all – why not me?
After Gwenddoleu no one will honour me,
No diversions attend me,
Nor fair women visit me.
Though at Arderydd I wore a golden torque
The swan-white woman despises me now.

VI

Sweet appletree, growing by the river,
Who will thrive on its wondrous fruit?
When my reason was intact
I used to lie at its foot
With a fair wanton maid, of slender form.
Fifty years the plaything of lawless men
I have wandered in gloom among spirits.
After great wealth, and gregarious minstrels,
I have been here so long not even sprites
Can lead me astray.
I never sleep, but tremble at the thought
Of my Lord Gwenddoleu, and my own native
  people.
Long have I suffered unease and longing –
May I be given freedom in the end.

VII

Sweet appletree, with delicate blossom,
Growing, concealed, in the wood!
At daybreak the tale was told me
That my words had offended the most
  powerful minister,
Not once, not twice, but thrice in a single day.

Christ! that my end has come
Before the killing of Gwendydd's son
Was upon my hands!

VIII

Sweet appletree with your delicate blossom,
Growing amid the thickets of trees!
Chwyfleian foretells,
A tale that will come to pass:
A staff of gold, signifyng bravery
Will be given by the glorious Dragon Kings.
The graceful one will vanquish the profaner,
Before the child, bright and bold,
The Saesons shall fall, and bards will flourish.

IX

Sweet appletree of crimson colour,
Growing, concealed, in the wood of Celyddon:
Though men seek your fruit, their search is
  vain,
Until Cadwaladyr comes from Cadfaon's
  meeting
To Teiwi river and Tywi's lands,
Till anger and anguish come from Aranwynion,
And the long-hairs are tamed.

X

Sweet appletree of crimson colour,
Growing, concealed, in the wood of Celyddon:
Though men seek your fruit, their search is
  vain,
Till Cadwaladyr comes from Rhyd Rheon's
  meeting,
And with Cynon advances against the Saesons.
Victorious Cymry, glorious their leaders,
All shall have their rights again,
All Britons rejoice, sounding joyful horns,
Chanting songs of happiness and peace!

OIANAU (Greetings)

Listen, little pig,
O happy little pig!
Do not go rooting
On top of the mountain,
But stay here,
Secluded in the wood,
Hidden from the dogs
Of Rhydderch the Faithful.

I will prophecy –
It will be truth! –

From Aber Taradyr
The Cymry will be bound
Under one warlike leader
Of the line of Gwynedd.
Usurpers of the Prydein
He will overcome.

Listen, little pig,
We should hide
From the huntsmen of Mordei
Lest we be discovered.

If we escape –
I'll not complain of fatigue! –
I shall predict,
From the back of the ninth wave,
The truth about the White One
Who rode Dyfed to exhaustion,
Who built a church
For those who only half believed.
Unti Cynan comes
Nothing will be restored.

Listen, little pig!
I lack sleep,
Such a tunmult of grief is within me.
Fifty years of pain I have endured.
Once I saw Gwenddoleu,
With the gift of Princes,
Garnering prey on every side;
Now, he's beneath the sod –
But still restless!
He was the chief of the North,
And the gentlest.

Listen, little pig,
Don't sleep yet!
Rumours reach me
Of perjured chieftains,
And tight-fisted farmers.
Soon, over the sea,
Shall come men in armour
Two-faced men,
On armoured horses,
With destroying spears.
When that happens,
War will come,
Fields will be ploughed
But never reaped.
Women will be cuckolds
To the corpses of their men.
Mourning will come to Caer Sallawg.

Listen, little pig,
O pig of truth!
The Sybil has told me
A wondrous tale.
I predict a Summer full of fury,
Treachery between brothers.
A pledge of peace will be required
From Gwynedd,
Seven hundred ships from Gynt
Blown in by the North wind.
In Aber Dyn they will confer.

Listen, little pig,
O blessed pig!
The Sybil has told me
A frightful thing:
When Llogria encamps
In the lands of Eddlyn,
Making Deganwy a strong fort
Between Llogrian and Cymru,
A child will appear, leaping,
And the Franks will flee.
At Aber Dulas they will fall,
Sweating in bloody garments.

Listen, little pig,
Go to Gwynedd,
Seek a mate when you rest.
While Rhydderch Hael feasts in his hall
He does not know
What sleeplessness I bear
Every night –
Snow to my knees,
Ice in my hair –
Sad my fate!

Listen, little pig,
O blessed pig!
If you had seen
All I have seen
You would not sleep,
Nor root on the hill.
Listen, little pig,
Is not the mountain green?
In my thin cloak
I get no respose!
I grow pale because
Gwendydd comes not.

Listen, little pig,
O bit of brawn!
Don't bury your snout.
Love is nether pledge nor play.
This advice I give to Gwernabwy:
Don't be a wanton youth.
I'll predict now the battle of Machawy,
Where ruddy spears will shine in Rhiw Dymdwy,
– the work of contentious chiefs.
Men will sit, breasts heaving, on their saddles,
And there will be mourning, and woeful mein.
A bear will arise in Deheubarth,
His men will infest Mynwy.
A blessed fate awaits Gwendydd
When Dyfed's prince comes to rule.

28

Listen, little pig,
Are not the thorn buds green
The mountain fair, the earth beautiful?
I will predict the battle of Argoed Llewifain,
Bloody biers after Owein's assault.
When stewards dispute,
When children are perjured,
When Cadwaladyr conquers Mona –
Then the Saeson will be driven out!

Listen, little pig,
Wonders there will be
In Prydein – but I
Shall not care.
When the people of Mona
Ask questions of the Brython,
That will be a troublesome time!
A superior lord will appear:
Cynan, from the banks of the Teiwi.
Confusion will follow –
But he shall have the music of Bards to follow!

Listen, little pig,
Do you hear the birds at Caerlleon?
I wish I stood on Mynydd Maon
Watching the bright ones dance.
Instead I'll prophesy
Battle on battle:
At Machawy, on a river,
At Cors Fochno, at Minron,
At Cyminawd, at Caerlleon,
And the battle of Abergwaith,
And the battle of leithion…
And when this music shall end,
A child will come,
And the Brython will know better days.

Listen, little pig,
O little, spotted friend!
Can you hear the sea-birds crying?
A day will come when even minstrels
Will be sent away, without their portion.
Though they stand at the door,
No gift will come.
A far-flying sea-gull told me

That strangers will come:
Gwyddyl, Brython, Romans.
There will be confusion then!
And the names of the Gods
Will be taken in vain!
Fighting on both banks of the Tywi.

Listen, little pig,
O stout-legged, little one!
Listen to the voices of the sea-birds –
Great their clamour.
Minstrels will get no honour,
No fair portion theirs;
In a time when hospitality's repugnant,
A youth of strong feelings will come.
Then two Idrises will contend for land,
And their contention will be long.

Listen, little pig,
It's no use my hearing,
The scream of the gulls.
My hair is thin,
My covering likewise.
The vales are my barn –
Short on corn.
My summer harvest
Brings little relief.
Once my passion was boundless;
Now I predict,
Before the world ends,
Shameless women,
Passionless men!

Listen, little pig,
O little trembling one!
Under this thin blanket,
I find no repose.
Since the battle of Arderydd
I no longer care,
If the sky falls
Or the seas overflows.
But I predict that after many kings
With one bridge on the Taw
And another on the Tywi,
There will be an end to war.

The Dialogue of Myrddin and Taliesin

Myrddin

How sad with me, how sad,
Cedfyl and Cadfan are fallen!
The slaughter was terrible,
Shields shattered and bloody.

Taliesin

I saw Maelgwn battling –
The host acclaimed him.

Myrddin

Before two men in battles they gather,
Before Erith and Gwrith on pale horses.
Slender bay mounts will they bring,
Soon will come the host of Elgan.
Alas for his death, after a great journey!

Taliesin

Gap-toothed Rhys, his shield a span –
To him came battle's blessing.
Cyndur has fallen, deplorable beyond
    measure.
Generous men have been slain –
Three notable men, greatly esteemed by
    Elgan.

Myrddin

Again and again, in great throngs they came,
There came Bran and Melgan to meet me.
At the last, they slew Dyel,
The son of Erbin, with all his men.

Taliesin

Swiftly came Maelgwn's men,
Warriors ready for battle, for slaughter armed.
For this battle, Arderydd, they have made
A lifetime of preparation.

Myrddin

A host of spears fly high, drawing blood
From a host of vigorous warriors –
A host, fleeing; a host, wounded –
A host, bloody, retreating.

Taliesin

The seven sons of Elifer, seven heroes,
Will fail to avoid seven spears in the battle.

Myrddin

Seven fires, seven armies,
Cynfelyn in every seventh place.

Taliesin

Seven spears, seven rivers of blood
From seven chieftains, fallen.

Myrddin

Seven score heroes, maddened by battle,
To the forest of Celyddon they fled.
Since I, Myrddin, am second only to Taliesin,
Let my words be heard as truth.

A Fugetive Poem of Myrddin in his Grave

He who speaks from the grave
Knows that before seven years
March will die.

I have drunk from a bright cup
With fierce and warlike lords;
My name is Myrddin, son of Morvran.

I have drunk from a goblet
With powerful warlords;
Myrddin is my given name.

When the black wheel of oppression
Comes to destroy exhausted Llogres
Defence will be bitter and sustained.
The White Mount will see sorrow
A long regret to the people of the Cymry.

Protection won't be found
From the Boar of the Hosts,
Even in the heights of Ardudwy
Or the Cymry's secret ports.

When the red Norman comes
And a castle is built at Aber Hodni
Greatly taxed will be the Llogrians –
Even predictions will be costly.

When the Freckled One comes
As far as Ryd Bengarn,
Men will face disgrace,
Their sword-hilts will break,
The new King of Prydain
Will be their judge.

When Henri comes to claim
Mur Castell on Eryri's border
Trouble across the sea will call him.

When the Pale One comes to London
Upon ugly horses
He will call out the lords of Caergain.

Scarce the acorns, thick the corn
When a young king appears
Who will cause men to tremble.

A youth of great renown
Conqueror of a hundred cities –
Tender and frail will be his life.

Strong to the weak will he be
Weak towards the strong of the upland –
One whose coming will bring dark days.

Wantonness will rule,
Women will be easy prey –
Even children will need to confess.
A time of order will follow
When even churls will do good deeds;
Maidens will be lovely
Youths resolute.

A time will follow, towards the end of the age,
When the young will fail from adversity
And cuckoos die in Maytime.

There will be a time of great hunting dogs,
And buildings in secret places,
When even a shirt will cost a fortune.

There will be a time of great profanity,
When vices are active, and churches empty.
Words and relics will be broken
Truth will vanish, falsehood spread
Faith will grow weak, and disputes abound.

There will be a time when everyone delights
    in clothing
When the lord's counsellors become like
    vagrants;

Bards will go empty-handed, through priests
    will be happy;
Men will be despised, and frequently refused.

There will be a time of windless days,
    without rain,
With little ploughing and less food,
One acre of land worth nine.

Men will be weak and unmanly
And corn grown under trees –
Though feasts will still occur.

When trees are held in high estate
There will be a new spring
An evil king –
The cowhouse worse than a single stake.

On Wednesday, a time of violence,
Blades will wear out,
Two will be bloodied at Cynghen.

At Aber Sor there will be a council
Of men following on the battle,
A bright ruler ruling the camp.

In Aber Avon the host of Mona congregate
Angles gather at Hinwedon;
Meryon's valour will be long remembered.

In Aber Dwyver the leader will fail
When the actions of Gwidig occur
After the battle of Cyvarllug.

A battle will be on the River Byrri,
Where Britons will have victory;
Gwhyr's men will be heroes.

An Aber Don a battle will occur
And the spears be unequal.
Blood on the brows of Saxons.
Servile you are today, Gwenddydd!

The mountain-spirits come to me
Here in Aber Carav.

A Dialogue Between Myrddyn and his Sister Gwenddydd

Gwenddydd

I have come hither to tell
Of the jurisdiction I have in the North;
Every region's beauty is known to me.

Myrddin

Since the action at Arderydd and Erydon
Gwendydd, and all that happened to me,
Dull of understanding I am –
Where shall I go for delight?

Gwenddydd

I will speak to my twin brother
Myrddin, wiseman and diviner,
Since he is used to making disclosures
When a girl goes to him.

Myrddin

I shall become a simpleton's song,
Ominous with the fears of the Cymry. The
     wind tells me
Rydderch Hael's standard cannot fall.

Gwenddydd

Though Rydderch is pre-eminent
And all the Cymry beneath him –
Who can possibly follow him?

Myrddin

Rydderch Hael, feller of foes,
Dealt out stabs aplenty
On the blissful day at the ford of Tawy.

Gwenddydd

Rydderch Hael, while he is the enemy
Of the bardic city in Clyd
Where will he come to the ford?

Myrddin

I will tell the fair Gwenddydd
Since she has asked so skilfully –
After tomorrow Rydderch will cease to be.

Gwenddydd

I ask my far-famed twin,
Intrepid battler,
Who comes after Rydderch?

Myrddin

As Gwenddoleu was slain at bloody Ardderyd,
And I have come from amid the furz –
Morgant Mawr, son of Sadyrnin.

Gwenddydd

I ask my far-famed brother,
Who fosters song amid the streams –
Who will rule after Morgant?

Myrddin

As Gwenddoleu was slain at bloody Ardderyd,
And as I wonder why anyone should see me –
The country will call to Urien.

Gwenddydd

As your hair is white as hoar-frost
And God has answered your need –
Who will rule after Urien?

Myrddin

Great affliction has fallen upon me,
And I am sick of life –
Maelgwyn Hir will rule over Gwynedd.

Gwenddydd

I pine every time I leave my brother,
Tears furrow my tired cheek –
After Maelgwyn who will rule?

Myrddin

Rhun is his name, impetuous in battle,
Foremost in the rank of the army –
Woe to Prydain when his day dawns.

Gwenddydd

As both friend and companion of slaughter
Men will name you leader –
Who will rule Gwynedd after Rhun?

Myrddin

Rhun, renowned in battle!
What I say will come to pass!
Gwynedd will fall next to Beli.

Gwenddydd

I ask my far-famed twin brother
Stalwart in the face of hardship –
Who rules after Beli?

Myrddin

Since mountain spirits have taken my reason
And I myself am full of thoughts –
After Beli, his son Iago.

Gwenddydd

Since mountain spirits have taken your
	reason,
And you are filled with thoughts –
Who will rule after Iago?

Myrddin

He that comes before me with a lofty brow,
Seeking social advancement –
After Iago, his son Cadvan.

Gwenddydd

Your words have always predicted
That one of universal fame shall appear –
Who will rule after Cadvan ?

Myrddin

The whole world shall hear of Brave
	Cadwallawn.
The heads of his enemeies shall fall
And the whole world will admire it.

Gwenddydd

Though I see tears on your cheeks,
I am bound to ask –
Who will come after Cadwallawn?

Myrddin

A tall man conferring with others
All of Prydain under one rule –
The Cymry's best son, Cadwaladyr.

Whoever comes after one so great
Is he not worthless?
After Cadwaladyr, Idwal.

Gwenddydd

I ask you gently,
far-famed, best of men –
Who will rule after Idwal?

Myrddin

There will rule after Idwal
As a result of another being summoned
White-shielded Howel, Cadwal's son.

Gwenddydd

I ask my far-famed twin brother,
Brave in war –
Who will come after Howel?

Myrddin

I will tell of his great fame,
Gwenddydd, before our parting,
After Howel, Rodri.

Cynan will come to Mona
Failing in his authority;
And before the son of Rodri is called
The son of Caeledigan will appear.

Gwenddydd

On the world's account I ask
And answer me gently if you will –
Who will rule after Cynan?

Myrddin

Since Gwenddoleu was slain at Ardderyd
You feel only fear –
Mervyn Vrych, from Manaw.

Gwenddydd

I will ask my renowned brother
Lucid in song, the best of men
Who will come after Mervyn?

Myrddin

I will declare, not with anger,
but from concern – Prydain will be oppressed:
After Mervyn will come Rodri Mawr.

Gwenddydd

I will ask my far-famed twin brother,
Intrepid at the sound of the war-cry
Who will rule after Rodri Mawr.

Myrddin

On Conway's banks in the midst of the
	conflict
Admired will be the eloquent lord –
Anarawd – the aged sovereign.

Gwenddydd

I will address my far-famed twin brother,
Who faced the mockers bravely –
Who will rule after Anarawd?

Myrddin

He who comes next
Is nearer the time of the unseen visitors –
Sovereignty will be in the hands of Howel.

The Borderers, men who hold back,
Will never reach Paradise –
Church or laity, both are as bad.

Gwenddydd

I will ask my beloved brother
Whom I have heard often celebrated –
Who will rule after the Borderers?

Myrddin

A year and a half to chattering barons
Whose rule shall be short-lived –
Any who stumble will be cursed.

Gwenddydd

As a companion of Cunllaith,
Mercy be to you –
Who will rule after the Barons?

Myrddin

One will arise from obscurity
Who nonetheless will fail –
Cynan of the Dogs will hold the Cymry.

Gwenddydd

On the world's behalf I ask you –
Answer me gently –
Who will rule after Cynan?

Myrddin

A man from a far country
Who will batter down our cities –
They say – a king from a baron.

Gwenddydd

On the world's account I ask,
Since you know the truth –
Who will come after the Baron?

Myrddin

I foretell the name of Serven Wyn,
A true and white-shielded messenger,
Brave, and strong as a prison wall.
He will cross the lands of the traitors
Who will tremble before him as far as Prydain.

Gwenddydd

I ask my blessed brother,
Indeed, I enquire it –
Who will rule after Serven Wyn?

Two white-shielded Belis
Will appear to cause tumult;
Golden peace will not be.

Gwenddydd

I ask my far-famed twin brother
Intrepid among the Cymry –
Who will rule after the Belis?

Myrddin

A passionate, beneficent lord
Who councils defence,
Will rule before a great disaster.

Gwenddydd

I ask my far-famed twin brother,
Brave in battle
Who is this passionate one
Whom you predict –
What name, what man, and when?

Myrddin

Gryffyd his name, brave and handsome,
He will throw lustre on all his kin,
And he will rule over Prydain.

Gwenddydd

I ask my far-famed brother
Intrepid in battle –
Who shall possess the land after Gryffyd?

Myrddin

I will declare it without rancour,
Oppression will follow –
After Gryffyd, Gwyn Gwarther.

Gwenddydd

I will ask my famous brother
Intrepid in war –
Who will rule after Gwyn Gwarther?

Myrddin

Alas! fair Gwenddydd, the oracle's words
Are as terrible as those of the Sybil
Of odious stock will be the two Idases;
For land admired, for judgement, vilified.

Gwenddydd

I will ask my far-famed brother,
Intrepid in battles –
Who will come after them?

Myrddin

I will predict what no youth will venture –
A king, a lion with a steady hand,
Gylvin Gevel with a wolf like grasp.

Gwenddydd

I ask my profound brother
Whom I have tenderly nourished –
After that who will reign?

Myrddin

To the number of the very stars
Will his followers be compared –
He is Mackwy Dau Hanner.

Gwenddydd

I asked my naked brother
The difficult key, the lords beneficence –
Who will rule after Dau Hanner?

Myrddin

There will be of tongues in the battle,
And fierce conflict among the Cymry –
He is a lord of eight Caers.

Gwenddydd

I will ask my pensive brother,
Who has read Cado's book –
Who will rule after this lord?

Myrddin

From Rheged he comes –
Since I am seriously questioned –
The whelp of illustrious Henri
Never in his time will there come deliverance.

Gwenddydd

I will ask my brother, renowned, famous,
Undaunted among the Cymry –
Who will rule after the son of Henri?

Myrddin

Two bridges there will be –
One on the Tav, one on the Tywi.
Confusion upon Llogres.
After the son of Henri
Such and such a king will bring trouble.

Gwenddydd

I will ask my blessed brother,
And it is I who ask it –
Who will rule after such and such a king?

Myrddin

A foolish king will come
And the men of Llogres will confuse him;
The land will cease to prosper under him.

Gwenddydd

Fair Myrddin, of fame-conferring song,
Wrathful concerning the world –
What will be in the age of the foolish one?

Myrddin

With Llogres groaning,
And Cymyr full of woe,
An army will traverse the land.

Gwenddydd

Fair Myrddin, gifted in speech,
Tell me no falsehood –
What will come after this army?

Myrddin

There will come one of six
Long hidden in concealment;
He will have mastery over Llogres.

Gwenddydd

Fair Myrddin, of fame-conferring stock,
Let the wind revolve in the house –
Who will rule after that?

Myrddin

Owein will come,
Right to the gates of London,
Bringing good tidings.

Gwenddydd

Fair Myrddin, most gifted and famed,
I will believe your word –
How long will Owein rule?

Myrddin

Gwenddydd, listen to rumours,
Let the wind whistle in the valley,
Seven years, as it was long since.

Gwenddydd

I will ask my profound brother,
Whom I have tenderly nourished,
Who will then be sovereign?

Myrddin

When Owein comes to Manaw,
Battle for Prydain will be close at hand,
There will be a man commanding others.

Gwenddydd

I ask my profound brother,
Whom I have tenderly nourished,
After that who will be sovereign?

Myrddin

A good and noble ruler will he be,
Who will conquer the land
And bring joy to all.

Gwenddydd

I ask my profound brother,
Whom I have tenderly nourished –
Who will be sovereign then?

Myrddin

Let there be a cry in the valley!
Beli Hir and his whirlwind warriors –
Blessed by the Cymry, woe to Gynt.

Gwenddydd

I ask my fair famed twin-brother,
Brave in battle –
After Beli who will possess the land?

Myrddin

Let there be a cry in the Aber!
Beli Hir and his numerous troops –
Blessed by the Cymry, woe to the Gwyddyl.

Gwenddydd

I address my far-famed brother,
Mighty in war –
Why woe to the Gwyddyl?

Myrddin

I predict that one prince above others
Will rule Gwynedd; yet after affliction
They will have victory over all.

Gwenddydd

The lord of Marvryn, how strong for us
Was Myrddin Vrych with his mighty host –
What will happen before this joy?

Myrddin

When Cadwaladyr descends
With a great host,
He will defeat the men of Gwenedd –
But then will the men of Caer Gamwedd come!

Gwenddydd

Don't depart from converse,
From a dislike of questioning –
In what place will Cadwaladyr descend?

Myrddin

When Cadwaladyr descends
To the valley of the Tywi,
Hard pressed will the Abers be,
Brythons will depose Brithwyr.

Gwenddydd

I ask my profound brother,
Whom I have tenderly nourished –
Who will rule after that?

Myrddin

When a fool knows three languages
In Mona, and his son be honoured –
Gwynedd will be rich.

Gwenddydd

Who will drive Llogres back from the borders?
Who will move upon Dyfed?
Who will succour the Cymry?

Myrddin

The great rout and tumult of Rydderch,
The armies of Cadwaladyr,
Above the river Tardennin
The key will be broken.

Gwenddydd

Don't leave me here
For dislike of converse –
What death will carry off Cadwaladyr?

Myrddin

A spear will pierce him
Made of wood from a ship.
That day will disgrace the Cymry.

Gwenddydd

Do not depart from me
For a dislike of converse –
How long will Cadwaladyr rule?

Myrrdin

Three months and the long years,
And full three hundred days
With many battles, he will rule.

Gwenddydd

Do not depart
For dislike of questioning –
Who will rule after Cadwaladyr?

Myrddin

I will declare to you Gwenddydd,
From age to age predict –
After Cadwaladyr, Cynda.

A hand on the cross of every sword,
Let everyone take care for his life –
With Cynda there is no reconciliation.

I foretell that one prince will come,
A prince of Gwynedd, after much affliction,
Who will over come all opposition. ...

From the time of Cymry suffer
Without help, and failing in their hope –
It is impossible to say who will rule.

Gwenddydd, delicate and fair,
First will be the greatest in Prydain –
Lament, wretched Cymry!

When killing becomes the first duty
From sea to sea across all the land –
Is the world at an end, lady...?

Gwenddydd

My twin-brother, well you have answered me,
Myrddin, son of Morvran the skilful –
Yet your tale is a sad one!

Myrddin

I will declare to you Gwenddydd,
Since you have asked me seriously,
Warfare, lady, will have an end.

All that I have predicted
To you Gwenddydd, glory of princes,
Will come to pass – to the smallest detail.

Gwenddydd

Twin-brother, since these things will happen
Even to the souls of our brethren –
What sovereign will come after?

Myrddin

Fairest Gwenddydd, courteous one –
I declare it powerfully –
There will be no more kings!

Gwenddydd

Alas, dear one! for the separation to be!
After the tumult to come
You may well be placed in the earth
By a king who is brave and fearless.

I am left cheerless by the thought
Of your dissolution –
A delay will be the best respite
For he who has spoken truth.

Arise from your rest,
Open the book of *Awen* without fear.
Hear the discourse of a maid,
Give repose to your dreams.

Dead is Morgenau, dead Cyvrennin Moryal.
Dead is Moryen, bulwark of battle –
The heaviest grief is for you, Myrddin.

Myrddin

I feel heavy affliction.
Dead is Morgenau, dead Mordav,
Dead is Moryen...I wish to die!

Gwenddydd

My only brother, chide me not.
Since the battle of Ardderyd I have suffered.
It is instruction I seek –
To God I commend you.

Myrddin

I also, I commend thee
To the Chieftain of Chieftains –
Fair Gwenddydd, refuge of songs.

Gwenddydd

Too long have my songs continued
Concerning universal events to be.
Would to God they had come to pass!

Myrddin

Gwenddydd, be not dissatisfied.
Has not the burden been consigned to earth?
Everyone must give up what he loves.

While I live, I will not forsake you,
And until death will keep you in mind –
Your fear is the heaviest blow!

Gwenddydd

Swift the steed, free the winds –
I commend my blameless brother
To God, the supreme ruler....

I will commend my blameless brother
To the supreme Caer –
May God take care of Myrddin!

Myrddin

I too command my blameless sister
To the supreme Caer –
May God take care of Gwenddydd!

THE STORY OF MYRDDIN WYLLT

THE TEXT WHICH follows here, in the translation of Thomas Jones, is taken from the sixteenth-century *Chronicle of Elis Gruffudd*, now in the National Library of Wales (MS 5276D). It is made up of two sections from this extensive body of material, compiled by Gruffudd, which traces the history of the world from its creation to the year 1552. Gruffudd compiled his material from many different sources, including French, English and Welsh, and in the latter included much original folklore and mythology which does not appear elsewhere. He tells the story of Merlin at some length, following in general the text of the French *Vulgate Merlin* and the *Vita Merlini* of Geoffrey of Monmouth. In addition he includes a series of dreams attributed to Merlin's sister Gwenddydd. He is careful to distinguish between the stories of Myrddin Wyllt and Myrddin Emrys, and in another portion of the manuscript states that Myrddin was widely believed to be a spirit in human form who appeared first in the time of Vortigern, again in the time of Maelgwn Gwynedd (when he was named Taliesin) and a third time in the time of Morfryn Frych, son of Esyllt, whose son he is believed to be. In between these times he is said to rest in Caer Siddi, one of the many names for the Celtic Otherworld.

This is an interesting attempt to reconcile the occasionally conflicting stories of Merlin and suggests that there was some recognition of Merlin as a spirit. Gruffudd also included the earliest written form of the story of Taliesin in his text and makes it clear that he perceived them as a single person – an idea supported by Taliesin's own words in the poem of his life which includes the lines:

John the wonderworker called me Myrddin;
At length everyone will call me Taliesin.

In the second extract from the *Chronicle* there is a fascinating dialogue between Myrddin and his sister which echoes the long poem given above. Gwenddydd is shown to be as remarkable a seeress as her brother is a seer and with Myrddin interpreting her dreams the two of them make a redoubtable team.

Of Elis Gruffudd himself we know only that he was born in Y Gronant Uchaf, Gwespyr, in the old cantref of Tegaingl, now Flintshire, and that he served as a soldier under the command of Sir Robert Wingfield. He was present at the Field of the

Cloth of Gold in 1520 and left a first-hand account of the events of that famous occasion as part of his chronicle. The original text, with commentary, was edited and translated by Thomas Jones in *Etude Celtique*, 1947.

According to the narrative of some authors there was about this time within the land which is called Nanconwy a man who was called Morfryn. But others show that [he was] Morfryn Frych, prince of Gwynedd, – which he could not be according to the tenor of his songs. Nevertheless the writing shows that a man of this name had a son, who was called Mryddin son of Morfryn, and a daughter who was called Gwenddydd. And as the story shows, the son was unstable in his senses; for at one time he would be witless and out of mind and reason, and at another time he would be in his mind, at which time he would be wise and discreet and prompt in his answers and good counsels concerning everything that would be asked of him. To him God had given the gift of prophecy, which [prophecies] he would declare in poetry in metre, when he would be in his mind, and especially to Gwenddydd his sister, who, as my copy shows, was wise and learned [and] who wrote a great book of his utterances, especially about such prophecies as related to this island. Some of these follow hereafter in this work, although there is hardly any profitable meaning to be gathered from any of them. But nevertheless, in order to ward off sloth, with God's help I will write down all those that I have been able to see in writing.

**The prophet Merlin dictating his prophecies to his scribe
(fifteenth-century medieval woodcut)**

The books show that this Myrddin was so unstable in mind and senses that he would not live within dwelling houses, especially during the three months of summer, but in caves in the rocks and in arbours of his own work in the glens and the woods on either side of the river Conway. To these parts and places Gwenddydd his sister would come many a time with his food, which she would set in a place so that he could take his nourishment when he came to his senses.

And at a certain time, as the narrative shows, it happened that Gwenddydd saw certain rare dreams on various nights. All these she carefully retained in her memory until she should find a place and time to relate them to Myrddin her brother. Against that time Gwenddydd prepared bread and butter on a herb cake of wheaten bread with various drinks in various vessels, every drink in its grade as its nature demanded, as wine in silver, and mead in a horn, and the beer in sycamore, and the milk in a white jug, and the water in an earthen jug. All these she placed in order besides the bread and butter inside the arbour to which Myrddin was wont to come, when he was in his senses, to take his nourishment.

To this part and place he came soon thereafter, as the writing shows. At which time Gwenddydd hid herself within the arbour or cell to listen to his declamations. At which time, as Gwenddydd shows at length, Myrddin took the finely wrought cake and the bread and butter upon it, to which he composed many songs. Of it he said:

> England will not muster hosts to every place;
> It is not from its centre that bread and butter is eaten.

And after he had eaten a portion of his bread and butter he complained to himself about drink. Thereupon Gwenddydd revealed herself to her brother, to whom she showed the drinks in order, as she had placed them in order. At which time, as [the story] shows, Myrddin asked his sister what kind of drink stood in the bright shining vessel. To which Gwenddydd answered saying, 'This drink, which is called wine, has been made from the fruit of the trees of the earth.' 'Aha!' said Myrddin, 'verily this drink is not suitable for me or for my people, for it is the nature of this drink to make such as are wont to drink it in these regions poor from being rich'. And after this he asked Gwenddydd what kind of drink was in the horn. To which answered Gwenddydd, who spoke thus: 'This drink, which is called mead amongst our people, has been made from water and honey.' 'Aha!' said Myrddin, 'much of this drink is not healthy for me or for anyone, for its nature is to make ill the healthy'. And afterwards he asked his sister what kind of drink was in the many coloured wood, to which Gwenddydd answered saying, 'This drink, which is called beer, has been made from water and from grains of barley.' 'Aha!' said Myrddin, 'this drink is not at all good for me, for its nature is to deprive the prudent of their senses.' And then Myrddin asked Gwenddydd what kind of drink was in the white jug. To which she answered saying, 'This drink is made from the produce of animals and is called milk.' Then Myrddin said thus: 'Verily this drink is good for me and my people, for this is natural to nurture the weak and to help the feeble and to strengthen the wretched and to increase energy for the strong.' And after this he asked what kind of drink stood in the earthen vessel. To which Gwenddydd answered saying, 'This is one of the four elements and it is called water, which God from Heaven has sent for the benefit of mankind.' Then Myrddin said thus, 'All thou hast said is true, and verily this is the one best drink till the Day of Judgement. Of this I will drink my fill to slake my thirst.'

And after this she begged of him to listen to her relating to him certain dreams which she had seen at certain times previously, begging him to interpret them and to show clearly to her what they represented. Upon which Myrddin asked her to state them, and she spoke as follows written in this work.

The First Dream

'My true brother and friend, of a night in my sleep I thought for certain within myself that I was standing on a great wide field which I saw full of stone cairns small in size and a few big cairns amongst the small ones. And I could see great numbers of peoples gathering the stones from the small cairns and casting them into the big ones without a pause. And yet in spite of this I could not see either the small cairns becoming smaller, however much I could see the peoples gathering from them, or the big cairns becoming bigger, however great the assiduity with which I could see the peoples collecting the stones from the small cairns and casting them into the big cairns. And with the marvel of the dream I awoke; but verily I cannot let the marvel of the dream out of my memory'.

How Myrddin interpreted the dream to his sister

'Gwenddydd and my dearest sister, do not marvel too much at thy vision, for no harm will come to thee from it. And be it known to thee that the field thou sawest represents this island. And the small cairns represent the husbandmen of the kingdom and its labourers of each and every grade who live lawfully and win their livelihood by the labour of their bodies, and who place their trust in God alone. And the big cairns represent the chiefs of the kingdom of each and every grade. And the peoples whom thou sawest gathering the stones from the small cairns and casting them into the big ones, represent the servants of noblemen who are and always will be ready to keep their servants to take the wealth of the labourers and the husbandmen without ceasing for ever, sometimes under pretence or semblance of the offices of the law, sometimes by force, sometimes by stealth. And in as much as thou sawest not the big cairns increasing however much the load thou sawest the peoples carrying from the small cairns to the big ones, that shows God's wrath and displeasure, for God does not allow the wealth that is wrongfully amassed to multiply with the gatherers and their descendants. And in as much as thou sawest not the small cairns smaller however much thou sawest the people taking away from them, that represents the grace of God, for it is certain that the noblemen of each and every grade oppress the common husbanding people for their worldly goods. And yet in spite of this, however much goods the noblemen and their peoples take from the husbandmen by oppression, the latter will not be the worse or the poorer; for as much as they may lose the one way God will send them twice as much another way, especially if they will take such oppression forbearingly with patience and restraint and by entrusting the punishment and vengeance to the Father of Heaven to Whom it is meet and rightful to punish all iniquity; for He ordained the weak and the strong. And verily, however much an innocent man may lose in this world, God will not allow him to want any wordly thing in this world, and an abundance of all goodness in the world that is to come. And verily this is what thy dream represents.'

And after this she showed him
the second dream, beginning in this wise:

'Myrddin the wise and my true brother, I saw the second dream, that is, in my sleep I thought that I was standing in an alder grove of the straightest and fairest trees which the heart of man could think of or imagine. Whither I saw great hosts of men coming with axes in their hands, and with these they were cutting the alder grove and felling them all to the ground from their trunks. And forthwith I saw the straightest and fairest yew trees which man could imagine, growing on the trunks of the alders. And with the marvel of the vision I awoke from my sleep, and from that to this day I cannot let it out of my memory.'

How Myrddin interpreted the second dream, speaking thus:

'Gwenddydd, my counsel to thee is that thou marvel not at the dream, for no harm or hurt will come to thee from it, for the alder grove thou sawest represents this island and its ancestral peoples, which [island] will be greatly impoverished, especially of its noblemen, whom the alder trees represent. All of them will be destroyed even as thou sawest the alders destroyed. Yet in spite of this, in the same way as thou sawest the yews growing forthwith on the trunks of the alders, so noblemen will again grow from the remnants of their lineage. At which time no wealth will remain in the hands of the noblemen, who will betroth their children to men of low rank, from whom there will grow mighty noblemen who will continue in that mode and state for a long time thereafter. And verily this is what thy dream represents.'

After this she showed him the third dream, speaking thus:

'My true brother, I saw the third dream, for as I was sound asleep I could see myself standing on a level circular strand upon which I could see a great number of high green hills or mounds. And to my mind and thought I could see the earth quaking so that the mounds subsided into level land. In place of these, to my mind and thought, there forthwith arose heaps of dung. And on these dunghills I could see various kinds of flowering scented herbs growing. There is a great marvel in my heart at the dream from that to this day.'

How Myrddin interpreted the third dream, speaking thus:

'Fair Gwenddydd, feel no worry in the matter, for the vision will do thee no harm; for the strand represents this island, and the mounds represent the chiefs of the island. And the quaking of the earth denotes that there will come war by which all the nobles will be destroyed in the same way as thou sawest the mounds destroyed. And the heaps thou sawest arising forthwith in their place denote that their dominions will be given to ignoble men. And the flowers denote that from these churls there will grow mighty noblemen. And yet it will be rare for the fifth descendant from the stock of these to possess the hearth of his father and grandfather and great-grandfather, for they will disappear like dung shoots. And this is the meaning of this dream.'

And after this she declared to him how she saw the fourth dream, speaking in this wise:

'Myrddin my brother, I thought at night in my sleep that I was standing in a park of the fairest wheat which a man could see with the sight of his eyes. The ears of the wheat I could see drily ripe and the stalks quite green. And I could see a mighty plague of swine coming and breaking down the hedge and coming into the park, where they caused grievous damage and destruction to the wheat so that the corn was level with the ground. At which time I saw coming into the wheat field a troop of white greyhounds, which forthwith ran at the swine and killed them nearly all. Because of the sight there is still a great marvel in my heart.'

How Myrddin interpreted the fourth dream,
saying:

'Fair Gwenddydd, feel no worry in the matter, for the wheat field represents this kingdom, and the wheat represents the people. And the ripe ears and the sappy stalks denote that men young in age will be whiteheaded at this time, which verily will be as rare a sight as seeing an ear of wheat quite ripe and the stalk quite green. And the swine thou sawest breaking into the wheat field denote that there will come to this kingdom a plague of foreigners who will destroy the people in the same way as thou sawest the swine destroying the wheat. And the greyhounds denote that there will come men who will avenge the whiteheaded people upon the swine; such of these as will have been left their lives the greyhounds will drive to flight out of the kingdom. And this is thy dream in full.'

And after this she declared to him the fifth dream,
saying:

'My brother, I saw the fifth dream, that is, I thought that I was standing in the middle of a grave-yard of exceeding size, which I could see full of girls or maidens of young age. All these I could see pregnant and near the time of their delivery. And I thought in myself that the children were conversing with one another from their mothers' wombs, which is a great marvel in my heart when I think of this vision.'

Then Myrddin said:

'Let there be no worry upon thee because of the dream. For this graveyard represents this island. And the girls or maidens denote that there will come a world and time when betrothals and marriage will be made between children under their snoods. Aye, and verily almost everyone of that age and generation will be married very young; and the children and offspring which will be begotten between them will be full of evil and cunning. And inasmuch as thou wert imagining that the children were speaking from their mothers' wombs, that denotes that a fifteen years old youth of this age will be wiser in that age than a man of sixty years at this time.'

Thus end the dreams.

Part 2

THE
MEDIEVAL
FIGURE

INTRODUCTION

THE MEDIEVAL FIGURE of Merlin is different in many ways from the character represented by the materials gathered in Part 1. Though he retains his role as a prophet, he becomes an enchanter as well, based in part on the figure of the Roman poet Virgil, who was seen as a magician by the medieval romance writers. In works such as Robert de Borron's poem of *Merlin* (*c*.1195), of which only the first 500 lines have survived, and the great epic *Vulgate Cycle*, Merlin becomes the creator of the Round Table, its prophet, and the guide and guardian not only of Arthur but also of the fellowship of knights who met at the table.

Chief among the texts which feature Merlin is the great work by Sir Thomas Malory known as *Le Morte D'Arthur*. This was completed in the fourteenth-century and remains the chief source for Arthurian literature. However, earlier versions exist, and apart from the extracts from Malory's book printed here, we have included four others: the *Vita Merlini* of Geoffrey of Monmouth; his collection of *The Prophecies of Merlin*; and two of the major English literary sources other than Malory, *The English Merlin*; and the powerful poem *Arthour and Merlin*.

Together these represent some of the best of the medieval writings on Merlin which have, far more than the earliest and primary Celtic sources, provided the sources for most subsequent literature. Only in the twentieth century have writers of both fiction and non-fiction begun to return to the earliest sources, and cut through the astonishing accumulation which has gathered, like layers of sedimentary rock, around the core figure of Merlin.

EXTRACTS FROM THE PROPHECIES OF MERLIN

by Geoffrey of Monmouth

THE PROPHECIES of Merlin have been almost overlooked by our contemporary craze for divinations and millennial pronouncements. I say almost, for the only modern edition with a commentary is my own (*The Prophetic Vision of Merlin,*

Arkana, 1986), now found in several translations. As is often the case, a prophet is not known in his own country, and though everyone has heard of Merlin, very few modern Britons know of his prophecies. While Nostradamus has become immensely popular with various editions and interpretations, ranging from thoughtful to banal or even ignorant, Merlin has been obscured by the range of fantasy fiction around his literary character. This is not a new obscurity, for the prophecies quoted by Thomas Heywood (see Part 3) in the seventeenth century are not the traditional ones, but something which he has compiled into verse from various sources, including his own imagination.

The true prophecies are a sequence of Latin verses, written down by Geoffrey of Monmouth in the twelfth century, but certainly not invented by him. While we can allow that Geoffrey elaborated some of the sequences to correspond to his own time and in the context of the political tensions of his own society, the bulk of the text is traditional. By traditional we should understand that these verses come from sets of prophecies preserved orally by Welsh or Breton bards. The bards were poets who retained the old wisdom traditions in verse and story form, and, despite the obviously pagan (pre-Christian era) content of much of their repertoire, they were integral to Welsh Celtic culture until as late as the eighteenth century.

An Elizabethan spy, sent out by Walshingham, concluded that when the Welsh gathered in secret on the hills to hear poets recite the prophecies of Merlin and the genealogies of the Welsh princes, they were not inciting one another to rebellion. The uneasy English dominance over Wales was not, it seems, threatened by these poetic gatherings, which must have been similar in many ways to the revived tradition of the *eisteddfod* as it is known today. This curious historical aside reminds us that the oral tradition lived on for centuries after Geoffrey wrote out the prophecies, including them in his greater book *The History of the British Kings*.

We can reconstruct the background to the text of the *Prophecies* that we know today: Geoffrey, a member of the privileged Norman ruling class, a churchman, but with a Welsh or Breton mother, could speak fluent Welsh and/or Breton. At this time the two languages were virtually identical, and we know that Geoffrey was a witty maker of puns in Welsh, for he uses multilayered jokes that work in both Welsh and Latin in his *History*, a huge book which he amplified from older traditional sources of legendary and factual history.

The *Prophecies*, however, have a less literary tone than the *History*, and have the feeling of verses copied down almost verbatim. My personal guess is that Geoffrey talked with a bard or bards, and that someone, perhaps a scribe who spoke Welsh in the first instance, or Geoffrey himself, wrote down the prophetic verses from recitation. They are not edited or polished and it is likely that even uncertain phrases or entire sections were quoted as they occurred, for traditional prophecies, in any culture, have a sanctity of their own. By comparison, the *Vita Merlini*, which is quoted below on pages 52–61, is in sophisticated Latin poetry, yet is still clearly drawn from traditional bardic sources.

The *Prophecies* are non-Christian, and contain much imagery and metaphysics of both Celtic and ancient Greek origin. They include visions of goddesses, magical transformations and a chronological sequence which extends into the twenty-first century, when there will be an apocalypse. The apocalyptic vision is not drawn from the Christian Book of Revelation, but from older traditions, in which a weaver goddess unravels the web of the stars and, as a result, the familiar Zodiac collapses. The astrology of this goddess vision is not Arabic, but ancient Greek.

In our extracts we have included the most striking prophecies that seem to refer to historical events that Geoffrey could not have known about, as they came after his death. It seems that many of these have come true, and the verses that relate to the twentieth and twenty-first centuries are particularly resonant for us.

51 After these things shall come forth a heron from the forest of Calaterium, which shall fly round the island for two years together. With her nocturnal cry she shall call together the winged kind, and assemble to her all sorts of fowls. They shall invade the tillage of husbandmen, and devour all the grain of the harvests.

52 Then shall follow a famine upon the people, and a grievous mortality upon the famine. But when this calamity shall be over, a detestable bird shall go to the valley of Galabes, and shall raise it to be a high mountain. Upon the top thereof it shall also plant an oak, and build its nest in its branches. Three eggs shall be produced in the nest, from whence shall come forth a fox, a wolf, and a bear.

53 The fox shall devour her mother, and bear the head of an ass. In this monstrous form shall she frighten her brothers, and make them fly into Neustria. But they shall stir up the tusky boar, and returning in a fleet shall encounter with the fox; who at the beginning of the fight shall feign herself dead, and move the boar to compassion.

54 Then shall the boar approach her carcass, and standing over her, shall breathe upon her face and eyes. But she, not forgetting her cunning, shall bite his left foot, and pluck it off from his body. Then shall she leap upon him, and snatch away his right ear and tail, and hide herself in the caverns of the mountains.

55 Therefore shall the deluded boar require the wolf and bear to restore him his members; who, as soon as they shall enter into the cause, shall promise two feet of the fox, together with the ear and tail, and of these they shall make up the members of a hog.

56 With this he shall be satisfied, and expect the promised restitution. In the meantime shall the fox descend from the mountains, and change herself into a wolf, and under pretence of holding a conference with the boar, she shall go to him, and craftily devour him.

57 After that she shall transform herself into a boar, and feigning a loss of some members, shall wait for her brothers; but as soon as they are come, she shall suddenly kill them with her tusks, and shall be crowned with the head of a lion.

58 In her days shall a serpent be brought forth, which shall be a destroyer of mankind. With its length it shall encompass London, and devour all that pass by it.

59 The mountain ox shall take the head of a wolf, and whiten his teeth in the Severn. He shall gather to him the flocks of Albania and Cambria, which shall drink the river Thames dry.

60 The ass shall call the goat with the long beard, and shall borrow his shape. Therefore

shall the mountain ox be incensed, and having called the wolf, shall become a horned bull against them. In the exercise of his cruelty he shall devour their flesh and bones, but shall be burned upon the top of Urian.

61 The ashes of his funeral-pile shall be turned into swans, that shall swim on dry ground as on a river. They shall devour fishes in fishes, and swallow up men in men.

62 But when old age shall come upon them, they shall become sea-wolves, and practise their frauds in the deep. They shall drown ships, and collect no small quantity of silver.

63 The Thames shall again flow, and assembling together the rivers, shall pass beyond the bounds of its channel. It shall cover the adjacent cities, and overturn the mountains that oppose its course.

64 Being full of deceit and wickedness, it shall make use of the fountain Galabes. Hence shall arise factions provoking the Venedotians to war. The oaks of the forest shall meet together, and encounter the rocks of the Gewisseans.

65 A raven shall attend with the kites, and devour the carcasses of the slain. An owl shall build her nest upon the walls of Gloucester, and in her nest shall be brought forth an ass.

66 The serpent of Malvernia shall bring him up, and put him upon many fraudulent practices. Having taken the crown, he shall ascend on high, and frighten the people of the country with his hideous braying.

67 In his days shall the Pachaian mountains tremble, and the provinces be deprived of their woods. For there shall come a worm with a fiery breath, and with the vapour it sends forth shall burn up the trees. Out of it shall proceed seven lions deformed with the heads of goats. With the stench of their nostrils they shall corrupt women, and make wives turn common prostitutes.

68 The father shall not know his own son, because they shall grow wanton like brute beasts. Then shall come the giant of wickedness, and terrify all with the sharpness of his eyes. Against him shall arise the dragon of Worcester, and shall endeavour to banish him.

69 But in the engagement the dragon shall be worsted, and oppressed by the wickedness of the conqueror. For he shall mount upon the dragon, and putting off his garment shall sit upon him naked. The dragon shall bear him up on high, and beat his naked rider with his tail erected. Upon this the giant rousing up his whole strength, shall break his jaws with his sword. At last the dragon shall fold itself up under its tail, and die of poison.

70 After him shall succeed the boar of Totness, and oppress the people with grievous tyranny. Gloucester shall send forth a lion, and shall disturb him in his cruelty, in several battles. He shall trample him under his feet, and terrify him with open jaws.

71 At last the lion shall quarrel with the kingdom, and get upon the backs of the nobility. A bull shall come into the quarrel, and strike the lion with his right foot. He shall

drive him through all the inns in the kingdom, but shall break his horns against the walls of Oxford.

72 The fox of Kaerdubalem shall take revenge on the lion, and destroy him entirely with her teeth. She shall be encompassed by the adder of Lincoln, who with a horrible hiss shall give notice of his presence to a multitude of dragons.

73 Then shall the dragons encounter, and tear one another to pieces. The winged shall oppress that which wants wings, and fasten its claws into the poisonous cheeks. Others shall come into the quarrel, and kill one another.

74 A fifth shall succeed those that are slain, and by various stratagems shall destroy the rest. He shall get upon the back of one with his sword, and sever his head from his body. Then throwing off his garment, he shall get upon another, and put his right and left hand upon his tail. Thus being naked shall he overcome him, whom when clothed he was not able to deal with.

75 The rest he shall gall in their flight, and drive them round the kingdom. Upon this shall come a roaring lion dreadful for his monstrous cruelty. Fifteen parts shall he reduce to one, and shall alone possess the people.

76 The giant of the snow-white colour shall shine, and cause the white people to flourish. Pleasures shall effeminate the princes, and they shall suddenly be changed into beasts.

77 Among them shall arise a lion swelled with human gore. Under him shall a reaper be placed in the standing corn, who, while he is reaping, shall be oppressed by him. A charioteer of York shall appease them, and having banished his lord, shall mount upon the chariot which he shall drive. With his sword unsheathed shall he threaten the East, and fill the tracks of his wheels with blood.

78 Afterwards he shall become a sea-fish, who, being roused up with the hissing of a serpent, shall engender with him. From hence shall be produced three thundering bulls, who having eaten up their pastures shall be turned into trees. The first shall carry a whip of vipers, and turn his back upon the next.

79 He shall endeavour to snatch away the whip, but shall be taken by the last. They shall turn away their faces from one another, till they have thrown away the poisoned cup.

80 To him shall succeed a husbandman of Albania, at whose back shall be a serpent. He shall be employed in ploughing the ground, that the country may become white with corn. The serpent shall endeavour to diffuse his poison, in order to blast the harvest.

81 A grievous mortality shall sweep away the people, and the walls of cities shall be made desolate. There shall be given for a remedy the city of Claudius, which shall interpose the nurse of the scourger. For she shall bear a dose of medicine, and in a short time the island shall be restored.

82 Then shall two successively sway the sceptre, whom a horned dragon shall serve.

One shall come in armour, and shall ride upon a flying serpent. He shall sit upon his back with his naked body, and cast his right hand upon his tail. With his cry shall the seas be moved, and he shall strike terror into the second.

83 The second therefore shall enter into confederacy with the lion; but a quarrel happening, they shall encounter one another. They shall distress one another, but the courage of the beast shall gain the advantage.

84 Then shall come one with a drum, and appease the rage of the lion. Therefore shall the people of the kingdom be at peace, and provoke the lion to a dose of physic. In his established seat he shall adjust the weights, but shall stretch out his hands into Albania. For which reason the northern provinces shall be grieved, and open the gates of the temples.

85 The sign-bearing wolf shall lead his troops, and surround Cornwall with his tail. He shall be opposed by a soldier in a chariot, who shall transform that people into a boar. The boar shall therefore ravage the provinces, but shall hide his head in the depth of Severn.

86 A man shall embrace a lion in wine, and the dazzling brightness of gold shall blind the eyes of beholders. Silver shall whiten in the circumference, and torment several wine presses. Men shall be drunk with wine, and regardless of heaven, shall be intent upon the earth.

87 From them shall the Stars turn away their faces and confound their usual course. Corn will wither at their malign aspects, and there shall fall no dew from Heaven.

88 A. Root and branch shall change places, and the newness of the thing shall pass as a miracle. The brightness of the Sun shall fade at the amber of Mercury, and horror shall seize the beholders. Stilbon of Arcadia shall change his shield; the Helmet of Mars shall call Venus.

89 The Helmet of Mars shall make a shadow; and the rage of Mercury shall exceed its orbit. Iron Orion shall unsheathe his sword; the marine Phoebus shall torment the clouds. Jupiter shall go out of his lawful paths; and Venus forsake her appointed circuits.

90 The malignity of the star Saturn shall fall down in rain, and slay mankind with a crooked sickle. The Twelve Houses of the Stars shall lament the irregular excursions of their inmates.

91 The Gemini shall omit their usual embrace, and will call the Urn (Aquarius) to the fountains. The Scales of Libra shall hang awry, till Aries puts his crooked horns under them. The tail of Scorpio shall produce lightning, and Cancer quarrel with the Sun. Virgo shall mount upon the back of Sagittarius, and darken her Virgin flowers.

92 The Chariot of the Moon shall disorder the Zodiac, and the Pleiades break forth into weeping. No offices of Janus shall return hereafter, but his gate being shut shall lie hid in the chinks of Ariadne.

93 The seas shall rise up in the twinkling of an eye, and the dust of the Ancients be restored. The winds shall fight together with a dreadful blast, and their Sound shall reach to the Stars.

EXTRACTS FROM VITA MERLINI

by Geoffrey of Monmouth

THE *Vita Merlini* or *Life of Merlin* is a poetic allegory written in or around 1150 by Geoffrey of Monmouth. It is woven around the figure of Merlin, with many traditional themes and sub-poems interlaced and included. I say sub-poems, but the shorter poems that stand out so vividly in the main text are likely to be Latin translations and reworkings of Welsh originals. I have examined the *Vita* in detail in *The Mystic Life of Merlin* (Arkana, 1986) and its symbolic structure in *The Merlin Tarot* (Aquarian Press, 1988), with cards based on the vivid images in the text, painted by Miranda Gray. Such a complex and rich text cannot be fully described by a short introduction and extracts, so three main themes have been chosen out of the many possibilities.

The first theme is that of mad Merlin uttering insights, and asking naïve questions out of grief and suffering. This theme revolves around the four seasons and the four directions, just as the greater creation utters the four elements.

The second theme is the threefold death, linking the idea of the fool and the hanged man, known to us today through the popularity of tarot. But the entire sacrificial sequence in Geoffrey's poem is some three or four hundred years earlier than the first tarot cards, hand-painted for the Renaissance princes and nobles of Italy. Clearly the images were the property of a mythic poetic tradition, later to be formalized as picture cards.

The threefold death, in which someone falls, hangs and drowns simultaneously, is drawn from the traditions of sacrificial kingship, known in ancient Ireland and Europe. It has strong connections with the self-sacrifice of Odin in Norse mythology, and is thematically connected to the Christian myth of the Crucifixion and Resurrection. The ancient world abounded in death and resurrection myths and cults, as death and rebirth are an essential feature of human life.

The third theme is the creation vision, which is uttered to the wild, bedraggled Merlin by the knowledgeable bard Taliesin. This creation balances the pagan apocalypse that Geoffrey had rendered into Latin in 1135 when he included the *Prophecies* in his *History of the British Kings*. The two visions, one of creation, one of destruction, are the beginning and end of the bardic, druidic and possibly pre-druidic wisdom tradition of Northern Europe. They can be linked to Celtic, Norse and Germanic, and Greek and Roman mythology in many ways. The predominant mythic and cultural source is Celtic, though there are also traces of Gnostic philosophy and metaphysics.

The creation vision begins with four universal powers and culminates in the multitudes of living creatures in the manifest planet. It is a holistic vision of interconnection and extends into the Celtic Otherworld.

In this extract we find the story of Merlin travelling with the wounded Arthur to the Fortunate Isle, where the king awaits healing from Morgen, a Celtic goddess of healing arts, flight and shape-changing. This reveals the resurrection theme that was later to flourish in Arthurian texts in the form of the Grail mystery and the wounded Fisher King.

Merlin and Madness

I am preparing to sing the madness of the prophetic bard, and a humorous poem on Merlin; pray correct the song, Robert, glory of bishops, by restraining my pen. For we know that Philosophy has poured over you its divine nectar, and has made you famous in all things, that you might serve as an example, a leader and a teacher in the world. Therefore may you favor my attempt, and see fit to look upon the poet with better auspices than did that other whom you have just succeeded, promoted to an honor that you deserve. For indeed your habits, and your approved life, and your birth, and your usefulness to the position, and the clergy and the people all were seeking it for you, and from this circumstance happy Lincoln is just now exalted to the stars. On this account I might wish you to be embraces in a fitting song, but I am not equal to the task, even though Orpheus, and Camerinus, and Macer, and Marius, and mighty-voiced Rabirius were all to sing with my mouth and all the Muses were to accompany me. But now, Sisters, accustomed to sing with me, let us sing the work proposed, and strike the cithara.

Well then, after many years had passed under many kings, Merlin the Briton was held famous in the world. He was a king and a prophet; to the proud people of the South Welsh he gave laws, and to the chieftains he prophesied the future. Meanwhile it happened that strife arose between several of the chiefs of the kingdom, and throughout the cities they wasted the innocent people with fierce war. Peredur, king of the North Welsh, made war on Gwenddoleu, who ruled the realm of Scotland; and already the day fixed for the battle was at hand, and the leaders were ready in the field, and the troops were fighting, falling on both sides in a miserable slaughter. Merlin had come to the war with Peredur and so had Rhydderch, king of the Cumbrians, both savage men. They slew the opposing enemy with their hateful swords, and three brothers of the prince who had followed him through his wars, always fighting, cut down and broke the battle lines. Thence they rushed fiercely through the crowded ranks with such an attack that they soon fell killed.

The Battle Lament

At this sight, Merlin, you grieved and poured out sad complaints throughout the army, and cried out in these words, 'Could injurious fate be so harmful as to take from me so many and such great companions, whom recently so many kings and so many remote kingdoms feared? O dubious lot of mankind! O death ever near, which has them always in its power, and strikes with its hidden goad and drives out the wretched life from the body! O glorious youths, who now will stand by my side in arms, and with me will repel the chieftains coming to harm me, and the hosts rushing upon me? Bold young men your audacity has taken from you your pleasant years and pleasant youth! You who so recently were rushing in arms through the troops, cutting down on every side those who resisted you, now are beating the ground and are red with red blood!' So among the hosts he lamented with flowing tears and mourned for the men, and the savage battle was unceasing. The lines rushed together, enemies were slain by enemies, blood flowed everywhere, and people died on both sides. But at length the Britons assembled their troops from all quarters and all together rushing in arms they fell upon the Scots and wounded them and cut them down, nor did they rest until the hostile battalions turned their backs and fled through unfrequented ways.

Merlin called his companions out from the battle and bade them bury the brothers in a richly colored chapel; and he bewailed the men and did not cease to pour out laments, and he strewed dust on his hair and rent his garments, and prostrate on the ground rolled now hither and now thither. Peredur strove to console him and so did the nobles and the princes, but he would not be comforted nor put up with their beseeching words. He had now lamented for three whole days and had refused food, so great was the grief that consumed him. Then when he had filled the air with so many and so great complaints, new fury seized him and he departed secretly, and fled to the woods not wishing to be seen as he fled. He entered the wood and rejoiced to lie hidden under the ash trees; he marvelled at the wild beasts feeding on the grass of the glades; now he chased after them and again he flew past them; he lived on the roots of grasses and on the grass, on the fruit of the trees and on the mulberries of the thicket. He became a silvan man just as though devoted to the woods. For a whole summer after this, hidden like a wild animal, he remained buried in the woods, found by no one and forgetful of himself and of his kindred.

The Winter Lament

But when the winter came and took away all the grass and the fruit of the trees he had nothing to live on, he poured out the following lament in a wretched voice.

'Christ, God of heaven, what shall I do? In what part of the world can I stay, since I see nothing here I can live on, neither grass on the ground nor acorns on the trees? Here once there stood nineteen apple trees bearing apples every year; now they are not standing. Who has taken them away from me? Whither have they gone all of a sudden? Now I see them – now I do not! Thus the fates fight against me and for me, since they both permit and forbid me to see. Now I lack the apples and everything else. The trees stand without leaves, without fruit; I am afflicted by both circumstances since I cannot cover myself with the leaves or eat the fruit. Winter and the south wind with its falling rain have taken them all away. If by chance I find some roots deep in the ground the hungry swine and the voracious boars rush up and snatch them from me as I dig them up from the turf. You, O wolf, dear companion, accustomed to roam with me through the secluded paths of the woods and meadows, now can scarcely get across the fields; hard hunger has weakened both you and me. You lived in these woods before I did and age has whitened your hairs first. You have nothing to put into your mouth and do not know how to get anything, at which I marvel, since the wood abounds in so many goats and other wild beasts that you might catch. Perhaps that detestable old age of yours has taken away your strength and prevented your following the chase. Now, as the only thing left you, you fill the air with howlings, and stretched out on the ground you extend your wasted limbs.'

These words he was uttering among the shrubs and dense hazel thickets when the sound reached a passer-by who turned his steps to the place whence the sounds were rising in the air, and found the place and found the speaker. As soon as Merlin saw him he departed, and the traveller followed him, but was unable to overtake the man as he fled. Thereupon he resumed his journey and went about his business, moved by the lot of the fugitive. Now this traveller was met by a man from the court of Rhydderch, King of the Cumbrians, who was married to Ganieda and was happy in his beautiful wife. She was sister to Merlin and, grieving over the fate of her brother, she had sent her retainers to the woods and the distant fields to bring him back. One of these retainers came toward the traveller and the latter at once went up to him and they fell into conversation; the one who had been sent to find Merlin asked if the other had seen him in the woods or the glades. The latter admitted that he had seen such a man among the bushy glades of the Calidonian forest, but, when he wished to speak to him and sit down with him, the other had fled away swiftly among the oaks. These things he told, and the messenger departed and entered the forest; he searched the deepest valleys and passed over the high mountains; he sought everywhere for his man, going through the obscure places.

On the very summit of a certain mountain there was a fountain, surrounded on every side by hazel bushes and thick with shrubs. There Merlin had seated himself, and thence through all the woods he watched the wild animals running and playing. Thither the messenger climbed, and with silent step went on up the heights seeking the man. At last he saw the fountain and Merlin sitting on the grass behind it, and making his complaint. ...

The Question of the Four Seasons
[...]
'O Thou who rulest all things, how does it happen that the seasons are not all the same, distinguished only by their four numbers? Now spring, according to its laws, provides flowers and leaves; summer gives crops, autumn ripe apples; icy winter follows and devours and wastes all the others, bringing rain and snow, and keeps them all away and harms with its tempests. And it does not permit the ground to produce variegated flowers, or the oak trees acorns, or the apple trees dark red apples. O that there were no winter or white frost! That it were spring or summer, and that the cuckoo would come back singing, and the nightingale who softens sad hearts with her devoted song, and the turtle dove keeping her chaste vows, and that in new foliage other birds should sing in harmonious measures, delighting me with their music, while a new earth should breathe forth odors from new flowers under the green grass; that the fountains would also flow on every side with their gentle murmurs, and near by, under the leaves, the dove would pour forth her soothing laments and incite to slumber.

Lament for Guendoloena
The messenger heard the prophet and broke off his lament with cadences on the cither he had brought with him that with it he might attract and soften the madman. Therefore making plaintive sounds with his fingers and striking the strings in order, he lay hidden behind him and sang in a low voice, 'O the dire groanings of mournful Guendoloena! O the wretched tears of weeping Guendoloena! I grieve for wretched dying Guendoloena! There was not among the Welsh a woman more beautiful than she. She surpassed in fairness the goddesses, and the petals of the privet, and the blooming roses and the fragrant lilies of the fields. The glory of spring shone in her alone, and she had the splendor of the stars in her two eyes, and splendid hair shining with the gleam of gold. All this has perished; all beauty has departed from her, both color and figure and also the glory of her snowy flesh. Now, worn out with much weeping, she is not what she was, for she does not know where the prince has gone, or whether he is alive or dead; therefore the wretched woman languishes and is totally wasted away through her long grief. With similar laments Ganieda weeps with her, and without consolation grieves for her lost brother. One weeps for her brother and the other for her

husband, and both devote themselves to weeping and spend their time in sadness. No food nourishes them, nor does any sleep refresh them wandering at night through the brushwood, so great is the grief that consumes them both. Not otherwise did Sidonian Dido grieve when the ships had weighed anchor and Aeneas was in haste to depart; so most wretched Phyllis groaned and wept when Demophoon did not come back at the appointed time; thus Briseis wept for the absent Achilles. Thus the sister and the wife grieve together, and burn continually and completely with inward agonies.'

The messenger sang thus to his plaintive lyre, and with his music soothed the ears of the prophet that be might become more gentle and rejoice with the singer. Quickly the prophet arose and addressed the young man with pleasant words, and begged him to touch once more the strings with his fingers and to sing again his former song. The latter therefore set his fingers to the lyre and played over again the song that was asked for, and by his playing compelled the man, little by little, to put aside his madness, captivated by the sweetness of the lute.

Merlin's First Return

So Merlin became mindful of himself, and he recalled what he used to be, and he wondered at his madness and he hated it. His former mind returned and his sense came back to him, and, moved by affection, he groaned at the names of his sister and of his wife, since his mind was now restored to him, and he asked to be led to the court of King Rhydderch. The other obeyed him, and straightway they left the woods and came, rejoicing together, to the city of the king. So the queen was delighted by regaining her brother and the wife became glad over the return of her husband. They vied with each other in kissing him and they twined their arms about his neck, so great was the affection that moved them. The king also received him with such honor as was fitting, and the chieftains who thronged the palace rejoiced in the city.

But when Merlin saw such great crowds of men present he was not able to endure them; he went mad again, and, filled anew with fury, he wanted to go to the woods, and he tried to get away by stealth. Then Rhydderch ordered him to be restrained and a guard posted over him, and his madness to be softened with the cither; and he stood about him grieving, and with imploring words begged the man to be sensible and to stay with him, and not to long for the grove or to live like a wild beast, or to want to abide under the trees when he might hold a royal scepter and rule over a warlike people. After that he promised that he would give him many gifts, and he ordered people to bring him clothing and birds, dogs and swift horses, gold and shining gems, and cups that Wayland had engraved in the city of Segontium. Every one of these things Rhydderch offered to the prophet and urged him to stay with him and leave the woods.

The prophet rejected these gifts, saying, 'Let the dukes who are troubled by their own poverty have these, they who are not satisfied with a moderate amount but desire a great deal. To these gifts I prefer the groves and broad oaks of Calidon, and the lofty mountains with green pastures at their feet. Those are the things that please me, not these of yours – take these away with you, King Rhydderch. My Calidonian forest rich in nuts, the forest that I prefer to everything else, shall have me.'

Finally since the king could not retain the sad man by any gifts, he ordered him to be bound with a strong chain lest, if free, he might seek the deserted groves. The prophet, when he felt the chains around him and he could not go as a free man to the Calidonian forests, straightway fell to grieving and remained sad and silent, and took all joy from his face so that he did not utter a word or smile.

Meanwhile the queen was going through the hall looking for the king, and he, as was proper, greeted her as she came and took her by the hand and bade her sit down, and, embracing her, pressed her lips in a kiss. In so doing he turned his face toward her and saw a leaf hanging in her hair; he reached out his fingers, took it and threw it on the ground, and jested joyfully with the woman he loved. The prophet turned his eyes in that direction and smiled, and made the men standing about look at him in wonder since he was not in the habit of smiling. The king too wondered and urged the madman to tell the cause of his sudden laugh, and he added to his words many gifts. The other was silent and put off explaining his laugh. But more and more Rhydderch continued to urge him with riches and with entreaties until at length the prophet, vexed at him, said in return for his gift, 'A miser loves a gift and a greedy man labors to get one; these are easily corrupted by gifts and bend their minds in any direction they are bidden to. What they have is not enough for them, but for me the acorns of pleasant Calidon and the shining fountains flowing through fragrant meadows are sufficient. I am not attracted by gifts; let the miser take his, and unless liberty is given me and I go back to the green woodland valleys I shall refuse to explain my laughter.'Therefore when Rhydderch found that he could not influence the prophet by any gift, and he could not find out the reason for the laughter, straightway he ordered the chains to be loosed and gave him permission to seek the deserted groves, that he might be willing to give the desired explanation. Then Merlin, rejoicing that he could go, said, 'This is the reason I laughed, Rhydderch. You were by a single act both praiseworthy and blameworthy. When just now you removed the leaf that the queen had in her hair without knowing it, you acted more faithfully toward her than she did toward you when she went under the bush where her lover met her and lay with her; and while she was lying there supine with her hair spread out, by chance there caught in it the leaf that you, not knowing all this, removed.'

The Threefold Death

Rhydderch suddenly became sad at this accusation and turned his face from her and cursed the day he had married her. But she, not at all moved, hid her shame behind a smiling face and said to her husband, 'Why are you sad, my love? Why do you become so angry over this thing and blame me unjustly, and believe a madman who, lacking sound sense, mixes lies with the truth? The man who believes him becomes many times more a fool than he is. Now then, watch, and if I am not mistaken I will show you that he is crazy and has not spoken the truth.'

There was in the hall a certain boy, one of many, and the ingenious woman catching sight of him straightway thought of a novel trick by which she might convict her brother of falsehood. So she ordered the boy to come in and asked her brother to predict by what death the lad should die. He answered, 'Dearest sister, he shall die, when a man, by falling from a high rock.' Smiling at these words, she ordered the boy to go away and take off the clothes he was wearing and put on others and to cut off his long hair; she bade him come back to them thus that he might seem to them a different person. The boy obeyed her, for he came back to them with his clothes changed as he had been ordered to do. Soon the queen asked her brother again, 'Tell your dear sister what the death of this boy will be like.' Merlin answered, 'This boy when he grows up shall, while out of his mind, meet with a violent death in a tree.' When he had finished she said to her husband, 'Could this false prophet lead you so far astray as to make you believe that I had committed so great a crime? And if you will notice with how much sense he has spoken this about the boy, you will believe that the things he said about me were made up so that he might get away to the woods. Far be it from me to do such a thing! I shall keep my bed chaste, and chaste shall I always be while the breath of life is in me. I convicted him of falsehood when I asked him about the death of the boy.

Now I shall do it again; pay attention and judge.'

When she had said this she told the boy in an aside to go out and put on woman's clothing, and to come back thus. Soon the boy left and did as he was bid, for he came back in woman's clothes just as though he were a woman, and he stood in front of Merlin to whom the queen said banteringly, 'Say brother, tell me about the death of this girl.' 'Girl or not she shall die in the river,' said her brother to her, which made King Rhydderch laugh at his reasoning; since when asked about the death of a single boy Merlin had predicted three different kinds. Therefore Rhydderch thought he had spoken falsely about the queen, and did not believe him, but grieved, and hated the fact that he had trusted him and had condemned his beloved. The queen, seeing this, forgave him and kissed and caressed him and made him joyful.

Guendoloena remained sadly in the door watching him and so did the queen, both moved by what had happened to their friend, and they marveled that a madman should be so familiar with secret things and should have known of the love affair of his sister. Nevertheless they thought that he lied about the death of the boy since he told of three different deaths when he should have told of one. Therefore his speech seemed for long years to be an empty one until the time when the boy grew to manhood; then it was made apparent to all and convincing to many. For while he was hunting with his dogs he caught sight of a stag hiding in a grove of trees; he loosed the dogs who, as soon as they saw the stag, climbed through unfrequented ways and filled the air with their baying. He urged on his horse with his spurs and followed after, and urged on the huntsmen, directing them, now with his horn and now with his voice, and he bade them go more quickly. There was a high mountain surrounded on all sides by rocks with a stream flowing through the plain at its foot; thither the animal fled until he came to the river, seeking a hiding place after the usual manner of its kind. The young man pressed on and passed straight over the mountain, hunting for the stag among the rocks lying about. Meanwhile it happened, while his impetuosity was leading him on, that his horse slipped from a high rock and the man fell over a precipice into the river, but so that one of his feet caught in a tree, and the rest of his body was submerged in the stream. Thus he fell, and was drowned, and hung from a tree, and by this threefold death made the prophet a true one.

Creation of the World
Elements and circles

Meanwhile Taliesin had come to see Merlin the prophet who had sent for him to find out what caused wind or rainstorms, for both together were drawing near and the clouds were thickening. He drew the following illustrations under the guidance of Minerva his associate.

'Out of nothing the Creator of the world produced *four elements* that they might be the prior cause as well as the material for creating all things when they were joined together in harmony: the *heaven* which He adorned with *stars* and which stands on high and embraces everything like the shells surrounding a nut; then He made the *air*, fit for forming sounds, through the medium of which day and night present the stars; the *sea* which girds the land in four circles, and with its mighty refluence so strikes the air as to generate the *winds* which are said to be four in number; as a foundation He placed the earth, standing by its own strength and not lightly moved, which is divided into five parts, whereof the middle one is not habitable because of the heat and the two furthest are shunned because of their cold. To the last two He gave a moderate temperature and these are inhabited by *men* and *birds* and herds of *wild beasts*.

Clouds, rain, winds

He added clouds to the sky so that they might furnish sudden showers to make the fruits of the trees and of the ground grow with their gentle sprinkling. With the help of the sun these are filled like water skins from the rivers by a hidden law, and then, rising through the upper air, they pour out the water they have taken up, driven by the force of the winds. From them come rainstorms, snow, and round hail when the cold damp wind breathes out its blasts which, penetrating the clouds, drive out the streams just as they make them. Each of the winds takes to itself a nature of its own from its proximity to the zone where it is born.

Orders of spirits

Beyond the firmament in which He fixed the shining stars He placed the *ethereal heaven* and gave it as a habitation to troops of *angels* whom the worthy contemplation and marvellous sweetness of God refresh throughout the ages. This also He adorned with stars and the *shining sun*, laying down the law, by which a star should run within fixed limits through the part of heaven entrusted to it.

He afterwards placed beneath this the *airy heavens*, shining with the lunary body, which throughout their high places abound in troops of *spirits* who sympathize or rejoice with us as things go well or ill. They are accustomed to carry the prayers of men through the air and to beseech God to have mercy on them, and to bring back intimations of God's will, either in dreams or by voice or by other signs, through doing which they become wise.

The space below the moon abounds in evil *demons*, who are skilled to cheat and deceive and tempt us; often they assume a body made of air and appear to us and many things often follow. They even hold intercourse with women and make them pregnant, generating in an unholy manner. So therefore He made the heavens to be inhabited by *three orders of spirits* that each one might look out for something and renew the world from the renewed seed of things.

The sea

The sea too He distinguished by various forms that from itself it might produce the forms of things, generating throughout the ages. Indeed, part of it burns and part freezes and the third part, getting a moderate temperature from the other two, ministers to our needs.

That part which burns surrounds a gulf and fierce people, and its divers streams, flowing back, separate this from the orb of earth, increasing fire from fire. Thither descend those who transgress the laws and reject God; whither their perverse will leads them they go, eager to destroy what is forbidden to them. There stands the stern-eyed judge holding his equal balance and giving to each one his merits and his deserts.

The second part, which freezes, rolls about the foreshorn sands which it is the first to generate from the near-by vapor when it is mingled with the rays of Venus's star. This star, the Arabs say, makes shining gems when it passes through the Fishes while its waters look back at the flames. These gems by their virtues benefit the people who wear them, and make many well and keep them so. These too the Maker distinguished by their kinds as He did all things, that we might discern from their forms and from their colors of what kinds they are and of what manifest virtues.

The third form of the sea which circles our orb furnishes us many good things owing to its proximity. For it nourishes fishes and produces salt in abundance, and bears back and forth ships carrying our commerce, by the profits of which the poor man becomes suddenly rich. It makes fertile the neighboring soil and feeds the birds who, they say, are generated from it along with the fishes and, although unlike, are moved by the laws of nature. The sea is dominated by them more than by the fishes, and they fly lightly up from it through space and seek the lofty regions. But its moisture drives the fishes beneath the waves and keeps them there, and does not permit them to live when they get out into the dry light. These too the Maker distinguished according to their species and to the different ones gave each his nature, whence through the ages they were to become admirable and healthful to the sick.

Fish

For men say that the *barbel* restrains the heat of passion but makes blind those who eat it often. The *thymallus*, which has its name from the flower thyme, smells so that it betrays the fish that often eat of it until all the fishes in the river smell like itself. They say that the *muraenas*, contrary to all laws, are all the feminine sex, yet they copulate and reproduce and multiply their offspring from a different kind of seed. For often snakes come together along the shore where they are, and they make the sound of pleasing hissing and, calling out the muraenas, join with them according to custom. It is also remarkable that the *remora*, half a foot long, holds fast the ship to which it adheres at sea just as though it were fast aground, and does not permit the vessel to move until it lets go; because of this power it is to be feared. And that which they call the *swordfish*, because it does injury with its sharp beak, people often fear to approach with a ship when it is swimming, for if it is captured it at once makes a hole in the vessel, cuts it in pieces, and sinks it suddenly in a whirlpool. The *serra* makes itself feared by ships because of its crest; it fixes to them as it swims underneath, cuts them to pieces and throws the pieces into the waves, wherefore its crest is to be feared like a sword. And the *water dragon*, which men say has poison under its wings, is to be feared by those who capture it; whenever it strikes it does harm by pouring out its poison. The *torpedo* is said to have another kind of destruction, for if any one touches it when it is alive, straightway his arms and his feet grow torpid and so do his other members and they lose their functions just as though they were dead, so harmful is the emanation of its body.

Islands

To those and the other fishes God gave the sea, and He added to it many realms among the waves, which men inhabit and which are renowned because of the fertility which the earth produces there from its fruitful soil.

Of these *Britain* is said to be the foremost and best, producing in its fruitfulness every single thing. For it bears crops which throughout the year give the noble gifts of fragrance for the use of man, and it has woods and glades with honey dripping in them, and lofty mountains and broad green fields, fountains and rivers, fishes and cattle and wild beasts, fruit trees, gems, precious metals, and whatever creative nature is in the habit of furnishing.

Besides all these it has fountains healthful because of their hot waters which nourish the sick and provide pleasing baths, which quickly send people away cured with their sickness driven out. So *Bladud* established them when he held the scepter of the kingdom, and he gave them the name of his consort *Alaron*. These are of value to many sick because of the healing of their water, but most of all to women, as often the water has demonstrated.

Near to this island lies *Thanet* which abounds in many things but lacks the death-dealing serpent, and if any of its earth is drunk mixed with wine it takes away poison. Our ocean also divides the *Orkneys* from us. These are divided into thirty-three islands by the sundering flood; twenty lack cultivation and the others are cultivated. *Thule* receives its name 'furthest' from the sun, because of the solstice which the summer sun makes there, turning its rays and shining no further, and taking away the day, so that always throughout the long night the air is full of shadows, and making ice congealed by the benumbing cold, which prevents the passage of ships.

The most outstanding island after our own is said to be *Ireland* with its happy fertility. It is larger and produces no bees, and no birds except rarely, and it does not permit snakes to breed in it. Whence it happens that if earth or a stone is carried away from there and added to any other place it drives away snakes and bees. The island of *Gades* lies next to *Herculean Gades*, and there grows there a tree from whose bark a gum drips out of which gems are made, breaking all laws.

The *Hesperides* are said to contain a watchful dragon who, men say, guards the golden apples under the leaves. The *Gorgades* are inhabited by women with goats' bodies who are said to surpass hares in the swiftness of their running. *Argyre* and *Chryse* bear, it is said, gold and silver just as Corinth does common stones. *Ceylon* blooms pleasantly because of its fruitful soil, for it produces two crops in a single year; twice it is summer, twice spring, twice men gather grapes and other fruits, and it is also most pleasing because of its shining gems. *Tiles* produces flowers and fruits in an eternal spring, green throughout the seasons.

The Otherworld

The island of apples which men call '*The Fortunate Isle*' gets its name from the fact that it produces all things of itself; the fields there have no need of the ploughs of the farmers and all cultivation is lacking except what nature provides. Of its own accord it produces grain and grapes, and apple trees grow in its wood from the close-clipped grass. The ground of its own accord produces everything instead of merely grass, and people live there a hundred years or more.

There nine sisters rule by a pleasing set of laws those who come to them from our country. She who is first of them is more skilled in the healing art, and excels her sisters in the beauty of her person. *Morgen* is her name, and she has learned what useful properties all the herbs contain, so that she can cure sick bodies. She also knows an art by which to change her shape, and to cleave the air on new wings like Daedalus; when she wishes she is at Brest, Chartres, or Pavia, and when she wills she slips down from the air onto your shores.

And men say that she has taught mathematics to her sisters, Moronoe, Mazoe, Gliten, Glitonea, Gliton, Tyronoe, Thitis, Thitis best known for her cither. Thither after the battle of Camlan we took the wounded Arthur, guided by *Barinthus* to whom the waters and the stars of heaven were well known. With him steering the ship we arrive there with the prince, Morgen received us with fitting honor, and in her chamber she placed the king on a golden bed and with her own hand she uncovered his honorable wound and gazed at it for a long time. At length she said that health could be restored to him if he stayed with her for a long time and made use of her healing art. Rejoicing, therefore, we entrusted the king to her and returning spread our sails to the favoring winds.

ARTHOUR AND MERLIN

The Auchinleck Manuscript

THIS IS THE earliest English medieval verse romance of Merlin. It dates from the late thirteenth and early fourteenth centuries, and is drawn from the same source as *The English Merlin* (see below), though its approach is far more prosaic than that of its successor. Though it only includes about half of the *Estoire de Merlin* it totals some 9900 lines, retelling the story of Merlin's miraculous birth and his subsequent association with Uther Pendragon, Arthur's father, and later of the early days of Arthur himself. It exists in two manuscripts, one in the library of Lincoln's Inn, London, and the other in the National Library of Scotland. It has been edited in recent years by Dr Macrae-Gibson for the Early English Text Society (Oxford University Press, 1973) and the reader is recommended to obtain this version for a full rendition with extensive commentary. The version printed here, in the interests of readability, is from a transcript of the Auchinleck manuscript made by Sir Walter Scott in the nineteenth century and printed by George Ellis in 1848 as one of his *Specimens of Early English Metrical Romances*. In this form it is both easier to read and gives the student an opportunity to follow the complex story line with sufficient illustrative passages to give a flavour of the original. Of particular note are the short introductory passages to each section which evoke the seasons of the year.

CANTO I

After the death of Vortigern, Uther Pendragon marched to besiege Hengist in a castle to which he had retreated; but the efforts of the assailants being rendered abortive by the strength of the position, he was advised by five of his barons, who had witnessed the preceding feats of Merlin, to apply for the assistance of the magician. Accordingly, messengers were dispatched in search of him; and

> On a day, this messager,
> Sette hem alle to the diner.
> A beggar ther come in,
> With a long berd on his chin;
> A staff in his hond he hadde,
> And shoone on his fete bade.
> With his schuldres he gan rove,[1]
> And bade[2] 'good for Godys love'.
> They said he scholde nought share
> But strokes and bismare.[3]
>
> The eld man said anon,
> 'Ye be nice,[4] everych one,
> That sitten here and skorne me,

---

1. Shrug.
2. Prayed.
3. Infamy.
4. Foolish.

On the king's nedes that schuld be,
For to finde Merlin child!
The barouns ben witless and wild,
That senten men him to seche,[5]
That nought ne couthe[6] knowleche!
To day he hath yow oft met;
No know ye him never the bet.[7]
Wendeth[8] home by my rede![9]
For him to find ne shal ye spede.
Biddeth him and the barouns five
They come and spoken with him blyve;[10]
And seggeth,[11] Merlin wil hem abide
In the forest here byside.'

With these words he vanished; and the messengers, as 'telleth the letters black', were filled with wonder. Uther, having heard their relation, left the command of the army with his brother Aurilis Brosias (Aurclius Ambrosius), and repaired to the forest, where Merlin amused himself at his expense by assuming three several disguises: first that of a swine-herd; then that of a chapman with a pack at his back; and lastly that of a young and comely peasant, – in which shape he exhorted him to have patience, assuring him that Merlin would keep his assignation, though perhaps not till late at night. At last he arrived, announced himself as Merlin, though still in his peasant's shape, and related that by his advice Aurclius had just attacked and slain Hengist. Uther, rejoiced by this news 'as the birds by the first dawn of day', returned with Merlin to the camp, and found his brother not less astonished than delighted by his victory, of which he was unable to give a very intelligible account till he learnt from Uther the name of his powerful counsellor and assistant. At this time a message was received from the Saracens (Saxons) requesting leave to retire, with the assurance that they would never more return to infest the peace of Britain: and this proposal being by Merlin's advice accepted, and the tranquillity of the island restored by the departure of the enemy, Uther was elected sovereign, received the oath of fealty from the principal barons, and was solemnly crowned at Winchester, amidst the rejoicings of the whole nation.

Not long after this ceremony a vast army of Saracens from Denmark made an attack on Bristol. Merlin had forewarned the brothers of this invasion, and at the same time informed them that one of them was destined to fall in the dreadful conflict by which the triumph of the Britons must be purchased, but that the victim would be rewarded by the crown of martyrdom. Uther was directed to make head against the enemy on the land side, while Aurclius should attack them in the rear from the sea beach; and both exerted themselves with the most desperate valour. But Uther received from Merlin, during the engagement, a secret assurance that he was not the person destined to go immediately to heaven; and the romance tells us that he was very glad to hear it. He redoubled his efforts to secure the victory nearly gained by Aurclius, who fell when the enemy was already thrown into confusion; and these efforts were so successful,

---

5. To seek.
6. Knew no knowledge.
7. Better.
8. Go.
9. Advice.
10. Immediately.
11. Say.

> That of thritty thousand, and mo,[12]
> Ne let they five away go.
> Of our were slawen[13] then anon
> Three thousand, and ten, and one.
> Three mile wayes, other two,
> Ne might no man step, ne go,
> Neither on hill ne on den,
> Bot he stepped on dede men.
> The blode over-ran the countray,
> Over alle in the valley.

The body of Aurclius was, on the following day, carefully sought and interred with due solemnity.

Uther reigned seven years, and, scrupulously following in all things the advice of Merlin, distinguished every year by the most brilliant achievements. He overcame King Claudas,[14] the tyrant of Gaul, and became the suzerain of Hoel, king of Harman,[15] first husband of the beautiful Igerna, and lord of Gascony, Normandy and Boulogne, Poitou, Champagne, and Anjou. He also acquired the allegiance of Ban, king of Benoit in 'lesse Briteyne', and of his brother Bohort of Gannes, two of the first pillars of chivalry. Moreover, he instituted the round table, under Merlin's special guidance, intended to assemble the best knights in the world. High birth, great strength, activity, and skill, fearless valour, and firm fidelity to their suzerain, were indispensably requisite for an admission into this order. They were bound by oath to assist each other at the hazard of their own lives; to attempt singly the most perilous adventurers; to lead, when necessary, a life of monastic solitude; to fly to arms at the first summons; and never to retire from battle till they had defeated the enemy, unless when night intervened and separated the combatants.

> This table gan[16] Uther the wight;
> Ac it to ende had he no might.
> For, theygh alle the kinges under our lord
> Hadde y-sitten[17] at that bord,
> Knight by knight, ich you telle,
> The table might nought fulfille,
> Till they were born that should do all
> Fulfill the mervaile of the Greal.[18]

Happy are the kings whose ministers happen to be conjurers! Uther had the good fortune to close the list of his sanguinary conquests by the more flattering though not very honourable victory which he obtained, by the assistance of Merlin, over the beautiful Igerna, whom he enjoyed, under the shape of her husband the duke of Cornwall, in

12. More.
13. Slain.
14. This Claudas, the great enemy of Ban and Boort, makes a conspicuous figure in the romance of Sir Launcelot.
15. The country of Ilarman is unknown to modern geography, but appears in this place to mean Britany. Hoel, king of the country, is perhaps assumed to be the father of him who is celebrated in Geoffrey of Monmouth as the great assistant of Arthur in his victories; for, as our romancer has made him the first husband of Igerna, Arthur's mother, these heroes thus become very nearly related.
16. Commenced.
17. Sat.
18. The St. Graal was the vessel in which our Saviour ate the last supper with his apostles, and is fabled to have been preserved by Joseph of Arimathea.

Tintagel castle. It is unnecessary to repeat from the romance the same circumstances which are related by Geoffrey of Monmouth; but it will be proper to observe, that the subsequent union on Uther to his fair captive was accompanied by the marriages of the three daughters whom she had borne to Hoel, her first husband.

Nanters, king of Gerlot, married Blasine, the eldest, by whom he had a son named Galaas. King Lot espoused the second, named Belicent, who became the mother of Gawain, Guerehes, Agravain, and Gaheriet. The third was united to Urien, king of Scherham, whose son was the celebrated Ywain.

Merlin, it seems, had exacted from Uther, as the price of his complaisance in furthering his majesty's amours, the absolute right of directing, as he might think fit, the nurture and education of the boy who should result from them; and no sooner were the usual festivities concluded than he repaired to Uther, and reminded him of his promise. He had read in the stars that the wife of Antour, a nobleman high in Uther's esteem, would be the best possible nurse for the child; and therefore directed the king, in the first place, to obtain the consent of the intended foster-father. He then enjoined him to conceal carefully from Igerna the identity of her unknown ravisher with her present husband; and, when she should confess to him her pregnancy, that he should consent to forgive her supposed crime, only on condition that the child should be delivered to a person whom he would appoint, for the purpose of educating it in perfect obscurity. All this was punctually performed. Merlin received the child at the palace-gate; conveyed him to church, where he caused him to be christened by the name of Arthur; and then bore him to Antour's wife, who undertook to suckle him, having obtained another nurse for her own son Kay, of whom she had been recently delivered. As these secret ancedotes may require some attestation, the author assures us that 'he has found them *in the black*'; and soon after appeals to the *Brount*,[19] meaning perhaps the *Brut* or Chronicle.

Arthur grew and prospered under the care of Sir Antour –

> He was fair, and well agre,[20]
> And was a thild of gret noblay.
> He was curteys, faire and gent,
> And wight, and hardi, verament.[21]
> Curteyslich[22] and fair he spac;[23]
> With him was none evil lack.[24]

But he was kept in perfect ignorance of his high birth; and Uther, though he lived many years after this, expired without revealing the secret either to Arthur or to Igerna. Merlin however, who attended him on his death-bed, assured him that his son should succeed him, and that in his reign should be fulfilled all the wonders of the San-Gréal; and with this promise the king was perfectly satisfied. He died, and was buried by Bishop Brice, a personage of great sanctity and no small importance.

As soon as the obsequies of the late king were finished, a parliament was convened for the purpose of electing a successor, and was attended by all the independent lords and princes of the island. But as Uther's family was supposed to be extinct, and numerous candidates brought forward their claims to the throne, the assembly continued to

---

19. This is no doubt a misreading. The Brut is, of course, the work alluded to.
20. Pleasing; agreeable.
21. Truly.
22. Courteously.
23. Spoke.
24. Fault.

deliberate during six months; at the end of which they were so divided into factions as to preclude all rational hope of accommodation. Bishop Brice, on Christmas eve, took occasion to address them; and represented that, as no human means were likely to produce unanimity in their councils without the special interference of heaven, it would well become them to put up their prayers, at that solemn season, for some token which should manifest the intentions of providence respecting their future sovereign. This advice was adopted; all parties prayed with the greatest fervour – and with such success, that the service was scarcely ended when a miraculous stone was discovered before the church-door, and in the stone was firmly fixed a sword with the following words engraved on its hilt:

> 'Ich am y-hote[25] Esealibore;
> Unto a king fair tresore.'
> (On Inglis is this writing,
> Kerve steel, and yren, and al thing.')

Bishop Brice, after exhorting the assembly to offer up their thanksgivings for this signal miracle, proposed a law, that whoever should be able to draw out that sword from the stone should be immediately acknowledged as sovereign of the Britons; and his proposal was instantly decreed by general acclamation.

King Lot, King Nanters, King Clarien, and all the principal candidates, successively put their strength to the proof; but the miraculous sword resisted all their efforts. It stood till Candlemas; it stood till Easter; it stood till Pentecost, when the best knights in the kingdom usually assembled for the annual tournament; and no one had been able to move it. In the mean time Arthur had been placed, for the purpose of finishing his education, in the service of King Lot: but when Kay was received, previously to the feast of Pentecost, into the order of knighthood, he was advised by his father to take Arthur as his squire; and the young hero accordingly attended his foster-brother, in that capacity, to the lists. Sir Kay was a youth of great valour and address, (though, as the romancer tells us, he 'stammered a little,') and, having overthrown a competent number of knights with his spear, proceeded into the medley with his sword – which unfortunately broke in his hand, – so that he was forced to send Arthur to his mother for a new one. Arthur hastened home, but did not find the lady: he had however observed near the church a sword sticking in a stone, and on his return galloped to the place, drew it out with great ease, and, perfectly unconscious of having performed a mighty feat, delivered it to his master. Kay, who was better aware of its value, swore him to secresy, and then, showing the weapon to his father, professed his intention of claiming the throne.

Sir Antour, who was rather incredulous, insisted that his son should repeat the feat, lest he should only cover himself with ridicule by failing in the experiment before the general assembly; and Kay, who hoped that the charm was now broken, readily replaced the sword in the stone; to which the blade instantly adhered so strongly that he was utterly unable to remove it. Somewhat abashed by this discovery of the imposture, he confessed to his father that he had received the sword from his squire; and Antour, carrying Arthur to the cathedral, intrusted him with the secret virtues of the sword, promised his best assistance in placing him on the throne, and only requested of his foster-son, in return for all his service, the promise of nominating Sir Kay to the office of high steward; a request with which Arthur joyfully complied.

---

25. Called.

Sir Antour now hastened to invest him with the order of knighthood, and equipped him with a degree of splendour suited to his high pretensions.

> First he fond him cloth and cradel,
> Tho he fond him stede and sadel;
> Helm, and briny, and hauberjoun,
> Saumbers, quissers, and aketoun.[26]
> Quarré shield, gode swerd of steel,
> And launce stiff, biteand[27] wel.
> There he gave him, anon-rights,[28]
> To his service forty knights.
> A-morwe[29] they went to tournament.
> And so there dede, verament,
> That, eche day, Sir Arthour
> The los[30] he bare and the honour.

Antour then repaired to Bishop Brice, to inform him that Arthur had performed the conditions pointed out by heaven; upon which the good prelate summoned the general meeting, before whom the trial of the sword was several times repeated; Arthur was unanimously proclaimed, and an early day appointed for his solemn coronation.

During the preparations for this ceremony Merlin arrived, and communicated to the bishop the whole mystery of Arthur's birth. He at the same time forewarned him that the approaching festival would not pass off without a severe contest, and the effusion of much blood; he recommended that Arthur's party should be strengthened as quickly as possible by the accession of Sir Jordain, Sir Bretel, and all the adherents of Igerna; and above all, that they should be constantly armed, and prepared for the attack of their enemies.

CANTO II

> Mirie it is in time of June,
> When fenil hangeth abroad in toun;
> Violet, and rose flower,
> Woneth[31] then in maiden's bower.
> The sonne is hot, the day is long.
> Foulis maketh miri song.
> King Arthour bar coroun
> In Cardoile that noble town.

Among the competitors for the crown were six kings, distinguished by superior power or merit; these were Lot of Lothian; Nanters of Gerlot; Urien of Reged; Carodas king of Strangore; Yder king of the Marches; and Anguisant king of Scotland. Each of these conducted a small army of adherents to Arthur's coronation; attended, in sullen

---

26. Cradel, perhaps from Cratula, a species of dress which Du Cange supposes to have been clerical; briny, and hauberjoun, different sorts of breastplates; saumbers, the coverings for the arm; quissers, covering for the thigh; aketoun, a coat of mail.
27. Cutting.
28. Immediately.
29. On the morrow.
30. Praise; glory.
31. Dwell.

silence, the religious ceremonies; listened without any symptoms of impatience to the exhortations of Bishop Brice; and even condescended to partake of the venison, of the swans, peacocks, bustards, pheasants, partridges, and cranes, as well as of the piment and claré,[32] by which the mass was immediately followed. But when, at the conclusion of the feast, Arthur proceeded according to custom to confer on his guests the investiture of the great fiefs and offices of the crown, they suddenly rose with one accord, exclaimed that a misbegotten adventurer was unfit to reign over them, and attempted to seize the king's person. Merlin, who was present, defended the legitimacy of Arthur's birth, and told, as intelligibly as the noise would permit, his whole story; but his eloquence was unavailing –

> The barouns said to Merlin,
> 'He was found thurgh witching thine!
> 'Traitour,' they said, 'verament,
> For al thine enchantement,
> No shall never no hore's stren[33]
> Our king, no heved[34] ben,
> Ac he shal sterve[35] right anon!' –

Luckily Arthur's friends, being perfectly armed, very soon drove before them their immense crowd of enemies, and chasing them quite out of the town, shut the gates against them. But though forced to retreat to their tents, they still threatened a speedy vengeance; and their great numbers, their valour, and the smallness of Arthur's party, which did not amount to more than three hundred and ten knights and about three thousand seven hundred ill-armed infantry, seemed to promise them a certain and speedy victory. Bishop Brice, however, having assembled the whole inhabitants of the town, explained to them the divine right of Arthur to the crown, as well as his hereditary claim as son to Uther; assured them of the assistance of heaven; and concluded his harangue by these energetic words:

> 'Ae, for he is king, and king's son,
> Y curse alle, and y dom
> His enemies with Christes mouth,
> By East, by West, by North, and South!'

Merlin, on his part, was not less active. He cast, by his enchantments, a sort of magical wild-fire into the spacious camp of the enemy, which spread a general conflagration; and whilst they were bewildered in the smoke and almost deprived of their senses, directed a sally from the town; by which they were instantly put to flight, with the loss of four hundred and fifteen (our author is very exact in his numbers) of their most forward combatants.

But the panic could not last for ever. Nanters, king of Gerlot, at last succeeded in rallying the fugitives, of whom he collected about ten thousand in a valley, and threatened to crush at once the small army of his pursuers.

---

32. Piment was a species of spiced wine, and claré was a wine made of grapes, honey, and aromatic spices. Wine mixed with honey and spices, and afterwards strained, was also called claré. In the east of England any sort of red wine is called clarry or claret, and perhaps the term may be a relic of our ancient language.
33. Race; progeny. A.S.
34. Head.
35. Die; perish.

> Arthur seighe[36] where he cam,
> A stiff launce anon he nam:[37]
> His fete in the stiropes he streight;[38]
> The stirop to-bent, the hors aqueight:[39]
> The stede he smot, and he forth slode:[40]
> Ogain[41] the king Nanters he rode.

Arthur, as might be expected, speedily, overthrew this antagonist, and afterwards King Lot; and drawing the terrible Escalibore, rushed into the thickest part of the press, and spread destruction round him. But being stopped by an impenetrable multitude, and assailed by the six kings at once, his horse was finally killed, and himself in inminent danger of suffocation; when he was rescued by Sir Kay, who by one thrust of his lance overthrew Anguisant and Carodas, and, assisted by Ulfin and Bretel, mounted the king on a fresh horse. But though all these knights performed prodigies of valour, they did not wholly engross the honour of the day.

> Here ye shal understond,
> That men o-foot, of this lond,
> Helden with King Arthour,
> And did him well gret honour.
> With axes, staves, and with bowe,
> Did so that alle the other flowe,[42]
> And this kinges flowen also.

Arthur, after a long pursuit, collected his men, bestowed on them the plunder of the enemy's camp, returned to Carlisle, and after a solemn thanksgiving, and a festival of fourteen days in honour of his victory, was advised by Merlin to march to London, and there to summon round him all the great vassals of the kingdom, for the purpose of receiving their oaths of allegiance.

At this assembly, Merlin, after representing the very formidable conspiracy which was formed against Arthur, recommended that an embassy should be sent to King Ban of Benoit, and King Bohort of Gannes, two of the best knights in the world, to request their immediate presence, and that Sir Bretel and Sir Ulfin should be the bearers of the invitation. They passed the sea; found on the frontiers of France and Britany a vast wilderness, the effect of the long wars carried on by Claudas, the French tyrant, against the Bretons; and during their passage through this desolated country were attacked by seven knights, partisans of King Claudas, of whom they slew six, put the seventh to flight, executed their commission, and returned to England accompanied by Ban and Bohort, and by a third brother named Grimbaut, a clerk, only inferior to the arch-conjurer Merlin.

On their arrival they were welcomed at Portsmouth, and in all the towns from thence to London, by songs and by 'hoppings' or dances:

---

36. Saw.
37. Took.
38. Stretched.
39. Shook; trembled.
40. Slid.
41. Against.
42. Fled.

> . . . . . . every strete
> Was bi-honged[43], ich say forsoth,
> With many pall, and many cloth.
> Everich man of each mester[44]
> Hem riden again with fair attire.
> In everich strete, damiseles
> Carols[45] ledden, fair and feles.[46]

Arthur met them in great state, and led them to a splendid entertainment; and after dinner the royal guests were much edified by listening to a conversation between Merlin and Grimbaut, which they could not understand, concerning the 'quaintise' and contrivance of the sphere, the sun, moon, stars, and other 'privy works'. They then, being fully satisfied by Merlin as to the validity of Arthur's title, swore fealty to him, and afterwards proceeded to a tournament; which must have been very magnificent, because the author enumerates fourteen knights whose feats of arms were particularly noticed. These were Sir Kay, Sir Lucan the Butler, Sir Grifles, Sir Maruc, Sir Gumas, Sir Placides, Sir Driens, Sir Holias, Sir Graciens, Sir Marlians, Sir Flandrius, Sir Melcard, Sir Drukius, and Sir Breoberius. These festivities being ended, Merlin at length explained to the two kings the great purposes for which he had requested their presence; the first of which was, that they should assist King Arthur in obtaining the hand of Guenever, the daughter of Leodigan, king of Carmalide, and that with this view they should discomfit King Rion, who, at the head of twenty tributary sovereigns, was making war on the said Leodigan. The other, that they should join Arthur with a body of twenty-five thousand men; whereby he would be enabled to overcome eleven kings and one duke, who were at that moment in rebellion against him, and were actually encamped, with a vast army, in the forest of Rockingham.

Ban and Bohort readily admitted the importance of both these objects, but alleged that they were themselves in hourly danger from the enterprises of their old enemy Claudas, who was then soliciting a powerful alliance against them; and that before they could reach Britany, collect their forces, and return to Rockingham, the eleven kings would probably be masters of London. Merlin, however, was by no means discouraged by these difficulties. He promised them, on the faith of a necromancer, that they should not suffer any damage from Claudas, and that the succours which he requested from them should be ready in due time. He then conducted Sir Ulfin and a strong garrison to Rockingham castle, with instructions to guard every pass, and to prevent the passage of any spies from the enemies' forces; after which, returning to London, and obtaining the rings of Ban and Bohort as symbols of the authority under which he acted, he passed *in one night* to Britany; assembled, with the assistance of Sir Leontes and Sir Farien, the lieutenants of the two kings, an army of forty thousand men; left fifteen thousand for the defence of the country; deposited twenty-five thousand at Rockingham; and, appearing very unexpectedly in the presence of Arthur and his two guests, advised that the royal army should immediately begin its march.

The rebel kings, who had formed their camp in the forest of Rockingham, were ten in number: viz. Clarion king of Northumberland, Brangores king of Strangore, Cradelman of North Wales, and a certain king called Agrugines, whose dominions lay very far north, and who is usually distinguished by the title of 'king of the hundred

---

43. Hung.
44. Trade, A.N.
45. Dances.
46. Numerous.

knights'; and the six who have been already enumerated. Estas or Enslaf, earl of Arundel, had also joined their forces, and this formidable confederacy had assembled an army of forty thousand men. They thought themselves secure of victory, because they knew that Arthur's forces amounted to no more than fifteen thousand; and were ignorant of the large reinforcements which Merlin, by a stroke of necromancy, had so recently smuggled over from Britany. They were therefore on the point of being surprised in their camp; but Lot, having very luckily dreamed a bad dream, sent out a number of scouts, who falling in with Arthur's army on its march, spread the alarm, and gave time to the troops to seize their arms. Merlin, however, by a new enchantment, caused all the tents to fall down at once; and the confusion thus produced forced the enemies to retreat some miles, during which they lost about one-fourth of their numbers. A long and obstinate encounter then took place, in which many fell on both sides by wounds which exhibit great anatomical variety; but at length the confederated kings were totally routed; and Arthur, after bestowing the pillage of their camp on his friends Ban and Bohort, returned with them to London.

Merlin now assured him that he had nothing more to fear from the rebels; that a dreadful famine, which would speedily be felt all over the country, and the approach of new Saxon invaders, would shortly compel his rivals to court his protection; that nothing remained for him but to amass a large stock of provisions, which he must disperse amongst his fortified towns, and to put his whole army in garrisons; that he should presently receive a strong reinforcement of young and valiant knights, who would become the instruments of his future victories; and that he might now dismiss his Breton auxiliaries, reserving only their two leaders. Ban and Bohort. Finally he invited him to a meeting, within a few days, at the town of Breckenho, between England and Carmelide, and suddenly vanished from their sight.

Arthur punctually followed the advice of his counsellor, and, having completed his preparations, repaired with his friends to Breckenho. But Merlin, though now by profession a minister of state, was always by taste a conjuror, and delighted in playing tricks upon the sovereigns whom he protected. He now met Arthur and his company in the disguise of an old 'charle' (peasant) with a bow and arrows, shot in their presence a couple of wild-ducks, and, on Arthur's proposing to cheapen them, took occasion to banter him pretty severely for his avarice. Having at length made himself known, he was received with due honours, and, finding it necessary to detain the court during some weeks at Breckenho, made Arthur amends by procuring for him an interview with the fair Lyanor, daughter of a certain Earl Sweyn, a damsel who had repaired to the king for the purpose of doing homage, and thus incidentally obtained the honour of giving birth to a son who was afterwards a knight of the round table. The name of this 'knight of mound' is not mentioned.[47]

CANTO III
In time of winter alange[48] it is!
The foules lesen her bliss!
The leves fallen off the tree;
Rain alangeth[49] the cuntree:
Maidens leseth[50] her hewe;
Ae ever hi lovieth[51] that be trewe!

---

47. In Malory's Morte d'Arthur he is called Borre.
48. Tedious, irksome.
49. Renders irksome.

50. Lose.
51. They love.

These moral reflections are occasioned by the author's change of his subject. He now carries us to the eleven kings, who, at the moment of their greatest distress in consequence of their late defeat, received intelligence that a vast body of Saxons was landed in the country, and that their whole remaining force would probably be insufficient to make head against this new and formidable enemy. In this exigency it was proposed by Cradelman, king of North Wales, that they should separate their forces; that each should collect around him a chosen body of men, and retire to the strongest posts in their respective dominions; and that, by carrying on a predatory war against the invaders, they should cut off by degrees their means of subsistence in the interior of the country. This advice was unanimously adopted; and they continued to defend themselves in their several capitals, (of which the names and situations are equally unintelligible,) during five years of bloody but obscure warfare; while their subjects, too much harassed to sow or gather in their harvests, were perishing in great numbers through want and misery. Cradelman himself was much infested by a wicked witch his neighbour, sister to a *soudan* called Hardogabran, a pagan conjurer. Her name was Carmile; and she was scarcely inferior, in knowledge of the black art, to the celebrated Morgain, who 'beguiled the good clerk Merlin'.

So general was the scene of misery, that Britain seemed to be on the verge of its total ruin: but heaven was now preparing the means of its deliverance, and a new generation was rising to repair the mischiefs produced by the rebellion of the confederate kings. Brangore had, about this time, espoused Indranes, the widow of the king of 'Hungary and Blaike'; and Sagremore, her son by this foreign husband, a knight of the most undaunted valour, was preparing to come to Britain, to receive the order of knighthood from the hands of King Arthur. The same project was formed about the same time by a small band of young heroes within this island; and the author of the romance has employed the remainder of this, and the whole of the following canto, in relating their achievements.

The reader will remember that Nanters, king of Gerlot, had married Blasine, uterine sister to Arthur, and had by her a son named Galachin. King Lot had married Belisent, the other daughter of Ygerna, and had four sons, Wawain or Gawain, Gueheret, Gaheriet, and Agravain. Galachin, having observed that the progress of the enemy was chiefly owing to want of union among the Britons, one day inquired of his mother Blasine whether Arthur was indeed his uncle; and on being told by her that it was so, and that he could not be better employed than in producing a reconciliation between his uncle and his father, he determined to undertake the task, and to associate, if possible, his cousin Gawain in the same project. Gawain was on a hunting party when Galachin's messenger arrived; and, returning to his mother with his three greyhounds in one hand and three *raches*[52] in the other, was received with reproaches for the futility of his amusements.

> 'Thou lesest[53] thy time with unright;
> Thou hast age to ben knight.
> Thou shult leten[54] thy folie,
> Thy rage[55] and thy ribaudie.[56]
> Think on thine eme[57] King Arthour,

---

52. Scenting hounds.
53. Losest.
54. Leten, leave.
55. Rage, wantonness.
56. Ribaudie, profligacy.
57. Uncle.

Knight that is of mest[58] valour.
And fond[59] to make good acord
Between him and Lot thy lord!'
Ther sehe told, him before,
How Arthour was bigeten and bore, &c.

Gawain excused himself by alleging his ignorance of these particulars. He redispatched the messenger of Galachin with assurances that he would shortly join him; and, finding that his three brothers were resolved on the same adventure, desired Belisent to furnish them with arms and a proper number of attendants; repaired at their head to 'the fair of Brockland' the appointed place of meeting; and, embracing Galachin, joyfully associated him in the enterprise, and fixed a day for their march towards London.

CANTO IV

Miri is th' entré of May;
The fowles make miric play;
Maidens singeth, and maketh play;
The time is hot, and long the day.
The jolif[60] nightingale singeth,
In the grene mede flowers springeth.

Lot and Belisent equipped their four sons for their great expedition with the utmost magnificence; and assembled to attend them five hundred young men, sons of earls and barons, all mounted on the best horses, with complete suits of choice armour, and all habited in the same cloth. Of this splendid troop, nine only had yet received the order of knighthood: the rest were candidates for that honour, and anxious to earn it by an early encounter with the enemy. The four princes received the parental benediction, and departed for the place of rendezvous appointed by Galachin, who met them with a similar troop of two hundred men appointed by Nanters and Blasine to attend him.

After a march of three days, they arrived in the vicinity of London, where they expected to find Arthur and his court, and very unexpectedly fell in with a large convoy belonging to the enemy, consisting of seven hundred sumpter horses, seven hundred carts, and five hundred waggons, all loaded with provisions, and escorted by three thousand men.

For the poudre[61] of this charging,
No might man see sonne shining.

Indeed the dust was considerably increased by the number of fugitives from the whole neighbouring country, who, with shrieks which 'shrilled into the cloud', attempted to escape from their burning houses, and from the indiscriminate slaughter exercised by the spoilers. Gawain's small army afforded a retreat to these frightened peasants, and a rallying point to about five hundred soliders who were also flying before the enemy; and from these he learnt the absence of Arthur, who was then conducted by Merlin to

---

58. Mest, most.
59. Try.
60. Joyful.
61. Dust.

the assistance of Leodegan; the general desolation of the country; and the necessity of a speedy effort to retrieve the affairs of the Britons. A single charge from Gawain's impetuous cavalry was sufficient to recover the convoy, which was instantly dispatched to London; and the escort, though much more numerous than the assailants, being thrown into confusion by this very unexpected attack, were so rapidly cut to pieces, that no more than twenty men were able to escape, and to carry to the neighbouring army of Saracens the news of this astonishing disaster. Their panic indeed was excusable, as they had never encountered any enemies at all comparable to these youthful heroes, and particularly to the formidable Gawain:

> For arme none, y-wrought with hond,
> Ogain his dent[62] no mighte stond.
> That he tok, he all to-rof,[63]
> So dust in wind; and aboute drof![64]

The author here takes occasion to inform us of a circumstance, very notorious at the time of these events, and certainly no less curious than important, viz., that the strength of Gawain, though always surpassing that of common men, was subject to considerable oscillations, depending on the progress of the sun. From nine in the morning till noon his muscular powers were doubled; from thence till three o'clock in the afternoon they relapsed into their ordinary state; from three till the time of evensong they were again doubled; after which this preternatural accession of strength again subsided till day-break. The poet, therefore, had reason to relate with some exultation that this great victory was achieved about noon, or shortly after.

In the mean time, one half of the twenty paynims who had escaped, fell in with a body of seven thousand unbelieving Irishmen, and brought them back to the attack of the five princes and of their little army. Gawain, singling out a king called Choas, who was fourteen feet high, began the battle by splitting him from the crown of the head to the breast. Galachin encountered King Sanigran, who was also very huge, and cut off his head. Agravain, having no kings immediately within his reach, amused himself with the necks of plebeians, which he cut through by dozens at a time, till he formed a circle of dead bodies to his satisfaction. Gaheriet was employed in the same manner, when he was called off from this vulgar prey by the desire of killing a certain King Grinbat, whom he saw in the act of overthrowing his brother Gueheret. Grinbat, who had witnessed Gaheriet's prowess, wished to decline the contest, and galloped off the field at full speed till he reached a valley, where a fresh army of eight thousand paynims, conducted by the other ten fugitives, was advancing to join the battle. Here he expected to find refuge; but Gaheriet, pursuing him into the crowd, discharged a blow at him, which cut off a quarter of his helmet, one of his cheeks, a shoulder, and an arm. The young prince now attempted, in his turn, to retreat; but though he easily cut his way through the enemy, he was closely pursued by numbers, till at length, his horse being killed under him, he was compelled to fight singly and on foot against a host of enemies.

Fortunately, one of his attendants, who had witnessed his impetuous pursuit of Grinbat, foresaw the danger, and hastened to Gawain with the intelligence. That prince, his two brothers, and Galachin instantly flew to the rescue of Gaheriet, bore down or killed all before them, and at length found the hero on the ground, nearly exhausted by

---

62. Stroke.
63. Crumbled to pieces.
64. Drove; rushed.

heat and fatigue, and surrounded by a crowd of vulgar enemies, who had already begun to unlace his helmet, and were preparing to cut off his head; when they were diverted from their purpose by the sudden amputation of their own. Gaheriet being now supplied with a fresh horse, the five knights made a desperate charge, cut their way out, and, though harassed in their retreat, rejoined their little army.

In the mean time, the convey, which they had intercepted and sent to London, having reached that city in safety, the *constable* or mayor, whose name was Sir Do, learnt the very unequal conflict in which the young princes had been engaged; and having proceeded to Algate, where he blew his horn, and thus collected the several aldermen of the city with their respective wards, amounting to seven thousand men, ordered them to arm, and, leaving two thousand to guard the city, put himself at the head of five thousand and marched out to the rescue of Gawain. It was now past three o'clock; and Gawain's strength becoming doubled, he astonished friends and foes by his supernatural prowess.

> In blood he stode, ich it abowe,[65]
> Of horse and man into the anclowe,[66]
> That he hadde himselve y-slawe,
> Withouten sleight of his felawe.[67]

In this situation he saw a pagan on the point of killing his brother Agrazain, and suddenly leaping two-and-twenty feet over the heads of his own assailants, clove the misbelieving wretch to the girdle, and, springing into the empty saddle, again dashed into the midst of his enemies.

The arrival of the Londoners soon decided the contest. Gimbating, one of the Saracen kings, was already slain; Medelan, his associate in the command, after felling Sir Do, was killed by Gawain; and the troops, now without a leader, fled in all directions, and were slaughtered without resistance. The princes, having thus in one day annihilated three armies of the enemy, proceeded to London, where Gawain directed Sir Do to divide the whole booty amongst the citizens, and thus added considerably to the acclamations with which they had already welcomed their noble deliverers.

CANTO V

> Marche is hot, miri, and long;
> Fowles singen her song;
> Burjouns springeth, medes greeneth;
> Of every thing the heart keeneth.[68]

Arthur departed from Breckenho and arrived at Carohaise, the capital of Carmelide, attended only by Merlin, and by thirty-nine knights whom the magician had selected for that service. Leodegan was at that moment sitting in council with his knights of the round table, two hundred and fifty in number, who had all been nominated by Uther Pendragon, and placed under the command of *Hervi the Rivel* and *Millot the Brown*, two knights of approved valour and experience: and they were then endeavouring, but with little prospect of success, to devise means of resisting the impending attack from

---

65. I maintain it, *avow* it to be true.
66. The ancle, A.S.
67. Without the help or contrivance of his companions.
68. Becomes earnestly inclined for.

Ryance, king of Ireland, who, with fifteen tributary kings and an almost innumerable army, had nearly surrounded the city, and was preparing to assault the walls.

Merlin halted his company at the door of the council-hall, caused them to alight, and marched them in procession up to the throne, where Ban was directed to address the king in a speech which he had previously learned at Breckenho. And here the author thinks that it will be very comfortable to his hearers to know the names of the illustrious characters who formed this procession; they are as follow:

Arthur was supported on his right by King Ban, and on his left by King Bohort; the rest followed hand in hand, but in pairs. These were, Sir Antour, Sir Ulfin, Sir Bretel, Sir Kay, Sir Lucan, Sir Do, son of the mayor of London, Sir Grifles, Sir Maroc, Sir Drians of the forest sauvage, Sir Belias of Maiden Castle, Sir Flandrin, Sir Lammas, Sir Amours the Brown, Sir Ancales the Red, Sir Bleobel, Sir Bleoberis, Sir Canode, Sir Aladan the Crisp, Sir Colatides, Sir Lampades, Sir Lercas, Sir Christopher of the Roche North, Sir Aigilin, Sir Calogrevand, Sir Angusale, Sir Agravel, Sir Cleodes the Foundling, Sir Ginures of Lambale, Sir Kehedin, Sir Merengis, Sir Gorvain, Sir Craddock, Sir Claries, Sir Bhehartis, Sir Amadan the Orgulous,[69] Sir Oroman hardy of heart, Sir Galescound, and Sir Bleheris, a godson of King Bohort. Merlin, who bore the white rod before Arthur, completed the number.

Those who may be disposed to glance their eye slightingly over this edifying catalogue should be told, that the names thus divulged to them were carefully concealed from King Leodegan; and that Ban was only permitted to tell him, in answer to his many inquiries respecting this noble troop, that 'they were strangers who came to offer him their services in his wars, but under the express condition that they should be at liberty to conceal their names and quality, until they should think proper to give him further information.' These terms were thought very strange and unprecedented, but were thankfully accepted; and the strangers, after taking the usual oath to the king, retired to the lodging which Merlin had prepared for them.

A few days after this, the enemy, regardless of a truce into which they had entered with Leodegan, suddenly issued from their camp to the number of sixty thousand men; made an unexpected attempt to surprise the city; and, being disappointed, spread themselves over the country, and, after carrying off as much booty as they could collect, proceeded to put all the inhabitants to the sword. On this alarm Cleodalis, the king's steward, assembled the royal forces with all possible dispatch; these amounted to about five thousand men. The two hundred and fifty knights of the round table soon joined him, and waited for the king's orders. Arthur and his companions also flew to arms; and Merlin appeared at their head, bearing a standard which excited, and not without reason, universal astonishment.

> Upon the top stode a dragoun,
> Swithe griselich,[70] with a litel croun;
> Fast him beheld alle in the town!
> For the mouthe he hadde grinninge,
> And the tonge out-platting,[71]
> That out kest sparkes of fer,[72]
> Into the skies thot flowen cler.
> This dragoun hadde a longe taile,

---

69. The proud, A.N.
70. *Griselich*, frightful.
71. *Out-platting*, lolling out.
72. *Fer*, fire.

That was wither-hooked,[73] sans faile.
Merlin cam to the gate,
And bade the porter him out late.

The porter, of course, refused, and requested him to await the king's orders; but Merlin, taking up the gate with all its appurtenances of locks, bolts, iron bars, &c., directed his troop to pass through; after which he, without dismounting, replaced it in perfect order, set spurs to his horse, and dashed at the head of his little troop into a body of two thousand Saracens who were leading to their camp a convoy of provisions. To discomfit these miscreants, and to retake the convoy, was the work of about twenty minutes; but on their return towards the city, they met a second convoy of a thousand carts escorted by sixteen thousand men. The disparity of numbers being so enormous, Merlin thought it worth while to cast a spell among the enemy, whom his troop charged with their usual gallantry, and proceeded to cut in pieces with all possible expedition. But the people in the city, who beheld this strangely unequal contest, were ashamed of leaving the small body of strangers to their fate.

Tho were up-undone the gate;
Cleodalis rode out thereat.
The steward, with five thousinde,
Opon the paynims[74] gun to wende.[75]
There was din! there was cry!
Many shaft broken, sikerly.[76]
For, in the coming of Cleodalis,
The payens might sen,[77] y-wis.
There was swiche contek[78] and wonder,
That it dinned so the thunder.

Leodegan, at the same time, charged at the head of two thousand picked men, and of fifty knights of his round table, and the remaining two hundred knights formed a third separate division of his small army. But the Saracens, having at length united all their forces, were enabled to oppose to each of these divisions a prodigious superiority. The knights of the round table, unable to bear up against the multitude of their opponents, made a desperate stand under the city walls; and while Cleodalis, with the assistance of Arthur and his companions, was gaining some slight advantages, the division commanded by the king in person was completely surrounded, and the monarch himself borne down and carried off by the enemy. Five hundred picked knights were chosen to conduct him to the camp of Ryance, whilst his attendants, though fighting with desperation, were unable to effect his rescue.

His dochter[79] stode on the city wall,
And beheld this misaventure[80] all.
Her hondes she set on her hair,

---

73. *Wither-hooked*, barbed.
74. Heathens.
75. Began to go.
76. Surely; certainly.
77. Might see; *i.e.*, they recovered their sight.
78. Debate. Hence, contest.
79. Daughter.
80. Misfortune.

And her fair tresses all to-tare.[81]
She her to-tare to her smok,
And on the wal her heved[82] gan knok,
And swooned oft, and said, 'Allas!'

But Merlin, aware of what passed in every part of the field, suddenly collected his knights, led them out of the battle, intercepted the passage of the five hundred who had conveyed away Leodegan, and, charging them with irresistible impetuosity, soon cut in pieces or dispersed the whole escort. The strokes of Arthur, Ban, Bohort, and the rest, fell 'like hail on the shingles'; and Merlin, having now near five hundred vacant horses, and as many suits of excellent armour, at his disposal, hastily equipped the king, and, leaving Cleodalis to fight as well as he could, returned at full speed to the city walls, and fell 'like a northern tempest' on the rear of the victorious Saxons.

The knights of the round table were, by this time, almost all unhorsed; but the very welcome sight of Merlin's fiery dragon, and the joyful shouts from the walls which hailed the unexpected return of their captive monarch, inspired them with fresh courage, and spread alarm through the ranks of the Saracens. The terrible 'forty-two' overcame, like a torrent, all opposition; and the boldest leaders of the Paynims, in attempting to check its progress, successively met their destruction. Caulang, a giant fifteen feet high, encountered Arthur: and the fair Guenever, who already began to feel a strong attachment to the handsome stranger, trembled for the issue of the contest; when the British monarch, dealing a dreadful blow on the shoulder of the monster, divided him to the navel so accurately, that the two sides hung over his horse, and he was thus carried about the field to the great horror of the Saracens. Guenever could not refrain from expressing aloud her wish, that the gentle bachelor who carved giants so dexterously were destined to become her husband; and the wish was re-echoed by her attendants. King Ban dispatched a second giant in a nearly similar manner; and Bohort meeting a third, who was standard-bearer to the army, cut away his shoulder, arm, and banner; after which the enemy began to fly with precipitation, and were closely pursued by Leodegan and his attendants.

But the Saracens had still in the field two large armies; one commanded by a king called Saphiran, who was opposed to Cleodalis, consisting of about fourteen thousand men; and a second, led by a certain King Sornegrex, amounting to eight thousand, including the fugitives who had rallied round him. Merlin led his forty-two against the latter, and was shortly joined by the two hundred and fifty knights of the round table, who had now supplied themselves with fresh horses; but as the heathens made a stout resistance, he directed his followers to turn their whole efforts against ten giant-champions on whom the Saracens placed their principal reliance. These, with Sornegrex at their head, being soon dispatched, the Christian knights quickly spread destruction through the rest, and drove them like straw before the wind. Yet even this victory was inefficient, because the beaten army took refuge with that of Saphiran, who by dint of numbers had already driven Cleodalis under the walls of the city, and began to anticipate the total destruction of the Christian forces.

Merlin though aware that no time was to be lost, ordered his knights to alight for a few moments, to relieve their horses, and then led them to this fresh contest. Cleodalis, who had exhausted all the arts of a commander, was almost in despair, when he was cheered by a general shout from the walls, announcing the rapid approach of the fire-

---

81. Tore in pieces.
82. Head.

casting dragon, of Leodegan, and of the knights of the round-table. The first charge of the forty-two was, as usual, irresistible; but Saphiran, who far surpassed all the Saracen kings in skill and valour, summoning round him his best knights, made a desperate attack upon these new assailants, and had the honour of breaking into this hitherto untouched phalanx, and of unhorsing many of Arthur's bravest champions. He then again returned, broke into them a second time, bore Leodegan to the ground, slew his horse, and was only prevented from killing him by the timely interposition of Arthur, who vented his rage in imprecations of vengeance agains the infidel; while Merlin, boiling with impatience, exclaimed,

'What abidest thou? coward king!
The paien[83] give anon meeting!'

Arthur, stung with this unexpected reproach, flew to meet Saphiran, whose spear was so strong and well directed, that it pierced his shield and hauberk, and wounded him in the side; but his lance at the same time passed through the body of Saphiran.

Quath Arthur, 'Thou hethen cokein,[84]
Wende to the devil Apolin!'
The payen fel dede to ground;
His soul laudht[85] hell-hound!

Ban, who on this occasion had first trembled for the days of his friend; Bohort, Kay, and the other worthies, now exerted themselves so well that the remaining leaders of the Saracens were soon dispatched; and the victory was so complete, that only five hundred survivors of this terrible day were able to reach the camp of Ryance.

The immense booty gained from the heathens was, by the king's order, presented to Arthur, who divided the whole amongst the subjects of Leodegan, having first particularly enriched the host with whom he had hiterto lodged, and whose house he now left for apartments at the palace. He was disarmed, and conducted to the bath by the princess Guenever, while his friends were attended by the other ladies of the court. Amongst these was a second Guenever, an illegitimate daughter of Leodegan, and so nearly resembling the princess that it was difficult to distinguish them. Her mother, a lady of exquisite beauty and maid of honour to the queen, had been married to Cleodalis, but, during his absence on some embassy, had resumed her functions, and habitually slept in the royal apartment. The queen, a woman of exemplary devotion, constantly rose to attend matins; and the amorous monarch had contrived on these occasions to indemnify himself for her absence and to share the bed of her attendant; whom, after the birth of a little Guenever, he secreted from her husband, and whom he continued to reserve as an occasional substitute for his devout consort, without exciting, as it should seem, any violent indignation in the tranquil Cleodalis.

The knights were now conducted to a magnificent entertainment, at which they were diligently served by the same fair attendants. Leodegan, more and more anxious to know the name and quality of his generous deliverers, and occasionally forming a secret wish that the chief of his guests might be captivated by the charms of his daughter, appeared silent and pensive, and was scarcely roused from his reverie by the ban-

---

83. Pagan; heathen.
84. Rascal.
85. Caught.

ters of his courtiers. Arthur, having had sufficient opportunities of explaining to Guenever, with that obscurity and circumlocution which a growing passion always inspires, his great esteem for her merit, was in the joy of his heart, and was still more delighted on learning from Merlin the late exploits of Sir Gawain in Britain; by means of which his immediate return to his dominions was rendered unnecessary, and he was left at liberty to follow those propensities which led him to protract his stay at the court of Leodegan.

CANTO VI

Listeneth now, fele and few;
In May the sunne felleth dew;
The day is miri, and draweth along;
The lark arereth[86] her song;
To meed[87] goth the damisele,
And faire flowers gadreth fele.

The poet now proceeds to describe the miseries to which the confederate kings in opposition to Arthur were exposed by the Saracen or Saxon invasion; but, unluckily, his geography is so very confused, that it is impossible to understand the position of the various battles which he paints with great minuteness.

Cradelman, king of North Wales, was first alarmed for the safety of his dominions, by the information that the enemy had landed in great force on both sides of Arundel, a city which, according to this romance, was not in Sussex but in Cornwall. Cradelman, taking with him ten thousand men, one-half of which he confided to the command of his steward Polydamas, attacked the pagans during the night, completely surprised them, and made a great slaughter; but the fugitives, having escaped to the neighbouring territories of Carmile, brought back a most powerful reinforcement, by which Cradelman was in his turn very nearly overpowered; but was finally rescued from destruction by a well directed sally of the garrison of Arundel, and by the assistance of the king of the hundred knights, who had accidentally heard the news of the invasion. The spoils of the enemy's camp were carried in triumph into Arundel.

About the same time,

Ther comen up, fer on north,
Ten riche soudans of grete worth;

and these soudans, or sultans, whose names are carefully enumerated, directed their forces, amounting to a million and a half of men against Anguisant, king of Scotland. Anguisant was then in his city of Comauges, and, hearing that the whole plain country was occupied by the infidels, hastily levied a body of fifteen thousand men, and riding to an eminence, beheld the extensive desolation of his territories.

His men there he shift a-two.[88]
Half he toke himself, and mo,
And halvendel[89] he tok[90] Gaudin,

---

86. Raises.
87. Mead, or meadow.
88. Divided into two portions.
89. Half.
90. Gave.

> That was knight hardi and fin,[91]
> That sithen,[92] of his mighty hand,
> Wan that maiden of the douke Brauland.

This little army performed prodigies of valour, but were finally overpowered by the enormous superiority of numbers. Leaving nine thousand of his followers on the field, Anguisant with great difficulty led back the remaining six to his fortified city; nor could he have effected this retreat but for the timely assistance of Urien, who, accompanied by his nephew Baldemagus, fell upon the rear of the Saracens with a body of twelve thousand picked soldiers.

> Ther was mani heved off weved,[93]
> And many to the middle cleved;[94]
> And mani of his horse y-lust;[95]
> For sothe, there ros so michel dust,
> That of the summe, schene and bright,
> No man might have no sight.
> Here and there cri, and honteye![96]
> Men might hem heren thre mile way!

The approach of night separated the combatants. Urien, on his return, unexpectedly fell upon a valuable convoy of the enemy, escorted by about eight thousand men, who were then unarmed and at table. He charged them, cut the escort to pieces without opposition, and carried off the convoy.

While this was passing in the north, Sagremor, who had embarked at Constantinople for the purpose of receiving the order of knighthood from King Arthur, arrived in Sussex with seven hundred noble companions who were ambitious of the same honour. They found the whole country overrun by a Saracen army under the command of King Oriens; but, having collected about five hundred adventurers whom they blended with their little troop, determined, with more boldness than wisdom, to cut their way through these infidels. They had scarcely formed this resolution, when an *old churl*, accosting Gawain, who was still in London, informed him that Sagremor was on the point of being surrounded and killed; urged him to hasten, with such forces as he could raise, to his assistance; and promised to conduct him by a very short route to the place of combat. To confirm his intelligence, he presented some letters apparently written by Sagremor; and Gawain was almost immediately ready to depart at the head of fifteen thousand citizens, who were joined on the march by numbers of volunteers, whilst the old churl conducted them without the least interruption, through roads unknown to the enemy, till they reached the field of battle.

Sagremor and his companions had successfully cut their way through some twenty thousands of miscreants, but at last found themselves, by repeated exertions of almost miraculous valour, hemmed in on all sides by the innumerable host of their assailants. They were then reduced to despair, and almost on the point of throwing down their arms when their spirits were restored by the unexpected appearance of Gawain and his

---

91. Perfect.
92. Since.
93. Heads taken off.
94. Cut through.
95. Lost.
96. Confusion; dishonour.

brethren, who joined them at the first charge, after killing or oversetting sixteen thousand infidels. Then

Mani mouthe the gras bot,[97]
And griselich yened,[98] God it wot!
Payens floated in her blod!
Ever is Christis mighte good.

Gawain, having luckily encountered King Oriens, gave him a blow on his helmet which threw him to the ground in a swoon, and was preparing to pursue his victory; when an unknown knight, suddenly accosting him in an imperious tone, ordered him to sound a retreat, and to lead his army to Camalot. Gawain obeyed, and had conducted his troops about a mile; when Oriens, recovering from his trance, called for a fresh horse and a new suit of armour, and galloped at the head of sixty thousand cavaliers to intercept the Christians. The result however was, that he was thrown into a second swoon by a blow from the sword of Gawain; and though the hardness of his skull and helmet resisted this repetition of the experiment, a considerable number of his best generals were slain around him by Gaheriet, Agravain, Galachin, Gueheret and Sagremor; and the Christians made good their retreat within the walls of Camalot, where the arrival of Sagremor was celebrated by all kinds of rejoicing.

Oriens, whose bruises did not tend to soften the ferocity of his temper, finding that it was hopeless to attempt the siege of Camalot, led his army into the territory of Caubernie, belonging to Estas, duke of Arundel, spoiled the whole country, and carried his ravages into the *adjoining* states belonging to King Clarion. Estas repaired to this monarch for the purpose of consulting him on the means of resisting, or at least of harassing, their inexorable enemy; and after a long discussion, which it is not worth while to repeat, they agreed to take post, with as many troops as they could levy, in the great forest of Rockingham, and there to watch an opportunity of taking their revenge on the Saracens.

CANTO VII

In May is miri time swithe;
Foules in wode hem maken blithe;
In every lond arist[99] song;
Jesus Christ be ous among!

The business of this short canto is not very interesting. The combined troops of Duke Estas and of King Clarion, having chosen a station in the forest where seven roads met, soon discovered a convoy –

Full of ich maner prey;
Of venisoun, and flesch, and brede,
Of brown ale, and win white and rede,
Of baudekins, and purple pall,
Of gold and silver, and cendal:[100]

---

97. Bit the grass, i.e. died.
98. Yawned frightfully.
99. Arises.
100. Baudkin was a rich and precious kind of cloth, composed of silk and gold thread. Cendal was also a kind of rich thin silken stuff, very highly esteemed. – See Halliwell's Dictionary of Archaisms, *in voce*.

and suddenly attacking the escort of five thousand horsemen, put them all to the sword, and seized the convoy, which they lodged in safety within the walls of Arundel. In returning from this capture they had an encounter with fifteen thousand Saracens, whom they also attacked and dispersed, after killing two or three giants who commanded them: but foreseeing that the enemy would be constantly strengthened by fresh reinforcements, they prudently secured their means of retreat into the forest. Oriens, on hearing of their success, became, as usual, very ferocious.

> 'Ah Mahoun!'[101] said Oriens, 'tho
> Thou nart[102] a god worth a sloe!
> Therefore the folk thou dost no gode,
> So for Christen doth her Gode!'

He then ordered forty thousand men to surround and destroy these insolent Christians; but they had already taken their measures, and under cover of the forest and of the night, retired with little loss to their several fastnesses.

CANTO VIII

> Mirie it is in somer's tide;
> Foules sing in forest wide;
> Swaines gin on justing ride;
> Maidens liffen hem in pride.

We have seen, that though Arthur had carried with him, to the assistance of Leodegan, the flower of British chivalry, a new race of heroes had since started up for the defence of the country. Gawain, his cousin Galachin, and his three brothers, together with Sagremor, already ranked with the most experienced commanders; and a new champion, the celebrated Ywain, was soon added to the number. It will be remembered that Urien

> Hadde spoused Hermesent,
> Blasine sister and Belisent.
> Thai had a young man hem bitwen,
> Michel Ywain, a noble stren.[103]
> He was yeleped[104] michel Ywain,
> For he hadde a brother knight, certain,
> Bast Ywain he was yhote,
> For he was bigeten a bast,[105] God it wote.
> Urien, by another quen,
> Yet hadde bigeten a gentil stren.
> That was hoten Morganor;
> A gode knight by Godis ore.[106]
> He hadde made him in al heir
> To the lond that of him com, veir.[107]

---

101. Mahomet.
102. Art not
103. Progeny.
104. Called.
105. A bastard.
106. Grace.
107. Truly.

> The lond that com of Hermesent
> Was Ywain's, thurgh right descent.

Mickle Ywain made the same request to Hermesent which Galachin and Gawain had addressed to Blasine and Belisent, and was, like them, strongly encouraged to forward a reconciliation between Arthur and his father Urien. Hermesent provided for him a hundred knights, and three hundred young bachelors, candidates, like himself, for the order of knighthood, with a proper supply of horses and armour; and Ywain, having received the maternal benediction, departed with his bastard brother, and began his march 'all by the forest of Bedingham, toward Arundel, in Cornwall'.

His road lay through the territories of King Yder; but they were at that time overrun by innumerable swarms of Saracens; and their ravages were so extensive that the report of them reached the ears of Gawain, who immediately marched to the rescue of Yder at the head of thirty thousand men; and, passing from London through Carduel, arrived at Bedingham about the time when Ywain quitted it on his way to Arundel. Yder himself at the same moment resolved on trying the fate of a battle with the enemy; and, putting himself at the head of fifteen thousand men, was accidentally encountered by the rear guard of the great Saracen army. Yder, though he perceived the superior numbers of the heathen forces, attacked them without hesitation, broke them, and was making a dreadful carnage of the unbelievers – when he was suddenly attacked by another division of their army, and owed his escape, together with that of a few attendants, to an unexpected diversion produced by Ywain, who issuing from the forest, and seeing the whole open country covered with enemies, instantly attacked the first who came in his way.

Ywain and his bastard brother were accompanied by a knight of great courage and experience named Ates, who quickly discovered, that, having passed a bridge, the only one which was to be found between Arundel and the forest which they had left, and this bridge having been immediately occupied by the Saracens, they had no longer any possibility of retreat. But the young bachelors made no reflections. By a desperate charge these four hundred destroyed five thousand infidels; and, finding themselves still 'whole and sound', began to anticipate a splendid and complete victory.

At this time a *little knave* (*i.e.* boy) delivered to Gawain a letter, which he professed to bring from Ywain; and he, having perused it, immediately called to arms, and, dividing a part of his troops into five bodies of three thousand each, gave the command of them to Sagremor, Galachin, and his three brothers, taking to himself the conduct of the rear guard, consisting of eight thousand.

> The knave taught her way sikerlich,
> Thai riden wel serrelich;[108]
> Ther gilt pensel,[109] with the wind
> Mirie ratled, of cendal ynde.[110]
> The stedes, so noble and so wight.[111]
> Lopen[112] and neighed with the knight.
> These beth alle so fast coming;
> The children, that whiles, wer fighting &c.

108. Closely.
109. Banner.
110. Indian.
111. Strong.
112. Leapt.

But to fight against such superiority of numbers as then assailed them was nearly hopeless, because they were gradually encompassed and attacked in every direction. Ywain now felt the consequences of the mistake which the more prudent Ates had discovered long before; and, in the hope of remedying it, proposed that they should unite all their efforts in one direction; make a violent charge towards the river; and, if it should prove fordable, retreat through it into the forest. But they were disappointed. The high banks of the river prevented all hope of escape, and beyond it they discovered fresh swarms of the enemy hastening towards the bridge. At this moment of desperation they beheld Agravain, who led the van of Gawain's forces, advancing rapidly to their assistance. They now again turned their horses, and, making a second effort, cut their way through the infidels, and joined their friends. The battle, being constantly supplied with fresh combatants by the successive succours of Gueheret, Gaheriet, Galachin, Sagremor, and Gawain, who were opposed by new reinforcements which arrived in the heathen army, was continued with great obstinacy; and our poet, who is never tired of describing such scenes, has painted every circumstance of the combat with the minuteness of an eye-witness, and with a degree of delight and satisfaction in which the modern reader would not easily participate. Suffice it to say, that, the sun approaching the meridian, Gawain's strength became double; and that of Ywain and the other Christian heroes being little diminished, they made as extensive a carnage amongst the infidels as the worst enemy of paganism could conscientiously wish to contemplate, and then marched in triumph and loaded with spoil to their former quarters at Bedingham.

Here Gawain was much surprised to learn that the letters 'written in Latin', which had brought him so opportunely to the assistance of Ywain, were counterfeits. The reader is probably aware that the 'little knave' who brought these letters, the 'old churl' who had announced the danger of Sagremor, and the unknown knight who advised the timely retreat into Arundel, were the same person; and that Merlin, under these and similar disguises, superintended all the enterprises of the British heroes during the absense of Arthur. After refreshing themselves during a few days at Bedingham, they were again summoned in great haste to Arundel.

Kaydestran and Kehedin, two noble young bachelors, with twenty-seven companions, arriving within sight of the walls, fell in with a party of the enemy, whom they instantly overthrew; but, being at length surrounded by greater numbers, and in imminent danger of being captured, were rescued by a sally of three hundred young men from the garrison of the city. The leaders of this little band were Ywain with the white hand, Ywain of Lyones, Ywain de la vis le bel, Ywain of Strangore, and Devidel the savage; all bachelors of approved courage, and all related to the family of Gawain. But before they could make good their retreat the whole were enveloped. At this instant Gawain arrived, and of course vanquished the infidels, rescued the Christian warriors, and was preparing to pursue the enemy, when Merlin, in the shape of an old knight, ordered him to enter Arundel with his young kinsmen, and there to wait for further instructions.

The infidels finding that the Britons could not be attacked with advantage in that part of the country, suddenly united all their forces, and, marching northwards, poured into Lothian, the territory of King Lot. That monarch, advancing against them with twenty thousand men, gained a great and bloody victory; but, having pursued his advantage too far, was totally defeated in his turn by a fresh army, and forced to take refuge, with only three thousand of his followers, in the city of Dorkeine. In this extremity he resolved, by the advice of his council, to make his way to the strong citadel of Glocedoine; to deposit there his wife Belisent and his infant son Modred, and to wait a more favourable opportunity of recovering his dominions.

Gawain was perfectly unconscious of the deplorable situation of his father, and was carelessly leaning with his companions on the walls of Arundel, when a strange knight, accoutred at all points, called to him precipitately to arm, and offered to conduct him to a scene where his assistance was wanted at that moment. Neither Gawain nor any of his companions knew Merlin in this disguise; but, having exacted from him an oath that his tale was strictly true, they hastily collected their forces, put themselves under his guidance, and galloped off in search of this unknown adventure.In passing through a forest they met a knight coming towards them at full speed, and bearing in his arms a child, whom Gawain at once recognized as his brother Modred. The knight informed them that Lot, having been surprised during his march, was severely wounded, and perhaps killed or taken; that Belisent was in the hands of the enemy at a very small distance; and that he, having with difficulty rescued the infant, was attempting to bear him to some place of safety. Gawain ordered the knight to follow his troops, and, keeping them concealed in the forest, cautiously proceeded towards the field of battle; where he soon discovered the infidel king, named Taurus, who, having seized a lady by the tresses of her hair, was endeavouring thus to draw her up and to fix her on his horse. This was Belisent. Her piteous cries for mercy reached the cars and thrilled the heart of Gawain, but, being mixed with invocations of the holy Virgin, drew down repeated buffets from the fist of the ruffian who held her. She fell from the horse's back; but Taurus still sustained her by the hair, scourged her, and bade her follow on foot; and when from weakness she entangled her feet in her long robes, and fell to the ground, he dismounted, tied her tresses to his horse's tail, and thus prepared to ride off with his mangled victim. But an attendant, seeing the rapid approach of Gawain, suddenly cut the lady's hair, and disengaged his master from this encumbrance.

> Wawain with spors his stede smot,
> And he forth sterte,[113] God it wot.
> He gred[114] aloud to King Taurous,
> 'Abide! thou thief malicious!
> Biche-son! thou drawest amiss!
> Thou shalt abeye it ywiss!'[115]

Accordingly, though Taurus was of the same gigantic dimensions with the rest of the infidel chiefs, Gawain passed his spear through his shield, hauberk and heart, and threw him dead amongst his troops, who were speedily exterminated to a man. Belisent, who had fallen into a swoon, was not a little surprised, on first opening her eyes, to find herself attended by her four sons; and her wonder and joy were complete, when, having expressed her fears for the infant Modred, the child was restored to her in health and safety. She then related that Lot, with only three hundred knights, had been attacked by many thousands of the enemy; that after a long and desperate resistance, he had seen her torn from him by the miscreant Taurus; and had only consulted his own safety by flight, when, his attendants being nearly all killed, and himself wounded in fifteen places, he could no longer hope to render her any assistance.

Belisent was now placed on a litter; and, being supplied with all possible conveniences from the sumpter carts of Taurus, six hundred in number, which attended her

---

113. Started.
114. Cried.
115. Certainly expiate it.

march, was conveyed by easy journeys to London, where she was received by the gallant Sir Do, and lodged with proper magnificence in the royal palace.

All these events, it is to be observed, were dictated by Merlin himself to his old master Blaise, – so that their veracity is unquestionable; and we must now follow Merlin to the court of Leodegan, where he related them to Arthur and his companions. He then condescended to inform the king, that the motive of their visit to his court had been to procure a suitable wife for their gallant leader; upon which Leodegan, going in search of Guenever, presented her to Arthur, telling him that, whatever might be his rank, his merit was sufficient to entitle him to the possession of the heiress of Carmelide. Arthur having accepted the lady with the utmost gratitude, Merlin then proceeded to satisfy the king respecting the rank of his son-in-law; upon which Leodegan, with the knights of the round table and his other barons, proceeded to do homage to their legitimate suzerain, the successor of Uther Pendragon. The beauteous Guenever was then solemnly betrothed to Arthur; and a magnificent festival was proclaimed, which lasted seven days, and would have been protracted much longer, but that, fresh succours having arrived in the camp of Ryance, it became necessary to prepare for military operations.

CANTO IX

Mirie is June that scheweth flower
The meden ben[116] of swete odour;
Lily and rose of swete colour;
The river clear withouten sour;[117]
This damiseles love paramour.

The whole of this canto, though it extends to no less than eleven hundred verses, is dedicated to the description of a single battle, which ended in the final discomfiture of King Ryance, and thereby left Arthur at liberty to accomplish the great adventures to which he was destined. The troops of Leodegan were marshalled by the particular advice of Merlin: but we cannot discover any advantages which resulted from the scientific distribution recommended by the magician; the ultimate success being solely owing to the efforts of individual valour.

It was a Monday, festival of Pentecost, that had been previously chosen for this great contest. The Christian knights rose at daybreak, and arrayed themselves in their most sumptuous suits of armour, which were ornamented with gold, silver, and jewels. Arthur, always eager for battle, was now doubly so, because he was to be armed by the hands of the beauteous Guenever; but, as the pieces which composed this iron dress were very numerous, and as the lady, on lacing on each, was required to pay a kiss as the forfeit of her awkwardness, or to receive one as the reward of her dexterity, the length of the ceremony excited the impatience of Merlin, who sternly enjoined the young warrior to remember these kisses[118] in the hour of distress and difficulty.

The main body of the army was divided by Merlin into seven parts of seven thousand men each. Of the first he took the personal direction, and in this body were comprehended the formidable *forty-two*, and the two hundred and fifty knights of the round table: the number being completed by a selection from the bravest of Leodegan's vassals. The commanders of the other six divisions were Gogenar, Leodegan's nephew; Elmadas; Belich le blond; Yder of north-land; Kandon, nephew of Cleodalis; and

---

116. Meads are.
117. Dirt; filth. This word occurs in the Promptorium Parvulorum.
118. One of the Northern chroniclers tells us that the 'amusement of kissing' was not known to the ancient Britons, but that it was introduced into this country by a daughter of Hengist!

Gempore molé; and besides these, a small but choice army of reserve, consisting of ten thousand men, was led by Leodegan in person, assisted by his good steward Cleodalis.

Merlin harangued the army, and promised them final success, notwithstanding the almost innumerable forces of the enemy, whom he proposed to surprise in their camp. This camp, it seems, was fortified on three sides; on the south by a rampart of wagons and carts, and on the west and east by a wall: 'but,' said Merlin, 'we shall attack them on the eastern side,

> 'And find them sleepand, and sle downright,
> For thai wer all dronken tonight.'

He then detached ten knights, with orders to destroy all the scouts who might give information of his approach; and, having unfurled his banner surmounted by the fiery dragon, advanced in silence to the camp, which he entered unperceived.

His first operation was to cast a spell into the air, by virtue of which great numbers of the tents fell down on the heads of the sleeping infidels; and it may be presumed, that those who were very drunken were irrecoverably stifled. Those who were more watchful or alert were punished for their sobriety by being trampled in their shirts under the horses' feet, or pierced by the lances of the assailants. Several thousands were thus slaughtered before a man in the camp had time to put on his armour. But at length a few knights appeared round the tent of King Ryance; these were followed by more; and, their numbers continually increasing, they were enabled to face the Christians, and began 'one of the greatest battles that ever was smitten.'

> Passed was the day-springing,
> The hot sunne was schining,
> Tho began knightes riding,
> Trumpes beting, tambours dassing;[119]
> Ther was fleing and withstonding,
> Tiring, togging,[120] and overthrowing!

Among the knights who distinguished themselves in this terrible day was one whom the author is particularly desirous to recommend to the grateful remembrance of his hearers. This was Nacien, a knight of great prowess and merit, and allied to many of the most renowned heroes of chivalry. His mother was Hamignes, sister to Joseph, a *knight of grace*, through whom he was cousin to the noble Perceval. His father was Ebron, who had sixteen more sons, all knights of great virtue; and through him Nacien was cousin to Celidoine the rich, son of Nacien of Betica, which Celidoine first saw all the mervail of the San Gréal. Nacien was also *sibbe* (i.e. related) to King Pelles of Listoncis,

> And sith then hadde Launcelot
> In his ward almost a yer,
> *So the Romauns seyth elles where:*[121]
> This Naciens, of whom y write,
> Sith then bicom eremite;[122]
> And lette knightschippe and al thing.

---

119. Beating
120. Tearing; tugging.
121. All this information, as well as that which is alluded to in the subsequent passage, is now lost.
122. A hermit.

And bicome preste, messe to sing.
Virgin of his bodi he was,
Whom sith them the holi Godes grace
Ravist into the thridde heven,
Where he herde angels' steven;[123]
And seighe Fader, Son, and Holi Ghost,
In on substaunce, in on acost.
This gave sith then the riche conseil
To the King Arthour, saunfaile,
Tho he was in gret peril
To lese his londes, and ben exil,
Ogaines the king Galahos,
The geauntes sone, of gret los,[124]
That gaf King Arthour batailing, &c.

Nacien was accompanied by Adregain the Brown; and these two had the honour of accompanying Arthur in a desperate attack on the standard of King Ryance, which represented four elephants with their castles. About this time the conflict became general all over the field; and the author has exhausted his powers of description in painting the horrors of the scene.

Al so thick the arwe schoten,[125]
In sunne-beam so doth the moten.
Gavelokes[126] al so thick flowe
So gnattes, ichil abowe.[127]
Ther was so michel dust rising,
That sene there nas sunne schining.
The trumping and the tabouring
Did togeder the knights fling.
The knights broken her speren
On thre,[128] thai smiten and to-teren.[129]
Knightes and stedes ther laien about,
The hevedes off smitten, the guttes out.
Heveden,[130] and fete, and armes, there
Lay strewed everich where
Under stedes' fete, so thick
In crowe's nest so doth the stick.
Sum sterven,[131] and sum gras gnowe;[132]
The gode steden her guttes drewe,
With blodi sadels in that pres.
Of swich bataile was no ses,[133]
To the night fram amorwe,[134]
It was a bataile of gret sorowe!

The main body of the Christian army, being overpowered by superior numbers, were at length driven in confusion under the walls of Denebleise; but again rallying, drove back

123. Voice; song.
124. Glory.
125. Arrows shot.
126. Javelins.
127. I will avow or maintain.
128. Into three parts.

129. Tear in pieces.
130. Heads.
131. Perished.
132. Gnawed the grass, died.
133. Cessation.
134. The morning.

their pursuers, and gave time to the knights of Arthur's company to refresh themselves, and to relieve their horses, who were incapable of carrying, during many hours, the enormous weight of iron which covered their riders. Merlin then, having at leisure taken his survey of the field, ordered his company to mount, and led them at full speed to the part of the battle where he discovered the 'crowns and beards', which were painted on the shield of King Ryance.

Arthur, glad of encountering the Irish monarch, made a violent blow at him, which cut off a quarter of his helmet, divided his shield, and falling on his shoulder, would have slit him to the middle, had not the sword been stopped by the toughness of a serpent's skin which he wore over his shirt. He fell to the ground: and though he was speedily replaced on his horse; though Arthur himself was overthrown and unhorsed by the crowd of giants who pressed forward to rescue their leader; the attack had been so well directed, that the great standard was taken, the infidels who guarded it dispersed in all directions, and Ryance at length, after an obstinate conflict, was obliged to fly before the victorious Arthur, who, singling him out from his companions, pursued him incessantly, and at length overtook him when on the point of joining another division of his army. At this second encounter Ryance received a dangerous and painful wound in the side, and dropped his excellent sword called Marandoise, which became the prey of Arthur.

As Escalibore was certainly the best sword in the world, Arthur seems to have had little occasion for Marandoise: but there is perhaps a pleasure in cutting off infidel heads with an infidel weapon; and in this pleasure Arthur indulged as long as his horse was able to carry him. In the mean time, Merlin had pursued a party of the flying enemy to a considerable distance, and had cast an enchantment on them, by means of which they mistook a valley which lay before them for a deep and spacious lake, into which they declined to venture –

> Hereafter some, in this write,[135]
> Why he did it ye shal it wite.[136]

But unfortunately this important piece of information is lost to posterity, because the whole remainder of the poem, as it now exists is employed in describing the confused scene of slaughter which followed the wound and flight of King Ryance.

The number of the infidels was still so great, and the field of battle so extensive, that no eye but that of a conjuror was capable of comprehending the whole scene; and Merlin alone was aware, that whilst the army of Leodegan was beginning to triumph in all quarters, the monarch himself was in the greatest jeopardy. Being accidentally separated from his body of knights, and attended only by his faithful steward Cleodalis, he had been suddenly attacked by a large troop of the enemy, and had seen his good steward unhorsed at the first onset. A dreadful blow from Colocaulucon, *a huge man*, brought the king also to the ground, and with such violence, that it was long before he began to exhibit any signs of life. Cleodalis, however, who was already on his feet, bestrode the body of his master, and, wielding his sword on all sides, manfully repelled the crowd of assailants till the king recovered his senses. Leodegan now recollected what the reader will perhaps have forgotten; viz., that he was then living in adultery with the beautiful wife of this good steward, and, kneeling before him, humbly implored his forgiveness in a long oration, concluding with

---

135. Writing; work.
136. Know.

> 'Forgive me now my trespas
> That I thee have done, alas!
> I pray thee, that never this misdede
> My soul into helle lede!'

Cleodalis, of course, forgave him as fast as he could, not only because he wished to waive a disagreeable subject, but because, as he properly observed to his master, their joint efforts were at this moment very necessary to preserve them both from being killed or captured. In fact, they were alternately felled to the ground so often, that their strength was at last completely exhausted; and they were on the point of being carried off by the enemy, when Merlin, who probably knew exactly their powers of endurance, and had been unwilling to interrupt the very edifying scene of their reconciliation, arrived with his knights, mounted them both on fresh horses, and in an instant destroyed their pertinacious assailants. Arthur, Ban, Bohort, Nacien, and their companions, who by Merlin's directions had taken time to rest themselves and their horses, now dispersed themselves over the field, and cut to pieces all the infidel leaders who fell in their way:

> The other paiens flowen swithe,[137]
> And our went again, bilive,[138]
> Into the cité of Carohaise;
> With her faren[139] hem made at aise;[140]
> They maden grete bliss and fest,
> And after, yeden[141] hem to rest.

Thus ends this fragment of more than ten thousand lines; the transcriber, as it should seem, thinking that he also had a right to rest from his labour, which he had not the courage to resume. The remainder of the column was occupied by part of another romance, which, as Sir W. Scott informs us, is totally effaced.

EXTRACTS FROM THE ENGLISH MERLIN

edited by H.B. Wheatley

SOMETIMES CALLED *The Prose Merlin*, this text was written some time around the mid-fifteenth century. It exists in a manuscript now in the Cambridge University Library (MS Ff 3 11), and was edited by Henry B. Wheatley for the Early English Text Society between 1865 and 1869. Like the version of *Arthour and Merlin* above, it is in fact a translation of the thirteenth-century Vulgate *Estoire de Merlin*

---

137. Flew quickly.
138. Immediately.
139. Companions.
140. Ease.
141. Went.

and as such covers Merlin's life from birth to his final imprisonment by Nimuë (here called Nimiane). In the course of the action Merlin plays a major role in the establishment of Arthur as king of Britain, and his subsequent wars and trials, his marriage and his struggle to maintain his authority in the face of political opposition. In this the text follows much the same course as Thomas Malory's *Le Morte d'Arthur* (see below), though it does contain several episodes which do not appear elsewhere. In the extracts which follow we have concentrated on three of these. In the first we learn of the birth and history of Nimiane, which differs extensively from other versions of the story. Interestingly, it suggests that she was the daughter of the goddess Diana and as such the inheritor of her power. The parallels between her birth and that of Merlin himself are not to be ignored, while the description of Merlin's wonder-workings designed to impress his sweetheart possess a wry humour. (The significance of this story is further explored in *Ladies of the Lake* by Caitlín and John Matthews, Thorsons, 1992).

The second episode, 'Merlin and Grisandole', forms a brief excursion from the main story and shows us some of Merlin's activities outside the area of Arthurian interest. It is a story rich in comic overtones and shows Merlin in his most teasing aspect. (It is retold, more fully, in *The Unknown Arthur* by John Matthews, Blandford, 1995.)

The third extract, 'The Last Words of Merlin', brings the story of his affair with Nimiane to a conclusion, as Sir Gawain, having suffered an unfortunate encounter with a magician, has been turned into a dwarf. Naturally he seeks the aid of Merlin, only to discover that the old wise man has been himself enchanted. The last words of Arthur's great adviser are moving and powerful, and make a fitting close.

We have chosen not to modernize the spelling of this text, despite its archaisms, since this detracts from its particular charm and personality. However, we have provided a number of glosses of more unfamiliar words at the end of this section. Reading the passages aloud will also help to make them more easily understood, since the medieval method of writing down words was often phonetic.

MERLIN AND NIMUË

Merlin...wente to se a maiden of grete bewte, and was right yonge, and was in a manner that was right feire and delitable and right riche, in a valee vnder a mounteyne rounde side be side to the forest of Briok, that was full delitable and feire, for to hunte at hertes and at hyndes, and bukke and doo and wilde swyn. This mayden of whom I spoke was the doughter of a vauasor of right high lynage, and his name was cleped Dionas, and many tymes diane com to speke with hym, that was the goddesse, and was with hym many dayes, for he was hir godsone; and whan she departed she yaf hym a yefte that plesed hym wele. 'Dionas,' quod diane, 'I graunte the, and so doth the god of the see and of the sterres shull ordeyne, that the firste childe that thow shalt haue female shall be so moche coveyted of the wisest man that euer was erthly or shall be after my deth, whiche in the tyme of kynge Vortiger of the bloy mountayne shall begynne for to regne, that he shall hir teche the moste parte of his witte and connynge by force of nygremauncye in soche maner, that he shall be so desirouse after the tyme that he hath hir seyn that he shall haue no power to do no-thinge a-gein hir volunte, and alle thinges that she enquereth he shall hir teche.' Thus yaf diane to Dionas hir yefte, and whan Dionas was grete he was right a feire knyght and a goode, of high prowesse of body, and he was moche and longe, and longe tyme serued a Duke of Burgoyne, that to hym yaf his nyece to ben his wif, that was right a feire maiden and a wise.

This Dionas loved moche the deduyt of the wode and the river while that he was yonge, and the Duke of Burgoyne hadde a parte in the foreste of brioke, so that was his the haluendell all quyte, and that other half was the kynge Ban. Whan the Duke hadde married his nyece he yaf to Dionas his part of this foreste and londe that he hadde a-boute grete plente, and whan Dionas wente it for to se it plesed hym wele, and he lete make a manner to repeire to, that was right faire and riche by the vyuier, and whan it was made he com thider to be ther for the deduyt of the wode and the river that was nygh, and ther a-boode Dionas longe tyme, and repeired ofte to the court of kynge Ban, hym serued with ix knyghtes, and in his seruise he yede at many a grete nede a-gein the kynge Claudas, to whom he dide many a grete damage, till that the kynge Ban and the kynge Boors hadden hym in grete love, ffor thei knewe hym so noble a knyght and so trewe, and the kynge Ban to hym so noble a knyght and so trewe, and the kynge Ban to hym graunted his parte of this foreste in heritage to hym and to his heyres, and londe and rentys grete foyson; and the kynge Boors yaf hym also a town and men and londe, for the grete trouthe that he saugh in hym, and he was so graciouse, that alle tho that a-boute hym repeyred loved hym a-bove all thinge. Thus dwelled Dionas in that londe longe tyme, till that he gat vpon his wif a doughter of excellent bewte, and hir name was cleped Nimiane, and it is a name of ebrewe, that seith in frensch, ment neu ferai, that is to sey in english, I shall not lye, and this turned vpon Merlin, as ye shall here her-after. This mayden wax till she was xij yere of age whan Merlin com to speke with leonces of Paerne, and Merlin spedde hym so that he com to the foreste of Brioke, and than he toke a semblaunce of a feire yonge squyre, and drowgh hym down to a welle, where-of the springes were feire and the water clere, and the grauell so feire that it seemed of fyn siluer. To this fountayn ofte tyme com nimiane for to disporte, and the same day that Merlin com thider was she come; and whan Merlin hir saugh he be-hilde hir moche, and a-vised hir well er he spake eny worde, and thought that a moche fole were he, yef he slepte so in his synne to lese his witte and his connynge for to haue the deduyt of a mayden, and hym-self shamed, and god to lese and displese. And whan he hadde longe thought, he hir salued, and she ansuerde wisely and seide, 'That lorde that alle thoughtes knoweth sende hym soche volunte and soche corage that hym be to profite, and hym not greve ne noon other, and the same welthe and the same honour hym sende as he wolde to other.' And when Merlin herde the maide thus speke, he sett hym down vpon the brinke of the welle and asked hir what she was; and she seide she was of this contrey, the daughter of a vauasour, a grete Gentilman, that was at a manoir ther-ynne, 'and what be ye, feire swete frende?' quod she. 'Damesell,' quod Merlin, 'I am a squyer traueillinge that go for to seehe my maister, that was wonte me for to teche, and moche he is for to preise.' 'And what maister is that?' seide the maiden. 'Certes,' quod he, 'he taught me so moche, that I cowde here reyse a Castell, and I cowde make with-oute peple grete plente that it sholde assaile, and with-ynne also peple that it sholde defende, and yet I sholde do mo maistries, ffor I cowde go vpon this water and not wete my feet, and also I cowde make a river where as neuer hadde be water.'

'Certes,' seide the maiden, 'these be queynte craftes, and fayn wolde I that I cowde do soche disportes.' 'Certes,' seide the squyer, 'yet can I mo delitable pleyes, for to reioise euery high astate more than these ben, ffor noon can devise nothinge but that I shall it do, and make it to endure as longe as I will,' 'Certes,' seide the maiden, 'yef it were to yow no gref, I wolde se somme pleyes by couenaunt that I sholde euer be youre love.' 'Certes,' seide Merlin, 'ye seme to me so plesaunt and deboneir, that for youre love I shall shewe yow a party of my pleyes, by couenaunt that youre love shall be myn, for other thinge will I not aske.' And she hym graunted that noon euell ne thought, and Merlin turned hym a-part and made acerne with a yerde in myddell of the launde, and than returned to the maiden, and satte a-gein down by the fountayn, and a-noon the mayden be-heilde and saugh come oute of the foreste of briogne ladyes and knyghtes and maydons and squyres, eche holdinge other by the hondes, and com singinge and made the grettest ioye that euer was seyn in eny londe, and be-fore the maiden com Iogelours and tymbres and tabours, and com be-fore the cerne that Merlin hadde made, and whan thei were with-ynne, thei be-gonne the caroles and the daunces so grete and so merveileuse, that oon myght not sey the fourthe parte of the ioye that ther was made, and for that the launde was so grete, Merlin lete rere a vergier, where-ynne was all manner of fruyt and alle manner of flowres, that yaf so grete swetnesse of flavour, that merveile it were for to telle; and the maiden that all this hadde seyn was a-baisshed of the merveile that she saugh, and was so at ese that sche ne a-tended to no-thinge but to be-holde and entende what songe thei seiden, saf that thei seiden in refreite of hir songe, 'Vraiement comencent amours en ioye, et fynissent en dolours.' In this maner dured the ioye and feste from mydday to evenesonge, that oon myght here the noyse from fer, ffor it was right high and clere, and plesaunt to heren, and it semed to be of moche peple, and oute of the Castel com Dionas and man and wif grete plente, and be-heilde and saugh the feire orcharde and the daunces and the caroles so feire and so grete, that neuer hadde thei seyn soche in theire lives; and thei merveilled gretly of the orcharde that thei saugh ther so feire ther noon was be-fore, and on that other side thei merveiled whens alle these ladyes and the knyghtes were come so wele a-pareiled of robes and Iuewelles. And whan the caroles hadde longe dured, the ladyes and the may-denys satte down vpon the grene herbes and fressh floures, and the squyres set vp a quyntayne in myddes of the medowes, and wente to bourde a partye of the yonge knyghtes, and on that other parte bourded the yonge squyres with sheldes oon a-gein a-nother that neuer ne lefte till euesonge tyme. And than com Merlin to the mayden and toke hir be the hande and seide, 'Damesell, how seme ye?' 'Ffeire swete frende,' seide the mayden, 'ye haue don so moche that I am all yours.' 'Damesell,' quod he, 'now holde my couenaunt.' 'Certes,' seide the mayden, 'so shall I with goode chere.' 'Also,' quod Merlin, 'be ye eny clerk, and I shall teche yow so many merveilles that neuer woman cowde so many.'

Quod the maiden, 'How knowe ye that I am a clerke?' 'Damesell,' quod Merlin, 'I knowe it well, ffor my maister hath me so well taught that I knowe alle thinges that oon doth.' 'Certes,' seide the mayden, 'that is the moste connynge that euer I herde, and moste myster were ther-of in many places, and that I wolde faynest lerne; and of thinges that be to come knowe ye ought?' 'Certes,' quod he, 'swete love, yee, a grete part.' 'God mercy!' quod the mayden, 'what go ye than sechynge?' 'Truly,' quod Merlin, 'of that ye moste yet a-bide yef it be youre plesier.' And while the Mayden and Merlin helde this Parlement, assembled a-gein the maidenes and the ladyes, and wente daun-singe and bourdinge toward the foreste fro whens thei were come firste; and whan thei were nygh thei entred in so sodaynly, that oon ne wiste where thei were be-come; but the orcharde a-bode stille ther longe tyme, ffor the maiden that swetly ther-of hym praide, aud was cleped ther by name the repeire of ioye and of feeste. And whan Merlin and the maiden hadde be longe to-geder, Merlin seyde at the laste, 'Ffeire maiden, I go, for I haue moche to do in other place than here.'

'How,' quod the maiden, 'feire frende, shull ye not teche me firste some of youre pleyes?' 'Damesell,' quod Merlin, 'ne haste yow not sore, ffor ye shull know I-nowe all in tyme, ffor I moste haue ther-to grete leyser and grete soiour, and on that other side I haue yet no suerte of youre love.' 'Sir,' quod she, 'what suerte wolde ye aske? devise ye, and I shall it make.' 'I will,' quod Merlin, 'that ye me ensure that youre love shall be myn, and ye also for to do my plesier of what I will.' And the maiden her be-thought a litill, and than she seide, 'Sir,' quod she, 'with goode will by soche forwarde, that after that ye haue me taught all the thinges that I shall yow aske, and that I can hem werke.' And Merlin seide that so it plesed hym well. Than he a-sured the maiden to holde coue-naunt like as she hadde devised, and he toke hir surete. Than he taught hir ther a pley that she wrought after many tymes, ffor he taught hir to do come a grete river ouer all ther as her liked, and to a-bide as longe as she wolde; and of other games I-nowe, where-of she wrote the wordes in perchemyn soche as he hir devised, and she it cowde full well bringe it to ende. And whan he hadde a-biden ther till euesonge tyme, he comaunded hir to god and she hym, but er he departed the maiden hym asked whan he sholde come a-gein; and he seide on seint Iohnes even; and thus departed that oon fro that other. And Merlin went to Tamelide, where the kynges made hym grete ioye whan that thei hym saugh.

[. . .]

MERLIN AND GRISANDOLE

As soone as Merlin was departed from Arthur, he wente in to the forestes of Rome that were thikke and depe, and in that tyme Julyus Cesar was Emperour; but it was not that Julyus Cesar that the deed knyght slough in his pavilion of Perce. But it was that Julius that Gawein, the nevew of kynge Arthur, slough in bateile vnder Logres at the grete dis-confiture that after was be-twene hym and the kynge Arthur that hym diffied, and what the cause was that Merlin wente that wey, it is reson it be declared. This is throuthe that this Julyus Cezar hadde a wif that was of grete bewte, and she hadde with hir xij[1] yonge men araied in gise of wymen, with whom she lay at alle tymes that the Emperour was oute of hir companye, ffor she was the most lecherouse woman of all Rome; and for the dredde that theire beerdes sholde growe she lete a-noynte her chynnes with certeyn oynementes made for the nones, and thei wre clothed in longe traylinge robes, and theire heer longe waxen, in gise of maydenes and tressed at theire bakkes, that alle that hem saugh wende wele thei were wymen; and longe thei endured with the Empress vn-knowen.

In this tyme that the Emperesse ledde this lif, it fill that a mayden com to the Emperours court that was the doughter of a prince, and the name of this prince was matan. Duke of Almayne; this mayden com in semblannce of a squyer, and this matan the Duke Frolle hadde disherited and driven out of his londe, and she com to serue[2] the Emperour, ffor she wiste not where her fader ne moder were be comen, and she was moche and semly, and well shapen and demened hir well in all maners that a man ought, saf only eny vylonye, and neuer was she knowen but for a man by no semblante, and so a-boode with the Emperour, and was of grete prowesse, and peyned tendirly to serue well the Emperour and plesed hym so well that she was lorde and gouernour of hym and his housolde; and the Emperour hir loved so well that he made hir knyght atte a feeste of seint John with other yonge squyers, wher-of were mo than CC,[3] and after made hir stiward of all his londe. Than the newe knyghtes reised a quyntayne in the mede of Noiron, and be-gonne the bourdinge[4] grete and huge, and many ther were

---

1. *xij* = 12.
2. *Serue* = serve.
3. *CC* = 200.
4. *Bourdinge* = jesting.

that dide right wele, but noon so well as dide Grisandoll, for so she lete hir be cleped; but in bapteme her name was Anable. This bourdinge endured all day on ende till euesonge that thei departed, and Grisandols bar a-wey the pris a-monge alle other, and whan the Emperour saugh Grisandoll of so grete prowesse, he made hym stiward of all his londe and comaunder a-bove alle that ther weren, and Grisandols was well beloved of riche and pore.

And vpon a nyght after it fill that the Emperour lay in his chamber with the Emperesse; and whan he was a-slepe he hadde a vision that hym thought he saugh a sowe in his court that was right grete be-fore his paleys, and he hadde neuer seyn noon so grete ne so huge, and she hadde so grete bristelis on her bakke that it trayled on the grounde a fadome large, and hadde vpon hir heed a cercle that semed of fyn golde, and whan the Emperour a-vised hym wele hym thought that he hadde seyn hir other tymes, and that he hadde hir norisshed vp; but he durste not sey of trouthe that she were hys, and while he entended to a-vise hym on this thinge he saugh come oute of his chamber xij lyonsewes,[5] and com in to the courte to the sowe, and assailed hir oon after a-nother, whan the Emperour saugh this merveile he asked his Barouns what sholde he do with this sowe by whom these lyonsewes hadde thus leyn, and thei seide she was not worthi to be conuersaunt a-monge peple, ne that no man sholde ete nothinge that of hir come, and luged[6] hir to be brente,[7] and also the lyonsewes to-geder; and than a-wooke the Emperour sore affraied and pensif of this a-vision. Ne neuer to man ne to wif wolde he it telle, for he was full of grete wisdom. On the morowe as soone as he myght se the day, he a-roos and yede to the mynster to here messe, and whan he was come a-gein he fonde the barouns assembled, and hadde herde messe at the mynster and the mete was all redy; and whan thei hadde waisshen thei satte to mete, and were well serued. Than fill that the Emperour fill in to a grete stodye, wher-fore all the courte was pensif and stille, and ther was noon that durste sey a worde for sore thei dredde for to wrathe the Emperour. But now we moste turne a litill to Merlin that was come in to the foreste of Romayne to certefie these thinges and these avisiouns.

While that the Emperour satte at his mete a-monge his Barouns thus pensif, Merlin come in to the entre of Rome and caste an enchauntement merveilouse, ffor he be-com an herte the gretteste and the moste merveilouse that eny man hadde seyn, and hadde oon of his feet before white, and hadde v braunches in the top, the grettest that euer hadde be seyn, and than he ran thourgh Rome so faste as all the worlde hadde hym chaced, and whan the peple saugh hym so renne, and saugh how it was an herte the noyse a-roos, and the cry on alle partyes, and ronne after grete and small with staves and axes, and other wepen, and chaced hym thourgh the town, and he com to the maister gate of the paleys where-as the Emperour satte at his mete, and whan thei that serued herde the noyse of the peple, thei ronne to the wyndowes to herkene what it myght be, and a-noon thei saugh come rennynge the herte and all the peple after; and whan the herte com to the maister paleys he drof in at the yate sodeynly, and than he ran thourgh the tables a bandon and tombled mete and drynke all on an hepe, and be-gan ther-in a grete trouble of pottis and disshes; and whan the herte hadde longe turned ther-ynne he com be-fore the Emperour, and kneled and seide, 'Julius Cezar, Emperour of Rome, wheron thinkest thow, lete be thi stodyinge for it a-vaileth nought, ffor neuer of thyne a-vision shalt thow not knowe the trouthe be-fore that man that is

---

5. *Lyonsewes* = lioncels (little lions-heraldic term).
6. *Iuged* = judged.
7. *Brente* = burnt.

sauage the certefie, and for nought as it that thow stodyest ther-on eny more.'

Than the herte hym dressed and saugh the yate of the paleyse cloos, and he caste his enchauntement that alle the dores and yates of the paleise opened so rudely that thei fly alle in peces, and the herte lept oute and fledde thourgh the town, and the chace be-gan a-gein after hym longe till that he com oute in to the playn feeldes; and than he dide vanysshe that noon sey where he be-com, and than thei returned a-gein, and whan the Emperour wiste the herte was ascaped he was wroth and lete crye thourgh the londe that who that myght brynge the sauage man or the herte sholde haue his feire doughter to wif, and half his reame, yef that he were gentill of birthe, and after his deth haue all; and lepe to horse many a vailaunt knyght and squyer of pris, and serched and sought thourgh many contrees, but all was for nought, ffor neuer cowde thei heere no tidings of that thei sought, and whan thei myght no more do thei returned a-gein. But euer Grisandols serched thourgh the forestes, oon hour foreward, another bakke that so endured viij[8] dayes full; and on a day as Grisandol was a-light vnder an oke for to praye oure lorde to helpe and to spede for to fynde that he sought, and as he was in is prayours the herte that hadde ben at Rome com be-fore hym and seide, 'Auenble,[9] thow chacest folye, ffor thow maist not spede of thy queste in no manner, but I shall telle the what thow shalt do. Purchese flessh newe and salt, and mylke and hony, and hoot breed newe bake, and bringe with the foure felowes, and a boy to turne the spite till it be I-nough rosted, and com in to this foreste by the moste vn-couthe weyes that thow canste fynde, and sette a table by the fier, and the breed, and the mylke, and the hony vpon the table, and hide the and thi companye a litile thens, and doute the nought that the sauage man will come.'

Than ran the herte a-grete walope thourgh the foreste, and Grisandol lept to horse and thought well on that the herte hadde seide and thought in his corage that it was somme spirituell thinge that by hir right name hadde hir cleped,[10] and thought well that of this thinge sholde come some merveile; and Grisandol rode forth to a town nygh the foreste vij myle, and toke ther that was myster, and com in to the foreste ther as he hadde spoke with the herte as soone as he myght, and roode in to the deepe of the foreste, where-as he fonde a grett oke full of leves, and the place semed delitable, and he a-light and sette theire horse fer thens, and made a grete fier, and sette the flesshe to roste, and the smoke and the sauour spredde thourgh the foreste, that oon myght fele the sauour right fer; and than sette the table be the fier, and whan all was redy thei hidde hem in a bussh.

And Merlin that all this knewe and that made all this to be don couertly that he were not knowen drough that wey that he were not knowen with a grete staffe in his nekke smytinge grete strokes from oke to oke, and was blakke and rough for rympled and longe berde, and bar-foote, and cloted in a rough pilche;[11] and so he com to the fier, ther as the flessh was roasted, and whan the boy saugh hym come he was so a-ferde that he fledde nygh oute of his witte; and he this com to the fier and be-gan to chacche and frote a-boute the fier, and saugh the mete and than loked all a-boute hym and be-gan to rore lowde as a man wood oute of mynde, and than be-heilde, and saugh the cloth spredde and soche mete ther-on as ye haue herde, and after he be-heilde towarde the fier, and saugh the flesshe that the knaue hadde rosted that was tho I-nough, and raced of it with his hondes madly, and rente it a-sonder in pieces, and wette it in mylke, and after in the hony, and ete as a wood man that nought ther lefte of the flessh; and

---

8. *viij* = 13.
9. *Auenable* = avenable.
10. *Cleped* = named.
11. *Pilche* = vest-like tunic.

than he eete of the hoot breed and hony that he was fuli and swollen grete, and somwhat was it colde, and he lay down by the fier and slepte; and whan Grisandol saugh he was on slepe she and hir felowes com as softely as thei myght, and stale a-wey his staffe, and than thei bounde hym with a cheyne of Iren streytely a-boute the flankes, and than delyured hym to oon of the companye by the tother ende of the cheyne; and whan he was so well bounde he a-wooke and lept vp lightly, and made sem-blaunt to take his staff as a wilde man, and Grisandolus griped hym in his armies right sore and hilde hym stille, and whan he saugh hym so bounde and taken, he hilde hym as shamefaste and mate; and than the horse were brought forth and he was sette vpon oon of hem; and bounden to the sadell with two bondes, and a man sette be-hynde hym that was bounde to hym and embraced hym by the myddill, and so thei rode forth her wey, and the sauage man loked on Grisandolus that rode by hym, and be-gan to laugh right harde, and whan Grisandolus saugh hym laughe he approched ner and rode side by side, and a-queynted with hym the beste that he myght, and enquered and asked many thinges, but he ne wolde nought ansuere, and Grisandol asked why he lough, but he wolde not telle. Saf that he seide, 'Creature formed of nature chaunged in to other forme fro hens-forth be-gilynge alle thinges venimouse as se[r]pent, holde thi pees, for nought will I telle the till that I com be-fore the Emperoure.'

With that the sauage man hilde his pees and spake no more, and rode forth to-geder, and Grisandolus of this that he hadde seide spake to his companye, and thei seide that he was wiser than he shewed, and that som grete merveile sholde falle in the londe. Thus thei ride spekynge of many thinges till thei passede be-fore an abbey, and saugh be-fore the yate moche pore peple a-bidinge almesse, and than the sauage man lowgh[12] right lowde; and than Grisandol com toward hym and swetly praide hym to telle wher-fore he lough, and he loked proudly on trauerse, and seide, 'Ymage repaired and disna-tured fro kynde, holde thy pees, ne enquere no mo thinges for nought will I telle the but be-fore the Emperour;' and whan Grisandolus this vndirstode, he lete hym be at that tyme and no more thinge hym asked, and here-of spake thei in many maners.

Thus thei ride forth all day till nyght, and on the morowe till the hour of prime, and fill that thei passed by-fore a chapell where a preste was toward masse, and fonde a knyght and a squyer heringe the seruyse; and whan Grisandolus saugh this, thei a-light alle the companye, and entred in to here the masse, and whan the knyght that was in the chapell saugh the man bounde with chaynes he hadde merveile what it myght be, and while the knyght be-heilde the man that was sauage, the squyer that was in an angle be-hynde the chapel dore come a-gein his lorde, and lifte yp his hande and yaf[13] hym soche a flap that alle thei in the chapell myght it here, and than returned thider as he com fro all shamefaste of that he hadde don, and whan he was come in to his place he ne rofte no-thinge, for the shame lasted no lenger; but while he was in returnynge, and whan the sauage man saugh this, he be-gan to laugh right harde, and the knyght that was so smyten was so a-baisshed that he wiste not what to sey but suffred; and Grisandolus and the other companye merveiled sore what it myght be. A-noon after the squyer com a-gein to his lorde, and yaf hym soche a-nother stroke as he dide be-fore, and wente a-gein in to his place, and the sauage man hym behilde and be-gan to laughe right harde, and yef the knyght be-fore were a-baisshed, he was than moche more, and the squyer that hadde hym smyten returned sorowfull and pensif to the place that he com fro, and hilde hym-self foule disceyved of that he hadde don, and whan he was in his place he rought neuer, and Grisandolus, and the companye merveiled right sore,

12. *Lowgh* = laugh.
13. *Yaf* = gave.

and herden oute the seruise be leyser,[14] and in the mene while that thei thoughten vpon these thinges that thei hadde seyn, the squyer com the thridde tyme and smote his lorde sorer than he hadde don be-fore, and ther-at lowgh the wilde man sore, and be that was the masse at an ende, and than Grisandolus and alle wente oute of the chapell, and the squyer that hadde smyten his lorde com after and asked Grisandolus what man it was that thei hadde so bounde, and thei seide that thei were with Julius Cezar, Emperour of Rome, and ledde to hym that sauage man that thei hadde founded in the foreste, for to certefie of a vision that was shewed hym slepinge. 'But, sir,' seide Grisandolus, 'tell me wherefore hath this squyer yow smyten thre tymes, and ye ne spake no words a-gein, haue ye soche a custome,' and the knyght ansuerde that he sholde it wite in tyme comynge.

Than the knyght cleped his squyer and asked hym be-fore Grisandolus wherefore he hadde hym smyten, and he was shamefaste, and seide he wiste neuer, but so it fill in his corage, and the knyght hym asked yef he hadde now eny talent hym for to smyte, and the squyer seide he hadde leuer be deed, 'but that,' quod he, 'it fill in my mynde that I myght not kepe me ther-fro,' and Grisandolus lough of the merveile. Than seide the knyght that he wolde go to court with hem for to here what the sauave man wolde sey, and with that thei rode forth on her wey, and Grisandolus by the sauage mannes side, and whan thei hadde a-while riden, he asked the wilde man wherfore he lough so thre tymes whan the squyer smote hir lorde, and he loked on hir a trauerse, and seide, 'Ymage repeyred, semblaunce of creature wherby men ben slayn and diffouled, rasour trenchaunt, ffountayne coraunt, that neuer is full of no springes holde thy pees, and nothinge of me enquere, but before the Emperour, for nought will I telle the,' and whan that Grisandolus vndirstode the fell wordes that he spake, he was all a-baisshed and pensef, and durste not no more enquere, and rode forth till thei come to Rome, and whan thei entred in to the town, and the peple hem parceyved thei wente all a-geins hym for to se the man that was sauage, and the noyse was grete of the peple that folowed, and be-hilde his facion as longe as thei myght, and so thei conveyed hym to the paleise, and whan the Emperour herde the tidings he com hem a-geins, and mette with hem comynge vpon the greces, and than com Grisandolus be-fore the Emperour, and seide, 'Sir, haue here the man that is sauage that I to yow here yelde, and kepe ye hym fro hens-forth for moche peyne haue I hadde with hym,' and the Emperour seide he wolde hem well guerdon,[15] and the man sholde be well kepte, and than he sente to seche a smyth to bynde hym in chaynes and feteres, and the sauage man badde hym ther-of not to entermete, 'ffor wite it right well,' quod he, 'I will not go with-oute youre leve,' and the Emperour hym asked how he ther-of sholde be sure, and he seide he wolde hym asur by his cristyndome. Quod the Emperour, 'Art thow than cristin?' and he seide, 'Ye with-oute faile,' 'How were thow than baptized,' seide the Emperour, 'whan thow art so wilde.'

'That shall I telle yow,' quod he, 'This is the trouthe that my moder on a day com from the market of a town, and it was late whan she entred in to the foreste of Brocheland,[16] and wente oute her way so fer that the same nyght be-hoved hir to lye in the foreste, and whan she saugh she was so a-lone be hir-self she was a-feerde and lay down vnder an oke and fill a-slepe, and than come a sauage man oute of the foreste and by hir lay, be-cause she was sool by hir-self. Durste she not hym diffende, ffor a woman a-loone is feerfull, and that nyght was I be-geten on my moder, and whan she was

---

14. *Be leyser* = at leisure.
15. *Guerdon* = reward.
16. *Brocheland* = Broceliande Forest (in Brittany).

repeired hom, she was full pensif longe tyme, till that she knewe verily that she was with childe, and bar me so till I was born in to this worlde and was baptised in a fonte, and dide me norishe till I was grete, and as soone as I cowde lyve with-outen hir[17] I wente in to the grete forestes for by the nature of my fader be-houeth me thider to repeire, and for that he was sauage I am thus wilde. Now haue ye herde what I am.'

'So god me helpe,' seide the Emperour, 'neuer for me shalt thow be putte in feteres ne in Irenes seth thow wilt me graunte that thow will not go with-oute my leve.' Than tolde Grisandolus how he dide laugh be-fore the abbey and in the chapell, for the squyer that hadde smyten his maister, and the dyuerse wordes that he hadde spoken, whan he asked where-fore he dide laugh, and he seide that neuer wolde he nought sey till he com be-fore yow, and now is he here, and therfore aske hym why he hath so often laughed by the wey, and than the Emperour hym asked, and he seide he sholde it knowe all in tyme, but sendeth first for all youre barouns and than shall I tell yow that and other thinges, with that entred the Emperour in to his chamber and the sauage man and his prive counseile, and ther thei rested and disported, and spake of many thinges, and on the morowe the Emperour sente to seche his barouns hem that he supposed sonest to fynde, and than thei come a-noon bothe oon and other from alle partyes.

On the fourthe day after the sauage man was comen, where that the lordes were assembled in the maister paleise, and the Emperour [brought in] this sauage man and made hym to sitte down by hym, and whan the barouns hadde I-nough hym be-holden thei asked why he hadde for hem sente, and he tolde hem for a vision that hym be-fill in his slepynge, 'ffor I will that it be expowned be-fore yow,' and thei seide that the significacion wolde thei gladly heren. Than the Emperour comaunded this man to telle the cause why that he was sought, and ansuerde and seide that he wolde nothinge telle till that the Emperesse and hir xij maydones were comen, and she com a-noon with gladde semblaunce as she that yaf no force of nothinge that myght be-falle, whan the Emperesse and hir xij maydones were come a-monge the barouns, the lordes roos a-gein hir and dide hir reuerence, and as soone as the sauage man hir saugh comynge he turned his heed in trauerse an be-gan to laughe in scorne, and whan he hadde a-while laughed he loked on the Emperour stadfastly, and than on Grisandolus, and than on the Emperesse, and than on hir xij Maydenys that weren with hir, and than he turned toward the barouns, and he be-gan to laughe right lowde as it were in dispite, whan the Emperour saugh hym so laughe he preied hym to telle that he hadde in couenaunt, and whi that he lough now and other tymes, with that he stode vp and seide to the Emperour so lowde that all myght it heren. 'Sir, yef ye me graunte as trewe Emperour be-fore youre barouns that ben here that I shall not be the werse ne no harme to me therfore shall come, and that ye will yeve me leve as soone as I haue yow certefied of youre a-vision I shall telle yow the trew significacion,' and the Emperour hym ansuerde and graunted that noon harme ne annoye to hym sholde be don, ne that he sholde come hym no magre to telle hym that he was so desirouse for to heren, and that he sholde haue leve to go whan hym liste. 'But I praye the telle me myn a-vision in audience of alle my barouns what it was, and than shall I the better be-leve the significacion whan thow haste me tolde, of that I neuer spake to no creature,' and he ansuerde as for that sholde hym not greve, and ther-fore wolde he not lette and than he be-gan the a-vision.

'Sir,' seide the sauage man to the Emperour, 'it fill on a nyght that ye lay by youre wif that is here, and whan ye were a-slepe ye thought ye saugh be-fore yow a sowe that was

---

17. *Hir* = her.

feire and smothe, and the heer that she hadde on her bakke was so longe that it trailed to grounde more than a fadome, and on hir heed she hadde a cercle of goolde bright shynynge, and yow semed that ye hadde norisshed that sowe in youre house, but ye cowde it not verily knowe, and ther-with yow semed that ye hadde hir othir tymes sein, and whan ye hadde longe thought on this thinge ye saugh come out of youre chamber xij lyonsewes full feire and smothe; and thei com by the halle thourgh the courte to the sowe and lay by hir oon after a-nother, and whan thei hadde do that thei wolde thei wente a-gein in to youre chamber; than com ye to your barouns and hem asked what sholde be do with this sowe, that he saugh thus demened, and the barouns and alle the people seide she was nothinge trewe, and thei Iuged to be brent, bothe the sowe and the xij lyonsewes, and than was the fier made redy grete and merveillouse in this courte, and ther-ynne was the sowe brente and the xij lyonsewes. Now haue ye herde youre sweuene[18] in the same forme as ye it saugh in your slepinge, and yef ye se that I haue eny thinge mys-taken, sey it be-fore your barouns.' And the Emperour seide he hadde of nothinge failed.

'Sir Emperour,' seide the barouns, 'seth that he hath seide what was youre a-vision, hit is to be-leve the significacion yef he will it telle, and it is a thinge that wolde gladly heren.' 'Certes,' seide the man, 'I shall it declare to yow so openly that ye may it se, and knowe a-pertly[19] that I yow shall sey. The grete sowe that he saugh signifieth my lady the Emperess, youre wif, that is ther; and the longe heer that she hadde on hir bakke betokeneth the longe robes that she is ynne I-clothed; and the sercle that ye saugh on her heed shynynge be-tokeneth the crowne of goolde that ye made her with to be crowned; and yef it be youre plesier I will no more sey at this tyme.' 'Certes,' seide the Emperour, 'yow be-hoveth to sey all as it is yef ye will be quyte of youre promyse.' 'Certes,' seide man, 'than I shall telle yow. Tho xij lyonsewes that he saugh come oute of a chamber, betokeneth the xij maydenes that be ther with the Emperess; and knowe it for very trouthe that thei be no wymen for it be men, and there-fore make hem be dispoiled, and shull se the trouthe; and as ofte as ye go oute of the town she maketh hem serue in hir chamber and in hir bedde. Now haue ye herde youre a-vision and the significacion, and ye may se and knowe yef that I haue seide to yow the soth.'

Whan the Emperour vunderstode th vntrouthe that his wife hadde don, he was so a-baisshed that he spake no worde a longe while; and than he spake and seide that that wolde he soone knowe, and than he cleped Grisandolus, and seide, 'Dispoile mo tho dameseles, for I will that alle the barouns that be here-ynne knowe the trouthe;' and a-noon Grisandolus and other lept forth and dispoiled hem be-fore the Emperour and his barouns, and fonde hem formed alle as other men weren; and than the Emperour was so wroth that he wiste not what to do. Than he made his oth that a-noon ther sholde be do Iustice soche as was right to be a-warded; and the barouns Iuged seth she hadde don hir lorde soch vntrouthe that she sholde be brente and the harlottes hanged, and some seide that thei sholde be flayn all quyk;[20] but in the ende thei acorded that thei sholde be brente in a fier, and a-noon as the Emperour herde the Iugement of the barouns, he comaunded to make the fier in the place, and a-noon it was don, and thei were bounde hande and foot, and made hem to be caste in to the brynynge fier, and in short tyme thei were all brent, ffor the fier was grete and huge. Thus toke Emperour vengaunce of his wif, and grete was the renomede that peple of hym spake whan it was knowen.

When the Emperesse was brente, and thei that she hadde made hir maydenes, the

---

18. *Sweuene* = dream.
19. *A pertly* = frankly.
20. *Flayn all quyk* = flayed alive.

barouns returned a-gein to the Emperour, and seide oon to a-nother that the sauage man was right wise and avisee, ffor yet shall he sey some other thinges wher-of shall come some grete merveile vs, and to all the worlde; and the Emperour hym-self seide that he hadde seide his a-vision as it was in trouthe. Thus wiste the Emperour the lyvinge of his wif, and than the Emperour hym called, and asked yef he wolde sey eny more, and he seide, 'Ye yef he asked hym whereof.' 'I wolde wite,' quod he, 'wherefore thow didist laughe whan thow were in the f[o]reste, and loked on Grisandolus, and also whan thow were ledde be-fore an abbey, and in the chapell whan the squyer smote his lorde, and why thow seidest tho wordes to my stiwarde whan he asked why thow loughe, and after telle me what be-tokeneth the laughter hereynne whan thow saugh the Emperesse come.'

'Sir,' seide the sauage man, 'I shall telle yow I-nowgh. I do yow to wite that the firste laughter that I made was for that a woman hadde me taken by her engyn',[21] that no man cowde not do; and wite ye well that Grisandolus is the beste maiden and the trewest with-ynne youre reame, and therefore was it that I lough; and the laughter that I made be-fore the abbey, was for ther is vnder erthe be-fore the yate[22] the grettest tresour hidde that eny man knoweth, and therefore I lough for that it was vnder feet of hem that a-boode after the almesse, ffor more richesse is in that tresour than alle the monkes beth worth, and all the abbey, and all that ther-to be-longeth, and the pore peple that ther-on stoden cowde it not take; and Avenable youre stywarde, that Grisandolus doth her clepen, saugh that I lowgh and asked me wherefore, and the couerte wordes that I to hir spake was for that she was chaunged in to the fourme of man, and hadde take a-nothir habite than hir owne; and alle the wordes that I spake thei ben trewe, ffor by woman is many a man disceyved, and therefore I cleped hir disceyaunt for by women ben many townes sonken and brent, and many a riche londe wasted and exiled, and moche people slayn; but I sey it not for noon euell that is in hir, and thow thy-self maist well perceyve that be women be many worthi men shamed and wratthed that longe haue loued to-geder, yef it were not for debate of women; but now rech the not for thy wif, that thou haste distroied, ffor she hath it well deserued, and haue therefore no mystrust to other, for as longe as the worlde endureth it doth but apeire, and all that cometh to hem by the grete synne of luxure that in hem is closeth; ffor woman is of that nature, and of that disire, that whan she hath the moste worthi man of the worlde to hir lorde, she weneth she haue the werse, and wite ye fro whens this cometh of the grete fragelite that is in hem; and the foule corage and the foule thought that thei haue where thei may beste hir volunte acomplish; but therefore be not wroth, for ther ben in the worlde that ben full trewe, and yef[23] thow haue be desceyved of thyn, yet shall thow haue soche oon that is worthy to be Emperesse, and to resceyve that high dignite, and yef thow wilt it be-leve thow shalt wynne ther-on more than thowe shalt lese.

'But the prophesie seith that the grete dragon shall come fro Rome that wolde distroie the reame of the grete Breteyne and put it in his subieccion; and the fierce lyon crowned maugre[24] the diffence of the turtill that the dragon hath norisshed vndir his wynges, and as soone as the grete dragon shall meve to go the grete Breteigne, the lyon crowned shall come hym a-geins, and shull fight so to-geder, that a fierce bore that is prowde, whiche the lyon shall bringe with hym smyte so the dragon with oon of his

---

21. *Engyn* = cunning.
22. *Yate* = gate.
23. *Yef* = if.
24. *Maugre* = despite.

hornes that he shall falle down deed, and thereby shall be delyuered the grete lyon. But I will not telle the significacion of these wordes, for I owe it nought to do, but all this shall falle in thy tyme, and therfore be well ware of euell counseile, for grete part longeth to the.

'The tother laughter that I made in the chapell was not for the buffetes that the squyer yaf his lorde, but for the be-tokenynges that ther-ynne ben. In the same place ther the squyer stode was entred, and yet ther is vndir his feet a merveillouse tresour. The firste buffet that the squyer yaf his lorde signifieth that for avoure the wo[r]lde becometh so prowde, that he douteth nother god ne his soule, no more than the squyer douted to smyte his maister, but the riche wolde oppresse the pore vnder theire feet; and that make these vntrewe riche peple whan enythinge cometh to hem by myschaunce thei swere and stare and sey maugre haue god for his yeftes,[25] and wite ye what maketh his nothinge but pride of richesse. The seconde buffet be-tokeneth the riche vserer[26] that deliteth in his richesse and goth s[c]ornynge his pore nyghebours that be nedy whan thei come to hym ought for to borough, and the vserer so leneth hem litill and litill that at laste thei moste selle theire heritage to hym that so longe hath it coveyted. The thridde buffet signifieth these false pletours, men of lawe, that sellen and a-peire theire neyghbours be-hinde here bakke for couetise and envye of that thei se hem thrive, and for thei be not in her daungier, ffor whan these laweers sen that her neighbours don hem not grete reverence and servise, thei thenken and a-spien how thei may hem a-noyen in eny wise, and to make hem lese that thei haue, and therfore men seyn an olde sawe, who hath a goode neighbour hath goode morowe. Now haue ye herde the significaciouns why the buffetes were yoven, but the squyer delited nothinge ther-ynne whan that he smote his maister, but he wiste not fro whens this corage to hym com. But god that is almyghty wolde haue it to be shewed in exsample that men sholde not be prowde for worldly richesse, for to the couetouse theire richesse doth hem but harme that slepen in auerice, and for-yete god and don the werkes of the deuell, that ledeth hem to euerlastinge deth, and all is for the grete delite that thei haue in richesse.

'But now shall I telle yow whi I lough to day whan I saugh the Emperesse comynge and hir lechours, I do yow to wite that it was but for dispite, ffor I saugh that she was youre wif, and hadde oon of the worthiest men of the worlde that eny man knoweth of youre yowthe, and she hadde take these xij harlottes and wende euer for to haue ledde this foly all hir lif; and ther-fore hadde I grete dispite for the love of yow and of youre doughter, ffor she is youre doughter with-oute doubte, and draweth litill after hir moder. Now haue ye herde alle the laughtres and wherefore thei were, and therfore may I go yef it be youre plesier.' 'Now a-bide a little,' seide the Emperour, 'and telle vs the trouthe of Grisandolus, and also we shull sende to digge after the tresour for I wite yef it be trewe,' and he ther-to dide assent; than the Emperour comaunded that Grisandolus were sought, and so she was founden oon of the feirest maydenes that neded to enquere in eny londe, and whan the Emperour knewe that Grisandolus, his stiwarde, that longe hadde hym serued was a woman, he blissed hym for the wonder that he ther-of hadde.

Than he asked the sauage man counseile what he sholde do of that he hadde promysed to yeve his doughter, and half his reame, ffor loth he was to falsen his promyse of couenaunt. 'I shall telle yow,' quod the man, 'what he shull do yef ye will do my counseile, and wite it well, it is the beste that eny man can yeven.' 'Sey on, than,'

---

25. *Yeftes* = gifts.
26. *Vserer* = usurer.

seide Emperour, ffor what counseile that thow yevest I shall it well be-leve, for I haue founde thy seyinge trewe.' Than seide the sauage man, 'Ye shall take Avenable to be yowre wif, and wite ye whos doughter she is. She is doughter to the Duke Matan that the Duke Frolle hath disherited and driven oute of his londe for enveye with grete wronge, and he and his wife be fledde, and his sone, that is a feire yonge squyer, in to Province in to a riche town that is called Monpellier; and sende to seche hem and yelde hem her heritage that thei haue loste with wronge, and make the mariage of youre doughter and Auenables brother that is so feire, and ye may her no better be setten.' And whan the Barouns vndirstode that the sauage man seide, thei spoke moche a-monge hem, and seiden in the ende that the Emperor myght do no better after theire advis; and than the Emperour asked his name, and what he was, and the hert that so pertly spake vnto hym, and than seide he, 'Sir, of that enquere no more, ffor it is a thinge the more ye desire to knowe the lesse ye shall witen.'

'Ffor sothe,' seide the Emperour, 'now suppose I well what it may be, but shull ye telle us eny more.' 'Ye,' quod he, 'I tolde yow right now of the lyon crowned and of the lyon volage,[27] but now shall I telle yow in other manere, for that ye shull be better remembred whan tyme cometh. Emperour of Rome,' quod he, 'this is trewe prophesie that the grete boor of Rome that is signified by the grete dragon, shall go agein the lyon, crowned of the bloy[28] Breteyne a-gein the counseile of the turtell that hath an heed of golde and longe hath ben his love. But the boor shall be so full of pride that he will nothir be-leve, but shall go with so grete pride with all his generacion in to the parties of Gaule to fight with the crowned lyon that shall come a-geins hym with alle his beestes. Ther shall be grete slaughter of beestes on both sides. Than shall oon of the fawnes of the lyon crowned sle the grete boor, and ther-fore I praye the yef thow wilt ought do for me er I departe that thow do nothinge a-gein the volunte of thy wif, after that day that thow haste her wedded, and wite well yef thow do thus thow shalt haue profite, and now I take my leve for here haue I no more to do.'

And the Emperour be-taught hym to god seth it myght no better be, and ther-with he wente on his wey, and whan he com to the halle dore he wrote letteres on the lyntell of the dore in grewe that seide, 'Be it knowe to alle tho that these letteres reden, that the sauage man that spake to the Emperour and expounded his dreme, hit was Merlin of Northumberlande, and the hert brancus with xv braunches that spake to hym in his halle at mete a-monge alle his knyghtes, and was chaced thourgh the Citee of Rome, that spake to Auenable in the foreste whan he tolde hir how she sholde fynde the man sauage; and lete the Emperour well wite that Merlin is maister counseller to kynge Arthur of the grete Breteyne.' And than he departed and spake no mo wordes. Whan this sauage man was departed from the Emperour, he sente in to Province to seche the fader and the moder of Auenable and Patrik hir brother, in the town of Monpellier, whider as thei were fledde; and a-noon thei com gladde and ioyfull of the auenture that god hadde hem sente, and whan thei were comen thei hadde grete ioye of theire doughter that thei wende neuer to haue seyn. Than thei a-bide with the Emperour longe tyme, and the Emperour restored hem to here herytage that Frolle hadde hem be-rafte. But as ffrolle myght he it agein seide, ffor he was of grete power, and so endured the werre longe tyme.

But in the ende the Emperour made the pees, and than he maried his doughter to Patrik, and hym-self toke Auenable to his wif, and grete was the ioye and the feeste that the Barouns maden, for moche was she be-loved bothe of riche and pore, and as the

---

27. *Volage* = wanton.
28. *Bloy* = great.

Emperour was in ioye and deduyt[29] of his newe spouse, ther com a massage to hym oute of Greece for a discorde that was be-twene the barouns of Greese and the Emperour Adrian, that sholde hem Iustise, ffor the Emperour Adrian myght vn-ethe ride for febilnesse of age, and whan the messagers hadde spoke to the Emperour and don all that he sholde, he toke his leve to go, and as he caste vp his yie vpon the halle dore and saugh the lettres that Merlin hadde writen in griewe, and a-noon he redde hem lightly, and than he gan to laughe right harde, and shewed hem to the Emperour, and seide, 'Sir, is this trewe that these lettres seyn.' 'What sey thei,' quod the Emperour, 'wote ye neuer.' Quod the messager, 'Thei seyn that he that tolde yow the vntrouthe of youre wif, and yoe d´reme expowned, and spake to yow in gise of an herte, that it was Merlin of Northumbirlande, the maister counseller of kynge Arthur of Breteyne, by whos counseile ye haue spoused youre wif Auenable.' And whan the Emperour vndirstode these wordes he merveiled sore; and than be-fill a grete merveile, wherof alle that were ther-ynne hadde wonder, and the Emperour hym-self; ffor as soone as the Emperour herde what the lettres mente, a-noon the lettres vanyssed so sodeynly that no man wiste how, and ther-of hadde their grete wonder, and moche it was spoken of thourgh the contrey. But now cesseth the tale of the Emperour of Rome that a-bode in his paleise gladde and myry with his wif Auenable, and ledde goode lif longe tyme, for bothe were thei yong epeople, ffor the Emperour was but xxvij yere of age at that hour, and his wife was xxij, and yef thei ledde myri lif, yet Patrik and Foldate, the doughter or the Emperour, lyved in more delite.

THE LAST WORDS OF MERLIN

Whan that sir Gawein was passed the duerf knyght, and the damesell wele a two bowe draught, a-noon he felte that the sleeves of his hauberk passed fer of lengthe ouer his hondes, and also the lengthe of his hauberk henge down be-nethe his feet, and his legges were waxen so short that thei passed not the skirtes of the sadill; and be-hilde and saugh how his hosen of stiell resten in the stiropes, and saugh how his shelde henge toward the erthe, and a-perceyved wele that he was be-come a duerf, and seide to hym-self that that it was that the damesell hadde hym promysed, and ther-with he wax so wroth, that for a litill he hadde gon oute of his witte, and rode forth so in that wrathe and in that anguyssh in the foreste, till he fonde a crosse and a ston therby; and thider he rode and a-light vpon the ston and toke his stiropes, and made hem shorter, and his hosen of stiell, and the renges of his swerde, and the gige of his shilde, and the sleves of his hauberk, with thonges of lether vpon his shuldres, and a-raied hym in the beste wise he myght, so wroth and angry, that he hadde leuer to be deed than on lyve; and after that he lepte vp and rode forth his wey, and cursed the day and the hour that euer he entred in to that quest, for shamed he was and dishonoured; and so hath he gon in this manner that neuer he lefte castell, ne town, ne burgh, but that he asked tidinges of Merlin of alle the men and women that he mette, and many oon he mette that grete shame and grete reproves hym seiden; and neuertheles he dide many prowesses, ffor though he were a duerf and mysshapen he hadde not loste his stengthe, neithir his hardinesse, and many a knyght he conquered; and whan he hadde serched the reame of logres vp and down, and saugh that he cowde not finde Merlin, he thought to passe the see, and go in to the litill Breteigne; and so he dide, and serched if fer and nygh, but neuer cowde he here no tidinge of Merlin, and so it drough nygh the terme that he hadde promysed to returne; and than he seide to hym-self, 'Allas, what shall I now do for the terme a-proched that I muste returne by the oth that I haue sworn to

---

29. *Deduyt* = pleasure.

myn oncle to repeire; returne moste I nede, for elles sholde I be for-sworn and vn-trewe, and that will I not in no maner, ffor the oth was soche that yef I were in my delyuer powste, and in my powste am I nought, for I am foule disfigured and a thinge of grete dispite, and I haue nought of my-self, and therfore may I wele a-bide of goinge to court. Certes now haue I euell seide, ffor neuer will I be for-sworne for to go ne to come what persone that euer I be, and for that I am not shet in prison I may go at my wille, and I may not a-bide but I be for-sworne, and ther-fore me be-houeth to go, ffor vntrouthe will I never do; but I pray to god to haue of me mercy and pite, ffor my body is shamefully and lothly arayed.' In these complayntes that sir Gawein ther made, he returned bak for to com to courte, and fill as he rode thourgh the foreste of Brocheliande, and wolde turne for to come to the see, and euer as he rode he made grete moone; and as he made this weymentacion he herde a voice a litill vpon the right side a-bove, and he turned that wey where he hadde herde the voice, and loked vp and down, and nothinge he saugh, but as it hadde ben a smoko of myste in the eyre that myght not passe oute; than he herde a voice that seide, 'Sir Gawein, disconfort you nothinge, for all shall falle as it be-houeth to falle.'

Whan sir Gawein herde the voyce that hadde hym cleped by his right name, he ansuerde and seide, 'Who is that in the name of god that to me doth speke?' 'How is that,' quod the voice, 'ne knowe ye me nought, ye were wonte to knowe me right wele, but so goth the worlde, and trewe is the proverbe that the wise man sieth that "who is fer from his iye is soone for-yeten," and so fareth it be me; ffor while that I haunted the Courte, and serued the kynge Arthur and his barouns. I was wele be-knowen of yow and of many other, and for that I haue left court I am vn-knowen, and that ought I not to be, yef feith and trouthe regned thourgh the worlde.' Whan sir Gawein herde the voice thus speke, he thought a-noon it was Merlin, and ansuerde a-noon, 'Certes, it is trouthe I ought you wele for to knowe, for many tyme haue I herde youre speche, and ther-fore I pray you that ye will a-pere to me so that I may yow se.' 'My lorde sir Gawein,' quod Merlin, 'me shull ye neuer se, and that hevieth me sore that I may do noon other; and whan ye be departed fro hens, I shall neuer speke with yow no more, ne with noon other saf only with my leef; for neuer man shall haue power hider for to come for nothinge that may be-falle. Ne fro hens may I not come oute, ne neuer I shall come oute, ffor in all the worlde is not so stronge a clos as is this where-as I am, and it is nother of Iren, ne stiell, ne tymbir, ne of ston, but it is of the aire withoute eny othir thinge be enchauntemente so stronge, that it may neuer be vn-don while the worlde endureth. Ne I may not come oute ne noon may entre, saf she that me here hath enclosed, that bereth me companye whan hir liked, and goth hens wham hir liste.'

'How is that, swete frende,' quod Gawein, 'that ye be in this maner with-holden, that noon may you delyuer by no force that may be do? Ne ye may not you shewe to me that be the wisest man of the worlde.' 'Nay, but the moste fole,' quod Merlin, 'for I wiste wele that sholde befalle, and I am soche a fole that I love a-nother better than my-self, and haue hir lerned so moche, where thourgh I am thus be-closed and shette in prison, ne noon may me oute bringe.' 'Certes,' seide sir Gawein, 'that me hevieth sore, and so will the kynge Arthur, myn vncle, whan he it knoweth as he that maketh you to be sought thourgh alle londes.' 'Now he moste it suffre,' quod Merlin, 'for he shall me se neuer more ne I hym, for thus is it be-falle. Ne neuer shall no man speke with me after you, ther-fore for nought meveth eny man me for to seche; ffor youre-self, a-noon as ye be turned fro hens, ye shull neuer here me speke; and ther-fore now returne and grete wele the kynge Arthur, and my lady the quene, and alle the barouns, and telle hem how it is with me, and ye shull fynde the kynge at Cardoell in wales; and whan ye come thider ye shull finde alle youre felowes ther that fro you were departed; and discounforte yow not of that is yow be-falle, ffor ye shall fynde the damesell that so hath yow mysshapen in the foreste, where-as ye hir mette, but for-yete not hir to salue, for it were folye.' 'Sir,' seide Gawein, 'ne nought I shall, yef god will.' 'Now,' quod Merlin, 'I be-teche yow to god that kepe the kynge Arthur and the reame of logres, as for the best peple of the worlde.'

[. . .]

EXTRACTS FROM LE MORTE D'ARTHUR

by Thomas Malory

SIR THOMAS MALORY'S great masterpiece of English prose storytelling is undoubtedly the most famous of the surviving Arthurian texts. Malory, whose colourful life has been the subject of much speculation in recent years (according to some sources he spent most of his life in prison on charges of rape, murder and treason), wrote his book between 1469 and 1470, drawing upon the vast thirteenth-century *Vulgate Cycle* of romances compiled and written by Cistercian scribes at the abbey of Clairvaux in France. Malory's version is much shorter than the original, and shows him consistently compressing his source to make a better and tighter story. His prose is lyrical, fast paced and savage by turns, according to the needs of the story, and his ear for dialogue is unsurpassed until the time of Shakespeare. The extracts included here all show Merlin in his role as helper and guide to the young Arthur. We read the story of Uther's infatuation with Igraine and Merlin's subsequent magical aid which enables Arthur to be engendered. Later we see him testing the young king in various ways: by disguising himself first as a youth and then as an old wise man; and finally by helping Arthur obtain his magical sword from the Lady of the Lake. The final extract concerns Merlin's obsession with Nimuë – the Nimiane of the *English Merlin* extracted above. That this story is a much altered version of that told in the *Vita Merlini* (see above) is almost certain. From this we can see how the medieval Christian scribes and authors who recorded the later Arthurian texts failed to recognize the magical relationship of Merlin and his sister, and turned it instead into a doomed affair in which an old man (which Merlin was very clearly not) falls helplessly in love with a young woman, with disastrous consequences.

BOOK I

CHAPTER I

How Uther Pendragon sent for the duke of Cornwall and Igraine his wife, and of their departing suddenly again

It befell in the days of Uther Pendragon, when he was king of all England, and so reigned, that there was a mighty duke in Cornwall that held war against him long time. And the duke was called the Duke of Tintagil. And so by means King Uther sent for this duke, charging him to bring his wife with him, for she was called a fair lady, and a passing wise, and her name was called Igraine.

So when the duke and his wife were come unto the king, by the means of great lords they were accorded both. The king liked and loved this lady well, and he made them great cheer out of measure, and desired to have lain by her. But she was a passing good woman, and would not assent unto the king. And then she told the duke her husband, and said, I suppose that we were sent for that I should be dishonoured; wherefore, husband, I counsel you, that we depart from hence suddenly, that we may ride all night unto our own castle. And in like wise as she said so they departed, that neither the king nor none of his council were ware of their departing. All so soon as King Uther knew of their departing so suddenly, he was wonderly wroth. Then he called to him his privy council, and told them of the sudden departing of the duke and his wife.

Then they advised the king to send for the duke and his wife by a great charge; and if he will not come at your summons, then may ye do your best, then have ye cause to make mighty war upon him. So that was done, and the messengers had their answers; and that was this shortly, that neither he nor his wife would not come at him.

Then was the king wonderly wroth. And then the king sent him plain word again, and bade him be ready and stuff him and garnish him, for within forty days he would fetch him out of the biggest castle that he hath.

When the duke had this warning, anon he went and furnished and garnished two strong castles of his, of the which the one hight Tintagil, and the other castle hight Terrabil. So his wife Dame Igraine he put in the castle of Tintagil, and himself he put in the castle of Terrabil, the which had many issues and posterns out. Then in all haste came Uther with a great host, and laid a siege about the castle of Terrabil. And there he pight many pavilions, and there was great war made on both parties, and much people slain. Then for pure anger and for great love of fair Igraine the king Uther fell sick. So came to the king Uther Sir Ulfius, a noble knight, and asked the king why he was sick. I shall tell thee, said the king, I am sick for anger and for love of fair Igraine, that I may not be whole. Well, my lord, said Sir Ulfius, I shall seek Merlin, and he shall do you remedy, that your heart shall be pleased. So Ulfius departed, and by adventure he met Merlin in a beggar's array, and there Merlin asked Ulfius whom he sought. And he said he had little ado to tell him. Well, said Merlin, I know whom thou seekest, for thou seekest Merlin; therefore seek no farther, for I am he; and if King Uther will well reward me, and be sworn unto me to fulfil my desire, that shall be his honour and profit more than mine; for I shall cause him to have all his desire. All this will I undertake, said Ulfius, that there shall be nothing reasonable but thou shalt have thy desire. Well, said Merlin, he shall have his intent and desire. And therefore, said Merlin, ride on your way, for I will not be long behind.

CHAPTER II

How Uther Pendragon made war on the duke of Cornwall, and how by the mean of Merlin he lay by the duchess and gat Arthur

Then Ulfius was glad, and rode on more than a pace till that he came to King Uther Pendragon, and told him he had met with Merlin. Where is he? said the king. Sir, said Ulfius, he will not dwell long. Therewithal Ulfius was ware where Merlin stood at the porch of the pavilion's door. And then Merlin was bound to come to the king. When King Uther saw him, he said he was welcome. Sir, said Merlin, I know all your heart every deal; so ye will be sworn unto me as ye be a true king anointed, to fulful my desire, ye shall have your desire. Then the king was sworn upon the four Evangelists. Sir, said Merlin, this is my desire: the first night that ye shall lie by Igraine ye shall get

Merlin taketh the child Arthur into his keeping (Aubrey Beardsley)

a child on her, and when that is born, that it shall be delivered to me for to nourish there as I will have it; for it shall be your worship, and the child's avail, as mickle as the child is worth. I will well, said the king, as thou wilt have it. Now make you ready, said Merlin, this night ye shall lie with Igraine in the castle of Tintagil; and ye shall be like the duke her husband, Ulfius shall be like Sir Brastias, a knight of the duke's, and I will be like a knight that hight Sir Jordanus, a knight of the duke's. But wait ye make not many questions with her nor her men, but say ye are diseased, and so hie you to bed, and rise not on the morn till I come to you, for the castle of Tintagil is but ten miles hence; so this was done as they devised. But the duke of Tintagil espied how the king rode from the siege of Terrabil, and therefore that night he issued out of the castle at a postern for to have distressed the king's host. And so, through his own issue, the duke himself was slain or ever the king came at the castle of Tintagil.

So after the death of the duke, King Uther lay with Igraine more than three hours after his death, and begat on her that night Arthur, and on day came Merlin to the king, and bade him make him ready, and so he kissed the lady Igraine and departed in all haste. But when the lady heard tell of the duke her husband, and by all record he was dead or ever King Uther came to her, then she marvelled who that might be that lay with her in likeness of her lord; so she mourned privily and held her peace. Then all the barons by one assent prayed the king of accord betwixt the lady Igraine and him; the king gave them leave, for fain would he have been accorded with her. So the king put all the trust in Ulfius to entreat between them, so by the entreaty at the last the king and she met together. Now will we do well, said Ulfius, our king is a lusty knight and wifeless, and my lady Igraine is a passing fair lady; it were great joy unto all, an it might please the king to make her his queen. Unto that they all well accorded and moved it to the king. And anon, like a lusty knight, he assented thereto with good will, and so in all haste they were married in a morning with great mirth and joy.

And King Lot of Lothian and of Orkney then wedded Margawse that was Gawaine's mother, and King Nentres of the land of Garlot wedded Elaine. All this was done at the request of King Uther. And the third sister Morgan le Fay was put to school in a nunnery, and there she learned so much that she was a great clerk of necromancy. And after she was wedded to King Uriens of the land of Gore, that was Sir Ewain's le Blanchemain's father.

CHAPTER III

Of the birth of King Arthur and of his nurture

Then Queen Igraine waxed daily greater and greater, so it befell after within half a year, as King Uther lay by his queen, he asked her, by the faith she owed to him, whose was the child within her body; then she sore abashed to give answer. Dismay you not, said the king, but tell me the truth, and I shall love you the better, by the faith of my body. Sir, said she, I shall you the truth. The same night that my lord was dead, the hour of his death, as his knights record, there came into my castle of Tintagil a man like my lord in speech and in countenance, and two knights with him in likeness of his two knights Brastias and Jordanus, and so I went unto bed with him as I ought to do with my lord, and the same night, as I shall answer unto God, this child was begotten upon me. That is truth, said the king, as ye say; for it was I myself that came in the likeness, and therefore dismay you not, for I am father of the child; and there he told her all the cause, how it was by Merlin's counsel. Then the queen made great joy when she knew who was the father of her child.

Soon came Merlin unto the king, and said, Sir, ye must purvey you for the nourishing of your child. As thou wilt, said the king, be it. Well, said Merlin, I know a lord of yours in this land, that is a passing true man and a faithful, and he shall have the nourishing of your child, and his name is Sir Ector, and he is a lord of fair livelihood in many parts in England and Wales; and this lord, Sir Ector, let him be sent for, for to come and speak with you, and desire him yourself, as he loveth you, that he will put his own child to nourishing to another woman, and that his wife nourish yours. And when the child is born let it be delivered to me at yonder privy postern unchristened. So like as Merlin devised it was done. And when Sir Ector was come he made fiaunce to the king for to nourish the child like as the king desired; and there the king granted Sir Ector great rewards. Then when the lady was delivered, the king commanded two knights and two ladies to take the child, bound in a cloth of gold, and that ye deliver him to what poor man ye meet at the postern gate of the castle. So the child was delivered unto Merlin, and so he bare it forth unto Sir Ector, and made an holy man to christen him, and named him Arthur; and so Sir Ector's wife nourished him with her own pap.

CHAPTER IV

Of the death of King Uther Pendragon

Then within two years King Uther fell sick of a great malady. And in the meanwhile his enemies usurped upon him, and did a great battle upon his men, and slew many of his people. Sir, said Merlin, ye may not lie so as ye do, for ye must to the field though ye ride on an horse-litter: for ye shall never have the better of your enemies but if your person be there, and then shall ye have the victory. So it was done as Merlin had devised, and they carried the king forth in an horse-litter with a great host towards his enemies. And at St. Albans there met with the king a great host of the North. And that day Sir Ulfius and Sir Brastias did great deeds of arms, and King Uther's men overcame the Northern battle and slew many people, and put the remnant to flight. And then the king returned unto London, and made great joy of his victory. And then he fell passing sore sick, so that three days and three nights he was speechless: wherefore all the barons made great sorrow, and asked Merlin what counsel were best. There is none other remedy, said Merlin, but God will have his will. But look ye all the barons be before King Uther to-morn, and God and I shall make him to speak. So on the morn all the barons with Merlin came to-fore the king; then Merlin said aloud unto King Uther, Sir, shall your son Arthur be king after your days, of this realm with all the appurtenance? Then Uther Pendragon turned him, and said in hearing of them all, I give him God's blessing and mine, and bid him pray for my soul, and righteously and worshipfully that he claim the crown, upon forfeiture of my blessing; and therewith he yielded up the ghost, and then was he interred as longed to a king. Wherefore the queen, fair Igraine, made great sorrow, and all the barons.

CHAPTER V

How Arthur was chosen king, and of wonders and marvels of a sword taken out of a stone by the said Arthur

Then stood the realm in great jeopardy long while, for every lord that was mighty of men made him strong, and many weened to have been king. Then Merlin went to the Archbishop of Canterbury, and counselled him for to send for all the lords of the realm, and all the gentlemen of arms, that they should to London come by Christmas, upon pain of cursing; and this cause, that Jesus, that was born on that night, that he would of his great mercy show some miracle, as he was come to be king of mankind, for to show some miracle who should be rightwise king of this realm. So the Archbishop, by the advice of Merlin, sent for all the lords and gentlemen of arms that they should come by Christmas even unto London. And many of them made them clean of their life, that their prayer might be the more acceptable unto God. So in the greatest church of London, whether it were Paul's or not the French book maketh no mention, all the estates were long or day in the church for to pray. And when matins and the first mass was done, there was seen in the churchyard, against the high altar, a great stone four square, like unto a marble stone; and in midst thereof was like an anvil of steel a foot on high, and therein stuck a fair sword naked by the point, and letters there were written in gold about the sword that said thus: Whoso pulleth out this sword of this stone and anvil, is rightwise king born of all England. Then the people marvelled, and told it to the Archbishop. I command, said the Archbishop, that ye keep you within your church and pray unto God still, that no man touch the sword till the high mass be all done. So when all masses were done all the lords went to behold the stone and the sword. And when they saw the scripture some assayed, such as would have been king. But none might stir the sword nor move it. He is not here, said the Archbishop, that shall achieve the sword, but doubt not God will make him known. But this is my counsel, said the Archbishop, that we let purvey ten knights, men of good fame, and they to keep this sword. So it was ordained, and then there was made a cry, that every man should assay that would, for to win the sword. And upon New Year's Day the barons let make a jousts and a tournament, that all knights that would joust or tourney there might play, and all this was ordained for to keep the lords together and the commons, for the Archbishop trusted that God would make him known that should win the sword.

So upon New Year's Day, when the service was done, the barons rode unto the field, some to joust and some to tourney, and so it happened that Sir Ector, that had great livelihood about London, rode unto the jousts, and with him rode Sir Kay his son, and young Arthur that was his nourished brother; and Sir Kay was made knight at All Hallowmass afore. So as they rode to the jousts-ward, Sir Kay lost his sword, for he had left it at his father's lodging, and so he prayed young Arthur for to ride for his sword. I will well, said Arthur, and rode fast after the sword, and when he came home, the lady and all were out to see the jousting. Then was Arthur wroth, and said to himself, I will ride to the churchyard, and take the sword with me that sticketh in the stone, for my brother Sir Kay shall not be without a sword this day. So when he came to the churchyard, Sir Arthur alighted and tied his horse to the stile, and so he went to the tent, and found no knights there, for they were at the jousting. And so he handled the sword by the handles, and lightly and fiercely pulled it out of the stone, and took his horse and rode his way until he came to his brother Sir Kay, and delivered him the sword. And as soon as Sir Kay saw the sword, he wist well it was the sword of the stone, and so he rode to his father Sir Ector, and said: Sir, lo here is the sword of the stone, wherefore I must be king of this land. When Sir Ector beheld the sword, he returned again and came to the church, and there they alighted all three, and went into the church. And anon he made Sir Kay swear upon a book how he came to that sword. Sir, said Sir Kay, by my brother Arthur, for he brought it to me. How gat ye this sword? said Sir Ector to Arthur. Sir, I will tell you. When I came home for my brother's sword, I found nobody at home to deliver me his sword; and so I thought my brother Sir Kay should not be swordless, and so I came hither eagerly and pulled it out of the stone without any pain. Found ye any knights about this sword? said Sir Ector. Nay, said Arthur. Now, said Sir Ector to Arthur, I understand ye must be king of this land. Wherefore I, said Arthur, and for what cause? Sir, said Ector, for God will have it so; for there should never man have drawn out this sword, but he that shall be rightwise king of this land. Now let me see whether ye can put the sword there as it was, and pull it out again. That is no mastery, said Arthur, and so he put it in the stone; wherewithal Sir Ector assayed to pull out the sword and failed.

CHAPTER VI
How King Arthur pulled out the sword divers times

Now assay, said Sir Ector unto Sir Kay. And anon he pulled at the sword with all his might; but it would not be. Now shall ye assay, said Sir Ector to Arthur. I will well, said Arthur, and pulled it out easily. And therewithal Sir Ector knelt down to the earth, and Sir Kay. Alas, said Arthur, my own dear father and brother, why kneel ye to me? Nay, nay, my lord Arthur, it is not so; I was never your father nor of your blood, but I wot well ye are of an higher blood than I weened ye were. And then Sir Ector told him all, how he was betaken him for to nourish him, and by whose commandment, and by Merlin's deliverance.

Then Arthur made great dole when he understood that Sir Ector was not his father. Sir, said Ector unto Arthur, will ye be my good and gracious lord when ye are king? Else were I to blame, said Arthur, for ye are the man in the world that I am most beholden to, and my good lady and mother your wife, that as well as her own hath fostered me and kept. And if ever it be God's will that I be king as ye say, ye shall desire of me what I may do, and I shall not fail you; God forbid I should fail you. Sir, said Sir

Ector, I will ask no more of you, but that ye will make my son, your foster brother, Sir Kay, seneschal of all your lands. That shall be done, said Arthur, and more, by the faith of my body, that never man shall have that office but he, while he and I live. Therewithal they went unto the Archbishop, and told him how the sword was achieved, and by whom; and on Twelfth-day all the barons came thither, and to assay to take the sword, who that would assay. But there afore them all, there might none take it out but Arthur; wherefore there were many lords wroth, and said it was great shame unto them all and the realm, to be over-governed with a boy of no high blood born. And so they fell out at that time that it was put off till Candlemas, and then all the barons should meet there again; but always the ten knights were ordained to watch the sword day and night, and so they set a pavilion over the stone and the sword, and five always watched. So at Candlemas many more great lords came thither for to have won the sword, but there might none prevail. And right as Arthur did at Christmas, he did at Candlemas, and pulled out the sword easily, whereof the barons were sore aggrieved and put it off in delay till the high feast of Easter. And as Arthur sped before, so did he at Easter; yet there were some of the great lords had indignation that Arthur should be king, and put it off in a delay till the feast of Pentecost.

Then the Archbishop of Canterbury by Merlin's providence let purvey then of the best knights that they might get, and such knights as Uther Pendragon loved best and most trusted in his days. And such knight were put about Arthur as Sir Baudwin of Britain, Sir Kay, Sir Ulfius, Sir Brastias. All these, with many other, were always about Arthur, day and night, till the feast of Pentecost.

[...]

Book II

CHAPTER XIX

How King Arthur rode to Carlion, and of his dream, and how he saw the questing beast

Then after the departing of King Ban and of King Bors, King Arthur rode into Carlion. And thither came to him, King Lot's wife, of Orkney, in manner of a message, but she was sent thither to espy the court of King Arthur; and she came richly beseen, with her four sons, Gawaine, Gaheris, Agravine, and Gareth, with many other knights and ladies. For she was a passing fair lady, therefore the king cast great love unto her, and desired to lie by her; so they were agreed, and he begat upon her Mordred, and she was his sister, on his mother's side, Igraine. So there she rested her a month, and at the last departed. Then the king dreamed a marvellous dream whereof he was sore adread. But all this time King Arthur knew not that King Lot's wife was his sister. Thus was the dream of Arthur: Him thought there was come into this land griffins and serpents, and him thought they burnt and slew all the people in the land, and then him thought he fought with them, and they did him passing great harm, and wounded him full sore, but at the last he slew them. When the king awaked, he was passing heavy of his dream, and so to put it out of thoughts, he made him ready with many knights to ride a-hunting. As soon as he was in the forest the king saw a great hart afore him. This hart will I chase, said King Arthur, and so he spurred the horse, and rode after long, and so by fine force oft he was like to have smitten the hart; whereas the king had chased the hart so long, that his horse lost his breath, and fell down dead. Then a yeoman fetched the king another horse.

So the king saw the hart enbushed, and his horse dead, he set him down by a fountain, and there he fell in great thoughts. And as he sat so, him thought he heard a noise of hounds, to the sum of thirty. And with that the king saw coming toward him the strangest beast that ever he saw or heard of; so the beast went to the well and drank, and the noise was in the beast's belly like unto the questing of thirty couple hounds; but all the while the beast drank there was no noise in the beast's belly: and therewith the beast departed with a great noise, whereof the king had great marvel. And so he was in a great thought, and therewith he fell asleep. Right so there came a knight afoot unto Arthur and said, Knight full of thought and sleepy, tell me if thou sawest a strange beast pass this way. Such one saw I, said King Arthur, that is past two mile; what would ye with the beast? said Arthur. Sir, I have followed that beast long time, and killed mine horse, so would God I had another to follow my quest. Right so came one with the king's horse, and when the knight saw the horse, he prayed the king to give him the horse: for I have followed this quest this twelvemonth, and either I shall achieve him, or bleed of the best blood of my body. Pellinore, that time king, followed the Questing Beast, and after his death Sir Palamides followed it.

CHAPTER XX

How King Pellinore took Arthur's horse and followed the questing beast, and how Merlin met with Arthur

Sir knight, said the king, leave that quest, and suffer me to have it, and I will follow it another twelvemonth. Ah, fool, said the knight unto Arthur, it is in vain thy desire, for it shall never be achieved but by me, or my next kin. Therewith he started unto the king's horse and mounted into the saddle, and said, Gramercy, this horse is my own. Well, said the king, thou mayst take my horse by force, but an I might prove thee whether thou were better on horseback or I. – Well, said the knight, seek me here when thou wilt, and here nigh this well thou shalt find me, and so passed on his way. Then the king sat in a study, and bade his men fetch his horse as fast as ever they might. Right so came by him Merlin like a child of fourteen year of age, and saluted the king, and asked him why he was so pensive. I may well be pensive, said the king, for I have seen the marvellest sight that ever I saw. That know I well, said Merlin, as well as thyself, and of all thy thoughts, but thou art but a fool to take thought, for it will not amend thee. Also I know what thou art, and who was thy father, and of whom thou wert begotten; King Uther Pendragon was thy father, and begat thee on Igraine. That is false, said King Arthur, how shouldest thou know if, for thou art not so old of years to know my father? Yes, said Merlin, I know it better than ye or any man living. I will not believe thee, said Arthur, and was wroth with the child. So departed Merlin, and came again in the likeness of an old man of fourscore year of age, whereof the king was right glad, for he seemed to be right wise.

Then said the old man, Why are ye so sad? I may well be heavy, said Arthur, for many things. Also here was a child, and told me many things that meseemeth he should not know, for he was not of age to know my father. Yes, said the old man, the child told you truth, and more would he have told you an ye would have suffered him. But ye have done a thing late that God is displeased with you, for ye have lain by your sister, and on her ye have gotten a child that shall destroy you and all the knights of your realm. What are ye, said Arthur, that tell me these tidings? I am Merlin, and I was he in the child's likeness. Ah, said King Arthur, ye are a marvellous man, but I marvel much of thy words that I must die in battle. Marvel not, said Merlin, for it is God's will your body to be punished for your foul deeds; but I may well be sorry, said Merlin, for I shall die a shameful death, to be put in the earth quick, and ye shall die a worshipful death. And as they talked this, came one with the king's horse, and so the king mounted on his horse, and Merlin on another, and so rode unto Carlion. And anon the king asked

Ector and Ulfius how he was begotten, and they told him Uther Pendragon was his father and Queen Igraine his mother. Then he said to Merlin, I will that my mother be sent for, that I may speak with her; and if she say so herself, then will I believe it. In all haste, the queen was sent for, and she came and brought with her Morgan le Fay, her daughter, that was as fair a lady as any might be, and the king welcomed Igraine in the best manner.

CHAPTER XXI

How Ulfius impeached Queen Igraine, Arthur's mother, of treason; and how a knight came and desired to have the death of his master revenged

Right so came Ulfius, and said openly, that the king and all might hear that were feasted that day, Ye are the falsest lady of the world, and the most traitress unto the king's person. Beware, said Arthur, what thou sayest; thou speakest a great word. I am well ware, said Ulfius, what I speak, and here is my glove to prove it upon any man that will say the contrary, that this Queen Igraine is causer of your great damage, and of your great war. For, an she would have uttered it in the life of King Uther Pendragon, of the birth of you, and how ye were begotten, ye have never had the mortal wars that ye have had; for the most part of your barons of your realm knew never whose son ye were, nor of whom ye were begotten; and she that bare you of her body should have made it known openly in excusing of her worship and yours, and in like wise to all the realm, wherefore I prove her false to God and to you and to all your realm, and who will say the contrary I will prove it on his body.

Then spake Igraine and said, I am a woman and I may not fight, but rather than I should be dishonoured, there would some good man take my quarrel. More, she said, Merlin knoweth well, and ye Sir Ulfius, how King Uther came to me in the Castle of Tintagil in the likeness of my lord, that was dead three hours to-fore, and thereby gat a child that night upon me. And after the thirteenth day King Uther wedded me, and by his commandment when the child was born it was delivered unto Merlin and nourished by him, and so I saw the child never after, nor wot not what is his name, for I knew him never yet. And there, Ulfius said to the queen, Merlin is more to blame than ye. Well I wot, said the queen, I bare a child by my lord King Uther, but I wot not where he is become. Then Merlin took the king by the hand, saying, This is your mother. And therewith Sir Ector bare witness how he nourished him by Uther's commandment. And therewith King Arthur took his mother, Queen Igraine, in his arms and kissed her, and either wept upon other. And then the king let make a feast that lasted eight days.

[. . .]

CHAPTER XXV

How Arthur by the mean of Merlin gat Excalibur his sword of the Lady of the Lake

Right so the king and he departed, and went unto an hermit that was a good man and a great leech. So the hermit searched all his wounds, and gave him good salves; so the king was there three days, and then were his wounds well amended that he might ride and go, and so departed. And as they rode, Arthur said, I have no sword. No force, said Merlin, hereby is a sword that shall be yours, an I may. So they rode till they came to a lake, the which was a fair water and broad, and in the midst of the lake Arthur was ware of an arm clothed in white samite, that held a fair sword in that hand. Lo! said Merlin, yonder is that sword that I spake of. With that they saw a damosel going upon the lake. What damosel is that? said Arthur. That is the Lady of the Lake, said Merlin; and within that lake is a rock, and therein is as fair a place as any on earth, and richly beseen; and this damosel will come to you anon, and then speak ye fair to her that she will give you that sword. Anon withal came the damosel unto Arthur, and saluted him, and he her again. Damosel, said Arthur, what sword is that, that yonder the arm holdeth above the water? I would it were mine, for I have no sword. Sir Arthur, king, said the damosel, that sword is mine, and if ye will give me a gift when I ask it you, ye shall have it. By my faith, said Arthur, I will give you what gift ye will ask. Well! said the damosel, go ye into yonder barge, and row yourself to the sword, and take it and the scabbard with you, and I will ask my gift when I see my time. So Sir Arthur and Merlin alighted and tied their horses to two trees, and so they went into the ship, and when they came to the sword that the hand held, Sir Arthur took it up by the handles, and took it with him, and the arm and the hand went under the water. And so [they] came unto the land and rode forth, and then Sir Arthur saw a rich pavilion. What signifieth yonder pavilion? It is the knight's pavilion, said Merlin that ye fought with last, Sir Pellinore; but he is out, he is not there. He hath ado with a knight of yours that hight Egglame, and they have foughten together, but at the last Egglame fled, and else he had been dead, and he hath chased him even to Carlion, and we shall meet with him anon in the highway. That is well said, said Arthur, now have I a sword, now will I wage battle with him, and be avenged on him. Sir, you shall not so, said Merlin, for the knight is weary of fighting and chasing, so that ye shall have no worship to have ado with him; also he will not be lightly matched of one knight living, and therefore it is my counsel, let him pass, for he shall do you good service in short time, and his sons after his days. Also ye shall see that day in short space, you shall be right glad to give him your sister to wed. When I see him, I will do as ye advise, said Arthur.

Then Sir Arthur looked on the sword, and liked it passing well. Whether liketh you better, said Merlin, the sword or the scabbard? Me liketh better the sword, said Arthur. Ye are more unwise, said Merlin, for the scabbard is worth ten of the swords, for whiles ye have the scabbard upon you, ye shall never lose no blood, be ye never so sore wounded; therefore keep well the scabbard always with you. So they rode unto Carlion, and by the way they met with Sir Pellinore; but Merlin had done such a craft, that Pellinore saw not Arthur, and he passed by without any words. I marvel, said Arthur, that the knight would not speak. Sir, said Merlin, he saw you not, for an he had seen you, ye had not lightly departed. So they came unto Carlion, whereof his knights were passing glad. And when they heard of his adventures, they marvelled that he would jeopard his person so, alone. But all men of worship said it was merry to be under such a chieftain, that would put his person in adventure as other poor knights did.

[...]

BOOK III

CHAPTER I

How King Arthur took a wife, and wedded Guenever daughter to Leodegrance, *King of the Land of Cameliard, with whom he had the Round Table*

In the beginning of Arthur, after he was chosen king by adventure and by grace; for the most part of the barons knew not that he was Uther Pendragon's son, but as Merlin made it openly known. But yet many kings and lords held great war against him for that cause, but well Arthur overcame them all, for the most part the days of his life he was ruled much by the counsel of Merlin. So it fell on a time King Arthur said unto Merlin, My barons will let me have no rest, but needs I must take a wife, and I will none take but by thy counsel and by thine advice. It is well done, said Merlin, that ye take a wife, for a man of your bounty and noblesse should not be without a wife. Now is there any that ye love more than another? Yea, said King Arthur, I love Guenever the king's

'Lo!' said Merlin, 'yonder is that sword that I spake of.' With that
they saw a damosel going upon the lake (Russell Flint,
The Morte D'Arthur, Book I, Chapter XXV)

daughter, Leodegrance of the land of Cameliard, the which holdeth in his house the
Table Round that ye told he had of my father Uther. And this damosel is the most
valiant and fairest lady that I know living, or yet that ever I could find. Sir, said Merlin,
as of her beauty and fairness she is one of the fairest alive, but, an ye loved her not so
well as ye do, I should find you a damosel of beauty and of goodness that should like
you and please you, an your heart were not set; but there as a man's heart is set, he will
be loath to return. That is truth, said King Arthur. But Merlin warned the king covertly
that Guenever was not wholesome for him to take to wife, for he warned him that
Launcelot should love her, and she him again; and so he turned his tale to the adventures of Sangreal.

Then Merlin desired of the king for to have men with him that should enquire of
Guenever, and so the king granted him, and Merlin went forth unto King Leodegrance
of Cameliard, and told him of his desire of the king that he would have unto his wife
Guenever his daughter. That is to me, said King Leodegrance, the best tidings that ever
I heard, that so worthy a king of prowess and noblesse will wed my daughter. And as for
my lands, I will give him, wist I it might please him, but he hath lands enow, him
needeth none; but I shall send him a gift shall please him much more, for I shall give
him the Table Round, the which Uther Pendragon gave me, and when it is full complete, there is an hundred knights and fifty. And as for an hundred good knights I have
myself, but I faute fifty, for so many have been slain in my days. And so Leodegrance
delivered his daughter Guenever unto Merlin, and the Table Round with the hundred
knights, and so they rode freshly, with great royalty, what by water and what by land,
till that they came nigh unto London.

[...]

Book IV

CHAPTER I

How Merlin was assotted and doted on one of the ladies of the lake, and how he
was shut in a rock under a stone and there died

So after these quests of Sir Gawaine, Sir Tor, and King Pellinore, it fell so that Merlin fell in a dotage on the damosel that King Pellinore brought to court, and she was one of the damosels of the lake, that hight Nimue. But Merlin would let her have no rest, but always he would be with her. And ever she made Merlin good cheer till she had learned of him all manner thing that she desired; and he was assotted upon her, that he might not be from her. So on a time he told King Arthur that he should not dure long, but for all his crafts he should be put in the earth quick. And so he told the king many things that should befall, and always he warned the king to keep well his sword and the scabbard, for he told him how the sword and the scabbard should be stolen by a woman from him that he most trusted. Also he told King Arthur that he should miss him, – Yet had ye liefer than all your lands to have me again. Ah, said the king, since ye know of your adventure, purvey for it, and put away by your crafts that misadventure. Nay, said Merlin, it will not be; so he departed from the king. And within a while the Damosel of the Lake departed, and Merlin went with her evermore wheresomever she went. And ofttimes Merlin would have had her privily away by his subtle crafts; then she made him to swear that he should never do none enchantment upon her if he would have his will. And so he sware; so she and Merlin went over the sea unto the land of Benwick, whereas King Ban was king that had great war against King Claudas, and there Merlin spake with King Ban's wife, a fair lady and a good, and her name was Elaine, and there he saw young Launcelot. There the queen made great sorrow for the mortal war that King Claudas made on her lord and on her lands. Take none heaviness, said Merlin, for this same child within this twenty year shall revenge you on King Claudas, that all Christendom shall speak of it; and this same child shall be the most man of worship of the world, and his first name is Galahad, that know I well, said Merlin, and since ye have confirmed him Launcelot. That is truth, said the queen, his first name was Galahad. O Merlin, said the queen, shall I live to see my son such a man of prowess? Yea, lady, on my peril ye shall see it, and live many winters after.

And so, soon after, the lady and Merlin departed, and by the way Merlin showed her many wonders, and came into Cornwall. And always Merlin lay about the lady to have her maidenhood, and she was ever passing weary of him, and fain would have been delivered of him, for she was afeard of him because he was a devil's son, and she could not beskift him by no mean. And so on a time it happed that Merlin showed to her in a rock whereas was a great wonder, and wrought by enchantment, that went under a great stone. So by her subtle working she made Merlin to go under that stone to let her wit of the marvels there; but she wrought so there for him that he came never out for all the craft he could do. And so she departed and left Merlin.

Part 3

THE
RENAISSANCE
MAGICIAN

INTRODUCTION

THE RENAISSANCE AND the so-called Age of Enlightenment which followed it were times of discovery, when old magics rubbed shoulders with dawning science. Practitioners of either discipline were regarded with a mixture of awe and suspicion. Not surprisingly then, Merlin, in this era, came to represent the magician and the alchemist, the proto-scientist and the visionary. Countless volumes of prophecies emerged at this time, many of them, like *England's Prophetical Merlin* by William Lilly (1602-81), attributed to Merlin.

After the fall of Constantinople in 1453, the Classical remnants of the great libraries found their way west into the ready soil of medieval Europe. Thus began the Renaissance, a rekindling of arts, philosophy and hermaneutics, where the narrow scope of medieval Christianity was expanded by contact with neo-Platonic and Classical world views. During this hermetic Renaissance, many physical embodiments of Merlin appeared throughout Europe. Figures like Marcilio Ficino (1453-99), Athanasius Kircher (1602-80) and Dr John Dee (1527-1608) revealed themselves as polymaths of comprehensive, druidic stature, prime movers in political strategy and in esoteric philosophy alike.

Dee made much of his Welsh descent and possible kinship with King Arthur. As Merlin to Queen Elizabeth's Arthur, Dee served as esoteric adviser, masterminding the discovery and colonization of the New World, as well as maintaining a closet coterie of esoteric practice. The account of his mediumistic discourse with spirits is well documented, revealing that his concern with mapping inner worlds matched his desire to chart the unexplored regions of the New World. Figures such as Dee actively demonstrated the practical and dynamic role of the magus in the public eye of the political world, recalling earlier archetypes to common consciousness. Gareth Knight has written of Merlin:

> He represents a humanized Western form of the ancient gods of learning and civilization, such as the Greek Hermes or the Egyptian Thoth. He is furthermore, one of those, akin to Melchizadek in the Old Testament, 'without father or mother, without descent.'
>
> *The Secret Tradition in Arthurian Legend*, 1984

Throughout the Renaissance, Reformation and Counter-Reformation, the figure of Merlin was an active constituent of state and imagination. But, by the early eighteenth century, the shake-down had begun; the fire of Renaissance had been replaced by the dim lamp of Reason. The mercurial and prophetic figure of the magus had become a side-show.

It was an era of grottos and romantic landscapes wherein a lone, elderly indigent man might be installed in a draughty cave as a rustic hermit to entertain weekend visitors. Merlin himself was not exempt from an appearance in an early Hanoverian Disneyland. His fame ensured him a starring role in the garden pavilion ordered by Queen Caroline, wife of George II. It was designed by the court architect William Kent (1685-1748) to represent 'Merlin's Cave'. Finished in 1735 the cave contained wax figures of Merlin and his secretary, Queen Elizabeth I and her nurse, and Elizabeth of York (Henry VII's queen) and Minerva. The royal ladies were probably modelled from their death-mask effigies housed at Westminster Abbey. So popular was the cave that, despite satirical attacks by Jonathan Swift and others, taverns were named after it and coffee-house owners set up models of it to entertain their customers. This popularity led to a revival of Dryden's opera *King Arthur* in 1736 as *Merlin, or the British Enchanter* (the text of which is printed below) with Kent's set designs. Kent later illustrated Spenser's *The Faerie Queen* (see below).

After this period, Merlin enters the realms of the nineteenth-century romance, save for one brief glittering exposition in the prophetic writings of William Blake. Blake saw Merlin as an exemplar of 'the immortal Imagination of the Vegetative [Natural] Man' and in his massive epic, *Jerusalem*, describes Merlin exploring 'the Three States of Ulro [the material world]: Creation, Redemption, & Judgement.' Merlin also appears in the same poem at the degeneration of the Cathedral Cities:

> Bath stood upon the Severn with Merlin [spirit] & Bladud [body] & Arthur [heart], the Cup of Rahab in his hand.
>
> *Jerusalem* 75:2, our brackets

For Blake, the Cathedral Cities represented the communion of saints, a direct link with the ancient druidic choirs or chairs which maintained the spiritual integrity of the country. He assigns Merlin to Bath, as its spiritual patron. In a long tradition of reattributed prophecy, Blake ascribed one of his own prophecies to Merlin:

> The harvest shall flourish in wintry weather,
> When two virginities meet together.
>
> The King and the Priest must be tied in a tether,
> Before two virgins can meet together.
>
> *Complete Poems*, Nonesuch, 1975

This is the last bitter blast of the Renaissance magus, harking back to the Platonic ideal outlined in *The Republic*, as well as an ironic comment upon the increasingly separated political and spiritual traditions which only the lone prophet can reunite.

EXTRACTS FROM THE LIFE OF MERLIN

by Thomas Heywood

The Life of Merlin with his strange Prophecies or Chronographical History by Thomas Heywood was first published in the reign of Charles I, with a later subscription edition in the nineteenth century. A facsimile of the nineteenth-century edition has been published by Jones publishers of Wales. It is, in essence, a reworking of the English and Welsh chronicles, such as those of Geoffrey of Monmouth, Hollinshed and others. Contrary to the title it is not a biography of Merlin and is not a version of the medieval *Vita Merlini*.

Heywood places a special emphasis upon Merlin, however, offering various metrical prophecies and other poems, which do not seem to come from traditional sources, but are, presumably, his own reworkings. In the chapters quoted here, Heywood follows Geoffrey's *History* closely, and the verses are typical doggerel, woven into the text as if they are extracts from a whole source.

We have also included the author's original foreword to the work, since this probably sums up what we ourselves would say as well as anything else!

A TRUE HISTORY OF THE STRANGE BIRTH OF
AMBROSIUS MERLIN,
AND HIS WONDERFUL PROPHECIES

To the reader
Courteous & considerate reader,
I have here exposed to thy especial perusal, *The Life and Prophecies of our famous Predictor, MERLINUS, surnamed AMBROSIUS*; who, though he lived in the time of profane paganism, was a professed Christian, and therefore, his auguries the better to be approved and allowed, which thou hast, with all their exposition and explanation, expressly and punctually, making plain and evident how genuinely and properly they comply with the truth of our chronology. In which you shall find (adding the supplement of the history from Brute, who laid the first foundation of our British Colony, to the time of king Vortigernus, or Vortigern, the usurper of the crown, under whose reign Merlin first flourished) a true catalogue of all the kings of this island, with a summary of all passages of state, ecclesiastical or temporal, of any remark or moment, during their principalities and dominions, insomuch that scarce any thing shall be here wanting to the best wishes, if thou art desirous to be instructed and faithfully informed in the knowledge of our English annals. For in the stead of a large study book, and huge voluminous tractate, able to take up a whole year in reading, and to load and tire a porter in carrying, thou hast here a small manuel, containing all the pith and marrow of the greater, made portable for thee (if thou so please) to bear in thy pocket, so that thou may'st say, that in this small compendium or abstract, thou hast Hollinshed,

Polychronicon, Fabian, Speed, or any of the rest of more giantlike bulk or binding. To which, my short abbreviary, I strive to make this my prologue or preface, to thee alike suitable, being as succinct and briefly contrived as the former summarily comprehended, desiring thee to read considerately, and withal to censure charitably, and so (without further compliment) wishing thy care in the one, and courtesy in the other, with a favourable pardon of some few errors committed in the Press, I bid thee farewell.

THOMAS HEYWOOD

CONTENTS OF CHAPTER THIRD
[...]

When Vortigern's architectures had caused the hill to be digged, and the foundation to be laid, on which, to erect this new structure, after the weak men had digged the circuit of the place, where the great stones were to be set in order, they were no sooner laid in the hollow of the earth, but they instantly sunk down, and were swallowed up, and no more seen. At which the workmen wondered, and the king himself was much astonished, and the more proofs they made, the greater cause of admiration they had; especially the situation being upon an hill, and no moorish or uncertain ground. Therefore the king commanded a cessation from the work for the present, and sent to the bards and wisards (of which that age afforded plenty) to know a reason of that prodigy, or at least what it might portend; who, being gathered together, and long consulted amongst themselves, and not finding by any natural or supernatural reason, what the cause thereof might be, concluded in the end, to save their credit, and to excuse their ignorance, to put the king off with an impossibility; and when he came to demand of them what they had done in the matter, they returned him this answer, that those stones could never be laid together, or the place built upon, till they were cemented with the blood of a man-child, who was born of a mother, but had no man to his father.

With this answer the king was satisfied, the soothsayers departed from him (not meanly glad that they had put him off, according to our English word, with a flam or delirement) without any disparagement to their art and cunning, who no sooner left his presence, but the king called his servants about him, commanding them to ride and search into, and through all provinces and countries till they could find such a one as the wisards had spoken of, and by fair or foul means to bring the party unto him, but not acquainting him with the cause, but that the king seeing such a one, would send him back richly and bountifully rewarded. Having received this commission (or rather imposition) from the king their master, we leave them to their several adventures, every one of them being sufficiently accommodated for so uncertain a journey.

One of them amongst the rest happened to come to a town or city called Caer-Merlin, which implies Merlin's town or Merlin's borough, which there is no doubt the same which we call to this day Caermarthen, but my author terms it a city; at whose gates the messenger of the king arriving, it happened that a great many young lads were sporting themselves without the walls; and of the company, two of them in gaming fell out, the one young Merlin, the other called Dinabutius, who, amongst other breathing words, cast into Merlin's teeth, that he was but some moon calf, as born of a mother, who knew not his father: the servant taking notice of this language, presently demanded what he was, and who were his parents? who returned him answer, that for any father he had, they knew none, but his mother was daughter to king Demetius, and lived a votaress in that city, in a nunnery belonging to the church of St. Peter: who presently went to the chief magistrates, and shewed his commission from the king, which they obeying, sent both the mother and son under his conduct, to attend the pleasure of his Majesty.

Of whose coming the king was exceeding joyful, and when they appeared before him (both ignorant of the occasion why they were sent for) the king first asked her, if that were her natural son? who replyed that he was, and born of her own body; he then desired to know by what father he was begot? to which she likewise answered, that she never had the society of any one mortal or human, only a spirit assuming the shape of a beautiful young man, had many times appeared unto her, seeming to court her with no common affection, but when any of her fellow-virgins came in, he would suddenly disappear and vanish, by whose many and urgent importunities, being at last overcome, I yielded, saith she, to his pleasure, and was comprest by him, and when my full time of teeming came, I was delivered of this son (now in your presence) whom I caused to be called Merlin. Which words were uttered with such modesty and constancy, considering withal the royalty of her birth, and the strictness of the order (in which she now lived) that the king might the more easily be induced to believe that whatsoever she spoke was truth.

When, casting his eye upon Merlin, he began to apprehend strange promising things in his aspect, as having a quick and piercing eye, an ingenious and gracious countenance, and in his youthful face a kind of austerity and supercilious gravity, which took in him such a deep impression, that he thought his blood too noble to be mingled with the dust and rubbish of the death, and therefore instead of sentencing him to death, and commanding him to be slain, he opened unto him the purpose he had to build this castle, and the strange and prodigious impediments, which hindred the work, then his assembly of the bards and wisards, and what answer they returned him of his demand, but bade him withal be of comfort, for he prized his life (being a christian) above ten such citadels, though erected and perfected with all the cost and magnificence that human art or fancy could devise.

To which words, Merlin (who had all this while stood silent and spoke not a word) thus replied, Royal Sir, blind were your bards, witless your wisards, and silly and simple your soothsayers; who shewed themselves averse to art, and altogether unacquainted with the secrets of nature, as altogether ignorant, that in the breast of this hill lies a vast moat, or deep pool, which hath ingurgitated and swallowed all these materials thrown into the trenches. Therefore command them to be digged deeper, and you shall discover the water in which your squared stones have been washed, and in the bottom of the lake you shall find two hollow rocks of stone, and in them two horrible dragons fast asleep: which having uttered, he with a low obeisance made to the king, left speaking.

Who instantly commanded pioneers with pickaxes, mattocks, and shovels, to be sent for; who were presently employed to dig the earth deep, where the pond was found, and all the water drained, so that the bottom thereof was left dry, then were discovered the two hollow rocks, which being opened, out of them issued two fierce and cruel dragons, the one red, the other white, and made betwixt them a violent and terrible conflict: but in the end the white dragon prevailed over the red. At which sight the king being greatly stupified and amazed, demanded of Merlin what this their combat might portend? Who fetching a great sigh, and tears in abundance issuing from his eyes, with a prophetical spirit, made him this following answer:

'Woe's me for the red Dragon, for alach,
The time is come, hee hasteth to his mach:
The bloudy Serpent, (yet whose souls are white)
Implys that Nation, on which thy delight
Was late sole-fixt, (the *Saxons*) who as friends
Came to thee first, but ayming at shrewd ends

> They shall have power over the drooping *red*,
> In which the British Nation's figured:
> Drive shall he them into caves, holes, and dens,
> To barren Mountains, and to moorish fens,
> Hills shall remove to where the valleyes stood,
> And all the baths and brooks shall flow with blood.
> The worship of the holy God shall cease.
> For in thilk dayes the Kirke shall have no peace:
> The Panims (woe the while) shall get the day,
> And with their Idols mawmetry beare sway,
> And yet in fine shee that was so opprest,
> Shal mount, & in the high rocks build her nest.
> For out of *Cornwall* shall proceed a Bore,
> Who shall the Kerk to pristine state restore,
> Bow shall all *Britaine* to his kingly beck,
> And tread he shall on the white Dragon's neck.'

Then casting a sad look upon the king, as reading his fate in his forehead, he muttered to himself and said,

> 'But well-away for thee, to *Britaine* deere,
> For I fore-see thy sad disaster's neere.'

Which accordingly happened, and that within a few years after, for Vortigern having builded this castle, and fortified it, making it defensible against any foreign opposition, the two sons of Constantine, whom Vortigern had before caused to be slain, assisted by their near kinsman Pudentius, king of Armorica, or little Britain, (where they had been liberally fostered and cherished) passed the sea with a compleat Army, and landed at Totness, whereof when the Britains who were dispersed in many provinces understood, they crept out of their holes and corners, and drew unto their host, which was no small encouragement to the two brothers, Ambrosius Aurelius and Uter-Pendragon, who now finding their forces to be sufficiently able both in strength and number, made their speedy expedition towards Wales, with purpose to distress Vortigern the usurper.

Who having notice of their coming, and not able in regard of the paucity of his followers to give them battle, he made what provision he could for the strengthening of his castle, to endure a long siege, and to oppose the rage of any violent battery, till he might send for supply elsewhere. But such was the fury of the assailants, that after many fierce and dangerous attempts finding the walls and gates to be impregnable; casting into the castle balls of wild fire, with other incendiaries, they burnt him and his people alive, amongst whom not one escaped. Of him it is reported, that he should have carnal society with his own daughter, in hope that kings should issue from them; thus died he most miserably when he had reigned, since his last inauguration, nine years and some odd months. The explanation of the rest of his prophecy, I will leave to the chapter following.

[...]

CONTENTS OF CHAPTER FOURTH
[...]

You have heard what the red and white dragons figured, namely, the British and Saxon people, we will now punctually examine the truth of his predictions in the rest. The caverns, corners, mountains, and moorish places, express into what sundry distresses

Merlin Ambrosius with attendant beasts (Thomas Heyward,
Life of Merlin, 1641)

the natives were driven into, by the merciless cruelty of the strangers; by the hills and valleys, shifting places, that there was no difference amongst the poor Britains, between the courtier and the cottager, the peer and the peasant; by the rivers flowing with blood, the many battles fought between the two nations; and that in those days religion and the true worship of God was supprest, happened under Hengist and Horsus, and their posterity. Octa the son of Hengist, who succeeded his father in the kingdom of Kent, Tosa, Pascentius, and Colgrinus, all pagans and princes of the Saxons. For when the Britains, from the time of Eleutherius, whom the Romists write was the fourteenth pope after the blessed St. Peter had received the Christian faith under king Lucius, of glorious memory, and had continued it for many years unto that time.

The Saxons, after coming into the land, being then miscreants, laboured by all means to suppress the same, and in the stead thereof, to plant their pagan idolatry, which they accomplished even to the coming of St. Augustine, sent hither by pope Gregory; in whose time again it began to flourish and get the upper hand, in the reign of Aurelius Ambrose, and his brother Uter-pendragon, (which is by interpretation the head of the dragon) who succeeded him. By the boar, which should come out of

Cornwall, and tread upon the neck of the white dragon, is meant the invincible king Arthur, who vanquished the Saxons, and subdued them in many battles, and was a great maintainer and exalter of the true Christian religion. Of whose begetting and birth, in this our History of Merlin, we shall have occasion to speak hereafter.

As Merlin was plentifully endued with the spirit of divination; so, by other authors, it is affirmed of him, that he was skilful in dark and hidden arts, as magic, necromancy, and the like; and relate of him, that when king Vortigern lived solitary in his late erected castle, forsaken of the greatest part of his followers and friends, and quite sequestered from all kingly honours, he grew into a deep and dumpish melancholy, delighting only (if any delight can be taken therein) in solitude and want of company. To expel which sad fits from him, which might be dangerous to impair his health, he would devise for his recreation and disport, many pleasant fancies to beget mirth, and sometimes laughter, by solacing his ear with several strains of music, both courtly and rural; the sound heard, but the persons not seen, as with the harp, bagpipes, cymbal, and tabret; and sometimes again with the lute, orphorian, viol, sackbut, cornet and organs. Then, to recreate his eyes, he would present him with stately masks and anti-masks; and again, for variety sake, with rustick dances, presented by swines and shepherdesses. And when these grew stale or tedious to his eye or ear, he would take him up into the top of one of his turrets, whereon he should see eagles and hawks fly after sundry games, and what fowl the king liked, they would strike it into his lap, to add to his slender provision for dinner and supper, which gave the king no small contentment.

Sometimes he would have an hare or hart, hunted and chased by a pack of dogs in the air, the game flying, the hounds, with open and audible mouths, pursing, with huntsmen winding their horns, and following the chase with all the indents and turnings, losses and recoveries; the champaign plains, the woods, and covers, appearing as visible and natural as if the sport had been upon the firm and solid earth.

Upon a time, being in the king's Summer parlour, who was desirous to be partaker of some novelty which he had never seen; there instantly appeared upon the table a pair of buts and whites in the middle to shoot at, where suddenly came in six dapper, and pert fellow like archers, in stature not above a foot high, and all other members accordingly proportioned, their bows were of the side bones of an overgrown pike; their strings of a small slivy silk, no bigger than the thread of a cobweb, their arrows less than picktooths, feathered with the wings of small flies, and headed with the points of Spanish needles, who made a show as if they were to shoot a match three to three, and roundly they went about it. In the middle of their game, there was a shot which rested doubtful; which, as it appeared, the gamesters could not well decide. Then, Merlin called to one of the servants (who had somewhat a big nose) and stood by, and bade him measure to the mark, and give it to the best; to which, while he stooped, and inclined his face, the better to impire the matter, one of the pigmy archers, who had an arrow to shoot, delivered it from his bow, and shot him quite through the nose, at which he started, and the king heartily laughed; (for there was no room to be seen) and the buts with the archers together disappeared.

But when Merlin knew the king's fate to draw nigh, and not willing to partake in his disaster, he fained occasions abroad, and though, with much difficulty, had at length leave to depart, leaving behind him a paper which he put into the king's closet, where, upon occassion, he might easily find, and read this ensuing prophecy.

'Fly from these fatall severall fires o King,
Which from less *Britain* the two exiles bring:
Now are their ships a rigging, now forsake,

> Th' *Armoricke* shoares, and towards *Albion* make,
> To avenge their murdered brothers bloud on thee,
> In *Totnesse* road to morrow they will bee,
> The *Saxon* Princes shall contend in vain,
> For young *Aurelius* having *Hengist* slain,
> Shall peaceably possesse the *British* throne,
> Striving the opposite Nations to attone.
> He the true faith shall seek to advance on high,
> But in the quest thereof, by poyson die,
> The Dragons head, his brother shall succeed,
> And after many a brave heroick deed,
> By him perform'd, the fates shall strive to waft,
> His sonle ore Styx, by a like poysnous draught,
> But those who sent them to th' *Elizian* bower,
> His sonne the Bore of *Cornwall* shall devoure.'

This history needs no comment, being so plain in itself by the success thereof; only this much, let me intreat the reader to bear in memory, that that Arthur, figured under the name of Aper Cornubiae, that is, the Boar of Cornwall, was son to Uter-pendragon, here called the head of the Dragon.

Amongst many brave heroical acts done by this Aurelius-Ambrose; after the death of Vortigern, he maintained the middle part of the kingdom of Britain, with all Cambria and Wales, endeavouring to repair all the ruined places in the land, as forts, castles, and citadels, but especially the temples which were much defaced by the pagan idolators, and caused divine service to be every where said in them, and after that, encountered the Saxons in the hill of Baden or Dadove, where he slew many of them, and utterly routed their whole army. After which defeat, another Saxon prince named Porthe, with his two sons, landed at an Haven in Sussex, after whom, as some authors affirms, the place is called Portsmouth unto this day, others landed also in several parts of the kingdom, so that Aurelius had with them many conflicts and battles, in which he sped diversly, being for the most part conqueror, and yet, at some times, repulsed and overset.

Our English chronicles, and others say, that he, by the help of Merlin, caused the great stones which stand till this day on the plain of Salisbury, to be brought in a whirl-wind one night out of Ireland, and caused them to be placed where they now stand in remembrance of the British lords there slain, and after buried in the time of the pretended treaty and communication had betwixt Vortigern and Hengist, as it formerly touched, but Polychronicon and others, ascribe the honour of their transportage to his brother, Uter-pendragon, at whose request to Merlin, that miraculous conveyance was performed; which, if by art he was able to do, no question to be made of the truth of those former prestigious feats, in this chapter before remembered.

CONTENTS OF CHAPTER FIFTH
[...]

Aurelius Ambrose, in the prime of his age and honour, being taken away by poison, his brother, Uter-pendragon, by the general suffrage both of the clergy, peers, and people, was made king; who, pursuing his brother's former victories, gave the Saxons many battles, in which he came off with great honour and victory, as awing them so far that they durst not once approach his confines and territories. Afterwards he began to repair the decayed and ruinated churches, and to provide that God should be carefully worshipped, restoring to his people all those goods and possessions, which by the enemy had been extorted from them. And afterwards, having slain Pascentius the son of Hengist in battle, with Guillamore king of Ireland, who came to his assistance, who had with great tyranny afflicted his subjects of the north with fire, sword, and sundry direptions and spoils; and having taken Octa, (who was also the son of Hengist) and Cosa his nephew, and put them in prison. He made a great solemnity at the feast of easter, to which he invited all his nobility and gentry with their wives and daughters, to gratulate with him his former victories. Among the rest of his peers, was then present Gorlais, duke of Cornwall, with his most beautiful Igerna, who was held to be the prime paramont of the whole English nation.

With whose beauty and demeanor, the king was so infinitely taken, that all other his most necessary affairs neglected, he could not restrain or bridle his extraordinary affection, but he must needs court and kiss her openly in the presence of her husband, at which he incensed with the rage of jealously, presently, without any leave taken of the king, or the rest of his fellow peers, rose from the table, and taking his wife with him along, by no persuasion could be moved to stay, but instantly posted with her into his country, which the king (being perditely enamoured of his lady) took in such ill part, that he sent for them back, pretending they must use his council in matters of state, to make his speedy return. But he more prizing his lady than all his other fortunes (whether favourable or disastrous) which way soever they should happen, disobeyed the kings command, with a peremptorily answer, *That he would not come*. At which, the king more inraged, sent him word, that if he persisted in his obstinacy, he would invade his dukedom and beat his towers and turrets (to which he trusted) about his ears, but vain were his menaces, for loath to loose so sweet a bed-fellow, he set the king at public defiance.

To chastise whose pride (as he pretended) Uter-pendragon gathered a strong army, and invaded his country with fire and sword, but Gorlais, perceiving himself unable to oppose so potent a prince, attended with such multitudes of experienced and tried soldiers, he betook himself to a strong castle, then called Dimilioch; and there fortified himself, daily expecting forces from Ireland; but because he would not hazard all his estate in one bottom; he, like a wise merchant, sent his wife to another impregnable fort called Tindagol, being round environed with the sea; and one way leading into it, which, three men elbowing one another, could not pass at once. A few days being past in the besieging of that former castle, which the duke maintained against him, he grew still the more besotted with the love of the lady, insomuch that he could neither enter nor escape. At length he uttered the impatience of his affection to one, who he had amongst many others, chosen for his familiar friend, whose name was Ulphin of Caer-Caradoc; who, when he had truly pondered the whole that the king had delivered unto him, he returned him answer, that he could perceive small hope for the king to attain his amorous ends, in regard that the fort in which she resided, by reason of the situation of the place (munified both by art and nature) was altogether inaccessible. For three armed men (so straight was the passage) might keep out his whole army; one refuge only remained, that if the prophet Merlin, who was then in the army, would undertake the business, it might be accomplished, but otherwise not.

The king, being attentive to his language, presently caused Merlin to be sent for, and told him, how ardently he was affected to the countess, without enjoying whose person he was not able to subsist alive; aggravating the trouble and perplexity of his mind, with much paleness in his face, many deep suspires and extraordinary passion; which Merlin commiserating, he told his majesty, that to compass a thing so difficult as that was, being but a little degree from impossibility, he must make proof of art mystical and unknown, by which he would undertake by such unctions and medicaments as he would apply, to metamorphose his highness into the true figure and resemblance of duke Gorlais; his friend Ulphin into Jordan of Tintegell, his familiar companion and counsellor; and himself would make the third in the adventure, changing himself into Bricel, a servant that waited for him in his chamber; and they three, thus disguised, would in the twilight of the evening, whilst the duke in one place was busied in the defence of his castle against the assailants, command their entrance into the other fort in the name and person of the duke, where they should be undoubtedly received.

This prestigious plot much pleased the king, who, impatient of delay, gave order to his chief captains and commanders concerning the siege, excusing to them his absence for some certain hours. He, in the mean time, the same night, committed himself to the charge and art of Merlin; who, disguised as aforesaid, knocked at the gates of Tindagol, to whom the porter (thinking he had heard his lord's voice demanding entrance) instantly opened the gate, and meeting him with Ulphin and Merlin, taking them for Jordan and Bricel; so that the king was presently conducted to the chamber of Igerna; who glady and lovingly received him as her lord and husband, where he was bountifully feasted, and bedded with her, he freely enjoyed her most loving embraces to the full satiating of his amorous desires, where betwixt them, that night, was begot the noble prince Arthur; who, for his brave facinorous, and high and heroical achievements, made his name glorious and venerable through the face of the whole earth. Of whom, Merlin, long before his begetting or birth, thus prophesied.

> 'The *Cornish Bore* shall fill with his devotion,
> The Christian World: the Islands of the Ocean,
> He shall subdue: the Flower de Lyces plant,
> In his own Garden, and prove Paramant,
> The two-neckt *Roman* Eagle hee shall make
> To flag her plumes, and her faint feathers quake.
> Pagans shal strive in vain to bend or break him,
> Who shall be meat to all the mouths that speake him,
> Yet shall his end be doubtfull: Him six Kings
> Shall orderly succeed, but when their wings
> Are clipt by death, a *German* Worme shall rise
> Who shall the *British* State anatomise.
> Him, shall a Sea-Wolfe waited on by Woods
> From *Africke* brought to passe Saint *Georges* floods
> Advance on high: then shall Religion faile,
> And then shall *London's* Clergie honour vaile
> To *Dorobernia*: he that seventy shall sit
> In the' *Eboracensick* Sea; he forc'd to flit
> Into *Armorica: Menevia* sad
> Shall with the Legion Cities Pall be clad,
> And they that in thilk days shall live, may see
> That all these changes in the Kirke shall bee.'

But before I come to the opening of this prophecy, which to the ignorant may appear rather a rhyming riddle. Then, to be grounded on truth or reason, it is necessary that I look back to where I late left, and proceed with the history which thus followeth: The king more ecstasied in the embraces of his sweet and desired bedfellow, his soldiers, without any commission by him granted, made a strange and terrible assault upon the other fort, in which Gorlais was besieged; who, being of a high and haughty spirit, scorning to be long immured, and coped up without making some expression of his magnanimity and valour, issued out of the castle, and with great rage and resolution sat upon the camp, in hopes, with his handful of men, to have disloged and routed a multitude, but it fell out far contrary to his expectation, for in the hotest brunt of the first encounter, he himself was slain, and all his soldiers without mercy offered, or quarter given, most cruelly put to the sword; the castle entered and seized, and the spoil divided amongst the soldiers.

Early in the morning before the king or the countess were ready in their wearing habits and ornaments, some of the besieged who had escaped the massacre, bounced at the gates of Tindagol, and, being known to be of the duke's party, were received; who told the porter and the rest, that they brought heavy news along, which they must first deliver to their lady; of which, she having notice, and knowing they came from that castle, caused them to be admitted into her presence, and demanding of them what news; they made answer: the tidings they brought was sad and disastrous, That the fort was, the preceding night, robustuously assaulted by the enemy, whom the duke, her husband, valiantly encountered without the gates, that all their fellow-soldiers were put to the sword, the castle taken and rifled, and that the general, her lord and husband, by his over hardness, was the first man slain in the conflict. At the relation of the first part of their news she seemed wonderously disconsolate and dejected, but, casting her eyes upon the king, she was again somewhat solaced in the safety of her husband.

They, also, when they saw the king, taking him for the duke, their general, began to blush at their report of his death, being wonderously astonished, that him, whom, to their thinking, they had left wounded and breathless in the field, they now see living and in health, amusing withal that they posting thither with so much speed would arrive thither before them, being altogether ignorant of the admirable transformation that Merlin's art had wrought upon them. In this anxiety and diversity of thoughts, the king more glad of the duke's fate than the rifling of his fort; thus bespoke to the duchess, Most beautiful, and my best beloved Igerna, I am not as these report dead, but as thou seest, yet alive; but much grieved both for the surprisal of my castle, and the slaughter of my soldiers; upon which victory, it may be feared, that the king, animated by his late success, may raise his army thence, and endanger us here in our fort of Tindagol; therefore, my best and safest course is to leave this place for the present, and to submit myself to the king in his camp; of whose acceptance and grace I make no question, as knowing him to be of a disposition flexible and merciful; then be you of comfort, for in a few hours you may expect to hear from me, with all things answerable to your desires and wishes. With which words, Igerna was much pleased and fully satisfied.

So, with a living kiss, they parted, she to her chamber, and he, with his two followers, towards the camp; who, no sooner from the sight of the citadel, but Merlin began to uncharm and dissolve his former incantations and spells, so that the king was no more Gorlais, but Uter-pendragon, and his friend ceased to be Jordan of Tindagol, but Ulphin of Caer-Caradoc; and the mage who had made this transformation, left the shape of Bricel, and turned again to be Merlin. And the king being now arrived at his army, first caused the body of Gorlais to be searched for amongst the slain soldiers; afterwards to be embalmed and honourably interred; and first, acquainting Igerna by letters, with all the former passages, how they stood, and how much he had hazarded his person for the fruition of her love, he invited her to her lord's funeral, at which the king and she both mourned; but after the celebration thereof ended, he, the second time, courted her, and in a few days made her his queen of a duchess; by whom he had Arthur and Anna; by which match, the fame of Merlin spread far abroad; the explanation of whose former prophecy, I leave to the following chapter.

CONTENTS OF CHAPTER SIXTH
[. . .]

Arthur, the son of Uter-pendragon and Igerna, succeeded his father in the principality; therefore, called the *Boar of Cornwall*, because begot and born in that country, and of a Cornish duchess. He was a great planter and supporter of religion and the Christian faith, for so all our British chronologers report of him. His conquests were many, and some of them miraculous. By the *Islands of the Ocean* are meant Ireland, Iceland, Scotland, and the Orcades, Goatland, Norway, and Dacia, all which are called Provincial Islands, which he brought under the obedience of his sceptre. By the *planting of the Flower de Lyces in his own garden*, is likewise intended his conquest of France, with sundry other appendant provinces, as Flanders, Poland, Burgundy, Aquitaine, Andegavia; and Normandy; all which, with divers others, paid him an annual tribute, and of which countries, for their long and faithful services, he gave the earldom of Andegavia to Gaius his taster, and the dukedom of Normandy to Bedverus his cup-bearer; in memory of whose regal bounty, it grew to a custom for the kings of France to make their tasters and cup-bearers, earls and dukes of Andegavia and Normandy.

By his *pluming and shaking off the eagle's feathers*, was his great victories over the Romans foretold; who, when their prince Lucius with ten other kings, invaded this his land of Britain, with a numberless army of soldiers, the most of them he slew, acquitting the tribute paid to Rome since the time of Julius Caesar, and those who survived, he made his feodaries and vassals, by which he got the sovereignty over many provinces before subjugate to the Roman empire, sending the dead body of their emperor back to Rome, to be interred there. Next, where it is said, His name shall be as meat to all those mouths that shall speak of his noble and notable achievements, by which no other thing is meant, but that the very relation of his brave guests shall be a refreshing and delight to all such as shall either read them or hear them with much pleasure by others reported, whose very begetting, conception, and birth, carry with them the novelty of a miracle. And where it is further said, *that his end shall be doubtful*; he that shall make question of the truth of Merlin's prophecy in that point (let him to this day) but travel into Armorica or Little Britain, and in many of their cities, proclaim in their streets, That Arthur expired after the common and ordinary manner of men; most sure, he shall have a bitter and railing language aspect upon him, if he escape a tempestuous shower of stones and brick-bats.

The six kings that succeeded him in order, were Constantinus, the eldest son of Cador duke of Cornwall, (and Arthur's cousin-german) the second was Constantinus' brother; the third Conanus Aurelius their nephew; the fourth Vortiporius; the fifth Malgo; the sixth Caretius; for, when Arthur in that great battle which he fought against his cousin the arch-traitor Mordred, whom he slew, being himself mortally wounded, and therefore had retired himself unto the vale of Avalan, in hope to be cured of his hurts; before his death, (and the manner of which is uncertain) he sent for his cousin Constantine, before-named, (a man of approved virtue, and expert in all martial discipline) and made him king, against whom, the Saxons, assisted by the two sons of Mordred, assembled themselves, who, having defeated them in sundry battles, the elder son of Mordred, who had for his refuge fortified Winchester, he took in the church of St. Amphibalus, (whither he had fled for sanctuary) and slew him before the altar: the younger he found hid in a monastery in London, whom he likewise caused to be slain; this happened in the 543rd year of the incarnation of our blessed Saviour; but in the third year after he was perfidiously betrayed to death by the practice of his nephew; Conanus Aurelius, and his body was royally interred in mount Ambria near unto Uter-pendragon.

Then reigned his brother, whom Conanus suffered not to rest one hour in peace, till he had incarcerated him, and in the same year usurped the diadem; a young man of excellent parts and noble carriage, had he not been tainted with ambition, the love of civil wars and parricidial impiety, having slain one of his uncles, imprisoned the other, and killed his two sons to attain to the regal sovereignty, which not long he enjoyed, for in the next year he expired. Whom succeeded Vortiporius, against whom the Saxons made a new insurrection, and by whom they were utterly subverted, by which he became absolute monarch of this island; but, after four years, yielded his body to the earth, and left his crown to Malgo, who was invested in the year of grace, after some authors, 581.

This prince was strong in body, fortunate in arms, and of larger size and stature than any of his predecessors, who was a great suppressor of usurpers and tyrants, for he not only enjoyed this kingdom entire, but conquered by his sword all the six provincial islands. Of whom it is reported, that he was the fairest of all the British nation, but those excellent gifts of nature he shamefully abused, as being much addicted to sodomy: and as he was a proditor of other's chastities, he was also prodigal of his own; after whose death, in the year 586, Garetius was instituted on the throne, a prince hateful to good men, and incendiary of civil and domestic combustions, an exiler of his nobles, a slayer of his citizens, a robber of the rich, a suppressor of the poor, and indeed, subject to all the vices can be named.

By the *German Worm and the Sea Wolf waited on by Woods, brought from Africa, through St. George's channel, which shall support him*, our prophet would have us to know, that the Saxons are comprehended in the *Worm*; and in the *Wolf*, Gormundus king of Africa, who, in the time of this Garetius, came with a mighty navy upon the British seas; first, with 360,000 soldiers, who first invaded Ireland, and made great spoil of the country, and from thence he was invited by the Saxons to assist them against the British nation; to which, he assented, invaded the kingdom with fire and sword, committing many direptions and outrages, chasing the king from place to place, and from city to city, till he was in the end forced to fly to Wales, where they shut him up; and by this means, the German Worm, by the means of this Sea Wolf, had the upper hand on the red Dragon. Whilst these things were thus in agitation, there came to this great general of the Africans, from the transmarine parts of Gallia, one Isimbardus, nephew to Lewis the French king, who complained unto him that his uncle, against all justice, kept his rights from him, imploring his aid for the recovery thereof, promising him great rewards, in pledge whereof, like a wretched Apostata, he renounced his faith and christianity, of which proffer Gormundus accepted, and made his speedy expedition towards France.

But the miscreant Isimbardus, failed of his purpose, and was justly punished by the hand of God for his apostacy; for at their landing at the port of St. Waleric, a young gentleman called Hugo, son to Robert, earl of the Mount, having received an affront from this Isimbard, challenged him to a single duel, who entertaining the challenge, was, by the aforesaid king, left dead in the field, and the French setting upon the host of the pagans, gave them a great discomfiture, insomuch that of all that infinite number, scarce any were left to bear the tidings of their disaster into their country, but either perished by the sword, or were drowned in the ocean. *In which time*, saith the prophet, *religion shall fail*, which happened when this Gormundus with the Saxons rioted and made havock in this island, suppressing religious houses, and ruinating churches, so that scarce a christian native durst shew his head, but he was subject to persecution and torture.

But it follows in the prophecy, *that the honour of London's clergy shall give place to Dorobernia or Canterbury, that the seventh who sat in the Eboracensian see*, which is the arch-bishoprick of York, *shall be compelled to fly in Armorica or Little Britain, and that Menevia shall be adorned with the pall that belonged to the city of Legions.* Give me leave to use a little circumstance in the explaining of these, that finding the truth of his predictions by the success, the reader may be more easily induced to give credit unto the rest, in which I shall strive (though plain) to be brief.

The three prime seats or sees, were the three arch-bishopricks, which were London, York, and the city of Legions. Now, note, how punctually he comes to the purpose; the dignity of London's metropolitanship was transferred to Canterbury by St. Augustine, whom pope Gregory sent hither with others to preach the gospel, who also gave the primacy of the city of Legions to Menevia, a city of Wales, situate near to the Demetical see, but the city of Legions stands upon the river Osca, not far from the Severn sea, which was first erected by king Belinus, whose valiant brother Brennus, being general of the Senon Galls, after many honourable exploits and glorious victories by him achieved, assaulted the famous city of Rome, took, sacked, and spoiled it in the days of Ahasuerus and Esther; Gabinus and Porsenna, being consuls, the first of whom he slew in battle, and the other took prisoner, &c.

By the arch-bishop of York, the seventh inaugurated into that see, who should be compelled to seek shelter in Little Britain, is intimated Samson, then resident; who, in that great prosecution made by the Africans and Saxons, with six of his brothers, all clergymen, and of great sanctity of life, fled into Little Britain, and there established his metropolitan cathedral. The rest of his six brothers, whose names were Melanius, Matutus, Maclovius, Pabutaus, Paternus and Waslovius, being all divines, were made the rectors of other churches, and became, in a short time, to be capable of episcopal dignities; which seven brothers, not only the natives of the country, but all the bordering provinces, call the seven saints of Britain (meaning the less Britain) even to this day, now let it be held any deviation or digression from the subject now in hand. If I borrow so much patience of the reader to acquaint him with a strange and almost miraculous story or legend, by what accident, or rather divine providence these seven holy and devout brothers, were by the mutual congress of two noble parents, (the father and mother) begot and conceived in one womb, and after mature time of teeming, delivered into the world at one day. But because I am loath to swell the pages of this chapter beyond the limits of the former, I will refer the relation thereof unto the next ensuing.

EXTRACTS FROM THE FAERIE QUEEN
by Edmund Spenser

EDMUND SPENSER'S GREAT epic poem *The Faerie Queen*, begun in the 1570s and only half finished before his death in 1599, is one of the truly great masterpieces of the Renaissance. It is also one of the very few literary or historical works dating from this period which deal with Arthurian themes. The epic begins with the war between Uther Pendragon, Arthur's father, and the Saxon leader Octa, son of Hengist. At the time Arthur is still a prince, and having dreamed of the Faerie Queen, Gloriana (a thinly disguised symbolic portrait of Elizabeth I), he sets out on a long quest in which he encounters various highly symbolic tests and trials. Through this Spenser sought to celebrate the return of the Tudor monarchy to Britain and to demonstrate the power of magnanimity.

Throughout the poem Merlin appears in a traditional guise, advising Arthur in matters of the spirit, prophesying about the future progency of the wholly fictional character Artegall (Arthur's half-brother) and transporting Arthur to the country of Faery after the battle of Camlan. In the extract below we find Britomart (a woman disguised as a man to enable her to pursue a knightly destiny) and her confidante, Glauce, visiting the tomb of Merlin, who, in a manner curiously reminiscent of Myrddin's dialogues with Gwenddydd (see Part 1 above), prophesies of the future kings of Britain.

But it is his power over the elements and the natural world which marks him out as the epitome of the Renaissance magician. He is, in many ways, modelled on the great magician Dr John Dee, who was the adviser to Queen Elizabeth I. It is certainly in this guise that we hear of his creation of a wall of brass (later known as Merlin's Enclosure) around the city of Carmarthen and in his creation of a magical mirror in which could be seen events happening anywhere in the world. He also creates a magic suit of armour for Prince Arthur. Despite the complexity of the language and its many symbolic references to political events of Elizabeth's reign, the portrait of Merlin which emerges from this makes a powerful addition to the canon.

BOOK III

CANTO III

Merlin bewrayes to Britomart,
the state of Artegall,
And shewes the famous Progency
which from them springen shall

I

Most sacred fire, that burnest mightily
  In living brests, ykindled first above,
  Emongst th'eternall spheres and lamping sky,
  And thence pourd into men, which men call Love;
  Not that same, which doth base affections move
  In brutish minds, and filthy lust inflame
  But that sweet fit, that doth true beautie love,
  And choseth vertue for his dearest Dame,
Whence spring all noble deeds and never dying fame:

2

Well did Antiquite a God thee deeme,
  That over mortall minds has so great might,
  To order them, as best to thee doth seeme,
  And all their actions to direct aright;
  The fatall purpose of divine foresight,
  Thou doest effect in destined descents,
  Through deepe impression of thy secret might,
  And stirredst up th'Heroes high intents,
Which the late world admyres for wondrous moniments.

3

But thy dread darts in none doe triumph more,
  Ne braver proofe in any, of thy powre
  Shew'dst thou, than in this royall Maid of yore,
  Making her seeke an unknowne Paramoure,
  From the worlds end, through many a bitter stowre:
  From whose two loynes thou afterwards did rayse
  Most famous fruits of matrimoniall bowre,
  Which through the earth have spred their living prayse,
That fame in trompe of gold eternally displayes.

4

Begin then, O my dearest sacred Dame,
  Daughter of *Phœbus* and of *Memorie*,
  That doest ennoble with immortall name
  The warlike Worthies, from antiquitie,
  In thy great volume of Eternitie:
  Begin, O *Clio*, and recount from hence
  My glorious Soveraines goodly auncestrie,
  Till that by dew degrees and long protense,
Thou have it lastly brought unto her Excellence.

5

Full many wayes within her troubled mind,
  Old *Glauce* cast, to cure this Ladies griefe:
  Full many waies she sought, but none could find,
  Nor herbes, nor charmes, nor counsell, that is chiefe
  And choisest med'cine for sicke harts reliefe:
  For thy great care she tooke, and greater feare,
  Least that it should her turne to foule reprife,
  And sore reproch, when so her father deare
Should of her dearest daughters hard misfortune heare.

6

At last she her avisd, that he, which made
  That mirrhour, wherein the sicke Damosell
  So straungely vewed her straunge lovers shade,
  To weet, the learned *Merlin*, well could tell,
  Under what coast of heaven the man did dwell,
  And by what meanes his love might best be wrought:
  For though beyond the *Africk Ismaell*,
  Or th'Indian *Peru* he were, she thought
Him forth through infinite endevour to have sought.

7

Forthwith themselves disguising both in straunge
  And base attyre, that none might them bewray,
  To *Maridunum*, that is now by chaunge
  Of name *Cayr-Merdin* cald, they tooke their way:
  There the wise *Merlin* whylome wont (they say)
  To make his wonne, low underneath the ground,
  In a deepe delve, farre from the vew of day,

That of no living wight he mote be found,
When so he counseld with his sprights encompast round.

8

And if thou ever happen that same way
   To travell, goe to see that dreadfull place:
   It is an hideous hollow cave (they say)
   Under a rocke that lyes a little space
   From the swift *Barry*, tombling downe apace,
   Emongst the woodie hilles of *Dynevowre*:
   But dare thou not, I charge, in any cace,
   To enter into that same balefull Bowre,
For fear the cruell Feends should thee unwares devowre.

9

But standing high aloft, low lay thine eare,
   And there such ghastly noise of yron chaines,
   And brasen Caudrons thou shalt rombling heare,
   Which thousand sprights with long enduring paines
   Doe tosse, that it will stonne thy feeble braines,
   And oftentimes great grones, and grievous stounds,
   When too huge toile and labour them constraines:
   And oftentimes loud strokes, and ringing sounds
From under that deepe Rocke most horribly rebounds.

10

The cause some say is this: A litle while
   Before that *Merlin* dyde, he did intend,
   A brasen wall in compas to compile
   About *Cairmardin*, and did it commend
   Unto these Sprights, to bring to perfect end.
   During which worke the Ladie of the Lake,
   Whom long he lov'd, for him in hast did send,
   Who thereby forst his workemen to forsake,
Them bound till his returne, their labour not to slake.

11

In the meane time through that false Ladies traine,
   He was surprisd, and buried under beare,
   Ne ever to his worke returnd againe:
   Nath'lesse those feends may not their worke forbeare,
   So greatly his commaundement they feare,
   But there doe toyle and travell day and night,
   Until that brasen wall they up doe reare:
   For *Merlin* had in Magicke more insight,
Than ever him before or after living wight.

12

For he by words could call out of the sky
   Both Sunne and Moone, and make them him obay:
   The land to sea, and sea to maineland dry,
   And darkesome night he eke could turne to day:

Huge hostes of men he could alone dismay,
And hostes of men of meanest things could frame,
When so him list his enimies to fray:
That to this day for terror of his fame,
The feeds do quake, when any him to them does name.

13

And sooth, men say that he was not the sonne
Of mortall Syre, or other living wight,
But wondrously begotten, and begonne
By false illusion of a guilefull Spright,
On a faire Ladie Nonne, that whilome hight
Matila daughter to *Pubidius*,
Who was the Lord of *Mathravall* by right,
And coosen unto king *Ambrosius*:
Whence he indued was with skill so marvellous.

14

They here ariving, staid a while without,
Ne durst adventure rashly in to wend,
But of their first intent gan make new dout
For dread of daunger, which it might portend:
Untill the hardie Mayd (with love to frend)
First entering, the dreadfull Mage there found
Deepe busied bout worke of wondrous end,
And writing strange characters in the ground,
With which the stubborn feends he to his service bound.

15

He nought was moved at their entrance bold:
For of their comming well he wist afore,
Yet list them bid their businesse to unfold,
As if ought in this world in secret store
Were from him hidden, or unknowne of yore.
Then *Glauce* thus, Let not it thee offend,
That we thus rashly through thy darkesome dore,
Unwares have prest: for either fatall end,
Or other mightie cause us two did hither send.

16

He bad tell on; And then she thus began.
Now have three Moones with borrow'd brothers light,
Thrice shined faire, and thrice seem'd dim and wan,
Sith a sore evill, which this virgin bright
Tormenteth, and doth plonge in dolefull plight,
First rooting tooke; but what thing it mote bee,
Or whence it sprong, I cannot read aright:
But this I read, that but if remedee
Thou her afford, full shortly I her dead shall see.

17

Therewith th'Enchaunter softly gan to smyle
  At her smooth speeches, weeting inly well
  That she to him dissembled womanish guyle,
  And to her said, Beldame, by that ye tell.
  More need of leach-craft hath your Damozell,
  Than of my skill: who helpe may have elsewhere,
  In vaine seekes wonders out of Magicke spell.
  Th'old woman wox half blanck, those words to heare;
And yet was loth to let her purpose plaine appeare.

18

And to him said, If any leaches skill,
  Or other learned meanes could have redrest
  This my deare daughters deepe engraffed ill,
  Certes I should be loth thee to molest:
  But this sad evill, which doth her infest,
  Doth course of naturall cause farre exceed,
  And housed is within her hollow brest,
  That either seemes some cursed witches deed,
Or evill spright, that in her doth such torment breed.

19

The wisard could no lenger beare her bord,
  But brusting forth in laughter, to her sayd;
  Glauce, what needs this colourable word,
  To cloke the cause, that hath it selfe bewrayed?
  Ne ye faire *Britomartis*, thus arayd,
  More hidden are, than Sunne in cloudy vele;
  Whom thy good fortune, having fate obayd,
  Hath hither brought, for succour to appele:
The which the powres to thee are pleased to revele.

20

The doubtfull Mayd, seeing her selfe descryde,
  Was all abasht, and her pure yvory
  Into a cleare Carnation suddeine dyde;
  As faire *Aurora* rising hastily,
  Doth by her blushing tell, that she did lye
  All night in old *Tithonus* frosen bed,
  Whereof she seemes ashamed inwardly.
  But her old Nourse was nought dishartened,
But vauntage made of that, which *Merlin* had ared.

21

And sayd, Sith then thou knowest all our griefe,
  (For what doest not thou know?) of grace I pray,
  Pitty our plaint, and yield us meet reliefe.
  With that the Prophet still awhile did stay,
  And then his spirite thus gan forth display;
  Most noble Virgin, that by fatall lore
  Hast learn'd to love, let no whit thee dismay

The hard begin, that meets thee in the dore,
And with sharpe fits thy tender hart oppresseth sore.

22

For so must all things excellent begin,
  And eke enrooted deepe must be that Tree,
  Whose big embodied braunches shall not lin,
  Till they to heavens hight forth stretched bee.
  For from thy wombe a famous Progenie
  Shall spring, out of the auncient *Trojan* blood,
  Which shall revive the sleeping memorie
  Of those same antique Peres the heavens brood,
Which *Greeke* and *Asian* rivers stained with their blood.

23

Renowmed kings, and sacred Emperours,
  Thy fruitfull Ofspring, shall from thee descend;
  Brave Captaines, and most mighty warriours,
  That shall their conquests through all lands extend,
  And their decayed kingdomes shall amend:
  The feeble Britons, broken with long warre,
  They shall upreare, and mightily defend
  Against their forrein foe, that comes from farre,
Till universall peace compound all civill jarre.

24

It was not, *Britomart* thy wandring eye,
  Glauncing unwares in charmed looking glas,
  But the streight course of heavenly destiny,
  Led with eternall providence, that has
  Guided thy glaunce, to bring his will to pas:
  Ne is thy fate, ne is thy fortune ill,
  To love the prowest knight, that ever was.
  Therefore submit thy wayes unto his will,
And do by all dew meanes thy destiny fulfill.

25

But read (said *Glauce*) thou Magitian
  What meanes shall she out seeke, or what wayes take?
  How shall she know, how shall she find the man?
  Or what needs her to toyle, sith fates can make
  Way for themselves, their purpose to partake?
  Then *Merlin* thus; Indeed the fates are firme,
  And may not shrinck, though all the world do shake:
  Yet ought mens good endevours them confirme,
And guide the heavenly causes to their constant terme.

26

The man whom heavens have ordaynd to bee
  The spouse of *Britomart*, is *Arthegall*:
  He wonneth in the land of *Fayeree*,
  Yet is no *Fary* borne, ne sib at all

To Elfes, but sprong of seed terrestriall,
And whilome by false *Faries* stolne away,
Whiles yet in infant cradle he did crall;
Ne other to himselfe is knowne this day,
But that he by an Elfe was gotten of a *Fay*.

27

But sooth he is the sonne of *Gorlois*,
  And brother unto *Cador* Cornish king,
  And for his warlike feates renowmed is,
  From where the day out of the sea doth spring,
  Untill the closure of the Evening.
  From thence, him firmely bound with faithfull band,
  To this his native soyle thou backe shalt bring,
  Strongly to aide his countrey, to withstand
The powre of forrein Paynims, which invade thy land.

28

Great aid thereto his mightly puissaunce,
  And dreaded name shall give in that sad day:
  Where also proofe of thy prow valiaunce
  Thou then shalt make, t'increase thy lovers pray.
  Long time ye both in armes shall beare great sway,
  Till thy wombes burden thee from them do call,
  And his last fate him from thee take away,
  Too rathe cut off by practise criminall
Of secret foes, that him shall make in mischiefe fall.

29

With thee yet shall he leave for memory
  Of his late puissaunce, his Image dead,
  That living him in all activity
  To thee shall represent. He from the head
  Of his coosin *Constantius* without dread
  Shall take the crowne, that was his fathers right,
  And therewith crowne himselfe in th'others, stead:
  Then shall he issew forth with dreadfull might,
Against his Saxon foes in bloudy field to fight.

30

Like as a Lyon, that in drowsie cave
  Hath long time slept, himselfe so shall be shake,
  And comming forth, shall spred his banner brave
  Over the troubled South, that it shall make
  The warlike *Mertians* for feare to quake:
  Thrise shall he fight with them, and twise shall win,
  But the third time shall faire accordaunce make:
  And if he then with victorie can lin,
He shall his dayes with peace bring to his earthly In.

3I

His sonne, hight *Vortipore*, shall him succeede
  In kingdome, but not in felicity;
  Yet shall be long time warre with happy speed,
  And with great honour many battels try:
  But at the last to th'importunity
  Of froward fortune shall be forst to yield.
  But his sonne *Malgo* shall full mightily
  Avenge his fathers losse, with speare and shield,
And his proud foes discomfit in victorious field.

32

Behold the man, and tell me *Britomart*,
  If ay more goodly creature thou didst see;
  How like a Gyaunt in each manly part
  Beares he himselfe with portly majestee,
  That one of th'old *Heroes* seemes to bee:

**The Lady of the Lake telleth Arthur of the sword Excalibur
(Aubrey Beardsley)**

142

He the six Islands, comprovinciall
In auncient times unto great Britainee,
Shall to the same reduce, and to him call
Their sundry kings to do their homage severall.

33

All which his sonne *Careticus* awhile
Shall well defend, and *Saxons* powre suppresse,
Untill a straunger king from unknowne soyle
Arriving, him with multitude oppresse;
Great *Gormond*, having with huge mightinesse
Ireland subdewd, and therein fixt his throne,
Like a swift Otter, fell through emptinesse,
Shall overswim the sea with many one
Of his Norveyses, to assist the Britons fone.

34

He in his furie all shall overrunne,
And holy Church with faithlesse hands deface,
That thy sad people utterly fordonne,
Shall to the utmost mountaines fly apace:
Was never so great wast in any place,
Nor so fowle outrage doen by living men:
For all thy Cities they shall sacke and race,
And the greene grasse, that groweth, they shall bren,
That even the wild beast shall dy in starved den.

35

Whiles thus thy Britons do in languour pine,
Proud *Etheldred* shall from the North arise,
Serving th'ambitious will of *Augustine*,
And passing *Dee* with hardy enterprise,
Shall backe repulse the valiaunt *Brockwell* twise,
And *Bangor* with massacred Martyrs fill;
But the third time shall rew his foolhardise:
For *Cadwan* pittying his peoples ill,
Shall stoutly him defeat, and thousand *Saxons* kill.

36

But after him, *Cadwallin* mightily
On his sonne *Edwin* all those wrongs shall wreake;
Ne shall availe the wicked sorcery
of false *Pellite*, his purposes to breake,
But him shall slay, and on a gallowes bleake
Shall give th'enchaunter his unhappy hire;
Then shall the Britons, late dismayd and weake,
From their long vassalage gin to respire,
And on their Paynim foes avenge their ranckled ire.

37

Ne shall he yet his wrath so mitigate,
Till both the sonnes of *Edwin* he have slaine,

Offricke and *Osricke*, twinnes unfortunate,
  Both slaine in battell upon Layburne plaine,
  Together with the king of *Louthiane*,
  Hight *Adin*, and the king of *Orkeny*,
  Both joynt partakers of their fatall paine:
  But *Penda*, fearefull of like desteny,
Shall yield him selfe his liegeman, and sweare fealty.

38

Him shall he make his fatall Instrument,
  T'afflict the other *Saxons* unsubdewd;
  He marching forth with fury insolent
  Against the good king *Oswald*, who indewd
  With heavenly powre, and by Angels reskewd,
  All holding crosses in their hands on hye,
  Shall him defeate withouten bloud imbrewd:
  Of which, that field for endlesse memory,
Shall *Hevenfield* be cald to all posterity.

39

Where at *Cadwallin* wroth, shall forth issew,
  And an huge hoste into Northumber lead,
  With which he godly *Oswald* shall subdew,
  And crowne with martyrdome his sacred head.
  Whose brother *Oswin*, daunted with like dread,
  With price of silver shall his kingdome buy,
  And *Penda*, seeking him adowne to tread,
  Shall tread adowne, and do him fowly dye,
But shall with gifts his Lord *Cadwallin* pacify.

40

Then shall *Cadwallin* dye, and then the raine
  Of *Britons* eke with him attonce shall dye;
  Ne shall·the good *Cadwallader* with paine,
  Or powre, be hable it to remedy,
  When the full time prefixt by destiny,
  Shalbe expird of *Britons* regiment.
  For heaven it selfe shall their successe envy,
  And them with plagues and murrins pestilent
Consume, till all their warlike puissaunce be spent.

4I

Yet after all these sorrowes, and huge hills
  Of dying people, during eight yeares space,
  Cadwallader not yielding to his ills.
  From *Armoricke*, where long in wretched cace
  He liv'd, returning to his native place,
  Shalbe by vision staid from his intent:
  For th'heavens have decreed, to displace
  The *Britons*, for their sinnes dew punishment,
And to the *Saxons* over-give their government.

42

Then woe, and woe, and everlasting woe,
   Be to the Briton babe, that shalbe borne,
   To live in thraldome of his fathers foe;
   Late King, now captive, late Lord, now forlorne,
   The worlds reproch, the cruell victors scorne,
   Banisht from Princely bowre to wastfull wood:
   O who shall helpe me to lament, and mourne
   To royall seed, the antique *Trojan* blood,
Whose Empire lenger here, than ever any stood.

43

The Damzell was full deepe empassioned,
   Both for his griefe, and for her peoples sake,
   Whose future woes so plaine he fashioned,
   And sighing sore, at length him thus bespake;
   Ah but will heavens fury never slake,
   Nor vengeaunce huge relent it selfe at last?
   Will not long misery late mercy make,
   But shall their name for ever be defast,
And quite from of the earth their memory be rast?

44

Nay but the terme (said he) is limited,
   That in this thraldome *Britons* shall abide,
   And the just revolution measured,
   That they as Straungers shalbe notifide.
   For twise foure hundreth yeares shalbe supplide,
   Ere they to former rule restor'd shalbee,
   And their importune fates all satisfide:
   Yet during this their most obscuritee,
Their beames shall oft breake forth, that men them faire may see.

45

For *Rhodoricke*, whose surname shalbe Great,
   Shall of him selfe a brave ensample shew,
   That Saxon kings his friendship shall intreat;
   And *Howell Dha* shall goodly well indew
   The savage minds with skill of just and trew;
   Then *Griffyth Conan* also shall up reare
   His dreaded head, and the old sparkes renew
   Of native courage, that his foes shall feare,
Least backe againe the kingdome he from them should beare.

46

Ne shall the Saxons selves all peaceably
   Enjoy the crowne, which they from Britons wonne
   First ill, and after ruled wickedly:
   For ere two hundred yeares be full outronne,
   There shall a Raven far from rising Sunne,
   With his wide wings upon them fiercely fly,
   And bid his faithlesse chickens overronne

The fruitfull plaines, and with fell cruelty,
In their avenge, tread downe the victours surquedry.

47

Yet shall a third both these, and thine subdew;
　　There shall a Lyon from the sea-bord wood
　　Of *Neustria* come roring, with a crew
　　Of hungry whelpes, his battailous bold brood,
　　Whose clawes were newly dipt in cruddy blood,
　　That from the Daniske Tyrants head shall rend
　　Th'usurped crowne, as if that he were wood,
　　And the spoile of the countrey conquered
Emongst his young ones shall divide with bountyhed.

48

Tho when the terme is full accomplishid,
　　There shall a sparke of fire, which hath longwhile
　　Bene in his ashes raked up, and hid,
　　Be freshly kindled in the fruitfull Ile
　　Of *Mona*, where it lurked in exile;
　　Which shall breake forth into bright burning flame,
　　And reach into the house, that beares the stile
　　Of royall majesty and soveraigne name;
So shall the Briton bloud their crowne againe reclame.

49

Thenceforth eternall union shall be made
　　Betweene the nations different afore,
　　And sacred Peace shall lovingly perswade
　　The warlike minds, to learne her goodly lore,
　　And civile armes to exercise no more:
　　Then shall a royall virgin raine, which shall
　　Stretch her white rod over the *Belgicke* shore,
　　And the great Castle smite so sore with all,
That it shall make him shake, and shortly learne to fall.

50

But yet the end is not. There *Merlin* stayd,
　　As overcomen of the spirites powre,
　　Or other ghastly spectacle dismayd,
　　That secretly he saw, yet note discoure:
　　Which suddein fit, and halfe extatick stoure
　　When the two fearefull women saw, they grew
　　Greatly confused in behavioure;
　　At last the fury past, to former hew
Hee turnd againe, and chearefull looks (as earst) did shew.

51

Then, when them selves they well instructed had
　　Of all, that needed them to be inquird,
　　They both conceiving hope of comfort glad,
　　With lighter hearts unto their home retird;

Where they in secret counsell close conspird,
How to effect so hard an enterprize,
And to possesse the purpose they desird:
Now this, now that twixt them they did devise,
And diverse plots did frame, to maske in strange disguise.

52

At last the Nourse in her foolhardy wit
　　Conceiv'd a bold devise, and thus bespake;
　　Daughter, I deeme that counsell aye most fit,
　　That of the time doth dew advauntage take;
　　Ye see that good king *Uther* now doth make
　　Strong warre upon the Paynim brethren, hight
　　Octa and *Oza*, whom he lately brake
　　Beside *Cayr Verolame*, in victorious fight,
That now all *Britanie* doth burne in armes bright.

53

That therefore nought our passage may empeach,
　　Let us in feigned armes our selves disguize,
　　And our weake hands (whom need new strength shall teach)
　　The dreadfull speare and shield to exercise:
　　Ne certes daughter that same warlike wize
　　I weene, would you misseeme; for ye bene tall,
　　And large of limbe, t'atchieve an hard emprize,
　　Ne ought ye want, but skill, which practize small
Will bring, and shortly make you a mayd Martiall.

54

And sooth, it ought your courage much inflame,
　　To heare so often, in that royall hous,
　　From whence to none inferiour ye came,
　　Bards tell of many women valorous
　　Which have full many feats adventurous
　　Performd, in paragone of proudest men:
　　The bold *Bunduca*, whose victorious
　　Exploits made *Rome* to quake, stout *Guendolen*,
Renowmed *Martia*, and redoubted *Emmilen*.

55

And that, which more than all the rest may sway,
　　Late dayes ensample, which these eyes beheld.
　　In the last field before *Menevia*
　　Which *Uther* with those forrein Pagans held,
　　I saw a *Saxon* Virgin, the which feld
　　Great *Ulfin* thrise upon the bloudy plaine,
　　And had not *Carados* her hand withheld
　　From rash revenge, she had him surely slaine,
Yet *Carados* himselfe from her escapt with paine.

56

Ah read, (quoth *Britomart*) how is she hight?
  Faire *Angela* (quoth she) men do her call,
  No whit lesse faire, than terrible in fight:
  She hath the leading of a Martiall
  And mighty people, dreaded more than all
  The other Saxons, which do for her sake
  And love, themselves of her name Angles call.
  Therefore faire Infant her ensample make
Unto thy selfe, and equall courage to thee take.

57

Her harty words so deepe into the mynd
  Of the young Damzell sunke, that great desire
  Of warlike armies in her forthwith they tyned,
  And generous stout courage did inspire,
  That she resolv'd, unweeting to her Sire,
  Advent'rous knighthood on her selfe to don,
  And counseld with her Nourse, her Maides attire
  To turne into a massy habergeon,
And bad her all things put in readinesse anon.

58

Th'old woman nought, that needed, did omit;
  But all things did conveniently purvay:
  It fortuned (so time their turne did fit)
  A band of Britons ryding on forray
  Few dayes before, had gotten a great pray
  Of Saxon goods, emongst the which was seene
  A goodly Armour, and full rich aray,
  Which long'd to *Angela*, the Saxon Queene,
All fretted round with gold, and goodly well beseene.

59

The same, with all the other ornaments,
  King *Ryence* caused to be hanged hy
  In his chiefe Church, for endlesse moniments
  Of his successe and gladfull victory:
  Of which her selfe avising readily,
  In th'evening late old *Glauce* thither led
  Faire *Britomart*, and that same Armory
  Downe taking, her therein appareled,
Well as she might, and with brave bauldrick garnished.

60

Beside those armes there stood a mighty speare,
  Which *Bladud* made by Magick art of yore,
  And usd the same in battell aye to beare;
  Sith which it had bin here preserv'd in store,
  For his great vertues proved long afore:
  For never wight so fast in sell could sit,
  But him perforce unto the ground it bore:

Both speare she tooke, and shield, which hong by it:
Both speare and shield of great powre, for her purpose fit.

61

Thus when she had the virgin all arayd,
    Another harnesse, which did hang thereby,
    About her selfe she dight, that the young Mayd
    She might in equall armes accompany,
    And as her Squire attend her carefully:
    Tho to their ready Steeds they clombe full light,
    And through back wayes, that none might them espy,
    Covered with secret cloud of silent night,
Themselves they forth convayd, and passed forward right.

62

Ne rested they, till that to Faery lond
    They came, as *Merlin* them directed late:
    Where meeting with this *Redcrosse* knight, she fond
    Of diverse things discourses to dilate,
    But most of *Arthegall*, and his estate.
    At last their wayes so fell, that they mote part:
    Then each to other well affectionate,
    Friendship professed with unfained hart,
The *Redcrosse* knight diverst, but forth rode *Britomart*.

THE SPEECHES AT PRINCE HENRY'S BARRIERS

by Ben Jonson

THIS WORK, by one of the greatest Jacobean dramatists, is one of a number of pageants or masques which contain an Arthurian element. Others that demonstrate the importance of Merlin as a character in this time include: *Merlin in Love* by Aaron Hill (1760); *Merlin, or the Devil of Stonehenge* by Lewis Theobald (1767); and later on the marvellously named *Merlin's Mount (or Harlequin Cymraeg and the Living Leek)* by T.J. Dibben (1825).

The masque, a kind of elaborate dramatic performance which combined the skills of dance, song and drama, was more often than not staged with great splendour and opulence. *The Speeches at Prince Henry's Barriers* cost £2466, a vast sum at the time. It was performed on Twelfth Night, 1610, in the banqueting hall of Whitehall Palace, as part of the celebrations for the investiture of King James I's 15-year-old son Henry as Prince of Wales. Costumes and sets were designed by the great architect Inigo Jones. In it Merlin lists the great kings of Britain, up to and including James, who claimed descent from Arthur.

Designed to mirror medieval chivalric pursuits, the 'barriers' referred to in the title are sets which suggested the medieval lists in which tournaments were held – though no actual armed combat took place. At the barriers of the work included here, Prince Henry himself took the part of the Arthurian knight Meliadus and, together with six companions, challenged all comers.

THE LADY OF THE LAKE, FIRST *DISCOUERED*

A silence, calme as are my waters, meet
Your raysd attentions, whilst my siluer fee(t)
Touch on the richer shore; and to this seat
Vow my new duties and mine old repeat.
Lest any yet should doubt, or might mistake
What *Nymph* I am; behold the ample lake
Of which I am stild; and neere it MERLINS tombe,
Graue of his cunning, as of mine the wombe.
By this it will not aske me to proclaime
More of my selfe, whose actions, and whose name
Were so full fam'd in *Brit[t]ish* ARTHVRS court;
No more then it will fit me to report
What hath before bene trusted to our squire
Of me, my knight, his fate, and my desire
To meet, if not preuent his destiny,
And stile him to the court of *Britany*;
Now when the Iland hath regain'd her fame
Intire, and perfect, in the ancient name,
And that a *monarch* æquall good and great,
Wise, temperate, iust, and stout, *claimes* ARTHVRS seat.
Did I say æquall? O too prodigall wrong
Of my o're-thirsty, and vnæquall tongue!
How brighter farre, then when our ARTHVR liu'd
Are all the glories of this place reuiu'd!
What riches doe I see; what beauties here!
What awe! what loue! what reuerence! ioy! and feare!
What ornaments of counsaile as of court!
All that is high and great, or can comport
Vnto the stile of maiesty, that knowes
No riuall, but it selfe, this place here showes.
Onely the house of *Chiualrie* (how ere
The inner parts and store be full, yet here
In that which gentry should sustaine) decayd
Or rather ruin'd seemes; her buildings layd
Flat with the earth; that were the pride of time
And did the barbarous *Memphian* heapes out-clime.
Those *Obelisks* and *Columnes* broke, and downe,
That strooke the starres, and raisd the *Brit[t]ish* crowne
To be a constellation: Shields and swords,
Cob-webd, and rusty; not a helme affords
A sparkle of lustre, which were wont to giue

Light to the world, and made the nation liue,
When in a day of honour fire was smit
To haue put out VVLCAN'S and haue lasted yet.
O, when this ædifice stood great and high,
That in the carcasse hath such maiesty,
Whose very sceleton boasts so much worth,
What grace, what glories did it then send forth?
When to the structure went more noble names
Then the *Ephesian* temple lost in flames:
When euery stone was laid by vertuous hands;
And standing so, (O that it yet not stands!)
More truth of *architecture* there was blaz'd,
Then liu'd in all the ignorant *Gothes* haue raz'd.
There *Porticos* were built, and seats for knights
That watchd for all *aduentures*, dayes and nights,
The *Nieces* filld with statues, to inuite
Young valures forth, by their old formes to fight.
With arkes triumphall for their actions done,
Out-striding the *Col[l]ossus* of the sunne.
And *Trophæes*, reard, of spoyled enemies,
Whose toppes pierc'd through the cloudes, and hit the skies

ARTHVR

And thither hath thy voyce pierc'd. Stand not maz'd,
Thy eyes haue here on greater glories gaz'd
And not beene frighted. I, thy ARTHVR, am
Translated to a starre; and of that frame
Or constellation that was calld of mee
So long before, as showing what I should bee,
ARCTVRVS, once thy king, and now thy starre.
Such the rewards of all good princes are.
Nor let it trouble thy designe, faire dame,
That I am present to it with my flame
And influence; since the times are now deuolu'd,
That MERLIN's misticke prophesies are absolu'd,
In *Brit[t]ain's* name, the vnion of this Ile;
And clayme both of my scepter and my stile.
    Faire fall his vertue, that doth fill that throne
In which I ioy to find my selfe so'out-shone;
And for the greater, wish, men should him take,
As it is nobler to restore than make.
    Proceed in thy great worke; bring forth thy knight
Preserued for his times, that by the might
And magicke of his arme, he may restore
These ruin'd seates of vertue, and build more.
Let him be famous, as was TRISTRAM, TOR,
LAVNC'LOT, and all our List of knight-hood: or
Who were before, or haue beene since. His name
Strike vpon heauen, and there sticke his fame.
Beyond the paths, and searches of the sunne
Let him tempt fate; and when a world is wunne,
Submit it duely to this state, and throne,

Till time, and vtmost stay make that his owne.
    But first receiue this shield; wherein is wrought
The truth that he must follow; and (being taught
The wayes from heauen) ought not be despisd.
It is a piece, was by the fates deuisd
To arme his maiden valure; and to show
Defensiue armes th'offensiue should fore-goe.
Indowe him with it, LADY of the lake.
And for the other mysteries, here, awake
The learned MERLIN; when thou shutst him there,
Thou buriedst valure too, for letters reare
The deeds of honor high, and make them liue.
If then thou seeke to restore *prowesse*, giue
His spirit freedome; then present thy knight:
For armes and arts sustaine each others right.

LADY

My error I acknowledge, though too late
To expiate it; There's no resisting fate.
Arise, great *soule*; Fame by surreption got
May stead vs for the time, but lasteth not.
    O, doe not rise with storme, and rage. Forgiue
Repented wrongs. I'am cause thou now shalt liue
æternally, for being deprest a while,
Want makes vs know the price of what we auile.

MERLIN

I neither storme, nor rage; 'tis earth; blame her
That feeles these motions when great sprits stirre.
She is affrighted, and now chid by heauen,
While we walke calmely on, vpright and euen.
    Call forth the faire MELIADVS, thy knight,
They are his fates that make the elements fight:
And these but vsuall throwes, when time sends forth
A wonder or a spectacle of worth.
At common births the world feeles nothing new:
At these she shakes; Mankind liues in a few.

LADY

The heauens, the fates, and thy peculiar starres,
MELIADVS, shew thee; and conclude all iarres.
                  MELIADVS, *and his sixe assistants here discouered.*

MERLIN

I, now the spheares are in their tunes againe,
What place is this so bright that doth remaine
Yet vndemolishd? or but late built! O
I read it now. ST. GEORGE's *Portico!*
The supreme head of all the world, where now
Knighthood liues honord with a crowned brow.
A noble *Scene*, and fit to shew him in
That must of all worlds fame the ghirland winne.

LADY

Do's he not sit like MARS, or one that had
The better of him, in his armor clad?
And those his sixe assistants, as the pride
Of the old *Græcian Heroes* had not died?
Or like APOLLO, raisd to the worlds view,
The minute after he the *Python* slew.

MERLIN

'Tis all too little, LADY, you can speake.
My thought growes great of him, and faine would breake.
Inuite him forth, and guide him to his tent,
That I may read this shield his fates present.

LADY

Glory of Knights, and hope of all the earth,
Come forth; your fostresse bids; who from your birth
Hath bred you to this hower, and for this throne.
This is the field to make your vertue knowne.
　　If he were now (he sayes) to vow his fires
Of faith, of loue, of seruice, then his squires
Had vttered nothing for him: But he hopes
In the first tender of himselfe, his scopes
Were so well read, as it wee no decor'me,
Where truth is studied, there to practise forme.

MERLIN

No, let his actions speake him; and this shield
Let downe from heauen, that to his youth will yeeld
Such copy of incitement: Not the deedes
Of antique knights, to catch their fellowes steedes,
Or ladies palfreyes rescue from the force
Of a fell gyant, or some score to vn-horse.
These were bold stories of our ARTHVRS age;
But here are other acts; another *stage*
And *scene* appeares; it is not since as then:
No gyants, dwarfes, or monsters here, but men.
His arts must be to gouerne, and giue lawes
To peace no lesse then armes. His fate here drawes
An empire with it, and describes each state
Preceding there, that he should imitate.
　　First, faire MELIADVS, hath shee wrought an Ile,
The happiest of the earth (which to your stile
In time must adde) and in it placed high
Britayne, the only name, made CAESAR flie.
Within the neerer parts, as apt, and due
To your first speculation, you may view
The eye of *iustice* shooting through the land,
Like a bright *planet* strengthned by the hand
Of first, and warlike EDWARD; then th'increase
Of trades and tillage, vnder lawes and peace,
Begun by him, but settled and promou'd

By the third *Heroe* of his name, who lou'd
To set his owne aworke, and not to see
The fatnesse of his land a portion bee
For strangers. This was he erected first
The trade of clothing, by which arte were nurst
Whole millions to his seruice, and releeu'd
So many poore, as since they haue beleeu'd
The golden fleece, and need no forrayne mine,
If industrie at home doe not decline.

    To proue which true, obserue what treasure here
The wise and seuenth HENRY heapt each yeere,
To be the strength and sinewes of a warre,
When MARS should thunder, or his peace but iarre.
And here how the eighth HENRY, his braue sonne,
Built forts, made general musters, trayn'd youth on
In exercise of armes, and girt his coast
With strength; to which (whose fame no tongue can boast
Vp to her worth, though all best tongues be glad
To name her still) did great ELIZA adde
A wall of shipping, and became thereby
The ayde, or feare of all the nations nigh.
These, worthyest Prince, are set you neere to reade,
That ciuill arts the martiall must precede.
That lawes and trade bring honors in and gayne,
And armes defensiue a safe peace maintayne.
But when your fate shall call you forth to'assure
Your vertue more (though not to make secure)
View here, what great examples shee hath plac'd.

    First, two braue *Britayne Heroes*, that were grac'd
To fight their *sauiours* battailes, and did bring
Destruction on the faithlesse; one a king,
RICHARD, surnamed with the *lyons hart*.
The other, EDWARD, and the first, whose part
(Then being but Prince) it was to lead these warres
In the age after, but with better starres.
For here though *Coeur de lion* like a storme
Powre on the *Saracens* and doth performe
Deedes past an angell, arm'd with wroth and fire,
Ploughing whole armies vp, with zealous ire,
And walled cities, while he doth defend
That cause that should all warres begin and end;
Yet when with pride, and for humane respect
The *Austrian* cullors he doth here deiect
With too much scorne, behold at length how fate
Makes him a wretched prisoner to that state;
And leaues him, as a marke of Fortunes spight,
When Princes tempt their starres beyond their light:
Whilst vpright EDWARD shines no lesse then he,
Vnder the wings of golden victorie,
Nor lets out no lesse riuers of the bloud
Of *Infidels*, but makes the field a floud,
And marches through it, with ST. GEORGES crosse,

Like *Israels* host to the *Ægyptians* losse,
Through the *red sea*: the earth beneath him cold
And quaking such an enemie to behold.
For which, his temper'd zeale, see Prouidence
Flying in here, and armes him with defence
Against th'assassinate made vpon his life
By a foule wretch, from whom he wrests the knife,
And giues him a iust hire: which yet remaynes
A warning to great chiefes, to keepe their traynes
About 'hem still, and not, to priuacie,
Admit a hand that may vse treacherie.
　　Neerer than these, not for the same high cause,
Yet for the next (what was his right by lawes
Of nations due) doth fight that MARS of men,
The black Prince EDWARD, 'gainst the *French*, who then
At *Cressey* field had no more yeeres then you.
Here his glad father has him in the view
As he is entring in the schoole of warre,
And powres all blessings on him from a farre,
That wishes can; whilst he (that close of day)
Like a yong lyon, newly taught to prey,
Inuades the herds, so fled the *french*, and teares
From the *Bohemian* crowne the plume he weares,
Which after for his crest he did preserue
To his fathers vse, with this fit word, *I SERVE*.
But here at *Poictiers* he was MARS indeed.
Neuer did valour with more streame succeed
Then he had there. He flow'd out like a sea
Vpon their troupes, and left their armes no way:
Or like a fire carryed with high windes,
Now broad, and spreading, by and by it findes
A vent vpright, to looke which way to burne.
Then shootes along againe, or round doth turne,
Till in the circling spoile it hath embrac'd
All that stood nigh, or in the reach to wast:
Such was his rage that day; but then forgot
Soone as his sword was sheath'd, it lasted not,
After the King, the *Dauphine*, and *french*, Peeres
By yeelding to him, wisely quit their feares,
Whom he did vse with such humanitie;
As they complayn'd not of captiuitie;
But here to *England* without shame came in.
To be his captiues was the next to win.
　　Yet rests the other thunder-bolt of warre,
HARRY the fift, to whom in face you are
So like, as *Fate* would haue you so in worth,
Illustrious Prince. This vertue ne'er came forth,
But *Fame* flue greater for him, then shee did
For other mortalls; *Fate* her selfe did bid
To saue his life: The time it reach'd vnto,
Warre knew not how to giue'him enough to doe.
His very name made head against his foes.

And here at *Agin-Court* where first it rose,
It there hangs still a comet ouer *France*,
Striking their malice blind, that dare aduance
A thought against it, lightned by your flame
That shall succeed him both in deedes and name.
    I could report more actions yet of weight
Out of this orbe, as here of *eightie eight*,
Against the proud *Armada*, stil'd by *Spaine*
The Inuincible; that couer'd all the mayne,
As if whole Ilands had broke loose, and swame;
Or halfe of *Norway* with her firre-trees came,
To ioyne the continents, it was so great;
Yet by the auspice of ELIZA beat:
That deare-belou'd of heauen, whom to preserue
The windes were call'd to fight, and stormes to serue.
One tumor drown'd another, billowes stroue
To out-swell ambition, water ayre out-droue,
Though shee not wanted on that glorious day,
An euer-honor'd HOWARD to display
ST. GEORGES ensigne; and of that high race
A second, both which ply'd the fight and chase:
And sent first bullets, then a fleet of fire,
Then shot themselues like ordinance; and a tire
Of ships for pieces, through the enemies moone,
That wan'd before it grew, and now they soone
Are rent, spoild, scatterd, tost with all disease,
And for their thirst of *Britayne* drinke the seas.
The fish were neuer better fed than then,
Although at first they fear'd the bloud of men
Had chang'd their element; and NEPTVNE shooke
As if the Thunderer had his palace tooke.
    So here in *Wales, Low Countries, France*, and *Spayne*,
You may behold both on the land and mayne
The conquests got, the spoiles, the *trophæes* reard
By *British* kings, and such as noblest heard
Of all the nation, which may make t[o]'inuite
Your valure vpon need, but not t[o]'incite
Your neighbour Princes, giue them all their due,
And be prepar'd if they will trouble you.
He doth but scourge him selfe, his sword that drawes
Without a purse, a counsaile and a cause.
    But all these spurres to vertue, seedes of praise
Must yield to this that comes. Here's one will raise
Your glorie more, and so aboue the rest,
As if the acts of all mankind were prest
In his example. Here are kingdomes mixt
And nations ioyn'd, a strength of empire fixt
Conterminate with heauen; The golden veine
Of SATVRNES age is here broke out againe.
HENRY but ioyn'd the *Roses*, that ensign'd
Particular families, but this hath ioyn'd
The *Rose* and *Thistle*, and in them combin'd

A vnion, that shall neuer be declin'd.
Ireland that more in title, then in fact
Before was conquer'd, is his *Lawrels* act.
The wall of shipping by ELIZA made,
Decay'd (as all things subject are to fade)
He hath new built, or so restor'd, that men
For noble vse, preferre it afore then:
Royall, and *mightie* IAMES, whose name shall set
A goale for all posteritie to sweat,
In running at, by actions hard and high:
This is the height at which your thoughts must fly.
He knowes both how to gouerne, how to saue,
What subjects, what their *contraries* should haue,
What can be done by power, and what by loue,
What should to *Mercie*, what to *Iustice* moue:
All *Arts* he can, and from the hand of *Fate*
Hath he enforc'd the making his owne date.
Within his proper vertue hath he plac'd
His guards 'gainst *Fortune*, and there fixed fast
The wheele of *chance*, about which Kings are hurl'd,
And whose outragious raptures fill the world.

LADY

I, this is hee, MELIADVS, whom you
Must only serue, and giue your selfe vnto:
And by your diligent practice to obay
So wise a Master learne the arte of sway.
    MERLIN, aduance the shield vpon his tent
And now prepare, faire Knight, to proue th'euent
Of your bold *Challenge*. Bee your vertue steeld,
And let your drumme giue note you keepe the field.
Is this the land of *Britaine* so renownd
For deeds of *Armes*, or are their hearings drownd
That none doe answere?

MERLIN

                    Stay, me thinkes I see
A person in yond' *caue*. Who should that bee?
I know her ensignes now: 'Tis *Cheualrie*
Possess'd with sleepe, dead as a *lethargie*:
If any *charme* will wake her, 'tis the name
Of our MELIADVS. I'll vse his *Fame*.
    Lady, MELIADVS, lord of the Iles,
Princely MELIADVS, and whom *Fate* now stiles
The faire MELIADVS, hath hung his shield
Vpon his tent, and here doth keepe the field,
According to his bold and princely word;
And wants employment for his pike, and sword.

CHEVALRY

Were it from death that name would wake mee. Say
Which is the Knight? O I could gaze a day

Vpon his armour that hath so reuiu'd
My spirits, and tels me that I am long liu'd
In his appearance. Breake, you rustie dores,
That haue so long beene shut, and from the shores
Of all the world, come knight-hood like a flood
Vpon these lists, to make the field, here, good,
And your owne honours, that are not call'd forth
Against the wish of men to proue your worth.

THE BARRIERS
After which MERLIN *speakes.*
Nay, stay your valure, 'tis a wisdome high
In Princes to vse fortune reuerently.
He that in deeds of *Armes* obeyes his blood
Doth often tempt his destinie beyond good.
Looke on this throne, and in his temper view
The light of all that must haue grace in you:
His equall *Iustice,* vpright *Fortitude*
And settled *Prudence,* with that *Peace* indued
Of face, as minde, alwayes himselfe and euen.
So HERCVLES, and good men beare vp *heauen.*
   I dare not speake his vertues for the feare
Of flattring him, they come so high and neare
To wonders: yet thus much I prophesy
Of him and his. All eares your selues apply.
You, and your other you, great King and Queene,
Haue yet the least of your bright *Fortune* seene,
Which shal rise brighter euery houre with *Time,*
And in your pleasure quite forget the crime
Of change; your ages night shall be her noone.
And this yong Knight, that now puts forth so soone
Into the world, shall in your ames atchieue
More *ghyrlands* for this state, and shall relieue
Your cares in gouernment; while that yong lord
Shall second him in *Armes,* and shake a sword
And launce against the foes of God and you.
Nor shall lesse ioy your royall hopes pursue
In that most princely *Mayd,* whose forme might call
The world to warre, and make it hazard all
His valure for her beautie, she shall bee
Mother of *nations,* and her Princes see
Riuals almost to these. Whilst you sit high,
And lead by them, behold your *Britaine* fly
Beyond the line, when what the seas before
Did bound, shall to the sky then stretch his shore.

EXTRACTS FROM THE BIRTH OF MERLIN

(or *The Child hath found his father*)

attributed to William Shakespeare and William Rowley

THIS ROLLICKING JACOBEAN farce was a vehicle for Will Rowley, one of the great comedians of Shakespearian theatre. Indeed, he claimed to have co-written it with Shakespeare, though this seems unlikely as Shakespeare was dead before it was assembled and performed. It may be possible that when the two Wills worked together they discussed using the Merlin theme for a play, but scholars cannot trace much of Shakespeare in this text. The entire subject is discussed in detail in *The Birth of Merlin*, a modern edition of the play I edited in 1986 (Element Books, 1989).

We have chosen first the lurid birth scene, which makes great play of the diabolical propaganda attached to Merlin by the late medieval Church. The origins of Merlin, son of a human mother and a spirit or otherworldly father, were too close to the wisdom of the pagan world for the Church, so, of course, he had to be the child of the Devil. Yet nothing of evil is associated with Merlin in the old tradition, only good.

Secondly, we have chosen some of the prophecies and visions worked into the play, which were highly popular at the time of their writing by Rowley, as they would have had many contemporary allusions and aspirations for the audience to identify.

ACT III

SCENE 3

Thunder and Lightning, Enter Devil

Devil: Mix light and darkness, earth and heaven dissolve, be of one piece agen, and turn to Chaos, break all your works you powers, and spoil the world, or if you will maintain earth still, give way and life to this abortive birth now coming, whose fame shall add unto your Oracles.

> Lucina, Hecate, dreadful Queen of Night,
> Bright Proserpine, be pleas'd for Ceres love,
> From stigian darkness, summon up the Fates,
> And in a moment bring them quickly hither,
> Lest death do vent her birth and her together,   *Thunder*
> Assist you spirits of infernal deeps,
> Squint ey'd Erictho, midnight Incubus.
> Rise, rise to aid this birth prodigious.

Enter Lucina, *and the three* Fates.

Devil: Thanks Hecate, hail sister to the Gods, there lies your way, haste with the Fates, and help, Give quick dispatch unto her laboring throws, to bring this mixture of infernal seed to humane being   *Exit* Fates.

And to beguil her pains, till back you come,
Anticks shall dance and Musick fill the room.   *Dance.*

Devil: Thanks Queen of Shades.
   Lucina: Farewel, great servant to th'infernal King,
In honor of this childe, the Fates shall bring
All their assisting powers of Knowledge, Arts,
Learning, Wisdom, all the hidden parts
Of all-admiring Prophecy, to fore-see
The event of times to come, his Art shall stand
A wall of brass to guard the Brittain Land,
Even from this minute, all his Arts appears
Manlike in Judement, Person, State, and years,
Upon his brest the Fates have fixt his name,
And since his birth place was this forrest here,
They now have nam'd him Merlin Silvester.
   Devil: And Merlins name in Brittain shall live,
Whilst men inhabit here, or Fates can give,
Power to amazing wonder, envy shall weep,
And mischief sit and shake her ebbone wings,
Whislt all the world of Merlins magick sings.   *Exit* Devil *and* Lucina.

SCENE 4
Enter Clown

   Clown: Well, I wonder how my poor sister does, after all this thundering, I think she's dead, for I can hear no tidings of her. Those woods yields small comfort for her, I could meet nothing but a swinherds wife, keeping hogs by the Forestside, but neither she nor none of her sowes would stir a foot to help us; indeed I think she durst not trust her self amongst the trees with me, for I must needs confess I offer'd some kindness to her; well, I would fain know what's become of my sister, if she have brought me a yong Cousin, his face may be a picture to finde his Father by, so oh, sister Joan Go-too't where are thou?
   Joan: (Within) Here, here brother, stay but a while, I come to thee.
   Clown: O brave, she's alive still, I know her voice, she speaks, and speaks cheerfully methinks, how now, what Moon-calf has she got with her?
Enter Joan *and* Merlin *with a Book*
   Joan: Come my dear Merlin, why dost thou fix thine eye so deeply on that book?
   Merlin: To sound the depth of Arts, of Learning, Wisdom, Knowledge.
   Joan: Oh my dear, dear son, those studies fits thee when thou art a man.
   Merlin: Why mother, I can be but half a man at best,
And that is your mortality, the rest
In me is spirit, 'tis not meat, nor time,
That gives this growth and bigness, no, my years
Shall be more strange then yet my birth appears,
Look mother, there's my Uncle.
   Joan: How doest thou know him son, thou never saw'st him?
   Merlin: Yet I know him, and know the pains he has taken for ye, to finde out my Father, give me your hand, good Uncle.
   Clown: Ha, ha, I'de laugh at that yfaith, do you know me sir?
   Merlin: Yes, by the same token that even now you kist the swinherds-wife 'ith' woods, and would have done more, if she would have let you, Uncle.

Clown: A witch, a witch, a witch, sister: rid him out of your company, he is either a witch or a conjurer, he could never have known this else.

Joan: Pray love him brother, he is my son.

Clown: Ha, Ha, this is worse then all the rest yfaith, by his beard he is more like your husband: let me see, is your great belly gone?

Joan: Yes, and this the happy fruit.

Clown: What, this Hartichoke? A Childe born with a beard on his face?

Merlin: Yes, and strong legs to go, and teethe to eat.

Clown: You can nurse up your self then? There's some charges sav'd for Soap and Candle, 'slid I have heard of some that has been born with teeth, but never none with such a talking tongue before.

Joan: Come, come, you must use him kindly brother, did you but know his worth, you would make much of him.

Clown: Make much of a Moncky? This is worse then Tom Thumb that let a fart in his Mothers belly, a Childe to speak, eat, and go the first hour of his birth, nay, such a Baby as had need of a Barber before he was born too; why sister this is monstrous, and shames all our kindred.

Joan: That thus 'gainst nature and our common births, he comes thus furnisht to salute the world, is power of Fates, and gift of his great father.

Clown: Why, of what profession is your father sir?

Merlin: He keeps a Hot-house 'ith' Low Countries, will you see him sir?

Clown: See him, why sister has the childe found his father?

Merlin: Yes, and Ile fetch him Uncle.   *Exit* Merlin.

Clown: Do not Uncle me, till I know your kindred, for my conscience some Baboon begot thee, surely thou art horribly deceived sister, this Urchin cannot be of thy breeding, I shall be asham'd to call him cousin, though his father be a Gentleman.

Enter Merlin *and* Devil

Merlin: Now my kinde Uncle see,
The Childe has found his Father, this is he.

Clown: The devil it is, ha, ha, is this your sweet-heart sister? have we run through the Countrey, haunted the City, and examin'd the Court to finde out a Gallant with a Hat and Feather, and a silken Sword, and golden Hangers, and do you now bring me to a Ragamuffin with a face like a Frying-pan?

Joan: Fie brother, you mistake, behold him better.

Clown: How's this? do you juggle with me, or are mine eyes matches? Hat and Feather, Sword, and Hangers and all, this is a Gallant indeed sister, this has all the marks of him we look for.

Devil: And you have found him now sir? give me your hand, I now must call you brother.

Clown: Not till you have married my sister, for all this while she's but your whore, sir.

Devil: Thou art too plain, Ile satisfie that wrong to her, and thee, and all, with liberal hand: come, why art thou fearful?

Clown: Nay I am not afriad, and you were the devil, sir.

Devil: Thou needst not, keep with thy sister still, and Ile supply your wants, you shall lack nothing that gold and wealth can purchase.

Clown: Thank you brother, we have gone many a weary step to finde you; you may be a husband for a Lady, for you are far fetcht and dear bought, I assure you: Pray how should I call you son, my cousin here?

Devil: His name is Merlin.

Clown: Merlin! Your hand, cousin Merlin, for your fathers sake I accept you to my kindred: if you grow in all things as your Beard does, you will be talkt on. By your Mothers side cousin, you come of the Go-too'ts, Suffolk bred, but our standing house is at Hocklye i'th Hole, and Layton-buzzard. For your father, no doubt you may from him claim Titles of

Worship, but I cannot describe it; I think his Ancestors came first from Hell-bree in Wales, cousin.

Devil: No matter whence we do derive our Name,
All Brittany shall ring of Merlin's fame,
And wonder at his acts. Go hence to Wales,
There live a while, there Vortiger the King
Builds Castles and strong Holds, which cannot stand
Unless supported by yong Merlins hand.
There shall thy fame begin, Wars are a breeding.
The Saxons practise Treason, yet unseen,
Which shortly shall break out: Fair Love, farewel,
Dear son and brother, here must I leave you all,
Yet still I will be near at Merlins call.   *Exit* Devil.

   Merlin: Will you go Uncle?

   Clown: Yes, Ile follow you, cousin: well, I do most horribly begin to suspect my kindred, this brother in law of mine is the Devil sure, and though he hide his horns with his Hat and Feather, I spi'd his cloven foot for all his cunning.   *Exit* Clown.

ACT IV

SCENE 4

Enter Cador *and* Edwin

   Candor: Bright Victor er self fights on our part, and buckled in a golden Beaver, rides triumphantly before us.

   Edwin: Justice is with her, who ever takes the true and rightful cause, let us not lag behinde them.

Enter Prince

   Candor: Here comes the Prince, how goes our fortunes Sir?

   Prince: Hopeful, and fair, brave Cador, proud Vortiger beat down by Edols sword, was rescu'd by the following multitudes, and now for safety's fled unto a Castle here standing on the hill: but I have sent a cry of hounds as violent as hunger,
To break his stony walls, or if they fail,
We'l send in wilde fire to dislodge him thence,
Or burn them all with flaming violence.   *Exeunt.*

SCENE 5

Blazing Star appears. Florish Tromp
Enter Prince, Uter, Edol, Cador, Edwin, Toclio *with* Drum *and* Soldiers

   Prince: Look Edol: Still this fiery exalation shoots his frightful horrors on th'amazed world, see in the beam that 'bout his flaming ring, a Dragons head appears, from out whose mouth two flaming snakes of fire, stretch East and West.

   Edol: And see, from forth the body of the Star, seven smaller blazing streams, directly point on this affrighted kingdom.

   Candor: 'Tis a dreadful Meteor.

   Edwin: And doth portend strange fears.

   Prince: This is no Crown of Peace, this angry fire hath something more to burn than Vortiger; if it alone were pointed at his fall, it would pull in his blasing Piramids, and be appeas'd, for Vortiger is dead.

   Edol: These never come without their large effects.

   Prince: The will of heaven be done, our sorrows this, we want, a mistick Pithon to expound this fiery Oracle.

Candor: Oh no my Lord, you have the best that ever Brittain bred, and durst I prophecy of your Prophet, sir, none like him shall suceed him.

Prince: You mean Merlin.

Candor: True sir, wonderous Merlin, he met us in the way, and did foretell the fortunes of this day successful to us.

Edwin: He's sure about the Camp, send for him sir.

Candor: He told the bloody Vortiger his fate, and truely too, and if I could give faith to any Wizards skill, it should be Merlin.

Enter Merlin *and* Clown

Candor: And see my Lord, as if to satisfie your Highness pleasure, Merlin is come.

Prince: See, the Comet's in his eye, disturb him not.

Edol: With what a piercing judgement he beholds it!

Merlin: Whither will Heaven and Fate translate this Kingdom?
What revolutions, rise and fall of Nations
Is figur'd yonder in that Star, that sings
The change of Brittains State, and death of Kings?
Ha! He's dead already, how swiftly mischief creeps!
Thy fatal end sweet Prince, even Merlin weeps.

Prince: He does foresee some evil, his action shows it, for e're he does expound, he weeps the story.

Edol: There's another weeps too. Sirrah dost thou understand what thou lamentst for?

Clown: No sir, I am his Uncle, and weep because my Cousin weeps, flesh and blood cannot forbear.

Prince: Gentle Merlin, speak thy prophetick knowledge, in explanation of this fiery horror, from which we gather from thy mournful tears, much sorrow and disaster in it.

Merlin: 'Tis true fair Prince, but you must hear the rest with patience.

Prince: I vow I will, tho' it portend my ruine.

Merlin: There's no such fear, this brought the fiery fall of Vortiger, and yet not him alone, this day is faln a King more good, the glory of our Land, the milde, and gentle sweet Aurelius.

Prince: Our brother!

Edwin: Forefend it heaven.

Merlin: He at his Palace Royal sir at Winchester, this day is dead and poison'd.

Candor: By whom? Or what means Merlin?

Merlin: By the Traiterous Saxons.

Edol: I ever fear'd as much: that devil Ostorius, and the damn'd witch Artesia, sure has done it.

Prince: Poison'd! oh look further gentle Merlin, behold the Star agen, and do but finde revenge for me, though it cost thousand lives, and mine the foremost.

Merlin: Comfort yourself, the heavens have given it fully, all the portentious ills to you is told, now hear a happy story sir from me, to you and to your fair posterity.

Clown: Me thinks I see something like a peel'd Onion, it makes me weep agen.

Merlin: Be silent Uncle, you'l be forc't else.

Clown: Can you not finde in the Star, Cousin, whether I can hold my tongue or no?

Edol: Yes, I must cut it out.

Clown: Phu, you speak without book sir, my Cousin Merlin knows.

Merlin: True, I must tie it up, now speak your pleasure Uncle.

Clown: Hum, hum, hum, hum.

Merlin: So, so – now observe my Lord, and there behold above yon flame-hair'd beam that upward shoots, appears a Dragons head, out of whose mouth two streaming lights point their flam-feather'd darts contrary ways, yet both shall have their aims:
Again behold from the ignifirent body, seven splendant and illustrious rays are spred, all

speaking Heralds to this Brittain Isle, and thus they are expounded:

The Dragons head is the Herogliphick that figures out your Princely self, that here must reign a King, those by-form'd fires that from the Dragons mouth shoot East and West, emblem two Royal babes, which shall proceed from you, a son and daughter.

Her pointed constellation Northwest bending,
Crowns Her a Queen in Ireland, of whom first springs
That Kingdom Title to the Brittain Kings.

Clown: Hum, hum, hum.

Merlin: But of your Son, thus Fate and Merlin tells, all after times shall fill their Chronicles with fame of his renown, whose warlike sword shall pass through fertile France and Germany; nor shall his conjuring foot be forc't to stand, till Romes Imperial Wreath hath crown'd his Fame with Monarch of the West, from whose seven hills, with Conquest, and contributory Kings, he back returns to inlarge the Brittain bounds, his Heraldry adorn'd with thirteen Crowns.

Clown: Hum, hum, hum.

Merlin: He to the world shall add another Worthy, and as a Loadstone for his prowess, draw a train of Marshal Lovers to his Court: It shall be then the best of Knight-hoods honor, at Winchester to fill his Castle Hall, and at his Royal Table sit and feast in warlike orders, all their arms round hurl'd, as if they meant to circumscribe the world.

He touches the Clowns mouth with his wand

Clown: Hum, hum, hum, oh that I could speak a little

Merlin: I know your mind Uncle, agen be silent.   *Strikes again*

Prince: Thou speakst of wonders Merlin, prithee go on, declare at full this Constellation.

Merlin: Those seven beams pointing downward, sir, betoken the troubles of this Land, which then shall meet with other Fate: War and Dissension strives to make division, till seven Kings agree to draw this Kingdom to a Hepterchy.

Prince: Thine art hath made such proof, that we believe thy words authentical, be ever neer us, my Prophet, and the Guide of all my actions.

Merlin: My service shall be faithful to your person, and all my studies for my Countries safety.

Clown: Hum, hum, hum.

Merlin: Come, you are releast, sir.

Clown: Cousin, pray help me to my tongue agen, you do not mean I shall be dumb still I hope?

Merlin: Why, hast thou not thy tongue?

Clown: Ha! yes, I feel it now, I was so long dumb, I could not well tell whether I spake or no.

Prince: I'st thy advice we presently pursue the bloody Saxons, that have slain my brother?

Merlin: With your best speed, my Lord, Prosperity will keep you company.

Cador: Take then your Title with you, Royal Prince, 'twil adde unto our strength, Long Live King Uter.

Edol: Put the Addition to't that Heaven hath given you: The Dragon is your Emblem, bear it bravely, and so long live and ever happy styl'd Uter-Pendragon, lawful King of Brittain.

Prince: Thanks Edol, we imbrace the name and title, and in our Shield and Standard shall the figure of a Red Dragon still be born before us, to fright the bloody Saxons. Oh my Aurelius,

Sweet rest thy soul; let thy disturbed spirit
Expect revenge, think what it would, it hath,
The Dragon's coming in his fiery wrath.   *Exeunt.*

Artesia: Ha, ha, ha.

Edol: Dost laugh Erictho?

Artesia: Yes, at thy poor invention, is there no better, torture-monger?

Donobert: Burn her to dust.

Artesia: That's a Phoenix death, and glorious.

Edol: I, that's to good for her.

Prince: Alive she shall be buried circled in a wall, thou murdress of a King, there starve to death.

Artesia: Then Ile starve death when he comes for his prey, and i'th' mean time Ile live upon your curses.

Edol: I, 'tis diet good enough, away with her.

Artesia: With joy, my best of wishes is before,
　　They brother's poison'd, but I wanted more.　　　　　　　　　　　　　　　　　*Exit.*

Prince: Why does our Prophet Merlin stand apart, sadly observing these our Ceremonies, and not applaud our joys with thy hid knowledge? Let thy divining Art now satisfie some part of my desires, for well I know 'tis in thy power to show the full event, that shall both end our Reign and Chronicle: speak learned Merlin, and resolve my fears, whether by war we shall expel the Saxons, or govern what we hold with beautious peace in Wales and Brittain?

Merlin: Long happiness attend Pendragons Reign, what Heaven decrees, fate hath no power to alter: The Saxons, sir, will keep the ground they have, and by supplying numbers still increase, till Brittain be no more. So please your Grace, I will in visible apparations, present you Prophecies which shall concern Succeeding Princes, which my Art shall raise, Till men shall call these times the latter days.

Prince: Do it my Merlin, and Crown me with much joy and wonder.

　　　　　　　　　　　　　　　　　　　　　　　　　　　　　　　Merlin *strikes.*

Hoeboys, Enter a King in Armour, his Shield quartered with thirteen Crowns.
At the other door enter divers Princes who present their Crowns to him
at his feet, and do him homage,
then enters Death *and strikes him, he growing sick,*
Crowns Constantine. *Exeunt*

Merlin: This King, my Lord, presents your Royal Son, who in his prime of years shall be so fortunate, that thirteen several Princes shall present their several Crowns unto him, and all Kings else shall so admire his fame and victories, that they shall be glad either through fear or love, to do him homage; but death (who neither favors the weak nor valliant) in the middest of all his glories, soon shall seize him, scarcely permitting him to appoint one in all his purchased Kingdoms to succeed him.

Prince: Thanks to our Prophet for this so wish'd for satisfaction, and hereby now we learn that always Fate must be observ'd, what ever that decree,
　　All future times shall still record this Story,
　　Of Merlin's learned worth, and Arthur's glory.　　　　　　　　　　　*Exeunt* Omnes.

MERLIN, OR THE BRITISH ENCHANTER

by John Dryden

JOHN DRYDEN'S 'Dramatick Opera', with music by Henry Purcell, was first performed in 1691, under the title *King Arthur, or the British Worthy*. It achieved a considerable success for both dramatist and composer, who were already well known to London audiences as the authors of several successful works, including *The Indian Queen*. In later performances it received the title change – a device which reflects the importance of the figure of Merlin. At this time Queen Caroline had established a curious rococo dairy and menagerie in Richmond Deer Park. Among the other attractions of this site were a hermitage and grotto called Merlin's Cave, where a resident soothsayer, dressed as the great enchanter, was available for consultation.

Dryden's immediate sources were Geoffrey of Monmouth and Bede, as well as the *Germania* and *Annales* of the Roman author Tacitus, to which he turned for information about the Saxons. The background is the familiar one of the struggle between the Britons and the invading 'heathens' from across the sea – but there all similarity between the traditional sources and the drama ceases. Dryden introduces new characters – like the blind Emmeline – and generally plays about with the story as it is usually told. None the less the work is not without merit and shows the way in which Merlin was regarded at the time – as still arranging the affairs of the Arthurian court and as exercising considerable magical power. In keeping with the literary interests of the time there are numerous spirits, and the goddess Venus appears at the end to bless the proceedings. The work is still performed today, and Purcell's powerful and lyrical music has assured it a place in the history of opera.

The text is printed here in its entirety (with the exception of the 'Prologue' and 'Epilogue') from the edition published by Curll in 1736.

Dramatis Personae

King *Arthur*.
Oswald, King of *Kent*, a Saxon and a Heathen.
Conon, Duke of *Cornwal* Tributary to King *Arthur*.
Merlin, a famous Inchanter.
Osmond, a Saxon Magician, and a Heathen.
Aurelius, Friend to *Arthur*.
Albanact, Captain of *Arthur*'s Guards.
Guillamar, Friend to *Oswald*.

Women

Emmeline, Daughter of *Conon*.
Matilda, her Attendant.
Philidel, an Airy Spirit.
Grimbald, an Earthy Spirit.

Officers and Soldiers, Singers and Dancers, &c.

Scene in *Kent*.

ACT I SCENE I
Enter Conon, Aurelius, Albanact

Con. Then this is the Deciding Day, to fix
Great Britain's Scepter in great Arthur's Hand.
   Aur. Or put it in the bold Invaders gripe.
Arthur and *Oswald*, and their different Fates,
Are weighing now within the Scales of Heaven.
   Con. In Ten set Battles have we driven back
These Heathen Saxons, and regain'd our Earth.
As Earth recovers from an Ebbing Tide,
Her half-drown'd Face, and lifts its o'er the Waves.

An engraving of Merlin's cave, commissioned by Queen Caroline
in 1735 (T. Bonles from *Merlin: or The British Inchanter and King Arthur,
The British Worthy*)

From *Severn*'s Banks, even to this *Barren-Down*,
Our foremost Men have prest their fainty Rear,
And not one Saxon Face has been beheld;
But all their Backs, and Shoulders have been stuck
With foul dishonest Wounds: Now here, indeed,
Because they have no further Ground they stand.
   Aur. Well have we chose a Happy Day, for Fight;
For every Man, in course of time, has found
Some days are lucky, some unfortunate.
   Alb. But why this day more lucky than the rest?
   Con. Because this day
Is Sacred to the Patron of our Isle;
A Christian, and a Souldiers Annual Feast.
   Alb. Oh, now I understand you, This is St. *George* of *Cappadocia*'s Day.
Well, It may be so, but Faith I was Ignorant; we Soldiers
Seldom examine the Rubrick; and now and then a Saint may
Happen to slip by us; But if he be a Gentleman Saint, he will
Forgive us.
   Con. Oswald, undoubtedly, will Fight it bravely.
   Aur. And it behoves him well, 'tis his last Stake.   *To* Alb.
But what manner of Man is this *Oswald*? Have ye ever seen him?
   Alb. Ne'er but once; and that was to my Cost too; I follow'd him too close;
And to say Truth, somewhat Uncivilly, upon a Rout;
But he turn'd upon me, as quick and as round, as a chaff'd Boar;
And gave me two Licks across the Face, to put me
In mind of my Christianity.
   Con. I know him well; he's free and open Hearted.
   Aur. His Countries Character: That Speaks a German.
   Con. Revengeful, rugged, violently brave; and once resolv'd, is never to be mov'd.
   Alb. Yes, he's a valiant Dog, Pox on him.

Con. This was the Character he then maintain'd,
When in my Court he sought my Daughters Love:
My Fair, Blind, *Emmeline.*

Alb. I cannot blame him for Courting the Heiress of *Cornwall.*
All Heiresses are Beautiful; and as Blind as she is, he would have had
No Blind Bargain of her.

Aur. For that Defeat in Love, he rais'd this War.
For Royal *Arthur* Reign'd within her Heart,
E're *Oswald* mov'd his Sute.

Con. Ay, now *Aurelius,* you have Nam'd a Man;
One, whom besides the Homage that I owe,
As *Cornwall's* Duke, to his Imperial Crown,
I wou'd have chosen out, from all Mankind,
To be my Soveraign Lord.

Aur. His worth divides him from the crowd of Kings;
So Born, without Desert to be so Born;
Men, set aloft, to be the Scourge of Heaven;
And with long Arms, to lash the Under-World.

Con. Arthur is all that's Excellent in *Oswald;*
And void of all his Faults: In Battle brave;
But still Serene in all the Stormy War,
Like Heaven above the Clouds; and after Fight,
As Merciful and Kind, to vanquisht Foes,
As a Forgiving God; but see, he's here,
And Praise is Dumb before him.

     Enter King Arthur, *reading a Letter, with Attendants*

 Arthur (reading) Go on, Auspicious Prince, the Stars are kind:
 Unfold thy Banners to the willing Wind;
While I, with Aiery Legions, help thy Arms:
Confronting Art with Art, and Charms with Charms.
So *Merlin* writes; nor can we doubt th'event,   *To* Con.
With Heav'n and you to Friends; Oh Noble *Conon,*
You taught my tender Hands the Trade of War;
And now again you Helm your Hoary Head,
And under double weight of Age and Arms,
Assert your Countries Freedom, and my Crown.

Con. No more, my Son.

Arth. Most happy in that Name!
Your *Emmeline,* to *Oswald's* Vows refus'd,
You made my plighted Bride:
Your Charming Daughter, who like Love, Born Blind,
Un-aiming hits, with surest Archery,
And Innocently kills.

Con. Remember, Son,
You are a General, other Wars require you.
For see the *Saxon* Gross begins to move.

Arth. Their Infantry Embattel'd, square and close,
March firmly on, to fill the middle space:
Cover'd by their advancing Cavalry.
By Heav'n, 'tis Beauteous Horrour:
The Noble *Oswald* has provok'd my Envy.

       Enter Emmeline, *led by* Matilda

Ha! Now my Beauteous *Emmeline* appears,
Anew, but Oh, a softer Flame, inspires me:
Even Rage and Vengeance, slumber at her sight.
Con. Haste your Farewel; I'll chear my Troops, and 5ye.   *Exit* Conon.
  Em. Oh Father, Father, I am sure you're here;
Because I see your Voice.
  Arth. No, thou mistak'st thy hearing for thy sight;
He's gone, my *Emmeline*;
And I but stay to gaze on those fair Eyes,
Which cannot view the Conquest thay have made.
Oh Star-like Night, dark only to thy self,
But full of Glory, as those Lamps of Heav'n
That see not when they shine.
  Em. What is this Heav'n, and Stars, and Night, and Day,
To which you thus compare my Eyes and me?
I understand you, when you say you love:
For, when my Father clasps my Hand in his,
That's cold, and I can feel it hard and wrinkl'd;
But when you grasp it, then I sigh and pant,
And something smarts, and tickles at my Heart.
  Arth. Oh Artless Love! where the Soul moves the Tongue,
And only Nature speaks what Nature thinks!
Had she but Eyes!
  Em. Just now you said I had:
I see 'em, I have two.
  Arth. But neither see.
Em. I'm sure they hear you then:
What can your Eyes do more?
  Arth. They view your Beauties.
  Em. Do not I see? You have a Face, like mine,
Two Hands, and two round, pretty, rising Breasts,
That heave like mine.
  Arth. But you describe a Woman,
Nor is it sight, but touching with your Hands.
  Em. Then 'tis my Hand that sees, and that's all one:
For is not seeing, touching with your Eyes?
  Arth. No, for I see at distance, where I touch not.
  Em. If you can see so far, and yet not touch,
I fear you see my Naked Legs and Feet
Quite through my Cloaths; pray do not see so well.
  Arth. Fear not, sweet Innocence;
I view the lovely Features of your Face;
Your Lips Carnation, your dark shaded Eye-brows,
Black Eyes, and Snowwhite Forehead; all the Colours
That make your Beauty, and produce my Love.
  Em. Nay, then, you do not love on equal terms:
I love you dearly, without all these helps:
I cannot see your Lips Carnation,
Your shaded Eye-brows, nor your Milk-white Eyes.
  Arth. You still mistake.
  Em. Indeed I thought you had a Nose and Eyes,
And such a Face as mine; have not Men Faces?

Arth. Oh, none like yours, so excellently fair.

Em. Then wou'd I had no Face; for I wou'd be
Just such a one as you.

Arth. Alas, 'tis vain to instruct your Innocence,
You have no Notion of Light or Colours.

Em. Why, is not that a Trumpet?   *Trumpet sounds within.*

Arth. Yes.

Em. I knew it.
And I can tell you how the sound on't looks.
It looks as if it had an angry fighting Face.

Arth. 'Tis now indeed a sharp unpleasant sound,
Because it calls me hence, from her I love,
To meet Ten thousand Foes.

Em. How does so many Men ee'r come to meet?
This Devil Trumpet vexes 'em, and then
They feel about, for one anothers Faces;
And so they meet, and kill.

Arth. I'll tell ye all, when We have gain'd the Field;
One kiss of your fair Hand, the pledge of Conquest,
And so a short farewel.

         Kisses her Hand, and Exit with Aurel. Alb. *and Attendants.*

Em. My Heart, and Vows, go with him to the Fight:
May every Foe be that, which they call blind,
And none of all their Swords have Eyes to find him.
But lead me nearer to the Trumpet's Face;
For that brave Sound upholds my fainting Heart;
And while I hear, methinks I fight my part.   *Exit, led by* Matilda.

            Enter Oswald *and* Osmond

The Scene represents a place of Heathen worship; The three Saxon Gods, Woden, Thor, *and*
Freya *placed on Pedestals. An Altar.*

Osmo. 'Tis time to hasten our mysterious Rites;
Because your Army waits you.

         Oswald *making three Bows before the three Images*

    Oswa. Thor, Freya, Woden, *all ye Saxon Powers,
Hear and revenge my Father *Hengist*'s death.

Osmo. Father of Gods and Men, great *Woden*, hear.
Mount thy hot Courser, drive amidst thy Foes;
Lift high thy thund'ring Arm, let every blow
Dash out a mis-believing Briton's Brains.

Oswa. Father of Gods and Men, great *Woden* hear;
Give Conquest to thy Saxon Race, and me.

Osmo. Thor, Freya, Woden, hear, and spell your Saxons,
With Sacred Runick Rhimes, from Death in Battle.
Edge their bright Swords, and blunt the Britons Darts.
No more, Great Prince, for see my trusty Fiend,
Who all the Night has wing'd the dusky Air.

         Grimbald, *a fierce earthy Spirit arises*

What News, my *Grimbald?*

Grim. I have plaid my part;
For I have Steel'd the Fools that are to dye;
Six Fools, so prodigal of Life and Soul,
That, for their Country, they devote their Lives

A Sacrifice to Mother Earth, and *Woden*.
    Osmo. 'Tis well; But are we sure of Victory?
    Grim. Why ask'st thou me?
Inspect their Intrails, draw from thence thy Guess:
Bloud we must have, without it we are dumb.
    Osmo. Say, Where's thy Fellow-servant, *Philidel*?
Why comes not he?
    Grim. For, he's a puleing Sprite.
Why didst thou chuse a tender airy Form,
Unequal to the mighty work of Mischief;
His Make is flitting, soft, and yielding Atomes:
He trembles at the yawning gulph of Hell,
Nor dares approach the Flame, lest he shou'd singe
His gaudy silken Wings.
He sighs when he should plunge a Soul in Sulphur,
As with Compassion, touch'd of foolish man.
    Osmo. What a half Devil's he?
His errand was, to draw the Low-land damps,
And Noisom vapours, from the foggy Fens:
Then, breath the baleful stench, with all his force,
Full on the faces of our Christned Foes.
    Grim. Accordingly he drein'd those Marshy-grounds;
And bagg'd 'em in a blue Pestiferous Cloud;
Which when he shou'd have blown, the frightd Elf
Espy'd the Red Cross Banners of their Host;
And said he durst not add to his damnation.
    Osmo. I'le punish him at leisure;
Call in the Victims to propitiate Hell.
    Grim. That's my kind Master, I shall break fast on 'em.
    Grimbald *goes to the Door, and Re-enters with 6 Saxons in White with Swords in their*
        hands. They range themselves 3 and 3 in opposition to each other.
            The rest of the Stage is fill'd with Priests and Singers.
Woden, first to thee,
A Milk-white Steed in Battle won,
We have Sacrific'd.
    Chor. *We have Sacrific'd.*
    Vers. *Let our next oblation be,*
To Thor, *thy thundering Son,*
Of such another.
    Chor. *We have Sacrific'd.*
    Vers. *A Third;* (of Friezland *breed was he,*)
To Woden's *Wife, and to* Thor's *Mother:*
And now we have atton'd all three
We have Sacrific'd.
    Chor. *We have Sacrific'd.*
    2 Voc. *The White Horse Neigh'd aloud.*
To Woden *thanks we render.*
To Woden, *we have vow'd.*
    Chor. *To* Woden, *our Defender.*   The four last Lines in *Chorus.*
    Vers. *The Lot is Cast, and* Tanfan *pleas'd*:
    Chor. *Of Mortal Cares you shal be eas'd,*
Brave Souls to be renown'd in Story.

Honour Prizing,
Death despising,
Fame acquiring
By Expiring,
Dye, and reap the fruit of Glory.
Brave Souls to be renown'd in Story.
Vers. 2. *I call ye all,*
To Woden's *Hall;*
Your temples round
With Ivy bound,
In Goblets Crown'd,
And plenteous Bowls of burnish'd Gold;
Where you shall Laugh,
And dance and quaff,
The juice, that makes the Britons bold.

> *The six Saxons are led off by the Priests, in Order to be Sacrific'd*

Osw. Ambitious Fools we are,
And yet Ambition is a Godlike Fault:
Or rather, 'tis no Fault in Souls Born great,
Who dare extend their Glory by their Deeds.
Now *Britany* prepare to change thy State,
And from this Day begin thy Saxon date.   *Exeunt* Omnes.

> *A Battle supposed to be given behind the Scenes,*
> *with Drums, Trumpets, and Military Shouts and Excursions:*
> *After which, the Britons, expressing their Joy for the Victory,*
> *sing this song of Triumph.*

Come if you dare, our Trumpets sound;
Come if you dare, the Foes rebound:
We come, we come, we come, we come,
Says the double, double, double Beat of the Thundring Drum.

Now they charge on amain,
Now they rally again:
The Gods from above the Mad Labour behold,
And pity Mankind that will perish for Gold.

The Fainting Saxons *quit their Ground,*
Their Trumpets Languish in the Sound;
They fly, they fly, they fly, they fly;
Victoria, Victoria, *the Bold* Britons *cry.*

Now the Victory's won,
To the Plunder we run:
We return to our Lasses like Fortunate Traders,
Triumphant with Spoils of the Vanquish'd Invaders.

ACT II
Enter Philidel

Phil. Alas, for pity, of this bloody Field!
Piteous it needs must be, when I, a Spirit,
Can have so soft a sense of Humane Woes!
Ah! for so many Souls, as but this Morn,

Were cloath'd with Flesh, and warm'd with Vital Blood,
But naked now, or shirted but with Air.

        Merlin, *with Spirits, descends to* Philidel, *on a Chariot drawn by Dragons*

  Mer. What art thou, Spirit, of what Name and Order?
(For I have view'd thee in my Magick Glass,)
Making thy moan, among the Midnight Wolves,
That Bay the silent Moon: Speak, I Conjure thee.
'Tis *Merlin* bids thee, at whose awful Wand,
The pale Ghost quivers, and the grim Fiend gasps.

  Phil. An Airy Shape, the tender'st of my kind,
That last seduc'd, and least deform'd of Hell;
Half white, and shuffl'd in the Crowd, I fell;
Desirous to repent, and loth to sin;
Awkward in Mischief, piteous of Mankind,
My Name is *Philidel*, my Lot in Air;
Where next beneath the Moon, and nearest Heav'n,
I soar, and have a Glimpse to be receiv'd,
For which the swarthy *Daemons* envy me.

  Mer. Thy Business here?

  Phil. To shun the Saxon Wizards dire Commands,
Osmond, the awful'st Name next thine below,
'Cause I refus'd to hurl a Noysom Fog
On Christen'd Heads, the Hue and Cry of Hell
Is rais'd against me, for a Fugitive Spright.

  Mer. Osmond shall know, a great Power protects thee;
But follow thou the Whispers of thy Soul,
That draw thee nearer Heav'n.
And, as thy Place is nearest to the Sky,
The Rays will reach thee first, and bleach thy Soot.

  Phil. In hope of that, I spread my Azure Wings,
And wishing still, for yet I dare not pray,
I bask in Day-light, and behold with Joy
My Scum work outward, and my Rust wear off.

  Mer. Why, 'tis my hopeful Devil; now mark me, *Philidel*,
I will employ thee, for thy future Good:
Thou know'st, in spite of Valiant *Oswald*'s Arms,
Or *Osmond*'s Powerful Spells, the Field is ours. —

  Phil. Oh, Master! hasten
Thy Dread Commands, for *Grimbald* is at Hand;
Osmond's fierce Fiend, I snuff his Earthy Scent:
The Conquering Britons, he misleads to Rivers,
Or dreadful Downfalls of unheeded Rocks;
Where many fall, that ne'er shall rise again.

  Mer. Be that thy care, to stand by falls of Brooks,
And trembling Bogs, that bear a Green-Sword show.
Warn off the bold Pursuers from the Chace:
No more, they come, and we divide the Task.
But lest fierce Grimbald's pond'rous Bulk oppress
Thy tender flitting Air, I'll leave my Band
Of Spirits with United Strength to Aid thee,
And Force with Force repel.

        Exit Merlin *on his Chariot.* Merlin's *Spirits stay with* Philidel.

Enter Grimbald *in the Habit of a Shepherd, follow'd by* King Arthur, Conon, Aurelius,
Albanact *and Soldiers, who wander at a distance in the Scenes*

Grim. Here, this way, Britons, follow Oswald's flight;
This Evening as I whistl'd out my Dog,
To drive my straggling Flock, and pitch'd my Fold,
I saw him dropping Sweat, o'er labour'd, stiff,
Make faintly as he could, to yonder Dell.
Tread in my Steps; long Neighbourhood by Day
Has made these Fields familiar in the Night.

Arth. I thank thee, Shepherd;
Expect Reward, lead on, we follow thee.

Phil. sings. *Hither this way, this way bend,*
Trust not that Malicious Fiend:
Those are false deluding Lights,
Wafted far and near by Sprights.
Trust 'em not, for they'll deceive ye;
And in Bogs and Marshes leave ye.

Chor. of Phil. Spirits. *Hither this way, this way bend.*
Chor. Of Grimb. Spirits. *This way, this way bend.*
Phil. sings. *If you step, no Danger thinking,*
Down you fall, a Furlong sinking:
'Tis a Fiend who has annoy'd ye;
Name but Heav'n, and he'll avoid ye.

Chor. of Phil. Spirits. *Hither this way, this way bend.*
Chor. of Grimb. Spirits. *This way, this way bend.*
Philidels Spirits. *Trust not that Malicious Fiend.*
Grimbalds Spirits. *Trust me, I am no Malicious Fiend.*
Philidels Spirits. *Hither this way,* &c.

Con. Some wicked Phantom, Foe to Human kind,
Misguides our Steps.

Alb. I'll follow him no farther.

Grimbald speaks. By Hell she sings 'em back, in my despight.
I had a voice in Heav'n, ere Sulph'rous Steams
Had damp'd it to a hoarseness; but I'll try.
He sings. *Let not a Moon-born Elf mislead ye,*
From your Prey, and from your Glory.
Too far, Alas, he has betray'd ye:
Follow the Flames, that wave before ye;
Sometimes sev'n, and sometimes one;
Hurry, hurry, hurry, hurry on.
See, see, the Footsteps plain appearing,
That way Oswald *chose for flying:*
Firm is the Turff, and fit for bearing,
Where yonder Pearly Dews are lying.
Far he cannot hence be gone;
Hurry, hurry, hurry, hurry on.

Aur. 'Tis true, he says; the Footsteps yet are fresh
Upon the Sod, no falling Dew-drops have
Disturb'd the Print,   *All are going to follow* Grimbald.

Philidel sings. *Hither this way.*
Chor. of Phil. Spirits. *Hither this way, this way bend.*
Chor. of Grimb. Spirits. *This way, this way bend.*

Philidels Spirits. *Trust not this Malicious Fiend.*
Grimb. Sprits. *Trust me, I am no Malicious Fiend.*
Philidels Spirits. *Hither this way,* &c.   *They all incline to* Philidel.
Grim. speaks, Curse on her Voice, I must my Prey forego;
Thou, *Philidel,* shalt answer this below.   Grimbald *sinks with a Flash.*
   Arth. At last the Cheat is plain;
The Cloven-footed Fiend is Vanish'd from us;
Good Angels be our Guides, and bring us back.
   Phil. singing. *Come follow, follow, follow me.*
   Chor. *Come follow,* &c.
   And me. And me. And me. And me.
   Verse 2. Voc. *And Green-Sword all you way shall be.*
   Chor. *Come follow,* &c.
   Verse. *No* Goblin *or* Elf *shall dare to offend ye.*
   Chor. *No, No, No,* &c.
No Goblin *or* Elf *shall dare to offend ye.*
   Vers. 3 Voc. *We Brethren of Air,*
You Hero's *will bear,*
To the Kind and the Fair that attend ye.
   Chor. *We Brethren,* &c.
Philidel *and the Spirits go off singing, with King* Arthur *and the rest in the middle of them.*
                    Enter Emmeline *led by* Matilda. *Pavilion Scene*
   Em. No News of my Dear Love, or of my Father;
   Mat. None, Madam, since the gaining of the Battel;
Great *Arthur* is a Royal Conqueror now
And well deserves your Love.
   Em. But now I fear
He'll be too great, to love poor silly me.
If he be dead, or never come agen,
I mean to die; But there's a greater doubt,
Since I ne'er saw him here,
How shall I meet him in another World?
   Mat. I have heard something, how two Bodies meet,
But now Souls joyn, I know not.
   Em. I shou'd find him,
For surely I have seen him in my Sleep,
And then, methought, he put his Mouth to mine,
And eat a thousand Kisses on my Lips;
Sure by his Kissing I cou'd find him out
Among a thousand Angels in the Sky.
   Mat. But what kind of Man do you suppose him?
   Em. He must be made of the most precious things:
And I believe his Mouth, and Eyes, and Cheeks,
And Nose, and all his Face, are made of Gold.
   Mat. Heav'n bless us, Madam, what a Face you make him!
If it be yellow, he must have the Jaundies,
And that's a bad Disease.
   Em. Why then do Lovers give a thing so bad
As Gold, to Women, whom so well they love?
   Mat. Because that bad thing, Gold, buys all good things.
   Em. Yet I must know him better: Of all Colours,
Tell me which is the purest, and the softest.

Mat. They say 'tis Black.

Em. Why then, since Gold is hard, and yet is precious,
His face must all be made of soft, black Gold.

Mat. But, Madam —

Em. No more; I have learn'd enough for once.

Mat. Here are a Crew of Kentish Lads and Lasses,
Wou'd entertain ye, till your Lord's return,
With Songs and Dances, to divert your Cares.

Em. O bring them in,
For tho' I cannot see the Songs, I love 'em;
And Love, they tell me, is a Dance of Hearts.

> *Enter Shepherds and Shepherdesses.*

1 Shepherd sings. *How blest are Shepherds, how happy their Lasses,*
While Drums & Trumpets are sounding Alarms!
Over our Lowly Sheds all the Storm passes;
And when we die, 'tis in each others Arms.
All the Day on our Herds, and Flocks employing;
All the Night on our Flutes, and in enjoying.

Chor. *All the Day,* &c.

Bright Nymphs of Britain, *with Graces attended,*
Let not your Days without Pleasure expire;
Honour's but empty, and when Youth is ended,
All Men will praise you, but none will desire.
Let not Youth fly away without Contenting;
Age will come time enough, for your Repenting.

Chor. *Let not Youth,* &c.

> *Here the Men offer their Flutes to the Women, which they refuse.*

2 Shepherdess. *Shepherd, Shepherd, leave Decoying,*
Pipes are sweet, a Summers Day:
But a little after Toying,
Women have the Shot to pay.
Here are Marriage-Vows for signing
Set their Marks that cannot write:
After that, without Repining,
Play and Welcom, Day and Night.

> *Here the Women give the Men Contracts, which they accept.*

Chor. of all. *Come, Shepherds, lead up, a lively Measure;*
The Cares of Wedlock, are Cares of Pleasure:
But whether Marriage bring Joy, or Sorrow,
Make sure of this Day, and hang to Morrow.

> *They Dance after the Song, and* Exeunt *Shepherds and Shepherdeses.*
> *Enter on the other side of the Stage,* Oswald *and* Guillamar

Osw. The Night has wilder'd us; and we are faln
Among their foremost Tents.

Guill. Ha! What are these!
They seem of more than Vulgar Quality.

Em. What Sounds are those? They cannot far be distant:
Where are we now, *Matilda?*

Mat. Just before your Tent:
Fear not, they must be Friends, and they approach.

Em. My *Arthur,* speak, my Love; Are you return'd
To bless your *Emmeline?*

Oswa. to Guilla. I know that Face:
'Tis my Ungrateful Fair, who, scorning mine,
Accepts my Rivals Love: Heav'n, thou-rt bounteous,
Thou ow'st me nothing now.
    Mat. Fear grows upon me:
Speak what you are; speak, or I call for help.
    Oswa. We are your Guards.
    Mat. Ah me! We are betray'd; 'tis *Oswald's* Voice.
    Em. Let 'em not see our Voices, and then they cannot find us.
    Osw. Passions in Men Oppress'd, are doubly strong.
I take her from King *Arthur*; there's Revenge:
If she can love, she buoys my sinking Fortunes:
Good Reasons both: I'll on. – Fear nothing, Ladies,
You shall be safe.
                              Oswald and Guillamar seize Emmeline and Matilda
    Em. & Matil. Help, help; a Rape, a Rape!
    Oswa. By Heav'n ye injure me, thô Force is us'd,
Your Honour shall be sacred.
    Em. Help, help, Oh *Britons* help!
    Oswa. Your *Britons* cannot help you:
This Arm, through all their Troops, shall force my way;
Yet neither quit my Honour, nor my Prey.   *Exeunt, the Women still crying.*
    An Alarm within: Some Soldiers running over the Stage: Follow, follow, follow.
             Enter Albanact *Captain of the Guards, with Soldiers.*
    Alb. Which way went th' Alarm?
ı *Sol.* Here, towards the Castle.
    Alb. Pox o' this Victory; the whole Camp's debauch'd:
All Drunk or Whoring: This way, follow, follow.   *Exeunt.*
      The Alarm renews: Clashing of Swords within for a while.
        Re-enter Albanact, *Officer and Soldiers*
    Officer. How sits the Conquest on great *Arthur's* Brow?
    Alb. As when the Lover, with the King is mixt,
He puts the gain of Britain in a Scale,
Which weighing with the loss of *Emmeline*,
He thinks he's scarce a Saver.   *Trumpet within.*
    Officer. Hark! a Trumpet!
It sounds a Parley.
    Alba. 'Tis from *Oswald* then;
An Eccho to King *Arthur's* Friendly Summons,
Sent since he heard the Rape of *Emmeline*,
To ask an Interview.   *Trumpet answering on the other side.*
    Officer. But hark! already
Our Trumpet makes reply; and see both present.
    Enter Arthur *on one side attended,* Oswald *on the other with Attendants, and* Guillamar.
               They meet and salute.
    Arthur. Brave *Oswald*! We have met on Friendlier Terms,
Companions of a War, with common Interest
Against the Bordering *Picts*: But Times are chang'd.
    Oswa. And I am sorry that those Times are chang'd:
For else we now might meet, on Terms as Friendly.
    Arth. If so we meet not now, the fault's your own;
For you have wrong'd me much.

Oswa. Oh you wou'd tell me,
I call'd more Saxons in, t'enlarge my Bounds:
If those be Wrongs, the War has well redress'd ye.
    Arth. Mistake me not, I count not War a Wrong:
War is the Trade of Kings, that fight for Empire;
And better be a Lyon, than a Sheep.
    Oswa. In what, then, have I wrong'd ye?
    Arth. In my Love.
    Oswa. Even Love's an Empire too; The Noble Soul,
Like Kings, is Covetous of single Sway.
    Arth. I blame ye not, for loving *Emmeline*:
But since the Soul is free, and Love is choice,
You shou'd have made a Conquest of her Mind,
And not have forc'd her Person by a Rape.
    Oswa. Whether by Force, or Stratagem, we gain;
Still Gaining is our End, in War or Love.
Her Mind's the Jewel, in her Body lock'd;
If I would gain the Gem, and want the Key,
It follows I must seize the Cabinet:
But to secure your fear, her Honour is untouch'd.
    Arth. Was Honour ever safe in Brutal Hands?
So safe are Lambs within the Lyons Paw;
Ungrip'd and plaid with, till fierce Hunger calls,
Then Nature shews it self; the close-hid Nails
Are stretch's, and open'd, to the panting Prey.
But if indeed, you are so Cold a Lover —
    Oswa. Not Cold, but Honourable.
    Arth. Then Restore her.
That done, I shall believe you Honourable.
    Oswa. Think'st thou I will forego a Victor's Right?
    Arth. Say rather, of an Impious Ravisher.
That Castle, were it wall'd with Adamant,
Can hide thy Head, but till to Morrow's Dawn.
    Oswa. And ere to Morrow, I may be a God,
If *Emmeline* be kind: But kind or cruel,
I tell thee, *Arthur*, but to see this Day,
That Heavenly Face, tho' not to have her mind,
I would give up a hundred Years of Life,
And bid Fate cut to Morrow.
    Arth. It soon will come, and thou repent too late;
Which to prevent, I'll bribe thee to be honest.
Thy Noble Head, accustom'd to a Crown,
Shall wear it still: Nor shall thy hand forget
The Sceptre's use: From *Medway*'s pleasing Stream,
To *Severn*'s Roar, be thine.
In short, Restore my Love, and share my Kingdom.
    Osw. Not, tho' you spread my Sway from *Thames* to *Tyber*;
Such Gifts might bribe a King, but not a Lover.
    Arth. Then prithee give me back my Kingly Word,
Pass'd for thy safe return; and let this Hour,
In single Combat, Hand to Hand, decide
The Fate of Empire, and of *Emmeline*.

Oswa. Not, that I fear, do I decline this Combat;
And not decline it neither, but defer:
When *Emmeline* has been my Prize as long
  As she was thine, I dare thee to the Duel.
  Arth. I nam'd your utmost Term of Life; To Morrow.
  Oswa. You are not Fate.
  Arth. But Fate is in this Arm.
You might have made a Merit of your Theft.
  Oswa. Ha! Theft! Your Guards can tell, I stole her not.
  Arth. Had I been present —
  Oswa. Had you been present, she had been mine more Nobly.
  Arth. There lies your way.
  Oswa. My way lies where I please.
Expect (for *Oswald*'s Magick cannot fail)
A long To Morrow, ere your Arms prevail;
Or if I fall, make Room ye blest above,
For one who was undone, and dy'd for Love.   *Exit* Oswald *and his Party.*
Arth. There may be one black Minute ere To Morrow:
For who can tell, what Pow'r, and Lust, and Charms,
May do this Night? To Arms, with speed, to Arms.   *Exit.*

Act III

Enter Arthur, Conon *and* Aurelius
  Con. Furle up our Colours, and Unbrace our Drums;
Dislodge betimes; and quit this fatal Coast.
  Arth. Have we forgot to Conquer?
  Aur. Cast off Hope:
Th' Imbattl'd Legions of Fire, Air, and Earth,
Are banded for our Foes.
For going to discover, with the Dawn,
Yon Southern Hill, which promis'd to the Sight
A Rise more easie to attack the Fort,
Scarce had we stept on the Forbidden Ground,
When the Woods shook, the Trees stood bristling up;
A Living Trembling Nodded through the Leaves.
  Arth. Poplars, and Aspen-Boughs, a Pannick Fright.
  Con. We thought so too, and doubled still our pace.
But strait a rumbling Sound, like bellowing Wings,
Rose and grew loud; confus'd with Howls of Wolves,
And Grunts of Bears; and dreadful Hiss of Snakes;
Shreiks more than Humane; Globes of Hail pour'd down
An Armed Winter, and Inverted Day.
  Arth. Dreadful, indeed!
  Aur. Count then our Labour's lost:
For other way lies none, to mount the Cliff,
Unless we borrow Wings, and sail through Air.
  Arth. Now I perceive a Danger worthy me.
'Tis *Osmond*'s work, a band of Hell-hir'd Slaves:
Be mine the Hazard, mine shall be the Fame.
  Arthur *is going out, but is met by* Merlin, *who takes him by the Hand, and brings him back.*
Enter Merlin
  Mer. Hold, Sir, and wait Heav'ns time; th'Attempts too dangerous.

There's not a Tree in that Inchanted Grove,
But numbred out, and given by tale to Fiends;
And under every Leaf a Spirit couch'd.
But by what Method to dissolve these Charms,
Is yet unknown to me.
    Arth. Hadst thou been here, (for what can thwart thy Skill?)
Nor *Emmeline* had been the boast of *Oswald*;
Nor I, fore-warn'd, been wanting to her Guard.
    Con. Her darkn'd Eyes had seen the Light of Heav'n;
That was thy promise too, and this the time.
    Mer. Nor has my Aid been absent, tho' unseen,
With Friendly Guides in your benighted Maze:
Nor *Emmeline* shall longer want the Sun.
    Arth. Is there an end of Woes?
    Mer. There is, and sudden.
I have employ'd a subtil Airy Spright
T' explore the passage, and prepare my way.
My self, mean time, will view the Magick Wood,
To learn whereon depends its Force.
    Con. But *Emmeline* —
    Mer. Fear not: This Vial shall restore her sight.
    Arth. Oh might I hope (and what's impossible
To *Merlin*'s Art) to be my self the bearer,
That with the Light of Heav'n she may discern
Her Lover first.
    Mer. 'Tis wondrous hazardous;
Yet I foresee th' Event, 'tis fortunate.
I'll bear ye safe, and bring ye back unharm'd:
Then lose not precious Time, but follow me.   *Exeunt Omnes,* Merlin *leading* Arthur.
                Enter Philidel. *Scene, a Deep Wood.*
    Phil. I left all safe behind;
For in the hindmost quarter of the Wood,
My former Lord, Grim *Oswald*, walks the Round:
Calls o'er the Names, and Schools the tardy Sprights.
His Absence gives me more security.
At every Walk I pass'd, I drew a Spell.
So that if any Fiend, abhorring Heav'n,
There sets his Foot, it roots him to the Ground.
Now cou'd I but discover Emmeline,
My Tast were fairly done.   *Walking about, and Prying betwixt the Trees.*
    Enter Grimbald *rushing out: He seizes* Philidel, *and binds him in a chain.*
    Grimb. O Rebel, have I caught thee!
    Phil. Ah me! What hard mishap!
    Grimb. What just Revenge!
Thou miscreant Elf, thou Renegado Scout,
So clean, so furbish'd so renew'd in White,
The Livery of our Foes; I see thee through:
What mak'st thou here? Thou trim Apostate, speak.
Thou shak'st for Fear, I feel thy false Heart Pant.
    Phil. Ah mighty *Grimbald*,
Who would not Fear, when seiz'd in thy strong Gripe;
But hear me, Oh Renown'd, Oh worthy Fiend,

The Favourite of our Chief.

Grimb. Away with fullsome Flattery,
The Food of Fools; thou know'st where last we met,
When but for thee, the Christians had been swallow'd
In quaking Bogs, and Living sent to Hell.

Phil. Aye, then I was seduc'd by *Merlin*'s Art,
And half persuaded by his soothing Tales,
To hope for Heav'n; as if Eternal Doom
Cou'd be Revers'd, and undecreed for me:
But I am now set Right.

Grimb. Oh still thou think'st to fly a Fool to Mark.

Phil. I fled from *Merlin*, free as Air that bore me,
T' unfold to *Osmond* all his deep Designs.

Grimb. I believe nothing, Oh thou fond Impostor,
When wert thou last in Hell? Is not thy Name
Forgot, and Blotted from th' Infernal Roll;
But since thou say'st, thy Errand was to *Osmond*,
To *Osmond* shalt thou go; March, know thy Driver.

Phil. Kneeling. Oh spare me, *Grimbald*, and I'll be thy Slave:
Tempt Hermits for thee, in their Holy Cells,
And Virgins in their Dreams.

Grimb. Canst thou, a Devil, hope to cheat a Devil?
A Spy; why that's a Name abhorr'd in Hell;
Haste forward, forward, or I'll Goad thee on,
With Iron Spurrs.

Phil. But use me kindly then:
Pull not so hard, to hurt my Airy Limbs;
I'll follow thee unforc'd; look, there's thy way.

Grimb. Ay, there's the way indeed; but for more surety
I'll keep an Eye behind: Not one Word more,
But follow decently.   Grimbald *goes out, dragging* Philidel.

Phil. aside. So, catch him Spell.

Grimb. within. Oh help me, help me, Philidel.

Phil. Why, What's the matter?

Grimb. Oh, I am ensnar'd:
Heav'ns Birdlime wraps me round, and glues my Wings.
Loose me, and I will free thee;
Do, and I'll be thy Slave.

Phil. What, to a Spy, a Name abhorr'd in Hell?

Grimb. Do not insult, Oh, Oh, I grow to Ground;
The Fiery Net draws closer on my Limbs.

Phil. Thou shalt not have the Ease to Curse in Torments:
Be Dumb for one half Hour; so long my Charm
Can keep thee Silent, and there lie
Till *Osmond* breaks thy Chain.   Philidel *unbinds his own Fetters.*

          Enter to him Merlin, *with a Vial in his Hand; and Arthur*

Mer. Well hast thou wrought they Safety with thy Wit,
My *Philidel*; go Meritorious on.
Me, other Work requires, to view the Wood,
And learn to make the dire Inchantments void.
Mean time attend King Arthur in my Room;
Shew him his Love, and with these Soveraign Drops

Restore her Sight.   *Exit* Merlin *giving a Vial to* Philidel.

   Phil. *We must work, we must haste;*
Noon-Tyde Hour, is almost past:
Sprights, that glimmer in the Sun,
Into Shades already run.
Osmond *will be here, anon.*

             Enter Emmeline *and* Matilda, *at the far end of the Wood*

   Arth. O yonder, yonder she's already found:
My soul directs my sight, and flies before it.
Now, Gentle Spirit, use thy utmost Art;
Unseal her Eyes; and this way lead her Steps.

            Arthur *withdraws behind the Scene.*
      Emmeline *and* Matilda *come forward to the Front.*
   Philidel *approaches* Emmeline, *sprinkling some of the Water over her Eyes, out of the Vial.*

   Phil. *Thus, thus I infuse*
These Soveraign Dews.
Fly back, ye Films, that Cloud her sight,
And you, ye Chrystal Humours bright,
Your Noxious Vapours purg'd away,
Recover, and admit the Day,
Now cast your Eyes abroad, and see
All but me.

   Em. Ha! What was that? Who spoke?
   Mat. I hear the Voice; 'tis one of *Osmond's* Fiends.
   Em. Some blessed Angel sure; I feel my Eyes
Unseal'd, they walk abroad, and a new World
Comes rushing on, and stands all gay before me.
   Mat. Oh Heavens! Oh Joy of Joys! she has her sight!
   Em. I am new-born; I shall run mad for Pleasure.   *Staring on* Mat.
Are Women such as thou? Such Glorious Creatures?
   Arth. *aside.*] Oh how I envy her, to be first seen!
   Em. Stand farther; let me take my fill of sight.   *Looking up.*
What's that above, that weakens my new Eyes,
Makes me not see, by seeing?
   Mat. 'Tis the Sun.
   Em. The Sun, 'tis sure a God, if that be Heav'n:
Oh, if thou art a Creature, best and fairest,
How well art thou, from Mortals so remote,
To shine, and not to burn, by near approach!
How hast thou light'ned even my very Soul,
And let in Knowledge by another sense!
I gaze about, new-born, to Day and thee;
A Stranger yet, an Infant of the World!
Art thou not pleas'd, *Matilda*? Why, like me,
Dost thou not look and wonder?
Mat. For these Sights
Are to my Eyes familiar.
   Em. That's my joy.
Not to have seen before: For Nature now
Comes all at once, confounding my Delight.
But ah! what Thing am I? Fain wou'd I know;
Or am I blind, or do I see but half?

With all my Care, and, looking round about,
I cannot view my Face.
   Mat. None see themselves,
But by Reflection; in this Glass you may.   *Gives her a Glass.*
   Em. taking the Glass, and looking. What's this?
It holds a Face within it: Oh sweet Face;
It draws the Mouth, and Smiles, and looks upon me;
And talks; but yet I cannot hear it Speak:
The pretty thing is Dumb.
   Mat. The pretty thing
You see within the Glass, is you.
Em. What, am I two? Is this another me?
Indeed it wears my Cloaths, has Hands like mine;
And Mocks what e'er I do; but that I'm sure
I am a Maid, I'd swear it were my Child.   Matilda *looks.*
Look, my *Matilda*; We both are in the Glass,
Oh, now I know it plain; they are our Names
That peep upon us there.
   Mat. Our Shadows, Madam.
   Em. Mine is a prettier Shaddow far, then thine.
I Love it; let me Kiss my to'ther Self.   *Kissing the Glass, and hugging it.*
Alas I've kiss'd it Dead; the fine Thing's gone;
Indeed it Kiss'd so Cold, as if 'twere Dying.
               Arthur *comes forward softly; shewing himself behind her.*
'Tis here again.
Oh no, this Face is neither mine nor thine;
I think the Glass has Born another Child.   *She turns and sees* Arthur.
Ha! What art thou, with a new kind of Face,
And other Cloaths, a Noble Creature too;
But taller, bigger, fiercer in thy Look;
Of a Comptrolling Eye, Majestick make?
   Mat. Do you not know him, Madam?
   Em. Is't a Man?
   Arth. Yes, and the most unhappy of my kind,
If you have chang'd your Love.
   Em. My dearest Lord!
Was my Soul Blind; and cou'd not that look out,
To know you e'er you Spoke? Oh Counterpart
Of our soft Sex; Well are ye made our Lords;
So bold, so great, so God-like are ye form'd.
How an ye Love such silly Things as Women?
   Arth. Beauty like yours Commands: and Man was made
But a more boisterous; and a stronger Slave,
To you, the best Delights of human Kind.
   Em. But are ye mine? Is there an end of War?
Are all those Trumpets Dead themselves, at last,
That us'd to kill Men with their Thundring Sounds?
   Arth. The Sum of War is undecided yet:
And many a breathig Body must be Cold,
Ere you are free.
   Em. How came ye hither then?
   Arth. By *Merlin*'s Art, to snatch a short-liv'd Bliss:

To feed my Famish'd Love upon your Eyes
One Moment, and depart.
    Em. O Moment, worth —
Whole Ages past, and all that are to come!
Let Love-sick *Oswald*, now, unpitied mourn;
Let *Osmond* mutter Charms to Sprights in vain,
To make me Love him; all shall not change my Soul.
    Arth. Ha! Des the Inchanter practice Hell upon you?
Is he my Rival too?
    Em. Yes, but I hate him;
For when he spoke, through my shut Eyes I saw him;
His Voice look'd ugly, and breath'd Brimstone on me:
And then I first was glad that I was Blind,
Not to behold Damnation.
    Phil. This time is left me to Congratulate
Your new-born Eyes; and tell you what you gain
By sight restor'd and viewing him you love.
Appear, you Airy Forms: *Airy Spirits appear in the Shapes of Men and Women.*
    Man sings. *O Sight, the Mother of Desires,*
What Charming Objects dost thou yield!
   'Tis sweet, when tedious Night expires,
To see the Rosie Morning guild
   The Mountain-Tops, and paint the Field!
But, when Clorinda *comes in sight,*
She makes the Summers Day more bright;
And when she goes away, 'tis Night.
    Chor. *When Fair* Clorinda *comes in sight,* &c.
    Wom. sings. *'Tis sweet the Blushing Morn to view;*
And Plains adorn'd with Pearly Dew:
But such cheap Delights to see,
   Heaven and Nature,
   Give each Creature;
They have Eyes as well as we.
This is the Joy, all Joys above
   To see, to see,
   That only she,
That only she we love!
    Chor. *This is the Joy, all Joys above,* &c.
    Man sings. *And, if we may discover,*
What Charms both Nymph and Lover,
'Tis, when the Fair at Mercy lies,
With Kind and Amorous Anguish,
To Sigh, to Look, to Languish,
On each others Eyes!
    Chor. of all Men & Wom. *And if we may discover,* &c.
    Phil. Break off your Musick; for our Foes are near.   *Spirits vanish.*
                    Enter Merlin
    Merl. My Soveraign, we have hazarded too far;
But Love excuses you, and prescience me.
Make haste; for *Osmond* is even now alarm'd,
And greedy of Revenge, is hasting home.
    Arth. Oh take my Love with us, or leave me here.

Merl. I cannot, for she's held my Charms too strong:
Which, with th' Inchanted Grove must be destroy'd;
Till when, my Art is vain: But fear not, *Emmeline*;
Th' Enchanter has no Pow'r on Innocence.

Em. to Arth. Farewel, Since we must part: When you are gone,
I'll look into my Glass, just where you look'd;
To find your Face again;
If 'tis not there, I'll think on you so long,
My Heart shall make your Picture for my Eyes.

Arth. Where'e'er I go, my Soul shall stay with thee:
'Tis but me Shadow that I take away;
True Love is never happy but by halves;
An *April* Sun-shine, that by fits appears,
It smiles by Moments, but it mourns by Years.

Exeunt Arthur *and* Merlin *at one Door.*
Enter Osmond *at the other Door, who gazes on* Emmeline, *and she on him*

Em. Matilda save me, from this ugly Thing,
This Foe to sight, Speak, dost thou know him:

Matil. Too well; 'tis *Oswald's* Friend, the great Magician.

Em. It cannot be a Man, he's so unlike the Man I Love.

Osm. aside. Death to my Eyes, she sees!

Em. I wish I cou'd not; but I'll close my Sight,
And shut out all I can — It wo'not be;
Winking, I see thee still, thy odious Image
Stares full into my Soul; and thre infects the Room
My *Arthur* shou'd possess.

Osm. aside. I find too late,
That *Merlin* and her Lover have been here.
If I was fir'd before, when she was Blind,
Her Eyes dark Lightning now, she must be mine.

Em. I prithee Dreadful Thing, tell me thy Business here;
And if thou canst, Reform that odious Face;
Look not so Grim upon me.

Osm. My Name is *Osmond*, and my Business Love.

Em. Thou hast a griezly look; forbidding what thou ask'st,
If I durst tell thee so.

Osm. My Pent-House Eye-Brows, and my Shaggy Beard
Offend your Sight, but these are Manly Signs;
Faint White and Red, abuse your Expectations;
Be Woman, know your Sex, and Love full Pleasures.

Em. Love from a Monster, Fiend!

Osm. Come you must Love, or you must suffer Love;
No Coiness, None, for I am Master here.

Em. And when did *Oswald* give away his Power,
That thou presum'st to Rule? Be sure I'll tell him:
For as I am his Prisoner, he is mine.

Osm. Why then thou art a Captive to a Captive.
O'er labour'd with the Fight, opprest with Thirst:
That *Oswald* whom you mention'd call'd for Drink:
I mix'd a Sleepy Potion in his Bowl:
Which he and his Fool Friend, quaff'd greedily,
The happy Dose wrought the desir'd effect;

Then to a Dungeons depth, I sent both Bound:
Where stow'd with Snakes and Adders now they lodge;
Two Planks their Beds; Slippery with Oose and Slime:
The Ratts brush o'er their Faces with their Tails;
And croaking Paddocks crawl upon their Limbs.
Since when the Garison depends on me;
Now know you are my Slave.
   Mat. He strikes a Horrour through my Blood.
   Em. I Freeze, as if his Impious Art had fix'd
My Feet to Earth.
   Osm. But Love shall thaw ye.
I'll show his force in Countries cak'd with Ice,
Where the pale Pole-Star in the North of Heav'n
Sits high, and on the frory Winter broods;
Yet there Love Reigns: For proof, this Magick Wand
Shall change the Mildness of sweet *Britains* Clime
To *Yzeland*, and the farthest *Thule*'s Frost;
Where the proud God, disdaining Winters Bounds,
O'er-leaps the Fences of Eternal Snow,
And with his Warmth, supplies the distant Sun.

Osmond Strikes the Ground with his Wand:

The Scene changes to a Prospect of Winter in Frozen Countries.

Cupid Descends

   Cup. sings. *What ho, thou* Genius *of the Clime, what ho!*
   Ly'st thou asleep beneath those Hills of Snow?
Stretch out thy Lazy Limbs; Awake, awake,
And Winter from thy Furry Mantle shake.

Genius Arises

   Genius. *What Power art thou, who from below,*
   Hast made me Rise, unwillingly, and slow.
From Beds of Everlasting Snow!
See'st thou not how stiff, and wondrous old,
Far unfit to bear the bitter Cold,
I can scarely move, or draw my Breath;
Let me, let me, Freeze again to Death.
   Cupid. *Thou Doting Fool, forbear, forbear;*
What, Dost thou Dream of Freezing here?
At Loves appearing, all the Skie clearing,
   The Stormy Winds, their Fury spare:
Winter subduing, and Spring renewing,
   My Beams create a more Glorious Year.
Thou Doting Fool, forbear, forbear;
What, Dost thou Dream of Freezing here?
   Genius. *Great Love, I know thee now;*
Eldest of the Gods art Thou:
Heav'n and Earth, by Thee were made.
   Humane Nature,
   Is Thy Creature,
Every where Thou art obey'd.
   Cupid. *No part of my Dominion shall be waste,*
   To spread my Sway, and sing my Praise,
   Ev'n here I will a People raise,

Of kind embracing Lovers, and embrac'd.
    Cupid *waves his Wand, upon which the Scene opens, and discovers a Prospect of Ice and*
                    Snow to the end of the Stage.
                Singers and Dancers, Men and Women, appear.
  Man. *See, see, we assemble.*
Thy Revels to hold:
Though quiv'ring with Cold,
We Chatter and Tremble.
    Cupid. *'Tis I, 'tis I, 'tis I, that have warm'd ye;*
In spight of Cold Weather,
I've brought ye together:
'Tis I, 'tis I, 'tis I, that have arm'd ye.
    Chor. *'Tis Love, 'tis Love, 'tis Love that has warm'd us.*
In spight of Cold Weather
He brought us together:
'Tis Love, 'tis Love, 'tis Love that has arm'd us.
    Cupid. *Sound a Parley, ye Fair, and surrender;*
Set your selves, and your Lovers at ease;
He's a Grateful Offender
Who Pleasure dare seize:
But the Whining Pretender
Is sure to displease.
Since the Fruit of Desire is possessing
'Tis Unmanly to Sigh and Complain;
When we Kneel for Redressing,
We move your Disdain:
Love was made for a Blessing,
And not for a Pain.   *A Dance; after which the Singers and Dancers depart*
    Em. I cou'd be pleas'd with any one but thee,
Who entertain'd my sight with such Gay Shows,
As Men and Women moving here and there,
That Coursing one another in their Steps,
Have made their Feet a Tune.
    Osmo. What, Coying it again!
No more; but make me happy to my Gust,
That is, without your struggling.
    Em. From my sight,
Thou all thy Devils in one, thou dar'st not force me.
    Osmo. You teach me well, I find you wou'd be Ravish'd;
I'll give you that excuse your Sex desires.
                 He begins to lay hold on her, and they struggle.
    Grimb. *within.* O help me, Master, help me!
    Osmo. Who's that, my *Grimbald*! Come and help thou me:
For 'tis thy Work t'assist a Ravisher.
    Grimb. *within.* I cannot stir; I am Spell-caught by *Philidel*,
And purs'd within a Net. With a huge heavy weight of Holy Words,
Laid on my Head, that keeps me down from rising.
    Osmo. I'll read 'em backwards, and release thy Bonds:
Mean time go in: —   *To* Emmeline.
Prepare your self, and ease my Drudgery:
But if you will not fairly be enjoy'd,
A little honest Force is well employ'd.   *Exit* Osmond.

Em. Heav'n be my Guard, I have no other Friend!
Heav'n ever present to thy Suppliants Aid,
Protect and pity Innocence betray'd.   *Exeunt* Emmeline *and* Matilda.

ACT IV SCENE I
Enter Osmond, *Solus*

Osmo. Now I am settled in my Force-full Sway;
Why then, I'll be Luxurious in my Love;
Take my full Gust, and setting Forms aside,
I'll bid the Slave, that fires my Blood, lie down.   *Seems to be going off.*
Enter Grimbald, *who meets him*

Grimb. No so fast, Master, Danger threatens thee:
There's a black Cloud descending from above,
Full of Heavens Venom, bursting o'er thy Head.

Osmo. Malicious Fiend, thou ly'st: For I am fenc'd
By Millions of thy Fellows, in my Grove:
I bad thee, when I freed thee from the Charm,
Run scouting through the Wood, from Tree to Tree,
And look if all my Devils were on Duty:
Hadst thou perform'd thy Charge, thou tardy Spright,
Thou wouldst have known no Danger threatn'd me.

Grim. When did a Devil fail in Diligence?
Poor Mortal, thou thy self art overseen;
I have been there, and thence I bring this News.
Thy Fatal Foe, great *Arthur*, is at hand;
Merlin has ta'en his time while thou wert absent,
T' observe thy Characters, their Force, and Nature,
And Counterwork thy Spells.

Osmo. The Devil take *Merlin*;
I'll cast 'em all anew, and instantly,
All of another Mould; be thou at hand.
Their Composition was, before, of Horror;
Now they shall be of Blandishment, and Love;
Seducing Hopes, soft Pity, tender Moans:
Art shall meet Art; and, when they think to win,
The Fools shall find their Labour to begin.   *Exeunt* Osm. *and* Grimb.
Enter Arthur, *and* Merlin *at another Door.*
Scene of the Wood continues.

Mer. Thus far it is permitted me to go;
But all beyond this Spot, is fenc'd with Charms;
I may no more; but only with advice.

Arth. My Sword shall do the rest.

Mer. Remember well, that all is but Illusion;
Go on; good Stars attend thee.

Arth. Doubt me not.

Mer. Yet in prevention
Of what may come, I'll leave my *Philidel*
To watch thy Steps, and with him leave my Wand;
The touch of which, no Earthy Fiend can bear,
In whate'er Shape transform'd, but must lay down
His borrow'd Figure, and confess the Devil.
Once more Farewel, and prosper.   *Exit* Merlin.

Arth. walking. No Danger yet, I see no Walls of Fire,
No City of the Fiends, with Forms obscene,
To grin from far, on Flaming Battlements.
This is indeed the Grove I shou'd destroy;
But where's the Horrour? Sure the Prophet err'd.
Hark! Musick, and the warbling Notes of Birds;   *Soft Musick.*
Hell entertains me, like some welcom Guest.
More Wonders yet; yet all delightful too,
A Silver Current to forbid my passage,
And yet to invite me, stands a Golden Bridge:
Perhaps a Trap, for my Unwary Feet
To sink, and whelm me underneath the Waves;
With Fire or Water, let him wage his War,
Or all the Elements at once; I'll on.
     As he is going to the Bridge, two Syrens *arise from the Water;*
        They shew themselves to the Waste, & Sing.

   I Syren. *O pass not on, but stay,*
And waste the Joyous Day
With us in gentle Play:
Unbend to Love, unbend thee:
O lay thy Sword aside,
And other Arms provide;
For other Wars attend thee,
And sweeter to be try'd.
   Chor. *For other Wars,* &c.
   Both Sing. *Two Daughters of this Aged Stream are we;*
And both our Sea-green Locks have comb'd for thee;
Come Bathe with us an Hour or two,
Come Naked in, for we are so;
What Danger from a Naked Foe?
Come Bathe with us, come Bathe, and share,
What Pleasures in the Floods appear;
We'll beat the Waters till they bound,
And Circle round, around, around,
And Circle round, around.

   Arth. A Lazie Pleasure trickles through my Veins;
Here could I stay, and well be Couzen'd here.
But Honour calls; Is Honour in such haste?
Can he not Bait at such a pleasing Inn?
No; for the more I look, the more I long;
Farewel, ye Fair Illusions, I must leave ye.
While I have Power to say, that I must leave ye.
Farewel, with half my Soul I stagger off;
How dear this flying Victory has cost,
When, if I stay to struggle, I am lost.
     As he is going forward, Nymphs *and* Sylvans *come out from behind the Trees.*
      Base and two Trebles sing the following Song *to a* Minuet.
       Dance with the Song, all with Branches in their Hands.

   Song. *How happy the Lover,*
How easie his Chain,
How pleasing his Pain?

How sweet to discover!
He sighs not in vain.
For Love every Creature
Is form'd by his Nature;
No Joys are above
The Pleasures of Love.   *The Dance continues with the Measure play'd alone.*

In vain are our Graces
In vain are your Eyes,
If Love you despise;
When Age furrows Faces,
'Tis time to be wise.
Then use the short Blessing:
That Flies in Possessing:
No Joys are above
The Pleasures of Love.

   Arth. And what are these Fantastick Fairy Joys,
To Love like mine? False Joys, false Welcomes all,
Begone, ye *Sylvan* Trippers of the Green;
Fly after Night, and overtake the Moon.
                Here the Dancers, Singers and Syrens vanish.
This goodly Tree seems Queen of all the Grove.
The Ringlets round her Trunk declare her guilty
Of many Midnight-Sabbaths Revell'd here.
Her will I first attempt.   Arthur *strikes at the Tree, and cuts it;*
           Blood spouts out of it, a Groan follows, then a Shreik.
Good Heav'ns, what Monstrous Prodigies are these!
Blood follows from my blow; the wounded Rind
Spouts on my Sword, and Sanguine dyes the Plain.
         He strikes again: A Voice of Emmeline *from behind.*
   Em. from behind. Forbear, if thou hast Pity, ah, forbear!
These Groans proceed not from a Senceless Plant,
No Spouts of Blood run welling from a Tree.
   Arth. Speak what thou art; I charge thee speak thy Being;
Thou that hast made my curdl'd Blood run back,
My Heart heave up; my Hair to rise in Bristles,
And scarcely left a Voice to ask thy Name.
         Emmeline *breaks out of the Tree, shewing her Arm Bloody.*
   Em. Whom thou hast hurt, Unkind and Cruel see;
Look on this Blood, 'tis fatal, still, to me
To bear thy Wounds, my Heart has felt 'em first.
   Arth. 'Tis she; Amazement roots me to the Ground!
   Em. By cruel Charms, dragg'd from my peaceful Bower,
Fierce *Osmond* clos'd me in this bleeding Bark;
And bid me stand expos'd to the bleak Winds,
And Winter Storms; and Heav'ns Inclemency,
Bound to the Fate of this Hell-haunted Grove;
So that whatever Sword, or sounding Axe,
Shall violate this Plant, must pierce my Flesh,
And when that falls, I dye. —
   Arth. If this be true,

O never, never, to be ended Charm,
At least by me; yet all may be Illusion.
Break up, ye thickning Foggs, and filmy Mists,
All that be-lye my Sight, and Cheat my Sense.
For Reason still pronounces, 'tis not she,
And thus resolv'd —   *Lifts up his Sword, as going to strike.*
   Em. Do, strike *Barbarian*, strike;
And strew my mangled Limbs, with every stroke
Wound me, and double Kill me, with Unkindness,
That by thy Hand I fell.
   Arth. What shall I do, ye Powers?
   Em. Lay down thy Vengeful Sword; 'tis fatal here:
What need of Arms, where no Defence is made?
A Love-Sick Virgin, panting with Desire,
No Conscious Eye t' intrude on our Delights:
For this thou hast the *Syren*'s Songs despis'd;
For this, thy Faithful Passion I Reward;
Haste then, to take me longing to thy Arms.
   Arth. O Love! O *Merlin*! Whom should I believe?
   Em. Believe thy Self, thy Youth, thy Love, and me;
They only, they who please themselves, are Wise:
Disarm thy Hand, that mine may meet it bare.
   Arth. By thy leave, Reason, here I throw thee off,
Thou load of Life: If thou wert made for Souls,
Then Souls shou'd have been made without their Bodies.
If, falling for the first Created Fair,
Was *Adam*'s Fault, great Grandsire I forgive thee,
Eden was lost, as all thy Sons wou'd loose it.
               Going towards Emmeline, *and pulling off his Gauntlet.*
               Enter Philidel *running*
Phil. Hold, poor deluded Mortal, hold thy Hand;
Which if thou giv'st, is plighted to a Fiend.
For Proof, behold the Virtue of this Wand;
Th' Infernal paint shall vanish from her Face,
And Hell shall stand Reveal'd.   *Strikes* Emmeline *with a Wand, who straight descends:*
         Philidel *runs to the Descent, and pulls up* Grimbald, *and binds him.*
Now see to whose Embraces thou wert falling.
Behold the Maiden Modesty of Grimbald,
The grossest, earthiest, ugliest Fiend in Hell.
   Arth. Horrour seizes me,
To think what Headlong Ruine I have tempted.
   Phil. Haste to thy Work; a Noble stroke or two
Ends all the Charms, and disenchants the Grove.
I'll hold thy Mistress bound.
   Arth. Then here's for Earnest;   *Strikes twice or thrice, and the Tree falls, or sinks:*
         A Peal of Thunder immediately follows, with dreadful Howlings.
'Tis finish'd, and the Dusk that yet remains,
Is but the Native Horrour of the Wood.
But I must lose no time; the Pass is free;
Th' unroosted Fiends have quitted this Abode;
On yon proud Towers, before the day be done,
My glittering Banners shall be wav'd against the setting Sun.   *Exit* Arthur.

Phil. Come on my surly Slave; come stalk along,
And stamp a mad-Man's pace, and drag thy Chain.
   Grim. I'll Champ and Foam upon't, till the blue Venom
Work upward to thy Hands, and loose their hold.
   Phil. Know'st thou this powerful Wand; 'tis lifted up,
A second stroke wou'd send thee to the Centre,
Benumb'd and Dead, as far as Souls can Die.
   Grim. I wou'd thou wou'dst, to rid me of my Sense:
I shall be whoop'd through Hell at my return,
Inglorious from the Mischief I design'd.
   Phil. And therefore since thou loath'st Etherial Light,
The Morning Sun shall beat on thy black Brows;
The Breath thou draw'st shall be of upper Air,
Hostile to thee; and to thy Earthy make,
So light, so thin, that thou sha't Starve, for want
Of thy gross Food, till gasping thou shalt lie,
And blow it back, all Sooty to the Sky.   *Exit* Philidel, *dragging* Grimbald *after him.*

ACT V

Enter Osmond *as affrighted*
   Osm. Grimbald made Prisoner, and my Grove destroy'd!
Now what can save me — Hark the Drums and Trumpets!   *Drums and Trumpets within.*
Arthur is marching onward to the Fort,
I have but one Recourse, and that's to *Oswald*;
But will he Fight for me, whom I have injur'd?
No, not for me, but for himself he must;
I'll urge him with the last Necessity;
Better give up my Mistress than my Life.
His force is much unequal to his Rival;
True; — But I'll help him with my utmost Art,
And try t' unravel Fate.   *Exit* Osmond.
               Enter Arthur, Conon, Aurelius, Albanact, *and Soldiers*
   Con. Now there remains but this one Labour more;
And if we have the Hearts of true Born *Britains*
The forcing of that Castle Crowns the Day.
   Aur. The Works are weak, the Garison but thin,
Dispirited with frequent Overthrows,
Already wavering on their ill mann'd Walls.
   Alb. They shift their places oft, and sculk from War,
Sure signs of pale Despair, and easie Rout;
It shews they place their Confidence in Magick,
And when their Devils fail, their Hearts are Dead.
   Arth. Then, where you see 'em clust'ring most, in Motion,
And staggering in their Ranks, there press 'em home;
For that's a Coward heap — How's this, a Sally?
               Enter Oswald, Guillamar, *and Soldiers on the other side*
Beyond my Hopes, to meet 'em on the square.
   Osw. advancing. Brave *Britains* hold; and thou their famous Chief
Attend what *Saxon Oswald* will propose.
He owns your Victory; but whether owing
To Valour, or to Fortune, that he doubts.

If *Arthur* dares ascribe it to the first
And singl'd out from a Crowd, will tempt a Conquest,
This *Oswald* Offers, let our Troops retire,
And Hand to Hand, let us decide our Strife:
This if Refus'd, bear Witness Earth and Heaven,
Thou steal'st a Crown and Mistess undeserv'd.

   Arth. I'll not Usurp thy Title of a Robber,
Nor will upbraid thee, that before I proffer'd
This single Combat, which thou didst avoid;
So glad I am, on any Terms to meet thee,
And not discourage thy Repenting shame;
As once *Eneas* my Fam'd Ancestor,
Betwixt the *Trojan* and *Rutilian* Bands,
Fought for a Crown, and bright *Lavinia's* Bed,
So will I meet thee, Hand to Hand oppos'd:
My Auguring Mind, assures the same Success.

   To his Men. Hence out of view; If I am Slain, or yield,
Renounce me Britains for the Recreant Knight,
And let the Saxon peacefully enjoy
His former footing in our famous Isle.
To Ratifie these Terms, I swear —

   Osw. You need not;
Your Honour is of Force, without your Oath
I only add, that if I fall, or yield,
Yours be the Crown, and Emmeline.

   Arth. That's two Crowns.
No more; we keep the looking Heav'ns and Sun
Too long in Expectation of our Arms.

*Both Armies go clear off the Stage. They Fight with Spunges in their Hands dipt in Blood,
after some equal Passes and Closeing, they appear both Wounded*: Arthur *Stumbles among
the Trees,* Oswald *falls over him, they both Rise*; Arthur *Wounds him again, then* Oswald
Retreats. Enter Osmond *from among the Trees, and with his Wand, strikes* Arthur's *Sword
out of his Hand, and* Exit. Oswald *pursues* Arthur. Merlin *enters, and gives* Arthur *his
Sword, and* Exit, *they close, and* Arthur *in the fall, disarms* Oswald.

Arth. Confess thy self o'ercome, and ask thy Life.
Osw. 'Tis not worth asking, when 'tis in thy Power.
Arth. Then take it as my Gift.
Osw. A wretched Gift,
With loss of Empire, Liberty, and Love.

> *A Consort of Trumpets within, proclaiming* Arthur's *Victory,
> while they sound,* Arthur *and* Oswald *seem to Confer.*

   'Tis too much Bounty to a vanquish'd Foe;
Yet not enough to make me Fortunate.

   Arth. Thy Life, thy Liberty, thy Honour Safe,
Lead back thy Saxons to their Ancient Elb:
I wou'd Restore thee fruitful *Kent*, the Gift
Of *Vortigern* for *Hengist*'s ill bought aid,
But that my *Britains* brook no Foreign Power,
To Lord it in a Land, Sacred to Freedom;
And of its Rights, Tenacious to the last.
Osw. Nor more then thou hast ofer'd wou'd I take.
I wou'd Refuse all *Britain*, held in Homage;

And own no other Masters but the Gods.
Enter on one side; Merlin, Emmeline, *and* Matilda. Conon, Aurelius, Albanact, *with British Soldiers, bearing King* Arthur's *Standard display'd.*
On the other side; Guillamar *and* Osmond, *with Saxon Soldiers, dragging their Colours on the Ground.*

Arth. *going to* ⎫ At length, at length, I have thee in my Arms;
Emm. *and em-* ⎬ Tho' our Malevolent Stars have strugled hard,
bracing her. ⎭ And held us long asunder:

   Em. We are so fitted for each others Hearts,
That Heav'n had err'd, in making of a third,
To get betwixt, and intercept our Loves.

   Osw. Were there but this, this only sight to see,
The price of Britain shou'd not buy my stay.

   Merl. Take hence that Monster of Ingratitude,
Him, who betray'd his Master, bear him hence,
And in that loathsom Dungeon plunge him deep,
Where he plung'd Noble *Oswald.*

   Osm. That indeed is fittest for me,
For there I shall be near my Kindred Fiends,
And spare my *Grimbald*'s Pains to bear me to 'em.   *Is carried off.*

   Mer. to *Arth.* For this Days Palm, and for thy former Acts,
Thy *Britain* freed, and Foreign Force expell'd,
Thou, *Arthur,* hast acquir'd a future Fame,
And of three Christian Worthies, art the first:
And now at once, to treat thy Sight and Soul,
Behold what Rouling Ages shall produce:
The Wealth, the Loves, the Glories of our Isle,
Which yet like Golden Oar, unripe in Beds,
Expect the Warm Indulgency of Heav'n
To call 'em forth to Light —
To *Osw.* Nor thou, brave Saxon Prince, disdain our Triumphs;
Britains and Saxons shall be once one People;
One Common Tongue, one Common Faith shall bind
Our Jarring Bands, in a perpetual Peace.

           Merlin *waves his Wand; the Scene changes, and discovers*
      the British Ocean in a Storm. Æolus *in a Cloud above: Four Winds hanging,* &c.

   Æolus singing. *Ye Blust'ring Brethren of the Skies,*
Whose Breath has ruffl'd all the Watry Plain,
Retire, and let Britannia *Rise*
In Triumph o'er the Main.
Serene and Calm, and void of fear,
The Queen of Islands must appear;
Serene and Calm, as when the Spring
The New-Created World began,
And Birds on Boughs did softly sing,
Their Peaceful Hmage paid to Man,
While Eurus *did his Blasts forbear,*
In favour of the Tender Year.
Retreat, Rude Winds, Retreat
To Hollow Rocks, your Stormy Seat;
There swell your Lungs, and vainly, vainly threat

                    Æolus *ascends, and the four Winds fly off.*

The Scene opens, and discovers a calm Sea, to the end of the House.
An Island *arises, to a soft Tune;* Britannia *seated in the* Island, *with Fishermen at her Feet, &c.*
The Tune changes; the Fishermen come ashore, and Dance a while;
After which, Pan *and a* Nereide *come on the Stage, and sing.*
Pan *and* Nereide *Sing.*

   Round thy Coasts, Fair Nymph of Britain,
     For thy Guard our Waters flow:
   Proteus *all his Herd admitting,*
     On thy Greens to Graze below.
   Foreign Lands thy Fishes Tasting,
   Learn from thee Luxurious Fasting.

Song of three Parts.

   For Folded Flocks, on Fruitful Plains,
   The Shepherds and the Farmers Gains,
   Fair Britain *all the World outvyes:*
   And Pan, *as in* Arcadia *Reigns,*
   Where Pleasure mixt with Profit lyes.

   Though Jasons *Office was Fam'd of old,*
   The British *Wool is growing Gold;*
   No Mines can more of Wealth supply:
   It keeps the Peasant from the Cold,
   And takes for Kings the Tyrian *Dye.*

   The last *Stanza* sung over again betwixt *Pan* and the *Nereide.*
   After which the former Dance is varied, and goes on.

Enter Comus *with three Peasants, who sing the following song in Parts.*

Com.   *Your Hay it is Mow'd, & your Corn is Reap'd;*
      Your Barns will be full, and your Hovels heap'd:
       Come, my Boys, come;
       Come, my Boys, come;
      And merrily Roar out Harvest Home;
       Harvest Home,
       Harvest Home;
      And merrily Roar out Harvest Home.
Chorus. *Come, my Boys, come, &c.*

I. Man. *We ha' cheated the Parson, we'll cheat him agen;*
      For why shou'd a Blockhead ha' One in Ten?
       One in Ten,
       One in Ten;
      For why shou'd a Blockhead ha' One in Ten?
Chorus. *One in Ten,*
      One in Ten;
      For why shou'd a Blockhead ha' One in Ten?

2. *For Prating so long like a Book-learn'd Sot,*
      Till Pudding and Dumplin burn to Pot;
       Burn to Pot,

Burn to Pot;
Till Pudding and Dumplin burn to Pot.
Chorus. *Burn to Pot,* &c.

3. *We'll toss off our Ale till we canno' stand,*
   And Hoigh for the Honour of Old England:
       Old England,
       Old England;
   And Hoigh for the Honour of Old England.
Chorus. *Old* England, *&c.*
           The Dance vary'd into a round Country-Dance.
                   Enter Venus.

Venus.   *Fairest Isle, all Isles Excelling,*
         Seat of Pleasures, and of Loves;
         Venus here, will chuse her Dwelling,
         And forsake her Cyprian *Groves.*

         Cupid *From his Fav'rite Nation,*
         Care and Envy will Remove;
         Jealousie, that poysons Passion,
         And Despair that dies for Love.

         Gentle Murmurs, sweet Complaining,
         Sighs that blow the Fire of Love;
         Soft Repulses, kind Disdaining,
         Shall be all the Pains you prove.

         Every Swain shall pay his Duty,
         Grateful every Nymph shall prove;
         And as these Excel in Beauty,
         Those shall be Renown'd for Love;

                   SONG by Mr. *HOWE*

She.   *You say, 'Tis Love Creates the Pain,*
         Of which so sadly you Complain;
         And yet wou'd fain Engage my Heart
         In that uneasie cruel part:
         But how, Alas! think you, that I,
         Can bear the Wound of which you die?

He.   *'Tis not my Passion makes my Care,*
         But your Indiff'rence gives Dispair:
         The Lusty Sun begets no Spring,
         Till Gentle Show'rs Assistance bring:
         So Love that Scorches, and Destroys,
         Till Kindness Aids, can cause no Joys.

She.   *Love has a Thousand Ways to please,*
         But more to rob us of our Ease:
         For Wakeful Nights, and Careful Days,

Some Hours of Pleasure he repays;
But Absence soon, or Jealous Fears,
O'erflow the Joys with Floods of Tears.

He.　　*By vain and senseless Forms betray'd,*
Harmless Love's th' Offender made;
While we no other Pains endure,
Than those, that we our selves procure:
But one soft Moment makes Amends
For all the Torment that attends.

Chorus of Both.

Let us love, let us love, and to Happiness haste;
Age and Wisdom come too fast:
Youth for Loving was design'd.
He alone. *I'll be constant, you be kind.*
She alone. *You be constant, I'll be kind.*
Both. *Heav'n can give no greater Blessing*
Than faithful Love, and kind Possessing.

After the Dialogue, a Warlike Consort:
The Scene opens above, and discovers the Order of the Garter.
Enter Honour, *Attended by* Hero's.
Merl. These who last enter'd, are our Valiant *Britains*,
Who shall by Sea and Land Repel our Foes.
Now look above, and in Heav'ns High Abyss,
Behold what Fame attends those future Hero's.
Honour, who leads 'em to that Steepy Height,
In her Immortal Song, shall tell the rest.

Honour sings.

Hon.　　*St.* George, *the Patron of our Isle,*
A Soldier, and a Saint,
On that Auspicious Order smile,
Which Love and Arms will plant.

Our Natives not alone appear
To Court this Martiall Prize;
But Foreign Kings, Adopted here,
Their Crowns at Home despise.

Our Soveraign High, in Aweful State,
His Honours shall bestow;
And see his Scepter'd Subjects wait
On his Commands below.

A full Chorus of the whole Song: After Which the Grand Dance.

Arth. to Merl. Wisely you have, whate'er will please, reveal'd,
What wou'd displease, as wisely have conceal'd:
Triumphs of War and Peace, at full ye show,

But swiftly turn the Pages of our Wo.
Rest we contented with our present State;
'Tis Anxious to enquire of future Fate;
That Race of Hero's is enough alone
For all unseen Disasters to atone.
Let us make haste betimes to Reap our share,
And not Resign them all the Praise of War.
But set th' Example; and their Souls Inflame,
To Copy out their Great Forefathers Fame.

THE ARGUMENT BETWEEN MERLIN AND MORIEN

by Elias Ashmole

THIS CURIOUS WORK is found among the copious manuscripts collected by the great seventeenth-century antiquarian Elias Ashmole. He included a fragment of the text in his *Theatrum Chemicum Britannicum*, an astonishing collection of alchemical and mystical source material compiled by him and published in 1652. A longer version, also apparently collected by Ashmole, is to be found in the Bodleian Library, Oxford (MS Ashmole 1445 vi. 27). The poem's only editor, F. Sherwood Anderson, commented that its language suggested that it was written towards the end of the fifteenth century. Most of the poem is taken up with an extended allegory describing the alchemical process and includes several names (Redrosman, Alkade, Osmura), which are unknown in most Western alchemical writings.

The poem reminds us that Merlin became a figure in whom all the subtle arts and sciences were vested. It is little wonder that a presentation of alchemy used the traditional form of a dialogue with Merlin as one of the protagonists. It is interesting to compare this text with the description of the creation given in the *Vita Merlini* (see Part 2), where Merlin and Taliesin discuss the making of the heavens and the creatures which live thereon. A world of learning and pseudo-knowledge separates the two, yet we cannot help feeling that the two bards would have felt at home with the unknown author of this poem.

The Argument between Morien the Father & Merline the Sonne;
How the Philosophers Stone Should be Wrought.

Son: As the Child Merlin sat on hys father's knee.
Blesse me Father he said for love and Charitie
For I have sought divers Countryes to and fro

And so will I yet do many mo,
To seeke Philosophy that Clarkes do reade
If I coude of the perfect knowledge thereof spede
And ther for ffather for charite
Som good comfort herin give thou me.

Fa: Son seech goodnes that grace thereof mai spryng
For fortune may be with thee by vertuous lyvyng.

Son: Quoth Merlyn wyth grace Father we must bigyn
Or else good end can we non ever wyn
Nowe dere Father for Chariti saye the
In thys Scyence now help thou me
I have sought and enquired ther for mani a day
But yet my purpose therein I coude never get I say
And ther for in mani wildsome Cuntrys have I gon
But as yet perfeit Elixir coude I find non.

Fa: What sekest thou therefor sayd Morien
All thie tyme therein thou spendest in vayne
Much Philosophy thou maist finde in Scripture

Son: Alle to mych quoth Merlyn for therin is but lytle sure
And therfor Father myne a vowe to mani have I made
That I will have one point therin that never was yet had.

Fa: It ys ympossible quoth Morien I wynn
For as good Philosophers bifor hath bynn
As ever was, or any other since thou wert borne
Wher for thy labor is alle forlorne
For reason would that he shoulde have the best
And ther for desyne thou now but that or the next.

Son: Never none quoth Merlyn as yet coude I fynde
For all they worketh agaynst nature and kynde
ffor they that Salte and Corasives do take
No cleane mettall can they ever make
ffor yt hath so much of saltnes
That yt swelleth it sone and makyth it full of rankness
Worke yt by nature and it shall not be soe
For thus thie work would alwayes be do.

Fa: Wythout Salte quoth Morien thou canst nought doe
Son: Naye quoth Merlyn ther schale come non therto
For yt ys but a poesie of Phylosofrys words derke
What weene ye ffurther that God wyll miracle warke.
Weene ye to graff good Peres upon an Elder tree
Or Cheryes on a Cole Stock nay nay father yt wyl not be
For brambles wyl beare no grapes greene
Nor the Walnut tre beare good Aples I weene
And ther for graff kyndly yee that graffers be
And then ye schale have good frute, prove and se
Braunches that be graff on stoke good and sure
The frute therof schale never rott but ever endure.
And yt schalbe the sweter of swete savour
And more comly of fresh colour
And thus worke by Nature kynde and cunning
For every nature by kynde hys nature wyll forthbring
And there for I preve the work all contrary

	For God never made thynge but one naturally
	And that was mankynde alone
	For all in other thyngs, nature is none.
Fa:	Yes quoth Morien and that schale I preve
Son:	Not by Astronomi quoth Merlyn I doe beleve
	For Man was made of one Nature I se
Fa:	One nature quoth Moryen what mai yt be
Son:	Of fowle corruption quoth Merlyn I weene
	And of a fowle matter that was unclene
	And that matter was tempered with the Elementes alle
	Wythout wych Elements no man mai live and yt prove I schale
	For God made the Elements hymselfe
	And so he dyd the Planets and sygnes twelfe
	And alsoe God made Man after hys owne lyknesse
	And Planets and Sygnes more and lesse
	In the mould of Man ther place thei tooke
	And of the figure of the shape of Chryst as sath the booke.
Fa:	What are planets and sygnes quoth Moryen.
	The Sun the Moone and Starrs quoth Merlyn agen
	The wych lightened unto Man as he on th'erth laye
	ffor he hath the similitude of our lord I saye
	And of the Man the woman was wrought
	And so much fruite forth they brought
	To multipli the worke of our heaven and kynge
	And yet come thei alle but of on only thyng
Fa:	Of on thyng quoth Moryen what mai yt be
Son:	The slipth or skyn of the Erth so saie I
Fa:	And Erth it was som men would saie
Son:	And yet yt was neyther clene erth sand nor clay
	But the feces of the Erth and yt was of Colour gray
	And it turned into Erth, as yt on the Erth laie
	And the water torned into blud to make men strong
	The Air and the Fire was medled these among
Fa:	How Air and Fire quoth Moryen
Son:	Through the worke of God quoth Merlyn.
	The brightness of the holy Ghost ys Air
	And the light that he gevith of lyfe in any lyvyng thyng ys fyr.
Fa:	Where hast thou gon to lerne all these
	For the thyng thou sayest is very true I wysse
	Son sayd Moryen who hath thi Master bee
	That thys high wysdome hath tought to the.
Son:	No other quoth Merlyn but our heavenly King
	And my symple wytt theron ever studyeing
Fa:	Yea but in thys Craft thou studyest and spedest nought
	And yet wyth foure spirits yt must be wrought.
Son:	Your Spyryts are to wyld quoth Merlyn againe.
	And therefore I will not have to do with them certaine
	ffor I would have to do wyth a spirit made by kynde naturally
	that wyll abyde with any body kyndly.
Fa:	Such a Spyryt coulde I make quoth Moryen
	But yer neer would hold yt but in vayne;
	And yet of alle worke yt ys the best

	And lest of Cost and most assurest
	flor yf that fayle then have we don alle
	flor the most perfit work we yt cale
	flor yt ys so rych when yt ys wrought
	That if alle the worlde were turn'd to nought
	As mani bodies would again make he
	As ever was or ever should be
	But I wyl teach yt to no manner of Creature
	Except he be of Condicion good and sure
Son:	Why so quoth Merlyn I you pray.
Fa:	ffor soth son quoth Moryen I shall to thee say
	Who so could thys work perfectly know and see
	The avayle thereof so great might be
	That some men thereof should be so proude and stoute
	That thei would not know the pore people that came them about
	And somme of them would be soe full of Joy and delight:
	That thei would forget the Lord God that ys so full of myght
	And then their sowles were lorne and yt were great pittie
	And therfore yt shall not be tought for me.
Son:	That ys well don quoth Merlyn that it so be
	But for chariti father teach yow yt me.
Fa:	My son quoth Moryen yt shall I not
	Nor no man els that ever yet had wrought
Son:	Yes truli father that must you do
	Or els my heart will soone burst in two
	Father of manners I am both stable and good
	And I am of your flesh and also of your blood
	Father to whome should you teach it but unto me.
Fa:	Nay my der Son yt schale never be
Son:	Alas father that ever I was borne
	ffor well I know that I am now forlorne
	Except there for that I this cunning have
	My lyfe truly can you not save.
	Then he fell downe ded short tale for to make
	And his father then did him up take.
Fa:	And said son upon condicion I shall thee leare
	So that thou wylt on the Sacrament sweare.
	That thou shalt never write it in scripture
	Nor teach yt to no man except thou be sure
	That he is a perfeit man to God and also full of chariti.
	Doing alle waies good deede and that he be full of humilitie
	And that you know him not in lowde words but alwaies soft & still
	And alle so preve whether his life be good or yll
	And alle this shal thou sweare and alle so make a vow
	If thou wylt have thys Cunning of me now
	And the same Oath on booke they make to thee
	Ere thou them let them any parte of thys scyence know or see
Son:	That Oath Father I am now ready to take
	And therein my vow to Jesus Christ I will make
Fa:	Yet soe I will not teach thee properli
	Of the measure the tyme wherefore and why.
Son:	And so likewise will I do said Merlyn truly.

Fa: And upon thys Condicion I wyl tech thee Son be of good cheere
       Then Merlyn made this Oath the sooth for to say me
       And then the Science of thys Father he began to frame.

Son: And saie ffather how shall we begyn

Fa: In principio Son begin
       With the helpe and grace of Jhesus
       The begynnying shalbe thus.
       First a father and a mother you must have beforne
       And a Chyld of them shall be conceived and borne
       For without a woman this thyng canot be doe
       But hyr heipe and worke must be ther unto

Son: Quoth Merlyn to me yt ys gret mervel
       That womans helpe should there unto avail.

Fa: May a Chyld wythout a woman into the world be brought

Son: Nay truly quoth Merlyn that maye yt nought.

Fa: Truly Son no more canst thou the Elixir make
       Except thou the helpe of a woman thereto take
       For thou mayst see in Scripture thee beforne
       How a Child of a Mother ys conceived and borne
       By a token thereof thou cannot misse
       For when the matrix of a woman receiving the sperme of Man
       The Chylde ys conceived soone and than
       The matrix of a woman closeth truly soe
       That no foule matter cometh then thereto
       And therfore take thou heede of thys ensample in the beginning.
       To close well the vessell, from any maner of thynge
       For if any Corrupcon come where the chylde ys
       It might never ingender then to be a man I wys
       No more shale truli thy work yf ani evil ayre come thereto
       And therefore close thy vessel well as thou shouldst doe
       That alle thie matter may therein abyde
       And not to go oute on never a side.
       Forty two dayes so let yt stand
       And then undoe it with thy hand
       For then ys the chyld borne and so forth brought.

Son: Then sayde Merlyn thys understand I nought
       Who shall the chyldes father be.

Fa: Silos son thus reade me
       And the moder Anul shalbe hyr name

Son: And no Moder els quoth Merlyn but the same.

Fa: Truly quoth Morien yt wyle non other be
       And theie schale dwelle in lowe Cuntrie
       And in a stronge Citty welle walled aboute
       That theie of there Enimyes thereof schale have no doubt
       The Cuntrie ys full good ingresse
       The wych ys called Homogenes
       Artevallo thus call me the Citty
       And the chylds name must be Mercury

Son: How high be the walls of the saide Citte
       And what wydenes wyth in them maye be

Fa: Five Sitigid it may be of wydenesse
       And but litle narrower thereto I gesse

And one sedep of hight sediprimus
And of the wydeness of five setigiderus.

Son: Whereby live they quoth Merlyn

Fa: Redrosman ys their meate and their drinke quoth Morien
Whiles they dwelle in that Citte
Those vittuals should wyth them be
The Father in that Cittee shal dye
But the moder shall live alway
And when the Chyld ys borne of the Moder free
Hee shalbe then brought out of the Cittee
And then he shalbe washed wyth water warme
So that the Chylde shalle take no harme
Looke that thou wash hym in waters twelve
And keepe each water by yt selfe
And the last water wilbe then cleere
Without any foule matter
And then hast thou a chylde fayre and bryght
But then yt ys younge and hath no myght
And then to make the Chyld hardy and stronge
I shall thee teach ere yt be longe
Fyrst thou must put hym to nourishying
Yet know her well that schale have hym in keeping
That she be of meane stature
And alsoe bryght of Colour
And looke that she be of body cleane and pure
And also perfeit good and sure
And looke that she be of a longe stature
And not massy but in a meane measure
And then take unto hyr Mercury the chylde
And she shalle hym tayme if he be wylde
And wyth hyr mylke she shalle make him white
And then ys the Chylde of grete myght
And put hym not to nurse beforne
Untyll he hath byne where he was borne
Wyth hys Moder let hym be alle naked
[Space in MS indicating lacuna, confirmed by missing rhyme]
And leave with hym both meate and drynke
For default of famishing
Soe by that tyme theie have dwelt there a long tyme
The Son schale by his Moder lyen
So that manie chyldren there schalbe borne
That through default of hunger they schalbe forlorne
And then take hym out of the Citty
And wash them as cleane as they may be
Untyll they be both faire and cleare
Wyth fayre lukewarme water as I said whileere
And thou put them to theire Gume and to none other
The wych wyth Mercuryes fathers brother
Twenty chyldren and foure and there ys the fyrst
And altogether him list
And so him XXV forth beare
And put then to nourish as I sayde whileere

203

	And she schale keepe them faire and cleane
	As young children ought to byn
	Wyth her mylke wythin the towne wall
	Tyll death comyth and slayeth them all
Son:	What is death quoth Merlyn I you pray
Fa:	It ys a change quothe Morien in fay
Son:	Warme fire. What ys the towne wherein the chyld doth dwell.
Fa:	It ys fusion Son I doe the tell
	And yt would be full hygh in hyghnes
	From the grounde to sedeprions and no lesse
	fior the hygher that she be
	The Kinder mylke have shall he
	ffor the mylke cometh out of the Ayre full sweete
Son:	What is yt quoth Merlyn that would I faine weete
Fa:	It ys called Alkade without blame
	And Auaruse ys the Nurses name
Son:	What shall alle the Chyldren dien
Fa:	Yea but one quoth Morven shall tourne to lyfe againe
Son:	Hoy may that be yt is marvel quoth Merlyn y wis
Fa:	Son quoth Moryen I shale thee say at this
	Thou shalt take the Chyldren from the Nurse true
	And thou shalt leade them to a Maister newe
Son:	I but say me quoth Merlyn at this tyde
	How longe shale they wyth the Nurse abide
Fa:	Till they have eate their Gumme I reade
	And they shall dye for that same deede
	And when they are deade take them againe
	And put them unto a Master Physitian
	And ere nyne dayes be all ygone
	He schale make one chylde of alle them
	And the Maister shall give hym a new name
	The wych ys called or said foresiall in fame
Son:	What schale the Masters name be then quoth Merlyn
Fa:	Acoravenesa is a right wyse man
	And the towne wherein he doth dwell
	Ys called Scaforusa truly to tell
Son:	Yt ys a wonderous Medcen quoth Merlyn so mought I thryve
	That maketh againe the chylde to live
Fa:	It is Trofie a good monument
	Jesus to the chylde did sende
Son:	How longe schale thys Chyld with hys Master be
Fa:	Tyll he waxen nygh as hygh as he
	And then schale the chyld be wondrous bryght
	Faire and strong and of great myght
	He shalbe so furious and so strong and myghty
	That of bodyes he shall get the victory
	And turne them alle unto hys beames
	For he schalbe Kyng of seaven Realmes
	And also he schalbe a conqueror wyth the best
	Wherever that he goe either by East or West
	Hys fathers death recover shall be
	And tourne them unto the sayd degree

Also all bodyes he wyll convert
Into hys fadyr & modyr being in desert
A thousand he wyll causen to be yelden in fyre
And make them of hys fathers power
Hee schall them make so strong of myght
Against 2000 that they mought well fight
And thus 3000 schalbe turned as I gesse
Unto the Emperor Osmura hys on likeness

Son: What ys that Emperour they lyken alle

Fa: Mercury he hyght fryst and after forisiall
and now ys called Osmura the Emperour
For of alle bodyes he beareth the flower

Son: Why maie not then the Emperour have a Queene
Yes truly Almaga hyr name shall been
And yet yt may be wrought as the other was
And of the said matter and in the said place
Thee same the besse a cage and do make cleane
And then unto the Emperour thou hast a Queene
Of alle weomen she vs the flower
And the most bryghtest of faire Colour
And as the Emperour doeth so wyl she
And be as good in hyr degree
And thus much fruite of them may spring
And yet all thys ys but on thyng

Son: Yes quoth Merlyn fadyr and modyr ys two

Fa: I quoth Morven but I meane not so
For truly thou maist change Silos in Anul sure
And also you maist change Anul into Silos with a liquor

Son: What is the liquor the fadyr I pray you tel me

Fa: Vinagrus Son thus call yt me

Son: It ys marvell quoth Merlyn that yt should so doe

Fa: Yet upon the fire white and red yt will be so

Son: Then understand I amiss quoth Merlyn.

Fa: Whie what meanest thou by Silos and anul Son.

Son: Sol and Luna fadyr and non other

Fa: Nay my son Sol ys but Silos brother

Son: Aha quoth Merlyn now have I understanding
ffor in thys ys more naturall workying
ffadyr now thys Elixer ys illered
May it not be multiplyed

Fa: Yes quoth Moryen that yt maie
Twelve tymes even in one day
Take one parte he said of sorifiall
And ten of sephider, ground small
And XIII of Osmura of Almuva
And do them together into a Arocamybusa
and make Alcagi fire stronge and mighti power
Arochite and more continually the space of an hower
Then merke the lyon yt ys of collour sable
Fie on hym for he ys nothing able
And therefore set thyne heart and thie delight
To gett the lyon that ys Collour white

But most intyrely above every each one
Take him that Colloured like the Carbuncle stone
For that noble Lyon in especiall
Of all other beasts he ys most Emperiali.

A FAMOUS
PREDICTION OF MERLIN

by Jonathan Swift

JONATHAN SWIFT (1667–1745) is best known for his polemical writings and for
the great satirical story *Gulliver's Travels*. The writing included here, one of many
occasional pieces, pokes fun at the array of pseudo-prophetical writings, such as
those complied by the astrologer William Lilly in his *England's Prophetical Merline*
of 1644, which put largely political suppositions into the mouth of the great Dark
Age prophet. By making the language deliberately obscure, Swift is able to extract
the maximum of meaning, and anything which is not clear is attributed to the
curious learning of the ancient prophet. Though written at the beginning of the
eighteeth century, the work looks both backwards to the seventeenth and forward
to the nineteenth centuries in its treatment of Merlin.

A Famous Prediction of Merlin, The British Wizard,
Written Above a Thousand Years Ago,
And Relating to the Year 1709
With Explanatory Notes by T. N. Philomath
Written in the Year 1709

Last year was published a paper of predictions, pretended to be written by one Isaac
Bickerstaff, Esq; but the true design of it was to ridicule the art of astrology, and expose
its professors as ignorant, or impostors. Against this imputation, Dr. Partrige hath
learnedly vindicated himself in his Almanack for that year.

For a farther defence of this famous art, I have thought fit to present the world with
the following prophecy. The original is said to be of the famous Merlin, who lived about
a thousand years ago: And the following translation is two hundred years old; for it
seems to be written near the end of Henry the Seventh's reign. I found it in an old edition of Merlin's Prophecies; imprinted at London by Johan Haukyns, in the year 1530.
Page 39. I set it down word for word in the old orthography, and shall take leave to subjoin a few explanatory notes.

SEVEN and Ten addyd to NINE,
Of Fraunce hir Woe thys is the Sygne,
Tamys Ryvere twys y-frozen,
Walke sans wetyng Shoes ne Hosen.
Then cometh foorthe, Ich understonde,
From Toune of Stoffe to fattyn Londe,
An herdie Chiftan, woe the Morne
To Fraunce, that evere he was borne.
Then shall the Fyshe beweyle his Bosse;
Nor shal grin Berrys make up the Losse.
Yonge Symnele shall again miscarrye:
And Norways Pryd again shall marrey.
And from the Tree where Blosums fele,
Ripe Fruit shall come, and all is wele.
Reaums shall daunce honde in honde,
And it shall be merye in old Inglonde.
Then old Inglonde shall be no more,
And no Man shall be sorie therefore.
Geryon shall have three Hedes agayne,
Till Hapsburge makyth them but twayne.

Explanatory Notes

Seven and Ten. This line describes the year when these events shall happen. Seven and ten make seventeen, which I explain seventeen hundred, and this number added to nine makes the year we are now in; for it must be understood of the natural year, which begins the first of January.

Tamys Ryvere twys, &c. The River Thames frozen twice in one year, so as men to walk on it, is a very signal accident; which perhaps hath not fallen out for several hundred years before; and is the reason why some astrologers have thought that this prophecy could never be fulfilled; because they imagined such a thing could never happen in our climate.

From Toune of Stoffe, &c. This is a plain designation of the Duke of Marlborough. One kind of stuff used to fatten land is called Marle, and every body knows, that *Borough* is a name for a town; and this way of expression is after the usual dark manner of old astrological predictions.

Then shall the Fyshe, &c. By the *Fish* is understood the Dauphin of France, as the Kings eldest sons are called: It is here said, he shall lament the loss of the Duke of Burgundy, called the *Bosse,* which is an old English word for *Hump-shoulder* or *Crookback,* as that Duke is known to be: And the prophecy seems to mean, that he should be overcome, or slain. By the *Grin Berrys,* in the next line, is meant the young Duke of Berry, the Dauphin's third son, who shall not have valour or fortune enough to supply the loss of his eldest brother.

Yonge Symnele, &c. By *Symnele* is meant the pretended Prince of Wales; who, if he offers to attempt any thing against England, shall miscarry as he did before. Lambert Symnel is the name of a young man noted in our histories for personating the son (as I remember) of Edward the Fourth.

And Norways Pryd, &c. I cannot guess who is meant by *Norways Pride,* perhaps the reader may, as well as the sense of the two following lines.

Reaums shall, &c. Reaums, or as the word is now, *Realms,* is the old name for *Kingdoms:* And this is a very plain prediction of our happy union, with the felicities that shall attend it. It is added, that Old England shall be no more, and yet no man shall be sorry for it. And, indeed, properly speaking, England is now no more; for the whole island is one kingdom, under the name of Britain.

Geryon shall, &c. This prediction, though somewhat obscure is wonderfully adapt. *Geryon* is said to have been a king of Spain, whom Hercules slew. It was a fiction of the poets, that he had three heads, which the author says he shall have again. That is, Spain shall have three kings; which is now wonderfully verified: For, besides the King of Portugal, which properly is part of Spain, there are now rivals for Spain; Charles and Philip. But Charles being descended from the Count of Hapsburgh, founder of the Austrian family, shall soon make those heads but two; by overturning Philip, and driving him out of Spain.

Some of these predictions are already fulfilled; and it is highly probable the rest may be in due time: And, I think, I have not forced the words, by my explication, into any other sense than what they will naturally bear. If this be granted, I am sure it must be also allowed, that the author (whoever he were) was a person of extraordinary sagacity; and that astrology brought to such perfection as this, is, by no means, an art to be despised; whatever Mr. Bickerstaff, or other merry gentlemen are pleased to think. As to the tradition of these lines, having been writ in the original by Merlin; I confess, I lay not much weight upon it: But it is enough to justify their authority, that the book from whence I have transcribed them, was printed 170 years ago, as appears by the title-page. For the satisfaction of any gentleman, who may be either doubtful of the truth, or curious to be informed; I shall give order to have the very book sent to the printer of this paper, with directions to let any body see it that pleases; because I believe it is pretty scarce.

Part 4

MERLIN IN FOLKLORE

INTRODUCTION

MERLIN HAS BEEN present in folklore from the beginning. It was almost certainly from such traditions that Geoffrey of Monmouth drew when he was writing and compiling his *Historia* and *Vita Merlini*, while strong associations with various sites such as Dinas Emrys in Wales, the supposed site of Vortigern's tower, the suggested derivation of Carmarthen (Caer Myrddin) from his name, and the various grave-mounds as far apart as Drumelzier in the Scottish Borders and Marlborough in Wiltshire (supposedly Latinized from 'Mereburgia', Merlin's Burgh), all contributed to an awareness of Merlin at a deep level within folk consciousness.

Tradition still says that Merlin's treasure is hidden somewhere on Bardsey Island off the coast of Wales, while a similar story is connected to both Dinas Emrys and Dinas Bran, where it is said that a youth with blue eyes and yellow hair will eventually arrive and discover the hidden treasures.

The legend which places Merlin's grave in Drumelzier was described by Alexander Pennecuik in his *Geographical, Historical Description of Tweeddale* (1715) where he says:

> There is one thing remarkable here. The Burn called Pausayl, which runs by the Eastside of this Church-yeard into Tweed, at the side of which Burn, a little below the Church-yeard, the famous Prophet Merlin is said to be buried. The particular place of his Grave, at the root of a Thorn-tree, was shown to me many ago, by the Old and Reverend Minister of the place Mr. Richard Brown, and here was the old prophecy fulfilled, delivered in Scots Rhyme to this purpose:
>
> > When Tweed and Pausayl, meet at Merlin's Grave,
> > Scotland and England, shall one Monarch have.

This refers to the tradition that on the day James VI of Scotland was crowned King James I of England, the River Tweed overflowed its banks and met the Powsail at this place. Since Merlin is believed to have experienced his triple death (see the extract from the *Vita Merlini* in Part 2) on or near the Tweed, as this story is referred to in the legend of Lailoken and the Scottish Saint Kentigern, it is possible that several traditions come together here.

The prophetic verse referred to is from the vernacular prophecies of Thomas Rhymer, a thirteenth-century seer and poet. Thomas left a series of Scottish prophecies, many of which seem to have come true. It is worth noting that the verses date from before the accession of James VI to the English throne. While Merlin's prophecies are inspired by the goddess of the land, those of Thomas are inspired by the fairy queen. Both, however, begin inside a hill or in the Underworld, which is the source of all prophecy.

MERLIN IN WALES

by Jan Knappert

IN THIS ESSAY Dr Jan Knappert, who is no stranger to the folklore of both Britain and other lands, records his encounter with the living tradition of Merlin in Wales. The story he records is familiar to us from Geoffrey of Monmouth and others, but it contains some fascinating variations. It is also interesting as a fragment of oral memory, which helped to preserve the myths of Merlin. Its teller, Llewellyn Jones of Llanwddyn, who was in his seventies when Dr Knappert met him in 1953, was an uneducated man who had not read the texts with which we have been concerned throughout this book. That the version of the story he relates is so close to the medieval texts is astonishing and says much about the tenacity of local folklore. I would add that on a visit to the area of Lake Vyrnwy in 1993, I noted that the local legend of the magician and healer Wddyn (pronounced Uthin) bears some resemblance to that of Merlin. Given the similarity of the two names, it is possible that the local story may well have originated in oral traditions concerning Myrddin.

Before the Romans, the Celts were the most powerful people in western and central Europe. Unlike the Romans, however, they left us very few inscriptions or other written records, so we are very incompletely informed about Celtic religion and mythology. We do know that their mythology was very complex and extensive, since many Roman writers, beginning with Caesar, have given us insight into it. The second source of data on Celtic religion is archaeology. Numerous monuments, statues, and other remains have been found and studied in Portugal, Spain, France, Belgium, the Netherlands, Germany, Switzerland, Austria, and Bohemia.

We know that in pre-Roman times there was close contact between the Celtic peoples on both sides of the Channel. Indeed, it was this contact that motivated Caesar to cross to Britain in order to punish the Belgae living there for their help to the Belgae in Belgium, whom he was fighting. The ancient Welsh traditions repeatedly mention Ireland and Scotland, where sister nations were ruled by kings whose names appear to have been well known in Wales.

Today, Celtic languages are spoken only in Scotland, Ireland, Wales, and Brittany. These peoples have preserved a rich heritage of ancient mythology, which supplements our data from archaeology and classical literature. Although several Celtic languages were spoken on the island of Britain in Roman days (Scottish, Pictish, Welsh, British, and perhaps others), the speakers' religions seem to have had many features in common.

One of the most mysterious characters in Welsh and British myths is Merlin, the magician and prophet who was born of a spirit. He sleeps, but he will wake up one day to save Britain from disaster. He is, no doubt, an ancient god, but which one? His name does not give us a clue. In modern English, merlin refers to a small falcon, so one might be tempted to seek comparison with the Egyptian sun-god, Horus, or the ancient Slavic sun-god Sokol; both gods are represented as falcons. However, the word *merlin* is of Frankish origin. The Welsh derivation of the word leads to the town of Carmarthen in Wales, which in Roman times was spelled Maridunum. It does not seem likely, however, that Merlin's name comes from the name of a town. This writer believes that Merlin is one of the names of the god Mercury, or Hermes, the European god of magic and prophecy, identified with the Germanic god Woden or Odin. Woden was associated with the forest, like Merlin, and also with the sea, which may partly explain the element *mer* or *mari* (a word for the sea) in Merlin's name. We know that Merlin, like Woden, could fly across the sea or walk on it.

Merlin is also associated with an even more mysterious Celtic goddess, Morgan le Fay, that is, the fairy Morgana, who can put a spell on people so that they see things that are not there. Such a vision is called a *fata morgana*, from the Latin name of this goddess. She must be identical with Margante, who in English versions of the Arthurian sagas is called the Lady of the Lake. For the peoples of antiquity, lakes and oceans were associated with the Other World, the Land of the Dead, and thus Margante is the queen of Avalon or Avallach, the Nether World of Annwn.

According to some sources, she was Merlin's sister; others say that she was Arthur's sister. Some sources assert she seduced Merlin in her secret cave on the coast, as queen Dido did Aeneas in the *Aeneid*. When King Arthur died, she came and carried his body to the shores of her lake. He is asleep in Avalon to this day. One day, when disaster threatens Britain, Arthur will rise again and defeat its enemies. Merlin too will come back as his counsellor and diviner. He lives now in the forests of the north, and will die only when the last tree in Britain is cut down.

For the people of antiquity, these myths were part of their religion. By the Middle Ages, however, the people of Britain had embraced Christianity, and were less interested in the mythical aspects of Arthur as the divine king than in the chivalric ideal of the noble, just, and valiant king, by the grace of God. The ancient Welsh bards sang the deeds of the heroes and gods across Britain, for even in Edinburgh, Welsh was spoken at that time. But by the time interest in these sagas revived, many new peoples had settled on Britain's sacred soil: Angles, Saxons, Vikings, Danes, and finally, the Norman knights who brought French as the language of their court.

The twelfth century witnessed the sudden efflorescence of great medieval poetry in French, singing the exploits of heroes and kings of an unknown past. Chrétien de Troyes and Geoffrey of Monmouth are the best-known writers of that time. They found their source material in the border districts, Brittany and Wales, where the language and poetry of the Celts were still alive. Of course, those court litterateurs selected what suited them and changed what they took to suit the taste of their patrons, the kings of France and England, the dukes of Normandy and Aquitaine. Thus King Arthur became a medieval knight in a twelfth-century Christian kingdom.

Merlin, however, pagan spirit that he was, had to be described as a child of the devil, for the old gods could not be tolerated. Yet, among the people of Britain, Merlin had, and has, many friends. He is, like so many characters in popular traditions, ambiguous – that is, not entirely saintly and angelic. Medieval scholars were absolutists: Merlin was not completely Christian, so he could not be good. But this literature already shows signs of a new taste, of the coming Renaissance. Arthur's queen has a lover, and that stain on his house will ruin his kingdom. And Merlin is unable to help since he is trapped in the spell of the beautiful Morgana.

Merlin is the mythical magician who enlivens the oldest stories of Wales. There, the oldest folktales of Britain are preserved, just as the oldest language is still spoken. In this mountainous province, all the people who did not want to be subjugated by the Saxon invaders of the late fifth century, nor to emigrate to Armorica (now called Brittany), congregated to make a determined stand against the Saxon kings. Sometimes they even invaded English territory, so that King Offa had to build an eighty-mile-long dyke to ward them off in 780. In those days the English still called the

Welsh Britons, showing that they were aware of their identity (Welsh, on the other hand, is a word identical with the Flemish *Walsch* [now *Waals*], referring to the Walloons).

The Britons of Roman times spoke several languages, of which only Welsh and Breton, and, I am told, Cornish survive. This is why the great wealth of myths and legends from ancient Britain has been mainly collected in Wales and Brittany. A discussion of the sources and the history of collecting this folklore would fill a volume. But even in the earliest written records the ancient myths have been Christianized. That is why Merlin is here called the 'son of the Devil'.

Before Christianity, Merlin was the god of the forest, which then covered most of Britain. Merlin may thus be regarded as the protecting deity of Britain itself, that is, of Logres (the land now called England) and Wales. The early missionaries, in their efforts to stamp out paganism, branded all native gods as dangerous devils and enemies of Christ. Merlin's divine nature is proven by his very immortality. Whenever Britain is in danger, he will rise from his sleep in the deepest forest and come to its rescue.

When I was busy with my Celtic studies in 1953, I had an experience that determined forever after my viewing angle on ancient Celtic mythology. In a small village called Llanwddyn, between Abertridwr and Pen-isar-Cwm, on the shores of Lake Vyrnwy, I met Llewellyn Jones, whom a friend later described as a grim philosopher. Jones, who was then in his seventies, was a true repository of Welsh lore. Being a philosopher, he had reflected for a long time on the value and original meaning of these traditions and had come to astonishingly original conclusions about these tales.

Although he was not anti-Christian, he had long since relinquished the church in which he had been brought up. He had come to the conclusion that the 'fairies' of Welsh folklore had once been gods, and were degraded to the rank of minor spirits by the teachings of the church.

This may not seem an epoch-making conclusion to a library-dwelling scholar who has read the endless debates of mythologists, but Jones had not read any of that. He had spent his early life listening to the sagas and epic songs of the late-Victorian bards. He was never a scholar, but spent his life farming. What made his conclusions valuable was that he had an inexhaustible knowledge of Welsh folklore and based his entire philosophy on it.

Jones was widely recognized in his district as the expert on local folklore. The following pages contain the few tales that I had the time to write down while I was staying in his village.

MERLIN, THE MAN OF MAGIC

It is related – but only God knows the full truth – that in the early days of Christianity, the Devil, the enemy of our Lord, was incensed upon seeing the success of the new religion of Jesus. The number of good people leading saintly lives increased every day, in spite of the danger and poverty that were the results of the great migrations and the fall of pagan Rome. So Satan devised a plan by which a man would be born with the ability to counteract the good works of the Christians. He himself would be that man's father.

As mother for the new man, Satan chose a young maiden, a good girl who lived a life of piety and devotion in a lonely house where she was visited only by her father confessor, a kindhearted monk of great wisdom and honesty.

One day, the Devil sent to the girl an old woman, who told her it was a shame that she was living there all on her own, without a nice man to keep her company night and day. 'Look at your pretty body, it is all going to waste. Shame!' Thus chattered the old woman, for whom only the pleasures of youth were worth talking about. That night the girl looked at her body, thinking that the old woman was perhaps right; but the next day, when she told everything to her confessor, the wise monk perceived that the Devil was playing a game with her. He told her: 'My daughter, be very careful never to be angry, never to despair. Make the sign of the cross when rising and when going to sleep, and always have a light in your room, for the Devil loves to work in the dark.'

Now this girl had a sister who was a loose woman. One day she suddenly arrived, accompanied by two mischievous young men. They uttered such shameless talk that the pious girl grew angry and told them to get out. Her sister protested that she was in their parent's house, which belonged just as much to herself. The young men gave the good girl a nasty beating, so that she had to escape to her room, locking the door. There she fell on her bed, sobbing and despairing until she fell asleep. It was in that night that the Devil came to visit her, because he knew that she had forgotten all the lessons of her good counsellor. She had neglected to light a candle, she had lost her temper, she was in despair, and she had not crossed herself before going to sleep. There are so many precautions necessary against the Devil that it is a miracle that many more people do not succumb to his wiles and tricks. It is not known in which form the Devil visited her. Did he look like a handsome young man or like the ugly, horrible incubus that women have nightmares about? The next morning the girl knew that he had been there, although she had neither seen him nor heard him.

Her father confessor would not believe her, but when she insisted, amid tears, that she just knew the Devil had been there, he instructed her to fast except on Fridays, and to avoid all enjoyment except sleeping. This she did, with great perseverance.

Soon her condition became evident for all to see, and the women of the village asked her who the father was. She said she did not know, so the women said: 'You must love him very much that you protect him thus by keeping his name secret. We hope that he will be grateful to you. Few men are. They just take!'

In those days, it was law in Wales that if a woman found herself pregnant without a husband, she had to name the man who had done that to her. The judge would then marry them so that disgrace for the town might be avoided and God would be pleased. If she refused to give the man's name, she would be executed by fire because she had brought impurity to her town. However, the judges decided to postpone the sentence until the baby was born, since the child was innocent.

Finally the baby was born, and a heavy boy it was, chubby-cheeked and smiling, a delight for any mother to have, except that his body was covered in soft black down, like a young bird. So they called him Merlin, which means blackbird. The girl asked her father confessor if he would baptize the child. The wise priest had no objection since he knew that Christianity is in the soul and charity is in the heart, not in the skin, no matter what people whispered about the baby.

His mother fed the boy herself, since no wet nurse would touch a hairy child. After a year she weaned him, and by that time he was as big as a child of two. She embraced him, saying: 'My poor fatherless child, soon you will be motherless as well, for I shall be executed because of you in spite of my innocence.' Suddenly the child opened his mouth and said, smiling: 'No, mother, you will not.' His mother was speechless with surprise. One day while she carried him through the village, they overheard two women saying: 'What a shame, such a nice girl, she has to go to the stake for that ill-starred child!' Suddenly the child turned to them and spoke: 'Leave my mother alone! Don't gossip behind her back! You are bigger sinners than she is! No one will be capable of harming her as long as I am alive.'

When these words reached the ears of the judge, he decided that justice had to be done or else who would believe that he must be obeyed? So he ordered the mother to be brought before him. When she appeared with her child in her arms, he began to read her sentence to her, according to the law of the land. However, little Merlin left him no time to finish. He cried: 'My mother still has plenty of time to live, by God's grace! If all the men and women who have deceived their spouses were to be condemned to death, there would not be many people left! I know who my father is, but you, Mr Judge, do not know yours! Your mother knows better of whom she conceived you than mine knows who my father is!'

The judge, at first speechless with surprise, soon found his voice and cried angrily: 'You vicious little slanderer, if you are lying I will have you burnt, together with your mother!' He sent a messenger to call his mother. Baby Merlin spoke: 'It would be better, Mr. Judge, if you let my mother go free and did not question your own either.' 'Oh no!' retorted the judge hastily, 'You will not get away with what you said so easily. You will burn, mark my words!'

At that time, the judge's mother arrive and he started asking her questions: 'Mother, am I not the son of your legal husband?' At first the venerable lady vehemently denied she had ever know another man, but the boy Merlin, who spoke like a man, knew all the details – even the name of the priest with whom she had lain while her husband was away for a day or two. At last, the mother of the judge bowed her head and spoke, trembling with shame: 'Alas, that it should come out even now. Thank God that my husband is dead so he will never know. Yes, the child is right. God knows where he gets his devil's wits. It is true, my son, you are the son of that priest who seduced me.'

The judge, equally ashamed, acquitted Merlin and his mother. 'Tell me, little boy who knows my father, who is yours?' asked he. 'My father was an evil spirit of the type they call an incubus. God permitted me to inherit the knowledge of the spirits concerning the past, but gave me in addition knowledge of the future, for the sake of my innocent mother whom the devil raped. Thus I will tell you that your natural father, the priest, will be told by your mother what happened here, and he will in turn be so ashamed that he will run from his house, fall in a lake, and die.'

That is what happened. The next day, the priest's body was found.

MERLIN AND THE KING OF BRITAIN

In those years, there reigned in Britain a king whose name was Constans. He had two young sons, Munk and Uter Pendragon. When King Constans died, his majordomo, Vortigern by name, usurped the throne, after the boy Munk was slaughtered by his henchman. The old king's most senior minister had left the city disguised as a shepherd, taking young Uter Pendragon with him, the prince disguised as a shepherd's boy. This act saved his life.

As soon as he had all the strings of power firmly in his hands, Vortigern decided he wanted to build a tower so big and strong that it would withstand a siege for many years. He chose a suitable (or so he thought) site and sent his masons to start building. They worked hard, but no sooner was the wall twenty feet high than it collapsed. The king scolded his masons, telling them to rebuild, using only the best mortar and the hardest stone. They did, but to no avail: The tower collapsed a second and a third time. The king now consulted his sages and astronomers, who answered that the tower would not stand unless a black-haired boy without a father were sacrificed on the spot.

The king at once sent messengers to all the towns and villages in the country. Finally they arrived in the village where Merlin was playing with other boys. As soon as he saw them, he went up to them, saying: 'I am the boy you are looking for. People say I have no father.' He was taken to the king at once. On the way, they saw a man walking up the path to his house. 'Watch that man!' said Merlin, 'that man is going to die!' He was right. A few moments later, the fellow stumbled and hit a stone with his head as he fell. He was dead by the time they came near him.

The king's messengers were so impressed by Merlin's knowledge of the future that they agreed when he asked them to tell the king what they had seen and to propose that he should tell the king why his tower could not be built on that spot. When they were admitted to the king's presence, the messengers told Vortigern how clever the boy was and assure him that he knew where to build the tower. They did not mention that he was the boy whose blood should be sacrificed for the tower.

The king believed the men and questioned Merlin about the building. Young Merlin spoke: 'Sire, under the spot you chose for your tower there live two dragons, one white and one red, in two subterranean chambers separated by a wall and covered by two enormous flat stones. As soon as they feel the weight of your tower, the dragons shake themselves and the tower collapses. Tell your men to dig here. If I am wrong, execute me. If I am right, I accuse your astrologers of ignorance.' The king, puzzled by what the boy said, ordered his workmen to dig. Soon they had uncovered two large, flat stones, and when at last these were removed, with great effort, they saw two dragons of colossal size, one white and one blood-red. As soon as the dragons saw each other, they attacked one another, beginning a battle that lasted all day. At nightfall the white dragon, though visibly tired, vomited out such a bright jet of flames that the red dragon was totally consumed by the heat and was burnt to ashes. Then the white dragon died as well.

Merlin told the king that he could now start building his tower without fear of its collapsing again. The king was grateful, but asked: 'Tell me, young sage, what is the reason for the dragons being locked up there, and why did they fight?' Merlin answered the king with a question: 'If your majesty wishes an answer, will you swear that I will come to no harm by telling you?' The king swore a solemn oath that he would spare Merlin's life, whatever he said. Then Merlin spoke: 'It has pleased God to show you a sign so as to warn you of the future. The red dragon represents yourself, the white dragon is Uter Pendragon, who is not dead. God warns you that if you continue to resist the only surviving son of the last rightful king of Britain, you will be burnt alive.'

Vortigern was deeply disturbed upon hearing this. He kept his word and let Merlin go, but he also prepared for battle against Uter Pendragon. That was a miscalculation: It is impossible to act against the will of God. Uter Pendragon landed near Winchester, and at once thousands of men gathered around him out of dissatisfaction with Vortigern's tyranny. Behind Uter's banners they marched against Vortigern, who could not stand his ground but fled north, taking refuge in an old castle. As soon as the new king's men arrived, they set fire to the castle. Vortigern was burnt to death, as Merlin had predicted.

Merlin retired to the great forest that covered most of Northumberland in those days. King Uter Pendragon wanted to make Merlin his chief counsellor, so he sent messengers to find him. They only found a woodcutter with shaggy hair and beard, who told them gruffly that if the king wanted to see Merlin, he would have to come himself. Of course, it was Merlin himself. 'Very well,' said the king, when he heard this, 'I will do just that.'

King Uter Pendragon mounted his horse and, with his senior courtiers, rode to Northumberland. The forest was majestically beautiful, and the knights were impressed by its grandeur. In a clearing, they found a shepherd herding his flock. 'Whose man are you?' the king demanded to know. 'I belong to a man who said that today the king would come in search of him, and when he comes I was to take him to Merlin.' Thus spoke the shepherd, enigmatically. 'Well then, what are you waiting for, take me to him!' impatiently ordered the king. 'He can only be found if he wants to be found.' 'Very well, tell him I am the king.' 'I am Merlin,' said the shepherd.

The king asked his courtiers if one of them recognized Merlin, but they had only seen him as the big boy who had come to foretell Vortigern's downfall. Suddenly, they all saw a big boy standing there, where a moment before there had been the old shepherd. Merlin could take on any appearance he wanted! The king invited Merlin to come and live at his court, to be his most honoured chief minister. But Merlin preferred to live in his forest, far from the intrigues of the court. Life in the forest is healthier and freer. However, Merlin assured the king of his lasting dedication to the House of Constans, adding that he would defeat the king's enemies for him.

And so he did. With Merlin's magical assistance, the king defeated the pagans known as the Saines. With magic incantations, Merlin erected an enormous circular monument of tall stones in the plain where the battle took place, now called Salisbury Plain. The monument is still there and is called Stonehenge, because of the 'hanging' stones.

After his victory, the young king built a new residence in Carduel in Wales, where he gave a splendid feast to celebrate the day of Pentecost, or Whitsunday, in May. Among the prominent guests were the duke and duchess of Cornwall, Hoell and Igerna Gorlois When he saw her, Uter Pendragon fell hopelessly in love with the beautiful Igerna, but she wanted to remain faithful to her husband. The king could think of only one solution to his heart's new problem. There was no one in the kingdom who knew an answer except Merlin. The king sent a messenger to Merlin, inviting him to a secret meeting. Of course, Merlin knew in advance what the king's desire was – indeed he knew more than that. He spoke: 'Sir, I will help you in your endeavor to conquer the Lady Igerna for one reason only: I know that it is God's decree that she shall give birth to your son, who will be a great emperor.'

Merlin had brought some rare herbs from his forest; he went with the king and one trusted confidant whose name was Ulfin, or Ulfius. The three of them went to a deserted place near the castle of Tintagel, the residence of the dukes of Cornwall. There Merlin made the king swear that his son would be entrusted to him as soon as he was weaned, to be educated with all the knowledge that a future king needed to know in statecraft. In the prospect of acquiring the love of the lady, Uter agreed. Merlin then ordered Ulfin to rub his face with the juice of the secret herb. Suddenly, his face changed and he looked exactly like Jordan, the duke of Cornwall's most trusted servant. Next, Merlin asked the king to rub his face with the juice, and at once Uter Pendragon became indistinguishable from the duke. Finally, Merlin rubbed his own face and took the appearance of Bretel, or Brastias, the duke's most faithful aide and adjutant.

The king's spies had told him that the duke resided at that time in a small hunting castle, Dimilioc, in the wooded hills. When the king and his two followers appeared before the gate of Tintagel, the gatekeepers opened the heavy door for the knight in whom they recognized their duke. The three horsemen entered the castle, and the king boldly walked into the personal chamber of the duchess. She received him as her husband, whom she loved.

Meanwhile, that same evening before sunset, the duke was killed. It is said that one of his huntsmen hit him by accident with an arrow, just as the king of France once hit a saint instead of a hind. It has also been said that the duke died fighting a gang of robbers who lived in the forest where the duke chose to hunt. The most likely explanation is that the duke's castle was invaded by a band of ruffians, probably on the king's orders, who 'accidentally' killed the duke. However that may be, it seems certain that the duchess, when she embraced the king that night, was already a widow, though she did not know it. Nor did she know that the man she embraced was not her wedded husband, but the king of Britain, to whom she owed loyalty. The magic spell of the great sorcerer was upon her so that whenever she looked at the king's face, she saw her husband, to whom she remained faithful until he died. In that night – and this was the third thing that happened to her in her ignorance – she conceived not an ordinary son, but the child whom God had predestined to become king of Logres, prince of Wales, emperor of Britannia.

The next day, the king and his two followers rode out from Tintagel to a forest where, in a grove, there was a well. Here, Merlin washed his face and advised the king and Ulfin to do the same. In this way all three recovered their normal appearance.

When the duke of Cornwall's death was reported at court, the king summoned his barons to consult about the best course of action. The duke and duchess had one daughter who would inherit the duchy of Cornwall. The duke of Orcania, Lot by name, begged his king's permission to ask her hand in marriage. Uter Pendragon assented to this request, promising to make him duke of Cornwall.

Meanwhile, Lady Igerna had come to see the king in private. She had to confess to him that a man who looked like her husband had come to her private chamber and had made love to her. The next day she had been told that her husband was already dead at that moment. 'And now I am expecting! What will people say?' The king knew an answer to her problem: 'Marry me and your child will become king after me; you will be the wife and mother of kings.'

Igerna consented, but she had another problem: 'When my child is born, it will be less than eight months after our wedding day. What will people say?' The king had an answer to that, too: 'We will hand over your son to my most trusted friend, Merlin, who will look after him better than anyone else, and no one will know about it.' Igerna agreed to this. In those days, even a loving mother had to give up her child for the sake of her good reputation, especially if she was a queen, even if she knew that the king himself was the father of her child.

When the child was born, it was a sturdy son, no seven-months' baby. The midwife, who had been sworn to silence, wrapped the baby in swaddling bands and carried him to a back door of the palace, where Merlin was waiting to receive him. Merlin took the child to Sir Ector (or Antor) whose wife nursed the young Arthur together with her own son Key or Keu, who thus became the future king's foster brother. Ector had the child baptized as Arthur.

Uter Pendragon lived happily with his lovely queen, Igerna, for sixteen peaceful and prosperous years. Alas, nothing is eternal. When it was revealed that the king was afflicted with a fatal illness, his enemies conspired to seize and divide the kingdom. Moved by the desire to keep Britain united, Uter Pendragon summoned his barons and their warriors, and explained his plans for a campaign. He even insisted on being carried to the battlefield in a litter. He died when the battle was won.

The king was dead! Who would succeed him? No one in Britain knew the answer to that question, except its faithful protector, Merlin. The country's noblemen asked him to designate the nobleman who would be worthy to succeed Uter Pendragon. Merlin promised them that on Christmas Day, all would be revealed.

On Christmas morning, all the nobles of the realm gathered in the ancient city of London to attend High Mass in St. Paul's old cathedral. When the faithful emerged from the church they saw, standing against the wall, something that had not been there when they went in. It was a large block of grey marble. On top of it there stood an anvil, and out of the anvil rose a long sword in its sheath, partly hidden in the anvil. All the old noblemen and young knights agreed that this was the finest sword they had ever seen. It shone light gold, and its sheath was encrusted with jewels. There was also an inscription on it, but no one could read it. They asked the bishop, who called one of his very scholarly clerics, who finally deciphered the inscription. It read: LIFT ME BY THY HAND. KING BE IN THIS LAND.

Of course, all the high noblemen and senior earls of the realm tried their hand at lifting the sword, but it could not be moved. The bishop smiled and spoke: 'Gentlemen, God's chosen king may be born in a stable of poor parents. David was only a shepherd boy. Saul was the son of a farmer; he was searching for his asses on the day before he was anointed king of Israel. God has His ways.'

When not even the strongest of the knights present could move the sword, they all went to partake of the Christmas banquet. After the banquet, a great tournament would be held, the finest the city had seen for many years. The knights expected that the winner would become king, but God had his own way.

Sir Ector had also come to London with his two sons, Key and the young Arthur, a handsome boy of sixteen, big for his age. On their way to the tournament they passed in front of the cathedral. Key was teasing his younger brother: 'You are a child still! You cannot participate in the tournament, you are too young! You do not even have a sword!' Stung by his elder brother's taunting words, young Arthur looked around for a sword, and suddenly he saw a big one, stuck in an anvil on top of a grey stone. Without dismounting he picked it up, sheath and all. It lay in his hand willingly, like a bride with her new husband; it shone in his hand, as bright as lightning.

Sir Ector had already heard of the magic sword and its mysterious inscription. He was also the only man alive, with Merlin in the forest, who knew Arthur's true father and his history. He dismounted and knelt down. Trembling with veneration for the sign of God he had just witnessed, the old nobleman exclaimed: 'Hail Arthur, king of Britain by the grace of God!'

Many people on the square heard this and, looking up, saw the young Arthur seated on his horse, his face illuminated by the miraculous sword he was holding aloft in his right hand, like David holding King Saul's spear. All the people followed Sir Ector's example and knelt before their king. Some ran to warn the bishop, who came forth from the church and, seeing Arthur with the royal sword in his hand, declared he would anoint him king.

And thus it happened! On the Day of Three Kings, that is the eve of Twelfth Night, Arthur was crowned king of Logres, the land we now call England. That same spring he led his armies – intrepid men, who were fired by the presence of their new leader – against the heathen invaders. Within a few years, Wales, Ireland, and even Scotland were freed from the scourge of Saxon raiders.

Additional Reading

Brian Branston, *The Lost Gods of England*, Thames & Hudson, London.
J. Douglas Bruce, *The Evolution of the Arthurian Romance from the Beginnings down to the Year 1300*, 2 vols, Peter Smith, Gloucester, Mass., 1958.
Norah Chadwick, *The Celts*, London, 1970.
Myles Dillon and N.K. Chadwick, *The Celtic Realms*, London, 1972
Jan Filip, *Celtic Civilization and Its Heritage*, Prague, 1960.
Ian Finlay, *Celtic Art*, London, 1973.
Kenneth Hurlstone Jackson, *A Celtic Miscellany*, Penguin, London, 1971.
—, *The Popular Tale and Early Welsh Tradition*, Cardiff, 1961.
Ivor B. John, *The Mabinogion*, London, 1901.
Gwyn Jones and Thomas Jones, *The Mabinogion*, Everyman, London, 1975.
Roger Sherman Loomis, *Celtic Myth and Arthurian Romance*, New York, 1927.
—, *Wales and the Arthurian Legend*, Cardiff, 1956.
A. MacBain, *Celtic Mythology and Religion*, New York, 1917.
Proinsias MacCana, *Celtic Mythology*, Paul Hamlyn, Boston, 1970.

John Armott MacCulloch, *Celtic Mythology*, Gray & Moore, Boston, 1918.

Alfred Nutt *Celtic and Mediaeval Romance*, London, 1904.

Cecile O'Rahilly, *Ireland and Wales, Their Historical and Literary Relations*, London, 1924.

S. Piggot, *The Druids*, London, 1974.

G. Paris and J. Ulrich, ed., *Merlin, Roman en Prose du Xiiième Siècle*, publié avec la mise en prose du poème de Merlin de Robert de Borron, Société des Anciens Textes Français, Paris, 1886.

Sir John Rhys, *Celtic Folklore, Welsh and Manx*, Oxford University Press, Oxford, 1901.

T. W. Rolleston, *Myths and Legends of the Celtic Race*, London, 1911.

Anne Ross, *Everyday Life of the Pagan Celts*, London 1970.

—, *Pagan Celtic Britain*, Routledge, Kegan Paul, London, 1967.

Marie Louise Sjoestedt-Jonval, *Gods and Heroes of the Celts*, trans. from the French by Myles Dillon, Methuen, London, 1949.

A. G. Van Hamel, *Aspects of Celtic Mythology*, London, 1934.

Ifor Williams, *Lectures on Early Welsh Poetry*, Dublin, 1944.

(From *The World and I*, September 1988. Reprinted with permission.)

CHILDE ROWLAND
by Joseph Jacobs

THIS STORY, from the collection of the great nineteenth-century folklorist Joseph Jacobs, offers one of the few examples which have survived in which Merlin appears as a character in a traditional folklore setting. We have no means of telling how old this tradition is, and Jacobs himself in his extended notes to the story, which follow on pages 223–8, indicated that at least some of the Arthurian references contained in his source were undoubtedly spurious. However, given Merlin's other appearances in folklore, detailed above, as well as the story collected by Dr Knappert, it is by no means unlikely that this tale represents a genuine folk memory of Merlin.

CHILDE Rowland and his brothers twain
    Were playing at the ball,
And there was their sister Burd Ellen
    In the midst, among them all.

Childe Rowland kicked it with his foot
    And caught it with his knee;
At last as he plunged among them all
    O'er the church he made it flee.

Burd Ellen round about the aisle
    To seek the ball is gone,
But long they waited, and longer still,
    And she came not back again.

They sought her east, they sought her west,
    They sought her up and down,

> And woe were the hearts of those brethren,
> For she was not to be found.

So at last her eldest brother went to the Warlock Merlin and told him all the case, and asked him if he knew where Burd Ellen was. 'The fair Burd Ellen,' said the Warlock Merlin, 'must have been carried off by the fairies, because she went round the church "widershins" – the opposite way to the sun. She is now in the Dark Tower of the King of Elfland; it would take the boldest knight in Christendom to bring her back.'

'If it is possible to bring her back,' said her brother, 'I'll do it, or perish in the attempt.'

'Possible it is,' said the Warlock Merlin, 'but woe to the man or mother's son that attempts it, if he is not well taught beforehand what he is to do.'

The eldest brother of Burd Ellen was not to be put off, by any fear of danger, from attempting to get her back, so he begged the Warlock Merlin to tell him what he should do, and what he should not do, in going to seek his sister. And after he had been taught, and had repeated his lesson, he set out for Elfland.

> But long they waited, and longer still,
> With doubt and muckle pain,
> But woe were the hearts of his brethren,
> For he came not back again.

Then the second brother got tired and tired of waiting, and he went to the Warlock Merlin and asked him the same as his brother. So he set out to find Burd Ellen.

> But long they waited, and longer still,
> With muckle doubt and pain,
> And woe were his mother's and brother's heart,
> For he came not back again.

And when they had waited and waited a good long time, Childe Rowland, the youngest of Burd Ellen's brothers, wished to go, and went to his mother, the good queen, to ask her to let him go. But she would not at first, for he was the last and dearest of her children, and if he was lost, all would be lost. But he begged, and he begged, till at last the good queen let him go; and gave him his father's good brand that never struck in vain, and as she girt it round his waist, she said the spell that would give it victory.

So Childe Rowland said good-bye to the good queen, his mother, and went to the cave of the Warlock Merlin. 'Once more, and but once more,' he said to the Warlock, 'tell how man or mother's son may rescue Burd Ellen and her brothers twain.'

'Well, my son,' said the Warlock Merlin, 'there are but two things, simple they may seem, but hard they are to do. One thing to do, and one thing not to do. And the thing to do is this: after you have entered the land of Fairy, whoever speaks to you, till you meet the Burd Ellen, you must out with your father's brand and off with their head. And what you've not to do is this: bite no bit, and drink no drop, however hungry or thirsty you be; drink a drop, or bite a bit, while in Elfland you be and never will you see Middle Earth again.'

So Childe Rowland said the two things over and over again, till he knew them by heart, and he thanked the Warlock Merlin and went on his way. And he went along, and along, and along, and still further along, till he came to the horse-herd of the King of Elfland feeding his horses. These he knew by their fiery eyes, and knew that he was at last in the land of Fairy. 'Canst thou tell me,' said Childe Rowland to the horse-herd, 'where the King of Elfland's Dark Tower is.' 'I cannot tell thee,' said the horseherd, 'but go on a little further and thou wilt come to the cow-herd, and he, maybe, can tell thee.'

Then, without a word more, Childe Rowland drew the good brand that never struck in vain, and off went the horse-herd's head, and Childe Rowland went on further, till he came to the cow-herd, and asked him the same question. 'I can't tell thee,' said he, 'but go on a little further, and thou wilt come to the hen-wife, and she is sure to know.' Then Childe Rowland out with his good brand, that never struck in vain, and off went the cow-herd's head. And he went on a little further, till he came to an old woman in a grey cloak, and he asked her if she knew where the Dark Tower of the King of Elfland was. 'Go on a little further,' said the henwife, 'till you come to a round green hill, surrounded with terrace-rings, from the bottom to the top; go round it three times "widershins", and each time say:

> "Open, door! open, door!
> And let me come in."

And the third time the door will open, and you may go in.' And Childe Rowland was just going on, when he remembered what he had to do; so he out with the good brand, that never struck in vain, and off went the henwife's head.

Then he went on, and on, till he came to the round green hill with the terrace-rings from top to bottom, and he went round it three times, 'widershins', saying each time:

> 'Open, door! open, door!
> And let me come in.'

And the third time the door did open, and he went in, and it closed with a click, and Childe Rowland was left in the dark.

It was not exactly dark, but a kind of twilight or gloaming. There were neither windows nor candles and he could not make out where the twilight came from, if not through the walls and roof. These were rough arches made of a transparent rock, incrusted with sheepsilver and rock spar, and other bright stones. But though it was rock, the air was quite warm, as it always is in Elfland. So he went through this passage till at last he came to two wide and high folding doors which stood ajar. And when he opened them, there he saw a most wonderful and gracious sight. A large and spacious hall, so large that it seemed to be as long, and as broad, as the green hill itself. The roof was supported by fine pillars, so large and lofty that the pillars of a cathedral were as nothing to them. They were all of gold and silver, with fretted work, and between them and around them wreaths of flowers, composed of what do you think? Why, of diamonds and emeralds, and all manner of precious stones. And the very key-stones of the arches had for ornaments clusters of diamonds and rubies, and pearls, and other precious stones. And all these arches met in the middle of the roof, and just there, hung by a gold chain, an immense lamp made out of one big pearl hollowed out and quite transparent. And in the middle of this was a big, huge carbuncle, which kept spinning round and round, and this was what gave light by its rays to the whole hall, which seemed as if the setting sun was shining on it.

The hall was furnished in a manner equally grand, and at one end of it was a glorious couch of velvet, silk and gold, and there sate Burd Ellen, combing her golden hair with a silver comb. And when she saw Childe Rowland she stood up and said:

> 'God pity ye, poor luckless fool,
> What have ye here to do?

'Hear ye this, my youngest brother,
    Why didn't ye bide at home?
Had you a hundred thousand lives
    Ye couldn't spare any a one.

'But sit ye down; but woe, O, woe,
    That ever ye were born,
For come the King of Elfland in,
    Your fortune is forlorn.'

Then they sate down together, and Childe Rowland told her all that he had done, and she told him how their two brothers had reached the Dark Tower, but had been enchanted by the King of Elfland, and lay there entombed as if dead. And then after they had talked a little longer Childe Rowland began to feel hungry from his long travels, and told his sister Burd Ellen how hungry he was and asked for some food, forgetting all about the Warlock Merlin's warning.

Burd Ellen looked at Childe Rowland sadly, and shook her head, but she was under a spell, and could not warn him. So she rose up, and went out, and soon brought back a golden basin full of bread and milk. Childe Rowland was just going to raise it to his lips, when he looked at his sister and remembered why he had come all that way. So he dashed the bowl to the ground, and said: 'Not a sup will I swallow, nor a bite will I bite, till Burd Ellen is set free.'

Just at that moment they heard the noise of someone approaching, and a loud voice was heard saying:

'Fee, fi, fo, fum,
I smell the blood of a Christian man,
Be he dead, be he living, with my brand,
I'll dash his brains from his brain-pan.'

And then the folding doors of the hall were burst open, and the King of Elfland rushed in.

'Strike then, Bogle, if thou darest,' shouted out Childe Rowland, and rushed to meet him with his good brand that never yet did fail. They fought, and they fought, and they fought, till Childe Rowland beat the King of Elfland down on to his knees, and caused him to yield and beg for mercy. 'I grant thee mercy,' said Childe Rowland; 'release my sister from thy spells and raise my brothers to life, and let us all go free, and thou shalt be spared.' 'I agree,' said the Elfin King, and rising up he went to a chest from which he took a phial filled with a blood-red liquor. With this he anointed the ears, eyelids, nostrils, lips, and finger-tips of the two brothers, and they sprang at once into life, and declared that their souls had been away, but had now returned. The Elfin King then said some words to Burd Ellen, and she was disenchanted, and they all four passed out of the hall, through the long passage, and turned their back on the Dark Tower, never to return again. So they reached home and the good queen their mother, and Burd Ellen never went round a church 'widershins' again.

NOTES TO CHILDE ROWLAND

SOURCE Jamieson's *Illustrations of Northern Antiquities*, 1814, p. 397 seq., who gives it as told by a tailor in his youth, *c.*1770. I have Anglicised the Scotticisms, eliminated an unnecessary ox-herd and swine-herd, who lose their heads for directing the Childe, and I have called the Erlkônig's lair the Dark Tower on the strength of the description and of Shakespeare's reference. I have likewise suggested a reason why Burd Ellen fell into his power, chiefly in order to introduce a definition of 'widershins'. 'All the rest is the original horse,' even including the erroneous description of the youngest son as the Childe or heir ... unless this is some 'survival' of Junior Right or 'Borough English', the archaic custom of letting the heirship pass to the younger son. I should add that, on the strength of the reference to Merlin, Jamieson calls Childe Rowland's mother Queen Guinevere, and introduces references to King Arthur and his Court. But as he confesses that these are his own improvements on the tailor's narrative, I have eliminated them. Since the first appearance of this book, I should add, Mr Grant Allen has made an ingenious use of *Childe Rowland* in one of his short stories now collected in the volume entitled *Ivan Greet's Masterpiece*.

PARALLELS The search for the Dark Tower is similar to that of the Red Ettin (cf. Köhler on Gonzebach, ii, 222). The formula 'Youngest best', in which the youngest of the three brothers succeeds after the others have failed, is one of the most familiar in folk-tales, amusingly parodied by Mr Lang in his *Prince Prigio*. The taboo against taking food in the underworld occurs in the myth of Proserpine, and is also frequent in folk-tales (Child, i, 322). But the folk-tale parallels to our tale fade into insignificance before its brilliant literary relationships. Browning has a poem under the title working upon a line of *King Lear*. There can be little doubt that Edgar, in his mad scene in *King Lear*, is alluding to our tale when he breaks into the lines:

> 'Childe Rowland to the Dark Tower came...
> His word was still: "Fie, foh and fum,
> I smell the blood of a British[1] man."'
> *King Lear*, Act iii., sc. 4, *ad fin*.

The latter reference is to the cry of the King of Elfland. That some such story was current in England in Shakespeare's time is proved by that curious *mélange* of nursery tales, Peele's *The Old Wives' Tale*. The main plot of this is the search of two brothers, Calypha and Thelea, for a lost sister, Delia, who had been bespelled by a sorcerer, Sacrapant (the names are taken from the *Orlando Furioso*). They are instructed by an old man (like Merlin in 'Childe Rowland') how to rescue their sister, and ultimately succeed. The play has besides this the themes of the Thankful Dead, the Three Heads of the Well (which see), the Life Index, and a transformation, so that it is not to be wondered at if some of the traits of 'Childe Rowland' are observed in it, especially as the title explains that it was made up of folk-tales.

But a still closer parallel is afforded by Milton's *Comus*. Here again we have two brothers in search of a sister, who has got into the power of an enchanter. But besides this, there is the refusal of the heroine to touch the enchanted food, just as Childe Rowland finally refuses. And ultimately the bespelled heroine is liberated by a liquid, which is applied to *lips and finger-tips*, just as Childe Rowland's brothers are unspelled by applying a liquid to their ears, eyelids, nostrils, lips, and finger-tips. There may be here a trace of the supreme unction of the Catholic Church. Such a minute resemblance as this cannot be accidental, and it is therefore probable that Milton used the original form of 'Childe Rowland', or some variant of it, as heard in his youth, and adapted it to the purposes of the masque at Ludlow Castle, and of his allegory. Certainly

---

1. 'British' for 'English'. This is one of the points that settle the date of the play; James I was declared King of Great *Britain*, October 1604. I may add that Motherwell, in his *Minstrelsy*, p. xiv, note, testifies that the story was still extant in the nursery at the time he wrote (1828).

no other folk-tale in the world can claim so distinguished an offspring.

REMARKS Distinguished as 'Childe Rowland' will be henceforth as the origin of *Comus*, if my affiliation be accepted, it has even more remarkable points of interest, both in form and matter, for the folk-lorist, unless I am much mistaken. I will therefore touch upon these points, reserving a more detailed examination for another occasion.

First, as to the form of the narrative. This begins with verse, then turns to prose, and throughout drops again at intervals into poetry in a friendly way like Mr Wegg. Now this is a form of writing not unknown in other branches of literature, the *cante-fable*, of which *Aucassin et Nicolette* is the most distinguished example. Nor is the *cante-fable* confined to France. Many of the heroic verses of the Arabs contained in the *Hamasa* would be unintelligible without accompanying narrative, which is nowadays preserved in the commentary. The verses imbedded in the *Arabian Nights* give them something of the character of a *cante-fable*, and the same may be said of the Indian and Persian story-books, though the verse is usually of a sententious and moral kind, as in the *gathas* of the Buddhist Jatakar. Even in remote Zanzibar, Mr Lang notes, the folk-tales are told as *cante-fables*. The contemporary Indian story-tellers, Mr Hartland notes, also commingle verse and prose. There are even traces in the Old Testament of such screeds of verse amid the prose narrative, as in the story of Lamech or that of Balaam. All this suggests that this is a very early and common form of narrative. (Cf. note on 'Connla' in *Celtic Fairy Tales*.)

Among folk-tales there are still many traces of the *cante-fable*. Thus, in Grimm's collection, verses occur in Nos. 1, 5, 11, 12, 13, 15, 19, 21, 24, 28, 30, 36, 38a, b, 39a, 40, 45, 46, 47, out of the first fifty tales, 36 per cent. Of Chamber's twenty-one folk-tales in the *Popular Rhymes of Scotland*, only five are without interspersed verses. Of the forty-three tales contained in this volume, three (9, 29, 33) are derived from ballads, and do not therefore count in the present connection. Of the remaining forty, 1, 3, 7, 16, 19, 21, 23, 25, 31, 35, 38, 41 (made up from verses), 43, contain rhymed lines; while 14, 22, 26, and 37 contain 'survivals' of rhymes ('let me come in – chinny chin-chin'; 'once again ... come to Spain'; 'it is not so – should be so'; 'and his lady, him behind'); and 10 and 32 are rhythmical if not rhyming. As most of the remainder are drolls, which have probably a different origin, there seems to be great probability that originally all folk-tales of a serious character were interspersed with rhyme, and took therefore the form of the *cante-fable*. It is indeed unlikely that the ballad itself began as continuous verse, and the *cante-fable* is probably the protoplasm out of which both ballad and folk-tale have been differentiated, the ballad by omitting the narrative prose, the folk-tale by expanding it. In 'Childe Rowland' we have the nearest example to such protoplasm, and it is not difficult to see how it could have been shortened into a ballad or reduced to a prose folk-tale pure and simple.

The subject-matter of 'Childe Rowland' has also claims on our attention, especially with regard to recent views on the true nature and origin of elves, trolls, and fairies. I refer to the work of Mr D. MacRitchie, *The Testimony of Tradition* (Kegan Paul, Trench, Trûbner & Co., 1889) – i.e. of tradition about the fairies and the rest. Briefly put, Mr MacRitchie's view is, that the elves, trolls, and fairies represented in popular tradition are really the mound-dwellers, whose remains have been discovered in some abundance in the form of green hillocks, which have been artificially raised over a long and low passage leading to a central chamber open to the sky. Mr MacRitchie shows that in several instances traditions about trolls or 'good people' have attached themselves to mounds, which have afterwards, on investigation, turned out to be evidently the former residence of men of smaller build than the mortals of today. He goes on further to identify these with the Picts – fairies are called 'Pechs' in Scotland – and other early races,

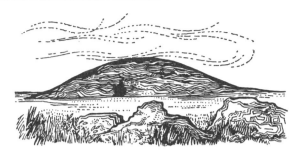

External view of hill and entrance

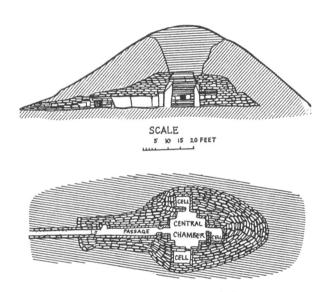

SCALE
5 10 15 20 FEET

Sectional view and ground plan

The Maes-How, Orkney

but with these ethnological equations we need not much concern ourselves. It is otherwise with the mound-traditions and their relation, if not to fairy tales in general, to tales *about* fairies, trolls, elves, etc. These are very few in number, and generally bear the character of anecdotes. The fairies, etc., steal a child, they help a wanderer to a drink and then disappear into a green hill, they help cottagers with their work at night, but disappear if their presence is noticed; human midwives are asked to help fairy mothers, fairy maidens marry ordinary men, or girls marry and live with fairy husbands. All such things may have happened and bear no such *a priori* marks of impossibility as speaking animals, flying through the air, and similar incidents of the folk-tale pure and simple. If, as archaeologists tell us, there was once a race of men in northern Europe very short and hairy, that dwelt in underground chambers artificially concealed by green hillocks, it does not seem unlikely that odd survivors of the race should have lived on after they had been conquered and nearly exterminated by Aryan invaders and should occasionally have performed something like the pranks told of fairies and trolls.

Certainly the description of the Dark Tower of the King of Elfland in 'Childe Rowland' has a remarkable resemblance to the dwellings of the 'good folk', which recent excavations have revealed. By the kindness of Mr MacRitchie, I am enabled to give the reader illustrations of one of the most interesting of these, the Maes-How of Orkney. This is a green mound some 100 feet in length and 35 in breadth at its broadest part. Tradition has long located a goblin in its centre, but it was not till 1861 that it was discovered to be pierced by a long passage, 53 feet in length, and only 2 feet 4 inches high, for half of its length. This led into a central chamber, 15 feet square and open to the sky. The illustrations on this page will give all further details.

Terraces at Newlands Kirk, Peeblesshire

Central chamber, Maes-How   **Childe Rowland (J. D. Batten)**

Now it is remarkable how accurately all this corresponds to the Dark Tower of 'Childe Rowland', allowing for a little idealisation on the part of the narrator. We have the long dark passage leading into the well-lit central chamber, and all enclosed in a green hill or mound. It is, of course, curious to contrast Mr Batten's frontispiece with the central chamber of the How, but the essential features are the same.

Even such a minute touch as the terraces on the hill have their bearing, I believe, on Mr MacRitchie's 'realistic' views of Faerie. For in quite another connection, Mr G. L. Gomme, in this book, *The Village Community* (W. Scott), pp.75-98, has given reasons and examples[2] for believing that terrace cultivation along the sides of hills was a practice of the non-Aryan and pre-Aryan inhabitants of these Isles. Here, then, from a quarter quite unexpected by Mr MacRitchie, we have evidence of the association of the King of Elfland with a non-Aryan mode of cultivation of the soil. By Mr Gomme's kindness I am enabled to give an illustration of this.

Altogether it seems not improbable that in such a tale as 'Childe Rowland' we have an idealised picture of a 'marriage by capture' of one of the diminutive non-Aryan dwellers of the green hills with an Aryan maiden, and her recapture by her brothers. It is otherwise difficult to account for such a circumstantial description of the interior of these mounds, and especially of such a detail as the terrace cultivation on them. At the same time it must not be thought that Mr MacRitchie's views explain all fairy tales, or that his identifications of Finns = Fenians = Fairies = Sidhe = 'Pechs' = Picts, will necessarily be accepted. His interesting book, so far as it goes, seems to throw light on tales about mermaids (Finnish women in their 'kayaks') and trolls, but not necessarily on fairy tales in general. Thus, in the present volume, besides 'Childe Rowland', there is only 'Tom Tit Tot' in his hollow, the green hill in 'Kate Crackernuts', 'The Cauld Lad of Hilton', and perhaps the 'Fairy Ointment', that are affected by his views.

Though *Childe Rowland* may contain traces of primitive custom, it is clear that in its present state it is of tolerably late date. We can, indeed, separate in it successive strata of social conditions. The extreme unction is Roman Catholic, and yet the latest indication of the story, which must therefore date before 1530. The reference to the Childe, if meant to indicate the heir, is feudal in character, while the heirship of the younger son carries us back to 'Borough English' and Anglo-Saxon times. The good brand that never struck in vain is at least of the Iron Age, while the Dark Tower, the terraces on the hills, and the Elfin King recall neolithic man with his cannibalism implied in the 'Fee-fi-fo-fum'. The story thus carries us through all the stages of civilisation up to the verge of modern times.

Finally, there are a couple of words in the narrative that deserve a few words of explanation: 'Widershins' is probably, as Mr Batten suggests, analogous to the German 'wider Schein', against the appearance of the sun, 'counter-clockwise' as the mathematicians say – i.e. W., S., E., N., instead of with the sun and the hands of a clock; Mr Gollancz, in the *Academy*, suggests 'Wider Sinn', i.e. in an opposite direction. 'Bogle' is a provincial word for 'spectre', and is analogous to the Welsh *bwg*, 'goblin', and to the English insect of similar name, and still more curiously to the Russian 'Bog' – God, after which so many Russian rivers are named. I may add that 'Burd' is etymologically the same as 'bride', and is frequently used in the early romances for 'Lady'.

(From *English Fairytales*, collected by Joseph Jacobs.)

---

2. To these may be added Iona (cf. Duke of Argyll, *Iona*, p.109).

MERLIN, THE REPUTED MAGICIAN

by Richard Roberts

RICHARD ROBERTS was a noted scholar and antiquarian whose book *Cambrian Popular Antiquities*, published in 1815, deserves to be better known than it is. In the course of an extended exploration of the writings and sources of Geoffrey of Monmouth, Nennius and other notable authors of the Celtic-Arthurian strain, he records much original folkloric detail which has not, to our knowledge, appeared elsewhere. In particular the episode in which King Arthur finds himself held captive in the cave of a hag, her son and daughter, offers a fascinating glimpse into the developing myth – suggesting that a story existed in which Arthur was associated with the Welsh Sow-Goddess Ceridwen, whose story occurs generally attached to the myth of Taliesin. This, together with the same unusual insights into the Merlin story proper, as well as some interesting local stories concerning Arthurian places, makes for a valuable as well as unusual addition to the present collection.

Two persons, of the name of Merlin, have obtained conspicuous places in the annals of the Welsh. The Caledonian Merlin, the author of some Druidical poems still in existence, and Merlin Ambrosius, the subject of the far-famed magician of romance, and, probably, the author of some portion of those prophecies, which stimulated the Welsh to a struggle for their rights, until they were happily amalgamated with those of England by the union. The account of his birth, as given by one of the writers of the history published by Geoffrey of Monmouth, is, probably, that of popular tradition, but wrought up into a somewhat more impressive form in the tales of the Troubadours. To them it was a professional, or at least a convenient idea, to attribute the birth of so eminent a magician to a supernatural origin. It was justifying to the imagination of credulity every subsequent description of the wondrous efficacy of his art. The progency of a demon who had violated the sanctuary of a religious order in the person of a nun, the mother of Merlin, must have been conceived, even as born of such parents, to be the devoted instrument of portentous effects, – for such was Merlin said to be. The place of his birth is said, in Welsh history, to have been Carmarthen, so called for *Caer* and *Myrdd*, and sygnifying, *the city of ten thousand* (soldiers), that is, of the legion. But, however just the derivation of the name of Carmarthen seems to be, and, I thought to be, when I published the translation of the Brut; a circumstance, which had not then occurred to my mind, induces me to believe, that the name and its derivation, have been substituted, by a mistake of Geoffrey of Monmouth's Carleon. Nennius says, that Merlin was born[1] 'In campo Electi,' that is *In the field of battle*, or, *Camp of Electus*. Now the Welsh for *campus Electi*, would be *maes Elect*; and not far from Carleon there is a village, called, in Welsh, *Maesaleg*, and commonly, at present,

---

1. Nennius, cap. 42. He says, it was *'In regione quæ vocatur Glevising.'* It is in the hundred of Gwaunllwg, of which *Glevising* is, perhaps, the error of the copyist.

Bassaleg. On a comparison of these names, the true reading of Nennius would be, 'In campo Allecti,' that is, *In the camp or field of battle of Allectus*, the Roman general; and this being the birth-place of Merlin, according to Nennius, the *city of the ten thousand* must, necessarily, have been Carleon, in this instance. The mistake of Geoffrey may have been caused by an explanation of the word *lleon*, that is, *legion*, in his original. It may now, on these circumstances, be assumed, that the birth-place of this celebrated character was Bassaleg, in Monmouthshire; and not, as the general opinion has prevailed, Carmarthen.

There is a kind of prejudice which pleases itself with the idea, that the birth and infancy of extraordinary characters are distinguished by some unusual circumstances, indicative of their future notoriety: and the prejudice is not wholly without foundation as to the latter, in which the first developing of the character often affords a clue to its subsequent preeminence; neither could the prejudice have been so readily acquiesced in, had not the fact sometimes seemed at least to justify it sufficiently for the purposes of the poet and the biographer. Hence the biographers of Merlin, esteeming him to be a magician, and, of course, potent in diabolical arts, have, in general, recorded him as the unhallowed issue of a demon and a nun; of an origin as monstrous, as his power was conceived to be supernatural and profane. This, however, appears to be the exaggeration of later writers of the Romish church, in order to discredit his prophecies; for Nennius, who wrote in the eighth century, says no more than that 'he was an illegitimate child whose mother, fearing that, if she acknowledged an illicit connexion, the king would put her to death, made oath that he had no father.' He, probably, was an illegitimate, and the mother, so far the more proper for the part she was called, and no doubt well instructed, to perform.

The idle narrative hitherto given, of his being brought into notice, has little that is satisfactory in its usual form; but the probable result of a consideration of all the circumstances is as follows.

The situation of Vortigern's affairs was, at this time, extremely, but deservedly, disastrous. Duped by his Saxon allies, and hated by the Britons for his attachment to the Saxons, dreading the effects which the just irritation of his own indignant people, after the treacherous massacre of the British chiefs at Stonehenge, might produce, he had fled to the recesses of Snowdon for security; and probably, also, as neither the influence nor the credit of the Druids was extinct, with a hope of engaging them in his favour. There seems also to have been another reason. Vortigern cannot reasonably be accused of entertaining any religious principle; and they who have no religious principle are, when in difficulties, the most superstitious. Endeavouring to console or encourage themselves by a principle of fatalism, their anxiety to know whether they have any thing to hope, or to know the worst, becomes a torment, and they apply with eagerness to any one whose plausible confidence and artifice has acquired an imaginary credit for a power of exploring the secrets of fate. With such an anxiety is Vortigern said to have applied to the Bards of Snowdon. But as the Bards were probably too wise to be gained over to his cause, and no less his enemies, it required no great artifice to render his design of building a fort ineffectual in a district where their influence was absolute, or to play upon the agitated mind of the king; and if as it seems, they were apprised of, and connected with, the intended landing of Ambrosius and Uther, the sons of Constantine, in order to dethrone Vortigern, it was an object to detain him there, and, at the same time, to prevent the building of the fort. Their declaration that the fort[2]

---

2. Dr. Jamieson, in his History of the Culdees, relates a similar traditional anecdote; from which it should seem that the sacrifice of a human victim was thought by the Druids a necessary propitiation, when the commencement of an undertaking was not

could not be built, unless the mortar were cemented with the blood of a child who had no father, seems to have been given with this view, and I am inclined to believe that the king perceived it, and, knowing Merlin to be brought up at Carleon with care, though as the child of no acknowledged father, and, suspecting him to be the son of Ambrosius, whether legitimate or not; sent for him thither in order to be revenged on the Bards for the death of the child, which the Bards, no doubt discovering, prevented, by giving the child instructions to perform his part, and, by some ceremonial illusions, which enabled them to secure the safety of the child, and impress the mind of Vortigern with apprehensions for his own safety if he remained there. To this purpose the giving to Merlin the prophetic character which the Bards themselves claimed was admirably adapted, and when the immediate purpose had been obtained; it was a character which remained with Merlin for the rest of his life. The impressions which extraordinary circumstances make on a young mind are durable, and something of the effect, combined with sagacity and the learning of the times, seems to have formed and established his subsequent character, and confirmed his reputation. This idea of his being a son of Ambrosius is not merely conjectural, though it was originally the result of the above consideration of circumstances: it is in a great measure confirmed by Nennius in chap. 44, who says, that when Merlin had concluded his explanation of the ominous representation, Vortigern demanded his name, to which Merlin replied, 'My name is Ambrosius.'[3] Then said the king, 'Of what family art thou?' He replied,[4] 'One of the Roman consuls is my father.'

The detail given by the British chronicle of Merlin's answers to Vortigern and the Bards, is in some respects difficult to be understood, as it relates to Druidic superstitions, of which no satisfactory account, that I know of, has been transmitted. The scene is laid at Dinas Emrys, where Vortigern intended to build his fort. Dinas Emrys signifies the city of Emrys, and as Stonehenge is also called Gwaith Emrys, that is, *the work of emrys*, or cor emrys, that is, *the circle*, or, *choir of emrys*: the intent of both were, probably, of the same kind, that is, I believe, as places of solemn assembly, convoked by the sovereign, whether of Bards or chieftains. Here Merlin is said to have upbraided the Bards with their ignorance, and the cruelty of their suggestions. As a proof of the former,[5] 'Tell me,' said he, (referring to the place where the fort was constructed, and on which there were rushes) 'what is below that heap of rushes?' When the Bards acknowledged their ignorance, he desired that the rushes might be cleared away, and there appeared a large pool water. 'Now,' said the boy to them, 'Tell me what is in that lake?'

---

successful. The anecdote is this: 'When Columba first attempted to build on Iona, the walls, as it is said, by the operation of some evil spirit, *fell down as fast as they were erected*. Columba received *supernatural* intimation that they would never stand unless *a human victim was buried alive*. According to one account, the lot fell on Oran, the companion of the saint, as the victim that was demanded for the success of the undertaking. Others pretend, that Oran voluntarily devoted himself, and was interred accordingly. At the end of three days, Columba had the curiosity to take a farewel look at his old friend, and caused the earth to be removed. Oran raised his swimming eyes, and said, "There is no wonder in death, and hell is not as it is reported." The saint was so shocked at this impiety, that he instantly ordered the earth to be flung in again, uttering the words of the proverb, viz., "*Earth, Earth, on the mouth of Oran, that he may blab no more*".' Page 20.

The traditions of Wales and Scotland, and particularly those of the legendary kind, have, in many instances, so near a connexion as to demonstrate the same origin, and to throw light the one on the other.

3. Nennius adds here Embreis glentic (Emrys gwledig) esse 'videbatur'. This may signify, *He was thought to be Ambrosius the Royal*: or the name AMBROSIUS *was thought to signify* ROYAL. The latter seems to be the sense intended here.

4. The Roman consuls here intended were not properly such, but noblemen, or chieftains of Roman origin, viz., the two brothers Ambrosius and Constantine, who claimed a descent from Constantine the Great.

5. Nennius gives the description of this exhibition with some variations. He says the dragons, or, as he calls them, worms, were found in a tent (probably a kind of shrine) inclosed in *two* vessels. I suppose he means that one of these vessels contained the other, and that *the tent* was in the inner vessel. He also adds, that the red worm drove the white out of the tent into the water, and that this *tent* signified the kingdom of Vortigern, which at the time was possessed both by Britons and Saxons, and 'that the pond denoted the world; more probably the ocean.'

They answered, 'We know not.' 'Then drain the lake,' said he, 'and, at the bottom, you will find a stone chest, in which there are two sleeping dragons. These, whenever they awake, fight with each other, and it is their violence that shakes the ground, and causes the work to fall.' The Bards, however, were unable to drain the lake, and Merlin effected it, by letting it out in five streams. Vortigern now commanded the stone chest to be opened, and out of it there came a white and a red dragon; which immediately began a fierce battle. At first the white dragon drove the red one to the middle of the pool, then the red one, provoked to rage, drove the white one thither in turn. Vortigern now asked what this should signify, and Merlin exclaimed, 'Woe to the red dragon, for her calamity draws nigh, and the white dragon shall seize on her cells. By the white dragon the Saxons are signified, and the Britons by the red one, which the white shall overcome. Then shall the mountains be made plains, and the glens and rivers flow with blood.[6] The Saxons shall possess almost all the island from sea to sea, and afterwards our nation shall arise, and bravely drive the Saxons beyond the sea.'

Such was the appearance exhibited, and the prophetic exposition: which, though naturally suggested by the hopes and fears prevalent at the time, made a deep and lasting impression on the minds of the nation to whom it was addressed.

When the conference was over, Vortigern, according to Nennius, made a grant to Merlin of a fort, and the western provinces, which, probably, means no more than that he left the Bards in possession of Carnarvonshire, as he himself hastily withdrew to South Wales, where, in his fort, which was in Monmouthshire, he was burned to death, in the burning of the fort by Ambrosius.

About this time, or at the conference, Merlin is said to have delivered what bears the name of his Great Prophecy, from its reputed importance. That, however, which has been published as such, is of no sufficient authority. Some passages of it are quoted by Giraldus Cambrensis, as traditional, others have, probably, been interpolated to make it conformable to real history. It is, however, so far useful as being, in some degree, a confirmation of the history.

On the death of Vortigern, Merlin appears to have returned to the neighbourhood of his native place, and to have chosen the delightful retirement of the vale of Euas, at a later period, adorned by Lanthoni Abbey, for his studies. From hence he is said to have been sent for by Ambrosius the Great, in order to give the plan of a monument to be erected in memory of the British chiefs massacred by the treachery of the Saxons on Salisbury plain. Men of profound studies, and ingenious powers and research, have, in all dark ages, been thought to hold a communication with beings of another world. To an ignorant mind the most satisfactory, as well as the readiest mode of accounting to itself and others, for a seclusion for which it is itself unfit; and for scientific discoveries, of which it can neither trace nor divine the origin, is to attribute them to the converse and communication of some beings of the invisible world; and any exhibitions of a surprising kind, though merely effects of natural knowledge and ingenuity, would be, of course, attributed to the power of such beings, and, if exhibited at pleasure by the artist, he would be conceived to have a power over them, by the means of either some superior being, or a compact of a tremendous nature. The latter idea is, perhaps, peculiar to the Christians, who applied a metaphorical expression of Scripture literally. If Merlin, therefore, was, as he appears to have been, a man of uncommon endowments, well versed in Bardic science, and perhaps, attached to their religion, the tale of tradition would have sufficient grounds for attributing magical powers to him: and, as Stonehenge was originally constructed upon scientific principles, and, no doubt, with

6. Nennius, chap. 43.

awful ceremonies, and was also distinguished by the epithet of Emrys, it is not surprising that the tradition should ascribe the construction to Merlin. Hence, in order to raise a monument worthy of the occasion, Merlin is said to have advised the king to send, not as it has usually been said, to Kildare, but to Killara, which is in the county of Meath, in Ireland, for a circle of stones, and transport them to Salisbury Plain. The tradition proceeds to state, that the plan being, on its first proposal, ridiculed by the king, Merlin persisted in his plan. 'Laugh not, sire,' said he, 'for my words are in seriousness and in truth. Those stones are of various efficacy and medicinal powers, and were brought thither formerly by the heroes from Spain, who placed them as they are at present. Their motive for bringing them was this: – In cases of sickness they medicated the stone, and poured water on it, and this water cured any disorder.' The king, informed of the efficacy of the stone, immediately determined upon the expedition, and sent out Uther Pendragon, accompanied by Merlin, and at the head of fifteen thousand men, to fetch them. After having gained a battle over the Irish forces, Uther and his men proceeded to Killara, and here the powers of Merlin were signally displayed. The army having in vain attempted to move the stones, Merlin, by his art alone, drew them freely and without labour to the ships, and thus they were brought, says the history, to Ambri, that is, Stonehenge.

Here are almost to a certainty, two distinct traditions confounded together, and an error as to the real object of the expedition. That the raising some monument, or perhaps the solemn interment of the remains of the chiefs, was one motive for the assembly on Salisbury Plain is probable, but, as I have already said in the Collectanea Cambrica, I am persuaded the principal motive was to settle the succession to the sovereignty, and other public affairs; and the great object of the expedition seems to have been the fatal stone on which the Irish kings were crowned: which Merlin, wishing to restore the power of Druidism, may have suggested; and he, therefore, would probably take a leading part in the enterprise, and make the removal to seem miraculously the effect of his art. As it was, I presume, brought to Stonehenge, this was sufficient, when the real fact was forgotten, to build the tradition of his having brought the immense stones which form the temple there. Though the history first mentions the circle of stones, yet it is remarkable, that in describing the medicinal virtues, these, in the oldest copy, are attributed to *a single stone*, which seems to confirm the conjecture.

The next occasion on which Merlin is noticed, is upon the appearance of a comet, about the time of the death of Ambrosius, when he was required to explain the intent of what was in those ages, supposed to be so portentous an event. This he did with equal policy and ingenuity, having had, as is most likely, private notice of the death of Ambrosius, so as to ensure the succession to the sovereignty to Uther. He burst out into an exclamation, that Ambrosius was dead, and, having bewailed the loss that Britain must sustain by his death, declared that the comet was significant of the fate of Uther and his son. The head of the comet, by the imagination of the multitude, was conceived to resemble a dragon, and this work of fancy was profitably converted to an important advantage. 'Thou, Uther,' said Merlin, 'art signified by this star with the head of a dragon. By the beam pointing towards France is denoted a son of thine, who shall be great in wealth, and extensive in sway, and by that directed towards Ireland a daughter, whose descendants shall successively govern the whole.' The result was, as might be expected, Uther was elected sovereign, and is said, from this circumstance, to have borne a dragon as his standard, and to have had the surname of Pendragon, that is, *The Dragon's head*.

Another exploit attributed to Merlin is far from doing honour to his memory, it being the transformation of Uther and his servant Ulphen, into the resemblances of

Gorlais, Earl of Cornwall, and his servant, in order to enable Uther to deceive the wife of the earl. This part of the story, however, bears so strong a resemblance to that of David and Uriah, and is so apparently intended to stigmatize the birth of Arthur, who was the son of Uther, that it can be esteemed only the idle fiction of a monk, or of a romance writer.

Whether Merlin survived Arthur or not has not been recorded in history, but it is most probable that he did, and through some apprehension of the Saxons endeavoured to escape them by sea. On this occasion he is said to have sailed in a ship of glass, and to have taken with him the thirteen precious curiosities of Britain. According to the account of this voyage given by Mr. Lewis Morris, he conveyed them to Bardsey Island, and died and was buried there, which is very probable; though one of the Triads says, that after he had sailed he was never heard of more, which, if the writer of the Triad lived in South Wales, might well be true *there*, considering the remote and unfrequented situation of Bardsey. The thirteen curiosities, with the explanation of the names or properties as given by Mr. Morris, are as follow.

1. Llen Arthur, (*the veil of Arthur*), which made the person who put it on invisible.

2. Dyrnwyn.

3. Corn Brangaled, (*the horn of Brangaled*), which furnished any liquor desired.

4. Cadair, neu carr Morgan mwynfawr, (*the chair, or car of Morgan mwynfawr*), which would carry a person seated in it wherever he wished to go.

5. Mwys Gwyddno, (*the hamper of Gwyddno*), meat for one being put into it, would become meat for a hundred.

6. Hogalen Tudno, (*the whetstone of Tudno*), which would sharpen none but the weapon of a brave man.

7. Pais Padarn, (*the cloak of Padarn*).

8. Pair Dyrnog, (*the caldron of Dyrnog*), none but the meat of a brave man would boil in it.

9. Dysgyl a gren Rhydderch, (*the dish and platter of Rhydderch*), any meat desired would appear on it.

10. Tawlbwrdd, (*a chess board*, or, rather *backgammon board*), the ground gold, and the men silver, and the men would play themselves.

11. Mantell, (*a robe*).

12. Madrwy Eluned, (*the ring of Eluned*), whoever put it on could make himself invisible at pleasure.

13. Cyllel Llawfrodedd, (*the knife or dagger of Llawfrodedd*).

Of the second of these Mr. Morris, I suppose, found no explanation, nor can I offer any thing that is satisfactory, the eleventh seems to have signified a magic robe; the last means, perhaps, the dagger of Druidic vengeance, as llawfrodedd may be interpreted, *the hand of havoc.*

The magical powers assigned to some of these curiosities are so similar to what is found in the Arabian tales, as to point out a common origin of great antiquity. The ship of glass is, by the author of the mythology of the Druids, ingeniously explained as signifying a sacred vessel, emblematic of the ark and the name of Bangor Wydrin, or *Glass Bangor*, an ancient name of Glastonbury, confirms the idea of Wydr, literally *glass*, signifying *sacred*. I believe gwydr, in these instances, has no connexion with, or relation to, the same sound when signifying glass, but that its true signification is sacred, though not now so used.

Here the tradition of Merlin ends. Of his art some traditionary information seems long to have remained, and the characters of poet, prophet, and magician, have been assigned to Robin Du of the 14th century. The most noted was, however, the celebrated

Dr. John Dee, whose real character has not, I think, been well understood. His learning is acknowledged, and a volume of his works published without the least apprehension of what they most probably contain: viz., the negociations of his time, in which he was employed in foreign courts. *The stone*, or *magic mirror*, seems in this book, though to the ignorant he shewed a piece of cannal coal, or a polished glass as such occasionally, really meant *the cypher*, which he used; *the spirits*, the *letters*, or *communications*; and the *fumigations*, the offers of advantage. It is, I think, most probable, that the utility of such men under a fictitious character, so well adapted to the gaining of intelligence and conveying it safely, that astrologers and dealers in the *Black Art*, as it was called found such protection: and it may have been in revenge for the defeat of some political project that Dee's library was destroyed. Kelly seems to have betrayed him; he at least deserted him. The cyphers used by Dee are still, I believe, in the British Museum.

[...]

The notices, which are afforded by the Welsh Chronicle, usually called the Brut, are in some parts, obscured apparently by the wish of the writer, or some of the transcribers, to suppress all reference to Druidism, and rendered less credible by an addition, or interpolation of circumstances borrowed by a later writer, probably from the compositions of the minstrels of the ninth or tenth century. Still, however, comparing the written with the oral traditions, a considerable portion of the obscurity will be removed, and the principal events of his life given, without making any violent demand on the faith of the reader, so as to be probably the truth, or very nearly so.

At the time of the birth of Arthur the state of Britain was, in several respects, a very unhappy one. The power of the Saxons continually increased from their first arrival by the successive influx of new hordes of adventurers into the realm, had established itself strongly on the southeastern counties, and the progress of the contest extended towards the Severn and the Humber, near which last the most important battle of this period was fought. But though the early historians seem to have thought it due to their attachment to Christianity to pass over any great conflict between its professors and those who adhered to Druidism, yet it is certain such did exist, and the dissensions of the Britons as to religion must have greatly favoured the enterprises of the Saxons, whose success is not upon any other supposition easily accounted for in its full extent. From the preceding transactions at Stonehenge, it should seem that Druidism had gained some advantage there, and that somewhat of a renewal of its rites had taken place under the superintendence of Merlin, who had, perhaps, brought back with him from Ireland some of its exiled priests, and with them the formularies of their worship. If this was the case, it was probably the last time of its celebration when Ambrosius was made sovereign, as there is no reference to any such in the succeeding reign, though Merlin in the beginning of it is said to have interpreted the prognostication of the comet. It is rather probable that Druidism was again on the decline. Thus much it appeared necessary to premise; and we may now enter on the history of our hero with a clearer view of the subject.

According to Nennius, this prince was the son of Uther Pendragon, which this historian states simply without any imputation of illegitimacy; and though it must be confessed, that what Nennius wrote has been dreadfully curtailed and corrupted, yet had he dropped a hint that could have tended to the prejudice of Arthur's fame, there can be little doubt but that it would have been carefully preserved. It is therefore the more probable, that the anecdote of an adulterous intrigue of Uther with the wife of Gorlais, Earl of Cornwall, the consequence whereof was the birth of Arthur, is the fabrication of a later writer than the author of the history. Even had it not been so, it was by the Welsh laws in the power of the father, by a public acknowledgement in presence of the heads of his family, to confer legitimacy on an otherwise illegitimate child.

According to the *Morte Arthur*, when this prince was born, Merlin desired that the child should be delivered to him *unbaptized*, but that he had him baptized before he delivered him to Sir Hector for his education. This intimates that he was educated in the principles of Druidism, and (perhaps on the death of Merlin) became a Christian. The Sir Hector of the romance, or Sir Autour, as he is called in the Life of Merlin, is, in the Welsh tale, called Cynhyrgain the bearded, the foster-father of Arthur, by whom he was instructed and brought forward to act upon the great scene which was to prove so renowned.

The death of Uther, when Arthur was about fifteen, or as Higden more probably states it, about eighteen years of age, embarrassed the British nobility much as to their choice of a successor; because of the youth of Arthur. In such cases it had been usual to elect the next of kin able to undertake the government; but at this time the promising hopes of the talents and spirit of the young prince, and possibly the concurrence of different parties as to one whose youth might open to each a prospect of attaching him to itself, decided in his favour. To give the decision a supernatural sanction in the eyes of the multitude. The artifice was simple, and the result easily effected by predetermination or compact. At Winchester, or more probably Silchester, there was said to be a stone,[7] in a cleft whereof was lodged a sword; and on the stone an inscription, the purport of which was, that he who could draw that sword out of the cleft was the right heir to the sovereignty of Britain. This, according to the tradition, none of the chieftains who were assembled could effect. At this time it chanced that the son of Arthur's foster-father in a contest broke his sword, and Arthur, recollecting the sword in the stone, ran for it, and drew it out with ease. The foster-brother knowing the importance of the sword, preferred his own claim upon the evidence of the sword, but, it being judged proper that the sword should be replaced in the cleft, and the experiment repeated, it was found that Arthur only could draw it out again, and thus his title was established. That this manoeuvre was Druidical the circumstances are sufficiently convincing, and though London and Winchester are, by different writers, mentioned as the scene of the transaction, it is more probable that it was either at Silchester or Stonehenge, as the one was a station of the army, the other of the national assembly, which is most likely to have been the place for that reason. The ceremony of the coronation is said to have been performed by Dubricius, archbishop of Carleon; and it may be inferred from its being so said, that the religious differences were, for a time, composed, in order to unite for the expulsion of the common enemy. The effect of such an union was soon felt by the Saxons; whom, according to Nennius, Arthur, at the head of his countrymen, defeated in twelve pitched battles, in each of which he displayed a prowess and sagacity far beyond his years. The last, and most celebrated, was the battle of Baddon-hill, near Bath, in which he is said to have killed upwards of six hundred with his own hand. In this battle Arthur is said to have worn a device called *Prydwen*, either on his helm, or his shield, and the sword Caliburn, which was made at Glastonbury. The device is said, in one copy of the Chronicle, to have been *a cross*; in another and later copy, *an image of the Virgin*. These are the interpretations of the writers, but, I am afraid, the name of the device proves that, at this time, Arthur was attached to Druidism, for it has, I think, been sufficiently proved, that it signifies *the sacred ship*, or *symbol of the ark of Noah*, exhibited in the Druidic ceremonies: and William of Malmesbury has very unconscious-

---

7. In the myddes thereof was lyk an anvyld of steel a ffote of hyght, and therein stake a fayre sword. *Morte Arthur.*

The Enchanter Merlin.

The enchanter Merlin (Howard Pyle, *The Story of King Arthur and his Knights*)

ly proved, that there was an establishment of a Druidical society at Glastonbury in this very period, having conceived it to be that of a Christian monastery. As the explanation is necessary to the history of the far-famed Caliburn, it may not be deemed superfluous to introduce it here. According to this author, 'twelve of the descendants of Cunedda, coming from the north, took possession of Venedotia, Demetia, Buthir, (Guhir, or Gower), and Kedweli, in right of their great grandfather,' (others say their father), 'Cunedda. One of them was called Glasteing, and this,' says Malmesbury, 'was that Glasteing, who, pursuing his *sow* through the midland territory of the Angles by the town of Escebtiorne, (*qu*. Shepton Mallet), to Wells, and from Wells, along a wet by-road, which we call Sugewege, (*Sow-way*), found her suckling her young under an *apple*-tree near the church we are speaking of: (viz., *Glastonbury*) and hence we even yet call the apples of that tree, *old-church apples*. The sow also was called, the old-church sow, because, though that other swine had but four legs, she had *eight*. Here Glasteing finding the situation advantageous in many respects, fixed the habitation of himself and family, and here he died.'

A story of the same kind is told in the Welsh Triads, and Cambrian Biography of Coll ap Coll Frewi, following the sow of Dallwaran Dalben, from Gwent in South Wales to

Lleyn in Carnarvonshire. The author of the Mythology of the Druids, considers the *sow* as symbolical of the ark, and it is remarkable that Malmesbury characterizes the *sow* of Glasteing as having had *eight* feet. As in the Welsh language *hwch* signifies a *sow*, and *cwch* a *boat*, I strongly suspect, that the former name was adopted to disguise the mystery: as approximating sufficiently in sound to intimate the sense to the initiated. The *sow* then with *eight* feet represents the *boat*, that is, the *ark*, with its *eight supporters*, or *eight priests*, as *representatives* of the *eight persons* saved in the ark; and these were what Glasteing found reposing under the *apple-tree*, a representative also, I presume, of the *tree of life*. When the boat was called a sow, for the same reason would its priests be called its *pigs*, whether for concealment by the friends, or in derision by the enemies, of the superstition.

Hence then it appears, that in the fifth or even sixth century (for Cunedda died at the close of the fourth) there was an establishment of Druids at Glastonbury, and, as the mighty sword Caliburn was wrought there, the reason of its having been so, was evidently to give it the credit of magic power, which no enemy could withstand, a credit which, in the hand of an Arthur, it was likely to sustain; and which the minstrel did not suffer to fall into oblivion.

The victory at Baddon-hill was of great importance to the British cause, and it is not improbable that many of the fugitives were pursued and driven to embark, having lost their leaders, or it being rumoured that they were slain, as the Welsh Chronicle states. The expressions of this Chronicle are too general to be taken strictly, and the fact seems to be taken strictly, and the fact seems to be as Higden has stated: that a peace was concluded between Arthur and Cerdic, upon the conditions that Arthur, ceding Wessex to Cerdic, should retain the title and privilege of sovereign paramount.

The interval between the conclusion of this peace, and Arthur's war with the Picts and Scots, as well as the motives to this war, are omitted by the Chronicle. Tradition has, however, preserved some circumstances from which, though involved in the fabulous guise of popular stories; some probable account may be elicited.

From what has been said it may be assumed, that Arthur was hitherto a votary of Druidism; but Christianity was, at the same time, making a rapid progress, and Druidism seeking shelter in the mountains of Snowdon, the recesses of Anglesey and Somersetshire. Arthur, now at peace with his neighbours, seems to have given himself up for some time to the idle and dangerous pursuits of youthful pleasures, and for those of the chace, to have made choice of Caerwys and Nannerch, in Flintshire, in North Wales. An anecdote of him whilst there may be seen in page 359 of the Collectanea Cambria, Vol. I., which will justify this opinion. In the mean time his people became dissatisfied, and he is said to have dreamed that his hair fell from his head, his fingers from his hands, and his toes from his feet, and having required an explanation of the dream was told, that his dominion was falling from him, and could be recovered only by means of a lion in steel, the entreaty of a blossom, and the advice of an old man. The dream may have been an invention to conceal secret intelligence, that his subjects were, as is usual in such cases, failing in their attachment; and could only be recovered when the lion should be clad in steel; when the monarch should arm, and exert himself for their safety. The two remaining particulars seem to present a choice of the parties of Druids or Christians. This I conceive from the explanation given of the second and third. Of the second it is said, that being separated from his train in the chace he lost his way, and coming to the mouth of a cave entered it, and found within three gigantic beings, viz., an old woman, and her son and daughter. The mother and son wishing, lest their retreat should be discovered, to put Arthur to death; the daughter by her entreaties prevailed so far, that the mother agreed to spare his life, if next morning he should be able to deliver a triad of truths. The conditions being accepted Arthur was well entertained, the son played also exquisitely on the harp to amuse him. But when Arthur went to repose, the son laid over him an ox-hide so heavy that he could not move under it, but was confined by it till the son came in the morning to take it off. Arthur then delivered his triad of truths. Addressing the son, 'You,' said he, 'are the best harper I ever heard.' 'True!' said the old woman. 'And you,' said he to her, 'are the ugliest hag I ever saw.' 'True again!' said she. 'If I were once from hence I would never come hither again,' said he. The truth of this was allowed, and Arthur set free.

In this tale the description of the hag, her son, and daughter, correspond with that of the Druidic deities, – Ceridwen, the prototype of witches, her son Avagddu, and her beautiful daughter, Flur, called in romance Blanche Fleur; as also Arthur's imprisonment under the ox-hide, to that of the aspirants previous to their initiation into the mysteries. The tale, therefore, intimates that Arthur was initiated, but conceived a disgust and hatred for the Druidical superstition, and perhaps, in consequence of some menacing apparitions exhibited which his mind was too well informed to regard, and too spirited to bear, as he could not be wholly ignorant of Christianity. It is dangerous to trifle with a sound understanding, and so the Druids seem to have found it. The advise of the old man is said to have been that of a hermit, and the purport of it was to rebuild, or restore the churches which had been destroyed by the Pagans; under the name Pagans, Druids, as well as Saxons, may have been comprehended; for as the Christian churches were generally built on the site of old Pagan temples, the Druids, no doubt, had endeavoured, when able, to destroy them. But their power was now falling, never more to rise. The light of Christianity was dispelling the mist and darkness of ignorance which shrouded its spells in horrors, and creating an abhorrence of the bloody sacrifices and superstitious delusions of Druidism.

It has been ingeniously conjectured by a learned Welsh antiquary from a comparison of circumstances, and names of places given in the romance of the Sangreal, that the borders of the Menai were the scenes of contest between Arthur and the Druids. What the Sangreal was in itself has been much doubted. In the romance itself the Sangreal is evidently described as a kind of cup, and in the passage referred to above, I have given my reasons for thinking it to have been, what I believe it was, the celebrated *Santo Catino*, now in Paris, a beautiful cup of composition (probably glass) resembling an emerald. The word *Graal* is said, by Mr. Lewis Morris, on the authority of the Speculum Historicum of Vincentius, to be derived from Gradale, an old French word signifying *a little dish*; and this seems to be the true signification. Was it originally *a divining cup* of the Druids? That divining cups were of the remotest antiquity we know from the history of Joseph, and a vestige of that kind of divination is yet observable in the practice of divining by the coffee or tea cup. If the Sangreal were such a cup, it would have been considered, when obtained by conquest, as the noblest trophy of the victory of Christians over the Druids; and, therefore, might have been represented as the object of the war itself. Of course the vessel would be deposited in the place of the greatest security; and whether this conjecture concerning its original history be, or be not, well founded; that the *Santo Catino* was at St. David's, and stolen and carried off from thence to Glastonbury, with other valuables, cannot now, I think, be doubted. I am not without some suspicion, that during the establishment of the Druids at Glastonbury, the *Catino*, or Sangreal, had been preserved there, and that it was from the celebrity of this vessel the place took the name of Ynys WYDRIN, or *the isle* (*or district*) of the LITTLE GLASS, and that Merlin, when he went to Bardsey, sailed not indeed in it, but with it, that is, carried it with him thither; and that it was recovered by Arthur, and consecrated to the use of the church by St. David. The supposition gives at least something like a clue to the[8] romance of the Sangreal; but, if correct, it does not admit of the idea, that it was the same as the *Altar of St. David*, which that saint is said to have brought from Jerusalem, unless it be thought, that this was the altar of St. David's, and not a divining cup, and had been carried off by the Druids and recovered from them; a supposition which appears to me less probable than the former.

The next transaction noticed by the Chronicle, is an expedition conducted by Arthur against *the Picts*, according to which it appears that he was victorious in three engagements. After the last battle, the Picts are said to have retired to the isles of *Loch Lomond*. Whilst the Picts were in this situation, an army under an Irish or Erse chieftain, came over to the assistance of the Picts, and was routed and compelled by Arthur to return to Ireland; and Arthur, at the entreaty of his nobles and clergy, received the submission of the Picts to his government, and pardoned their former opposition to him. In the narrative of these events the historian has, in rather a confused manner, introduced a very short and fabulous account of Loch Lomond, which Arthur went to view when the peace was concluded. But as it is evident this lake was the last retreat of these Picts, as the historian terms them, this is a strong argument, that they were in reality the party of the Druids, and as Arthur was able to explore the lake, that their sacred places were entered and subverted at this time, and that it was thought prudent to substitute the name of Picts for Druids, in the same manner as that of Pelagians probably is in the legend of Germanus.

This view of the subject is not only consistent with the subsequent part of the history, but is almost necessary to elucidate it, as Arthur, immediately after this battle, is stated to have returned to York, and to have re-established the Christian churches which had been injured or thrown down, and appointed an archbishop of York. His victory seems also to have tranquillized his dominions, as he now appointed also subordinate earls or princes of Scotland. At this time the peace with his Saxon neighbours continuing, he married Gwenhwyfar, daughter of the Earl of Cornwall, then esteemed the most beautiful of the British ladies; and some time after his marriage, whether from that spirit of adventure common in his time, or to employ his retainers, he built a fleet, sailed to Ireland, and from thence towards some isle, as it should seem, of the Hebrides. In a second voyage he extended his course northwards around Great Britain, and as the northern isles were probably peopled by Norwegians, or, perhaps, because it was really the fact, he is said to have reached Norway. As he is represented as victorious through the whole course of this voyage, it may have been successful, whatever was its real object; whether retaliation, investigation, or acquisition, of what was then deemed the honourable advantage of adventure. On his return he is said to have overcome one Frollo, or Rollo, at Paris. But the Paris of the Chronicle is Calais, or Witsan (the name being a mistake of the translator), and that such an encounter should have taken place there, is no way improbable. Between these two voyages an interval of twelve years of peace is interposed by this writer, during which the court of Arthur became the resort of men of talents and celebrity; his fame increased to an eminent degree of splendour; and he was himself excited to an ambition of universal conquest, by the complimentary adulation paid to his merits. This is too like the exaggeration of a romancer to gain full credit; but as he was in peace with his Saxon neighbours, he may have contemplated and performed the circumnavigation of the whole island, a labour of enterprise and difficulty in his time, which alone might justify, to a great degree, the exalted reputation his name has acquired. The second expedition is said to have taken up nine years,

---

8. The name of *Laucelot* du Lac, the Knight of the Sangreal, seems referable to that of Pedrogyl *Paladrddellt*, or *Pedrogyl of the shivered* LAUNCE, one of the knights of Arthur mentioned in the Triads.

including in this time a considerable portion passed in Gaul. According to Johannes Magnus, a Swedish historian, 'Harold, leader of the Danes, being overthrown in battle by Tordo, king of Sweden, fled to Britain to king Arthur, to collect succours in defence of his nation, which were granted, and a large fleet was assembled from Britain, Gaul, and Holland, and sent to the rescue of the Danes.' The historian, however, adds, that 'Arthur having at the head of the combined forces gained the victory, the Danes found a like oppression, under which they were long retained, not only from the Angles and Scots, but also from the Norwegians, Arthur having made his relation Loth their chief, as the Scottish history testifies.'

If this account be correct, the exploits of Arthur will assume a higher character than they have hitherto held in general estimation, and considering the confused, and perhaps, deserted state of the northern countries at this time, when the great irruption of the Northern nations was bearing down on the Roman empire, it is no great concession to grant that much of that might be true, as to Norway and Denmark, which is well known to have been true as to the more powerful and populous country of Britain. Countries drained of their warriors present an easy conquest to their invaders. The expedition may, however, have had an ulterior object, which seems to be intimated by Arthur's landing in Gaul; the more probable object is the transportation of troops from the north to reinforce the armies engaged with the Romans, an object which would require the junction and united aid of such a fleet as Magnus describes; and for which, as against a common foe, the northern nations had found it as necessary as it was eventually profitable to unite.

When Arthur had returned from Gaul he made Carleon the seat of his residence, which clearly marks that the Saxons were still in possession of the eastern districts. Here he is said to have once more devoted himself to the enjoyments of a more tranquil life. Whether his sovereignty had not been till now acknowledged by the subordinate kings, or whether his success, and the admiration of his conduct, had made it the more feasible to gratify his ambition and his taste for magnificence, does not appear; but as it was of great importance, and circumstances favourable, he now held a great festival for the formal coronation of himself and his queen Gwenhwyfar. The description of the ceremonial, and of the feast given in the Chronicle, is probably taken from the songs of the minstrels, who endeavoured to grace it with all their powers of decoration. Still, however, tradition gave the subject in such a favorable form as to be held a sufficient authority. The institution of the Round Table, to prevent any dissatisfaction among the guests, has been uniformly assigned to Arthur upon this occasion; and the novelty and adroitness of the expedient, could not fail to make a lasting impression on the minds of the guests so relieved from the constraint of punctilio without any loss of dignity; and prepared to enjoy the festivity with that pleasantry, which the sagacious good nature of their host, and the humorous proposal, tended to promote. To furnish the feast the writer has gone for guests, probably, the whole extent of his geographical knowledge, which is not very accurate. He may, however, have been less extravagant than he appears to be. The descendants of Roman legionaries may have retained the names of their original countries as family distinctions, and a prince of Spain have been, in fact, a chieftain of a clan of such Spanish origin, then resident in Britain.

Soon after this feast Arthur is said to have received a summons from a Roman general then in Gaul to pay a tribute as due to the Roman state, which, if the Roman affairs there wore any thing of a favourable aspect at the time, would not be likely to be omitted by a general of their's, who, it should seem, was pressing Britany. But as no time for such a message could be more unseasonable, or a proposal more irritating to a high-spirited king, he returned it by a defiance and a menace; which, as far as joining in opposition to the Romans, he appears to have put in execution: and, I am inclined to believe, that he was the person who is called Riothamar (probably a Gaelic designation), and said, by the historian, to have brought troops from Britain to Gaul, to act against the Romans. In this expedition he is said to have gone as far as Langres, and there may be some truth in it. But the history of what passed in Gaul in this age is so obscure, that there is little to be known, and that little seldom satisfactory. Human life seldom gives an advantage without a counterpoise. Whatever may have been Arthur's success abroad, the treachery of his wife, and of his nephew Mordred, to whom he had intrusted the care of his dominions, was preparing to destroy him on his return, which he hastened on receiving the intelligence; and found that his nephew joined with the Saxons were advancing to oppose re-entrance into his kingdom. The battle of Camlan, in Cornwall, soon followed, in which he slew the traitor Mordred in single combat, hand to hand: but died himself in a few days in the abbey of Glastonbury of the wounds he had received, and was buried there. Thus fell this noble prince, betrayed by those he trusted most; but lamented by his country; and leaving a record in the hearts of his people, which time has not been able to obliterate. Whether it was that his interment was concealed for some political purpose, and that there was a considerable time during which it was hoped he might recover, an idea of his resuscitation to rescue the Welsh was spread abroad, and the influence of such hope was great even down to the time of Henry II. This hope was founded on one of those prophecies which were, no doubt, originally published, like other false prophecies, for temporary purposes; and being once credited, and its accomplishment desirable, was retained in memory, and the hope flattered and indulged from age to age. Yet I imagine that the prediction may at first have had a different reference. The name of our hero was also the sacred name of a mythological personage in the Druidical mythology, and there is reason to believe, that the British chiefs were accustomed to assume such names either on their initiation, or on the commencement of a great undertaking: and somewhat of this is usual with the Welsh poets still, who, on their being acknowledged as such, though without any formality, assume the names of ancient poets as their own *poetic names*, and prefix or subjoin them as such to their works. Hence it appears probable to me, that the prophecy of the reviviscence of Arthur was originally intended of the reviviscence of Druidism, which its partisans might have no small hopes of, during the troubles which followed the death of Arthur. To their friends the meaning could be no secret, and to the public the more obvious reference was an encouragement to persist in the defence of their country, which they did with an unabated perseverance, till the happy union of Wales with England.

(From *Cambrian Popular Antiquities* by Peter Roberts, E. Williams, London, 1815).

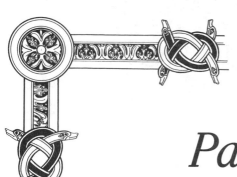

Part 5

MERLIN
IN THE
NINETEENTH
CENTURY

INTRODUCTION

IN THE NINETEENTH century the stories of Merlin, like the majority of literature associated with Arthur, became the source of literally hundreds of poems, plays and paintings. In this age Merlin becomes largely a symbolic figure, invested with an abiding power, and a deep reverence and connection with nature. He is, in fact, a kind of 'natural man' whose wisdom derives from nature rather than science. The question of his relationship with Vivien or Nimue posed a difficult problem for the moralizers of the Victorian era, and in this time Merlin appears cast more in the mould of the somewhat lascivious old man pursuing the young and innocent woman. Tennyson's poem *Merlin and Vivien* characterized Merlin's nemesis as 'wily' and 'saucy', a beautiful and sensual woman who uses her feminine wiles to enslave the old enchanter for ever. The end of the poem says it all:

> Then, in one moment, she put forth the charm
> Of woven paces and of weaving hands,
> And in the hollow oak he lay as dead,
> And lost to life and use and name and fame.
>
> Then crying 'I have made his glory mine,'
> And shrieking out 'O fool!' the harlot leapt
> Adown the forest, and the thicket closed
> Behind her, and the forest echo'd fool'.

Here Merlin loses everything; yet in another, later poem, included here, Tennyson saw in the character of Merlin something nobler, deeper, altogether more powerful than this; and it is this vision that we have endeavoured to capture in the selection of nineteenth-century writings which follow, which range from the pseudo-antiquarian work of Hersant de la Villemarqué to the dignified characterization of Merlin in the poems of the American philosopher Ralph Waldo Emerson.

THE MERLIN POEMS OF HERSANT DE LA VILLEMARQUÉ

THEODORE HERSANT de la VILLEMARQUÉ (1815-95) was a Breton nobleman who belongs in the ranks of the great eighteenth- and nineteenth-century antiquarian 'forgers', along with Iolo Morgannwg in Wales and James Macphearson in Scotland. All three were considerable scholars with an encyclopedic knowledge of their particular subject area – Iolo the ancient Welsh traditions, Macphearson those of Scotland and Villemarqué those of Brittany. Each produced extensive volumes which purported to be translations from their native 'bardic' literature. And each, finding insufficient genuine material, added their own imaginative 'reconstructions'. In so doing they made the work of scholars in succeeding generations that much more difficult, since in many cases it is virtually impossible to detect the fragments of genuinely original material from the additions.

For this reason we have chosen to place the three poems concerning Merlin, included by Villemarqué in his collection *Baraz Breiz* (The Breton Bards), published in 1839, here rather than in the part relating to the earliest records of Merlin. That Villemarqué's collection contained a number of genuine texts is beyond doubt, but what are we to make of the poems reproduced here? They are almost certainly the product of Villemarqué's imagination – yet at the same time they probably contain an element of genuine tradition. Villemarqué was exceptionally well read in his country's lore and literature, and he had also travelled throughout the land searching out fragments of oral tradition. It is by no means impossible therefore that both *The Verses of the Lore* (given here in a new translation by Caitlín Matthews) and *Merlin the Diviner* (translated by Thomas Stephens) contain echoes of genuine Breton traditions relating to Merlin. The third poem, translated by Charles Dent Bell, is a more extended episode relating more closely to literary tradition. They are included here as a further illustration of the revival of interest in the Arthurian legends which took place throughout the nineteenth century.

THE VERSES OF THE LORE

1. *Druid:*
   Child, fair druid's son, answer:
   Child, what shall I sing to you,
   What song shall I sing?
   Child:
   Sing me the lore of number one,
   So that I may learn it today.

   Druid:
   No verse is there for number one,
   Ankou, father of Anken;
   Nothing more, nothing less.

   Child, fair druid's son, answer:
   Child, what shall I sing to you,
   What song shall I sing?

2. *Child:*
    Sing me the lore of number two,
    So that I may learn it today.
    Druid:
    Two bulls yoked to a cockerel;
    They pull, they all but die;
    See with your eyes this wonder!
    No verse is there for number one,
    Ankou, father of Anken;
    Nothing more, nothing less.

    Child, fair druid's son, answer:
    Child, what shall I sing to you,
    What song shall I sing?

3. *Child:*
    Sing me the lore of number three,
    So that I may learn it today.
    Druid:
    Three verses (divisions) keep the world in
        check:
    Three the starts and three the ends,
    For man as for the oak.
    Two bulls yoked to a cockerel;
    They pull, they all but die;
    See with your eyes this wonder!
    No verse is there for number one,
    Ankou, father of Anken;
    Nothing more, nothing less.

    Child, fair druid's son, answer:
    Child, what shall I sing to you,
    What song shall I sing?

4. *Child:*
    Sing me the lore of number four,
    So that I may learn it today.
    Druid:
    Four are the whetstones,
    Whetstones of Merlin,
    Sharpening the swords of the brave.
    Three etc.

5. *Child:*
    Sing me the lore of number five,
    So that I may learn it today.
    Druid:
    Five are the earthly zones,
    Five are the ages of the world,
    Five are the stones on our sister.
    Four etc.

6. *Child:*
    Sing me the lore of number six,
    So that I may learn it today.
    Druid:
    Six are the children of wax,
    Enlivened by the moon's rays,
    If you know them not, I will tell:
    Six are the herbs in the cauldron,
    Fingerling mixes the brew,
    His little finger in his mouth.
    Five etc.

7. *Child:*
    Sing me the lore of number seven,
    So that I may learn it today.
    Druid:
    Seven suns and seven moons,
    Seven stars form the Hen, [Cygnus?]
    Seven elements in the dust of the air.
    Six etc.

8. *Child:*
    Sing me the lore of number eight,
    So that I may learn it today.
    Druid:
    Eight are the winds that blow,
    Eight fires with the Father of Fires,
    In the month of May, on the battle
        mount.
    Eight heifers white as the wave,
    Grazing on the isle of peace,
    Eight white beasts of the Lady.
    Seven etc.

9. *Child:*
    Sing me the lore of number nine,
    So that I may learn it today.
    Druid:
    Nine white hands on the stone table,
    Near the tower of Lezarmeur;
    And nine mothers keening on.
    They dance, the nine korrigans,
    Crowned with flowers, robed in white,
    About the fountain, in moonlight.
    The sow and her nine wild boars,
    At the threshold of the sty-door,
    Grunting and snuffling,
    Snuffling and grunting:
    'Torc, torc, torc! after the apple!
    The old boar will teach you a lesson!'
    Eight etc.

10. *Child:*
Sing me the lore of number ten,
So that I may learn it today.
Druid:
Ten ships of the foe sighted
Coming towards Naoned [Nantes;]
Ochone, Ochone, folk of Gwenned!
[Vannes]
Nine etc.

11. *Child:*
Sing me the lore of number eleven,
So that I may learn it today.
Druid:
Eleven Bel-druids in harness,
Travelling to Gwenned [Vannes]
With their swords broken.
And their robes are bloody,
And their hazel-wands muddy,
Of three hundred, only these eleven.
Ten etc.

12. *Child:*
Sing me the lore of number twelve,
So that I may learn it today.
Druid:
Twelve the months, twelve the signs,
Sagittarius, the last but one,
Lets loose his barbed arrow.
The twelve signs fall to warring.
The fair Cow, the jet-black Cow,
[Taurus?]
Leaves the Wasteland-Forest:
In her breast, the barbed arrow
Lets falls her lifeblood,
And she cries, head lifted.
The horn sounds: fire and thunder,
Rain and wind, thunder and fire,
Then nothing more, no further lore!

Eleven Bel-druids in harness,
Travelling to Gwenned [Vannes]
With their swords broken.
And their robes are bloody,
And their hazel-wands muddy,
Of three hundred, only these eleven.

Ten ships of the foe sighted
Coming towards Naoned [Nantes;]

Ochone, Ochone, folk of Gwenned!
[Vannes]
Nine white hands on the stone table,
Near the tower of Lezarmeur;
And nine mothers keening on.
They dance, the nine korrigans,
Crowned with flowers, robed in white,
About the fountain, in moonlight.
The sow and her nine wild boars,
At the threshold of the sty-door,
Grunting and snuffling,
Snuffling and grunting:
'Torc, torc, torc! after the apple!
The old boar will teach you a lesson!'

Eight are the winds that blow,
Eight fires with the Father of Fires,
In the month of May, on the battle
mount.
Eight heifers white as the wave,
Gazing on the isle of peace,
Eight white beasts of the Lady.

Seven suns and seven moons,
Seven stars form the Hen, [Cygnus?]
Seven elements in the dust of the air.

Six are the children of wax,
Enlivened by the moon's rays,
If you know them not, I will tell:
Six are the herbs in the cauldron,
Fingerling mixes the brew,
His little finger in his mouth.

Five are the earthly zones,
Five are the ages of the world,
Five are the stones on our sister.
Four are the whetstones,
Whetstones of Merlin,
Sharpening the swords of the brave.
Three verses [divisions] keep the world in
check:
Three the starts and three the ends,
For man as for the oak.
Two bulls yoked to a cockerel;
They pull, they all but die;
See with your eyes this wonder!
No verse is there for number one,
Ankou, father of Anken;
Nothing more, nothing less.

(Translated from the French of Hersant de la Villemarqué by Caitlín Matthews.)

MERLIN, THE DIVINER

Merlin! Merlin! where art thou going
So early in the day, with thy black dog?
Oi! oi! oi! oi! oi! oi! oi! oi! oi! oi!
Loi! oi! oi! oi! oi!

I have come here to search for the way
To find the red egg,
The red egg of the marine serpent,
By the sea-side in the hollow of the stone.

I am going to seek in the valley
The green water-cress and the golden grass;
And the top branch of the oak
In the wood by the side of the fountain.

Merlin! Merlin! retrace your steps:
Leave the branch on the oak,
And the green water-cress in the valley
As well as the golden grass.

And leave the red egg of the marine serpent
In the foam by the hollow of the stone
Merlin! Merlin! retrace thy steps;
There is no diviner but God.

(From *Welshmen. A sketch of their History, from the Earliest Time
To the Death of Llywelyn, The Last Welsh Prince* by Thomas Stephens, J.F. Spriggs,
Longon: Western Mail Ltd, Cardiff, 1901)

MERLIN, THE BARD

I

'List, list to me, good grandam mine: I to the feast would go,
Where holds the King a royal race in Kings pomp and show'
'Thou shalt not to this feast, my son, I do not hide my fears;
Thou shalt not to this feast, I say, for thy cheek is wet with tears
An I can stop thee, dearest son, thither thou may'st not go,
For in thy dreams the hot tears fell like rain in wintry flow
Kind Mother, little Mother mine, seek not thy son to keep
In going thither thou shalt sing, returning thou shalt weep'.

II

He has saddled his bay palfrey, all shod with polished steel,
The splendid housing decks his side, all o'er from head to heel.
He puts the bit within his mouth, round his neck a rig he throws;
And from his long and glossy tail a streaming ribbon flows,
Upon his shiny back he mounts, and to the feast he hies,
And gallops on right gallantly, as fleet as bird that flies,
Now, as he nears the longed for spot, the braying trumpets sound
And the people press in their gala dress, and prancing hoves bound
Then up and spake a herald bold, in voice heard far and near,
'To him who in the lists today the highest bar shall clear
To him who in a perfect life shall be given, a sweet and beauteous bride.'
Reared high the palfrey at the words, and, bounding, neighed aloud
The fire flashed brightly from his eyes, from his nostrils came the cloud;
Now curvets he, now prances he, now pawing sniffs the ground;
Now with the speed of light he clears the barrier at a bound,
Leaving all rivals in the race, at a distance far behind.
And now the victors voice is heard, floating along the wind:
'My lord the King, I claim as mine Lindore thy daughter fair,
In virtue of thy royal oath, my heart and home to share.'

'Lindore thy bride shall never be, ne'er wed with one so low,
No sorcerer shall be her lord, or hear her marriage vow',
Then whispered him an aged man, near to the King's right hand
Whose beard, all whiter than the wall, fell to his girdle'd band
All dight he was in woolen robe, fringed with bright silver lace
Such as doth oft in stary halls a monarch's person grace.
When heard the King the sage's words, three hasty blows struck he
With golden sceptre in his hand, on the table at his knee.
So loud he struck, the nobles all kept silence deep and still.
And harkened they with breathless awe. as the King spoke out his will
'If thou canst bring me Merlin's harp' so spake he out at last,
'Which with four golden chains is bound and from rich gold is cast.
If Merlin's harp thou bringest me, which layeth at his bed
Why, then mayhap, my daughter dear at the altar thou shall wed'.

III

'Kind grandam mine, dear grandam mine, as thou dost love me well
I pray thee by thy love to me, forthwith thy council tell
Or else this weary heart will break, its strings will weak with woe
And to the grave at once I'll pass, and lie the green sod below'
'This had not been,' his grandam said, 'had'st thou my bidding done'
'Then weep no more, my grandam dear, this golden hammer, like the sun
Beneath its stroke no sound is heard it falls like white snow flake'.

IV

'Rejoice ye in this palace all, since I've returned with speed
Bearing the harp of Merlin back to claim my promised maid'
Now, when the King's good son him heard, he whispered to his sire,
And the King himself outspoke right loud, and his eyes they flashed with fire
'Now by my royal crown, young sir, yea, by my king's life,
If thou old Merlin's ring wilt bring, my daughter is thy wife'.
Back to his grandam then he hies, in haste and burning tears,
And now in a rage, and now in grief, makes known to her his fears
'My lord the King has spoken thus, and so and so he said'.
'Grieve not for this, keep up thy heart, nay, never droop thy head:
Take thou that branch which yonder lies within my casket small;
From out it grow twelve little leaves which softly rise and fall –
Twelve little leaves, and brighter far than any burnished gold.
Seven nights I spent in seeking them, beneath the moonlight cold,
Full seven long years ago it was, in seven darkling woods,
Where the place is full of terrors, and blackness always broods
At midnight, when the cock he crows, your steed then quickly take,
And let not fear assail your heart, Merlin shall not awake
At dead of night, when crew the cock, the bay steed bounded on,
Scarce has the cock his crowing ceased ere Merlin's ring is won.'

V

Before the King at early morn again the young man stood,
Who at that sight rose up at once, in dazed and wondering mood
Astonished, too, were all the men gathered in presence there,
And eyed the youth all o'er and o'er with amazed and anxious stare
'Behold, his bride he's won', they cry 'his bride he's nobly won

And she shall be his lawful wife in the sight of yonder sun.'
The King now and his son withdrew, and the old man he retires
But soon returning with them both, the King spake his desires
'Tis true my son, as thou hast heard, this day thou'st won thy wife.
There's only one thing more I ask, I swear it by my life
It is the last, – in doing this, thou shalt be my true son,
My daughter then shall be thy bride, and all Leon is thine own
Of my forefathers bones, bring here great Merlin to our sight
And when he comes, I wreak that he shall bless the marriage rite'.

VI

'Oh, Merlin, Bard whence comest thou in weeds so sad and torn –
Where goest thou with naked feet, bare head, and face forlorn?
Oh whither, say, in this sad plight, old Merlin, dost thou go,
With oaken staff, and troubled brow, and eyes that overflow?'
'Seeking my harp in this sad world, my consolation woe, –
Seeking my harp, and eke my ring, their loss has brought me dole'
'Merlin, old Merlin, grieve thou not, let these tidings sooth thy pains
Nor lost are either harp or ring, they shall be there again;
Come in, come in, poor Merlin, and take some meat with me'
'No! No! I cannot cease my walk nor eat nor drink with thee;
No food shall ever pass these lips till I my harp have found
Till this is done, the world I pace is one long weary round.'
'Merlin, oh Merlin! heed me now, and thou thy harp shall find.'
So sore she pressed him that at last she won upon his mind,
And then he comes into her house, and quietly sits down
But still all woeful is his heart, and his tears they flow adown.
At evening comes the old dame's son, and finds old Merlin there
He shakes with fear as he glances round, and sees the minstrels chair
The minstrel's head droops on his breast, sleep binds him in its chain,
The son he thinks now can flee from his mothers house amain
'Hush, hush, my child, fear not at all, Merlin is wrapt in sleep;
You need not fear that he will start out from his slumber deep
Three ruddy apples, fair to see, I in the embers laid,
These roasted well, I gave to him; hush, son, be not afraid
He ate the three, he'll follow thee wherever thou dost go,
Through forest dark, o'er mound high, or in the valley low'.

VII

From out the royal bed the Queen then to her women said;
'What great arrival has there been? why has the trumpet brayed?
The mornings light had hardly fallen upon the dewy ground,
When the pillars of my bed did shake 'neath the loud and joyous sound.
Why shout the mob?' I pray you tell. What mean these voices loud?
Why rings the sky with praises high, as from a mighty crowd?'
'Merlin, the noble Bard is come', the citizens rejoice:
'Therefore you hear the trumpets flare, and the peoples shouting voice,
There comes with him an aged crone, and there walketh at her side
Your fair young son who is to have your daughter for his bride.'
When the King he hears the tidings, he hurries out right fast,
And runs to meet old Merlin, and the lord doth haste.
'Arise, good hereld, fly thy bed, awake, arise, arise,

And publish through the land the news, proclaim it in this wise
Who will may to the marriage come, may join the wedding feast:
All people in the land may come from highest to the least.
For eight days shall the feast be held in my palace here,
In honour of my sweet Lindore, my child, my daughter dear',
To the marriage all the nobles ride, the nobles of Betagne,
The judges and the gallant Knights, each true and princely man
And first the Counts and then the poor, and eke the rich beside
They swiftly to the palace come from all the countryside.

'Silence! keep silence, all who come, to hear the King's command
The marriage of the royal maid' for eight days from the land
But come she will – aye, come ye sirs, come ye both one and all
No matter what your rank or age, come ye both great and small
To the marriage all ye nobles hie, ye nobles of Betagne
Ye judges and ye gallant Knights, Churchmen and warlike man
Come first the mighty Count, and then come both ye rich and poor
The rich and poor, who shall not lack of gold or silver store
Nor shall they want, or meat or drink, or wine or hydromel
Or couches soft on which to rest, or men to serve them well.
The porkers fat shall here be slain, two hundred bulls or more,
Two hundred heifers and of deer as many as five score:
Two hundred steers, half black, half white, whose horns shall given be
To all who come from far and near this wedding high to see.
Then for the priests, an hundred robes of wool as white as snow,
An hundred collars all of gold, with pearls in every row;
Each warrior shall have one, – shall have it for his own,
And wear it as a loyal badge of fealty to the throne.
A chamber filled with cloaks all blue – blue as the sky above –
For ladies young and fair, and chaste, and gentle as the dove.
Eight hundred warm new garments to the poorest shall be given,
For well we know how dear they are, how cared for up in heaven,
And lately, in their seats aloft, both through the night and day,
One hundred well-skilled minstrels upon their harps shall play;
While Merlin, Bard, amid the court, shall celebrate, I ween;
The marriage-rite, and all shall say, such feast was never seen'.
'List, all ye skilful cooks, I pray, – What' is the marriage o'er?
It is, the splendid pageant's passed, such shall be seen no more.'

For fifteen joyous days it helde, and all was glad and gay,
And now unto their homes again they all have passed away,
Nor went they empty to their homes, but laden with rich store
Of royal gifts and venison which to their land they bore.
The bridegroom to fair Leon's land his bride with joy he bears,
And all are happy but the King, his eyes are full of tears,
His heart is sad and sorrowful: his heart is sick and sore,
His daughter she has left his home, he shall see her nevermore.
Merlin again is lost to sight, none knew where bideth he,
Whether in cavern of the earth, or air, or in the sea.
    (Translated by Charles Dent Bell in *Poems Old and New*, Edward Arnold, London, 1893.)

MERLIN AND THE GLEAM

by Alfred Tennyson

ALFRED LORD TENNYSON (1809-92) single-handedly did more to promote a revival of interest in the Arthurian legends during the nineteenth century than any other writer of the time. Reading Malory as a boy so inspired the young Tennyson that he embarked upon a huge cycle of poems, *The Idylls of the King*, which were begun in the 1850s and not completed until 1886. The power and sheer literary brilliance of these works provoked a spate of copies and imitations, as well as a legion of plays and a plethora of paintings which almost amount to a 'school' of Arthurian art. Much of this work, including that of Tennyson, is marked with a mawkish sentimentality which makes it hard going for twentieth-century readers. Yet there is no questioning Tennyson's devotion to the tradition, nor indeed his vast knowledge of the subject.

In 1852 he published two poems under the pseudonym of 'Merlin'; and in the poem *Merlin and Vivien* from the *Idylls* he rose to considerable heights, even though he did persist in presenting Vivien as a type of Victorian 'fallen woman'. The poem included here, *Merlin and the Gleam*, published in 1889, shows how important the character of the wise magician was to Tennyson. Here he represents the poet himself, and the poem describes the quest for knowledge through the person of Merlin, following 'the gleam' of poetic insight and wisdom.

I

O young Mariner,
You from the haven
Under the sea-cliff,
You that are watching
The gray Magician
With eyes of wonder,
I am Merlin,
And *I* am dying,
I am Merlin
Who follow The Gleam.

II

Mighty the Wizard
Who found me at sunrise
Sleeping, and woke me
And learn'd me Magic!
Great the Master,
And sweet the Magic,
When over the valley,
In early summers,
Over the mountain,
On human faces,
And all around me,
Moving to melody,
Floated The Gleam.

III

Once at the croak of a Raven who crost it,
A barbarous people,
Blind to the magic,
And deaf to the melody,
Snarl'd at and cursed me.
A demon vext me,
The light retreated,
The landskip darken'd,
The melody deaden'd,
The Master whisper'd
'Follow The Gleam.'

IV

Then to the melody,
Over a wilderness
Gliding, and glancing at
Elf of the woodland,
Gnome of the cavern,
Griffin and Giant,
And dancing of Fairies

In desolate hollows,
And wraiths of the mountain,
And rolling of dragons
By warble of water,
Or cataract music
Of falling torrents,
Flitted The Gleam.

V

Down from the mountain
And over the level,
And streaming and shining on
Silent river,
Silvery willow,
Pasture and plowland,
Horses and Oxen,
Innocent maidens,
Garrulous children,
Homestead and harvest,
Reaper and gleaner,
And rough-ruddy faces
Of lowly labour,
Sidled The Gleam. –

VI

Then, with a melody
Stronger and statelier,
Led me at length
To the city and palace
Of Arthur the king;
Touch'd at the golden
Cross of the churches,
Flash'd on the Tournament,
Flicker'd and bicker'd
From helmet to helmet,
And last on the forehead
Of Arthur the blameless
Rested The Gleam.

VII

Clouds and darkness
Closed upon Camelot;
Arthur had vanish'd
I knew not whither,
The King who loved me,
And cannot die;
For out of the darkness
Silent and slowly
The Gleam, that had waned to a wintry
    glimmer
On icy fallow

And faded forest,
Drew to the valley
Named of the shadow,
And slowly brightening
Out of the glimmer,
And slowly moving again to a melody
Yearningly tender,
Fell on the shadow,
No longer a shadow,
But clothed with The Gleam.

VIII

And broader and brighter
The Gleam flying onward,
Wed to the melody,
Sang thro' the world;
And slower and fainter,
Old and weary,
But eager to follow,
I saw, whenever
In passing it glanced upon
Hamlet or city,
That under the Crosses
The dead man's garden,
The mortal hillock,
Would break into blossom;
And so to the land's
Last limit I came –
And can no longer,
But die rejoicing,
For thro' the Magic
Of Him the Mighty,
Who taught me in childhood,
There on the border
Of boundless Ocean,
And all but in Heaven
Hovers The Gleam.

IX

Not of the sunlight,
Not of the moonlight,
Not of the starlight!
O young Mariner,
Down to the haven,
Call your companions,
Launch your vessel,
And crowd your canvas,
And, ere it vanishes
Over the margin,
After it, follow it,
Follow The Gleam.

FOUR MERLIN POEMS

by Ralph Waldo Emerson

RALPH WALDO EMERSON (1803–82), the American philosopher, essayist and educationalist, wrote altogether five poems in which Merlin figured as a main protagonist. Four of these are printed here as an expression of Emerson's transcendentalist teachings. He seems to have seen Merlin as an expression of the poetic imagination, as expressed in his bardic, prophetic and magisterial roles. Emerson's journals and notebooks display a continuing interest in Arthurian lore and legend, where he sees them as embodying a sense of national identity – a theme of great importance to Emerson himself. Though Victorian in style, these poems betray a sensibility which far outreaches that of most nineteenth-century writers.

MERLIN I

Thy trivial harp will never please
Or fill my craving ear;
Its chords should ring as blows the breeze,
Free, peremptory, clear.
No jingling serenader's art,
Nor tinkle of piano strings,
The kingly bard
Must smite the chords rudely and hard,
As with hammer or with mace;
That they may render back
Artful thunder, which conveys
Secrets of the solar track,
Sparks of the supersolar blaze.
Merlin's blows are strokes of fate,
Chiming with the forest tone,
When boughs buffet boughs in the wood;
Chiming with the gasp and moan
Of the ice-imprisoned flood;
With the pulse of manly hearts;
With the voice of orators;
With the din of city arts;
With the cannonade of wars;
With the marches of the brave;
And prayers of might from martyrs' cave.

Great is the art,
Great be the manners, of the bard.
He shall not his brain encumber
With the coil of rhythm and number;
But, leaving rule and pale forethought,
He shall aye climb
For his rhyme.

'Pass in, pass in,' the angels say,
'In to the upper doors,
Nor count compartments of the floors,
But mount to paradise
By the stairway of surprise.'

Blameless master of the games,
King of sport that never shames,
He shall daily joy dispense
Hid in song's sweet influence.
Things more cheerly live and go,
What time the subtle mind
Sings aloud the tune whereto
Their pulses beat,
And march their feet,
And their members are combined.

By Sybarites beguiled,
He shall no task decline;
Merlin's mighty line
Extremes of nature reconciled, –
Bereaved a tyrant of his will,
And made the lion mild.
Songs can the tempest still,
Scattered on the stormy air,
Mould the year to fair increase,
And bring in poetic peace.

He shall not seek to weave,
In weak, unhappy times,
Efficacious rhymes;
Wait his returning strength.

Bird, that from the nadir's floor
To the zenith's top can soar, –
The soaring orbit of the muse exceeds that
   journey's length.
Nor profane affect to hit
Or compass that, by meddling wit,
Which only the propitious mind
Publishes when 'tis inclined.

There are open hours
When the God's will sallies free,
And the dull idiot might see
The flowing fortunes of a thousand years; –
Sudden, at unawares,
Self-moved, fly-to the doors,
Nor sword of angels could reveal
What they conceal.

MERLIN II

The rhyme of the poet
Modulates the king's affairs;
Balance-loving Nature
Made all things in pairs.
To every foot its antipode;
Each color with its counter glowed;
To every tone beat answering tones,
Higher or graver;
Flavor gladly blends with flavor;
Leaf answers leaf upon the bough;
And match the paired cotyledons.
Hands to hands, and feet to feet,
In one body grooms and brides;
Eldest rite, two married sides
In every mortal meet.
Light's far furnace shines,
Smelting balls and bars,
Forging double stars,
Glittering twins and trines.
The animals are sick with love,
Lovesick with rhyme;
Each with all propitious time
Into chorus wove.

Like the dancers' ordered band,
Thoughts come also hand in hand;
In equal couples mated,
Or else alternated;

Adding by their mutual gage,
One to other, health and age.
Solitary fancies go
Short-lived wandering to and fro,
Most like to bachelors,
Or an ungiven maid,
Not ancestors,
With no posterity to make the lie afraid,
Or keep truth undecayed.

Perfect-paired as eagle's wings,
Justice is the rhyme of things;
Trade and counting use
The self-same tuneful muse;
And Nemesis,
Who with even matches odd,
Who athwart space redresses
The partial wrong,
Fills the just period,
And finishes the song.

Subtle rhymes, with ruin rife,
Murmur in the house of life,
Sung by the Sisters as they spin;
In perfect time and measure they
Build and unbuild our echoing clay
As the two twilights of the day
Fold us music-drunken in.

THE HARP

One musician is sure,
His wisdom will not fail,
He has not tasted wine impure,
Nor bent to passion frail.
Age cannot cloud his memory,
Nor grief untune his voice,
Ranging down the ruled scale
From tone of joy to inward wail,
Tempering the pitch of all
In his windy cave.
He all the fables knows,

And in their causes tells, –
Knows Nature's rarest moods,
Ever on her secret broods.
The Muse of men is coy,
Oft courted will not come;
In palaces and market squares
Entreated, she is dumb;
But my minstrel knows and tells
The counsel of the gods,
Knows of Holy Book the spells,
Knows the law of Night and Day,

Merlin (Aubrey Beardsley)

And the heart of girl and boy,
The tragic and the gay,
And what is writ on Table Round
Of Arthur and his peers;
What sea and land discoursing say
In sidereal years.
He renders all his lore
In numbers wild as dreams,
Modulating all extremes, –
What the spangled meadow saith
To the children who have faith;
Only to children children sing,
Only to youth will spring be spring.

Who is the Bard thus magnified?
When did he sing? and where abide?

Chief of song where poets feast
Is the wind-harp which thou seest
In the casement at my side.

Æolian harp,
How strangely wise thy strain!
Gay for youth, gay for youth,
(Sweet is art, but sweeter truth,)
In the hall at summer eve
Fate and Beauty skilled to weave.
From the eager opening strings
Rung loud and bold the song.
Who but loved the wind-harp's note?
How should not the poet doat
On its mystic tongue,
With its primeval memory,

Reporting what old minstrels told
Of Merlin locked the harp within, –
Merlin paying the pain of sin,
Pent in a dungeon made of air, –
And some attain his voice to hear,
Words of pain and cries of fear,
But pillowed all on melody,
As fits the griefs of bards to be.
And what if that all-echoing shell,
Which thus the buried Past can tell,
Should rive the Future, and reveal
What his dread folds would fain conceal?
It shares the secret of the earth,
And of the kinds that owe her birth.
Speaks not of self that mystic tone,
But of the Overgods alone:
It trembles to the cosmic breath, –
As it heareth, so it saith;
Obeying meek the primal Cause,
It is the tongue on mundane laws.
And this, at least, I dare affirm,
Since genius too has bound and term,
There is no bard in all the choir,
Not Homer's self, the poet sire,
Wise Milton's odes of pensive pleasure,
Or Shakespeare, whom no mind can measure,
Nor Collins' verse of tender pain,
Nor Byron's clarion of disdain,
Scott, the delight of generous boys,
Or Wordsworth, Pan's recording voice, –
Not one of all can put in verse,
Or to this presence could rehearse
The sights and voices ravishing

The boy knew on the hills in spring,
When pacing through the oaks he heard
Sharp queries of the sentry-bird,
The heavy grouse's sudden whir,
The rattle of the kingfisher;
Saw bonfires of the harlot flies
In the lowland, when day dies;
Or marked, benighted and forlorn,
The first far signal-fire of morn.
These syllables that Nature spoke,
And the thoughts that in him woke,
Can adequately utter none
Save to his ear the wind-harp lone.
Therein I hear the Parcæ reel
The threads of man at their humming wheel,
The threads of life and power and pain,
So sweet and mournful falls the strain.
And best can teach its Delphian chord
How Nature to the soul is moored,
If once again that silent string,
As erst it wont, would thrill and ring.

Not long ago at eventide,
It seemed, so listening, at my side
A window rose, and, to say sooth,
I looked forth on the fields of youth:
I saw fair boys bestriding steeds,
I knew their forms in fancy weeds,
Long, long concealed by sundering fates,
Mates of my youth, – yet not my mates,
Stronger and bolder far than I,
With grace, with genius, well attired,
And then as now from far admired,
Followed with love
They knew not of,
With passion cold and shy.
O joy, for what recoveries rare!
Renewed, I breathe Elysian air,
See youth's glad mates in earliest bloom, –
Break not my dream, obtrusive tomb!
Or teach thou, Spring! the grand recoil
Of life resurgent from the soil
Wherein was dropped the mortal spoil.

MERLIN'S SONG

Of Merlin wise I learned a song, –
Sing it low, or sing it loud,
It is mightier than the strong,
And punishes the proud.
I sing it to the surging crowd, –
Good men it will calm and cheer,
Bad men it will chain and cage.

In the heart of the music peals a strain
Which only angels hear;
Whether it waken joy or rage,
Hushed myriads hark in vain,
Yet they who hear it shed their age,
And take their youth again.

MERLIN

by Thomas Caldecott Chubb

THE AMERICAN WRITER Thomas Caldecott Chubb (1899-1979) is best
remembered as the biographer of Boccaccio and Aretino, but he was also a poet of
no small stature, whose volumes include *Ships and Lovers* (1933) and *Cornucopia*
(1953), as well as *The White God and Other Poems* (1920), from which the
following poem is extracted. His Merlin, like that of Alfred Noyes and Ralph Waldo
Emerson, reflects the idea of the magician having a great command over the forces
of nature, but finding this, ultimately, unsatisfactory. Though he lived through much
of the twentieth century, Chubb remains, at heart, an Edwardian poet, for which
reason he is included here.

A lonely man, his head among the stars
Walks on the clean sand white beside the sea, –
Merlin, the lonely man of Camelot,
Who left King Arthur and the tournaments
And decorous garlands and the sight of man
Dear to him, yea! the knights and pageantry
To walk beside the waves that curl in foam
And sparkling splendor round him.

       This because
His vague mysterious power – alchemy
Of mind, by which to purest testable gold
The baser man he strove to elevate
Through curious kabala, muttered words
And formulae, and fiery distillation
Of the elixirs red and white (for this
The allegorists hold to be the sum
And substance of the prime materia, –
Soul-purifier, leaving earth to rest
As 't was) – him lifted flaming far and far
Through unimagined distances of thought
And dream, by pathways metaphysical
To God's own face. And he had seen the face
Of glorious God. And God had looked upon
His eyes.

     So now he walks beside the sea
Alone. And nightly chants he: 'I have seen
The Moon, and far beyond her. I have seen
The ringèd planets curve around the Sun,
And the great Sun himself, and far beyond
Strewn stars and stars and filmy nebulae
Past them across the night, too, have I seen
And known that unapproachable face of God.
And now I walk alone lest man should see
Divinity reflected from mine eyes
Which I am granted only to behold.'
Thus Merlin. And the waves around his feet
Break in a fiery phosphorescence, while
The stars above are flaked in fire around,
And the moon floats among them like a barge
Of whitest silver on the unrippled mere.

MERLIN AND THE WHITE DEATH

by Robert Wiliams Buchanan

ROBERT WILLIAMS BUCHANAN (1841–1901) was the son of a Glasgow tailor who became a successful novelist, essayist and poet, and who also owned several socialist journals. He is best known for his attacks on the pre-Raphaelite movement, which he described as 'the fleshly school of poetry'. It is all the more surprising, therefore, that he should choose as a subject one of the favourite themes of the pre-Raphaelite poets and painters – the Arthurian legends. As well as *Merlin and the White Death*, which seems to be based upon a half-remembered idea of Merlin and Vivien and of Welsh folktales of the Lady of the Lake – he also wrote a brief poem about Mordred. In the poem reproduced here Merlin is not entrapped, but having once encountered 'Fair Uniun', is unable to forget her.

I

Darkly I sought, in shade and sun,
Fair Uniun, pale Uniun!
Long days I journeyed, fearing not,
 Through forests dark, by waters dire;
And far behind me Camelot
 Sank to its topmost spire.
Ay, wingëd as the summer wind,
I left the haunts of men behind:
By waters dire, through forests dark,
Under the white moon's silver arc;
O'er hill, down valley, far away.
Toward the sunset gathering gray,
 I, Merlin, fled, –
With aged limbs and hoary hair,
Arm'd with strange amulets to snare
The peerless Water-Witch, whose head
With lilies of sleep is garlanded,
 Under the earth and air, –
And all the viewless lures to break
Of that pale Lady of the Lake.

II

Swiftly I near'd her region dun,
Fair Uniun, pale Uniun!
Till, lastly, trees of hugest height,
 Below them, flowers of poppy red,
And weird deep whisperings of the night,
And breezes dropping dead,

Closed round my path; while in the sky
The moon shone like a great white eye
That watched me through a belt of cloud, –
What time, with head and shoulders bowed,
And lips that mutter'd unaware,
I gained the haunted region where
 White Uniun dwells;
And far away, through forest trees,
I caught a gleam like moonlit seas –
A glassy gleam of silver swells, –
The lake rimm'd round with lily-bells,
 Unstirr'd by rain or breeze; –
And trembled on, my own to make
The matchless Lady of the Lake.

III

Nor safely wooed, nor lightly won,
Fair Uniun, pale Uniun!
She dwells within her weed-hung cave,
 Deep in the green moon-lighted water,
She glimmers in the whispering wave –
A demon's awful daughter!
White, white as snow her oozy dress,
White as her face's loveliness;
Supple her boneless limbs as snakes,
And full of radiance, such as breaks
Around the cestus of a star,
And strange as eyes of serpents are
 Her haunting eyes;

And she had power, as stars aver,
To make the wight who conquered her
More young, and beautiful, and wise,
For good and ill, and great emprize,
   Than all men else that stir;
Wherefore I sought to win and take
This matchless Lady of the Lake!

IV

Colder than ice her blood doth run,
Fair Uniun, pale Uniun!
Pitiless to all things that range
   Below her, near her, or above,
Till, by some marvel dark and strange,
   She learn at last to love;
Knight after knight had thither gone,
Led by fierce impulse plunging on
To something that he loved with dread,
And each in turn been conquerëd;
Yea, each in turn been held and snared
By the pale syren, silver hair'd,
   Whom all men fear!
And side by side they lay at rest,
With folded hands upon the breast,
On beds of weed and darnel drear,
And foam-bells hung in every ear,
   And all in white were drest,
And all were watch'd till they should wake
By the pale Lady of the Lake.

V

Potent her spells in shade or sun,
Fair Uniun, pale Uniun!
Wherefore I, Merlin, old but strong,
   Sweeping by breast with hoary beard,
Skill'd in deep signs and magic song,
   Much honour'd and revered,
Vow'd, with a wise man's purpose stern,
To face the Water-Witch, and learn
What wondrous arts, unknown to me,
What superhuman witchery,
She used, those sleepers to enslave
That rested in her ocean cave,
   Nor felt, nor heard;
Nay, vowed by her strange love to free
My soul for immortality,
To woo her darkly, till I heard
The sigh of love, the whisper'd word
   That proved her love for me!
And then for aye her spells to break,
The wondrous Lady of the Lake.

VI

Thus arm'd, I near'd her region dun,
Fair Uniun, pale Uniun!
I passed from out the forests old,
   And 'tween two faintly purple hills,
Saw the smooth waters glitter cold,
   And throb with silvery thrills:
Under a heaven glassy gray,
Bare to the ghastly moon they lay.
And on their marge great lilies heaved,
Slimed with the water-snakes, huge-leaved
And monstrous, floating scores on scores,
With fire-sparks burning in their cores –
   Like eyes of flame;
Afar across the lake there passed
Great shadows, multiform and vast,
That with low murmurs went and came;
And crawling things, stingless and tame,
   Came creeping thick and fast
Upon me, as I silence brake
With, 'Rise, white Phantom of the Lake!'

VII

'The time has come, thy spells are spun,
Fair Uniun, pale Uniun!
And, lo! with hands uplifted thus,
   I weave a spell of strange device,
To awe thine eyes soul-perilous,
   And thaw thy blood of ice!'
Then, like a hum of waterfalls,
I heard a voice, 'Who calls, who calls?'
And, standing on the water's brim,
With heart stone-still and brain a-swim,
I wove the spell of strange device,
With whirling arms I wove it thrice,
   And audibly.
From the deep silence of the flood,
The answer smote me where I stood, –
'Who summons me, who summons me?'
And, straining dizzy eyes to see,
   With fingers gushing blood,
I shrieked aloud, 'Awake! awake!
Thou white-faced Phantom of the Lake.'

VIII

The deep caves murmur'd, all and one,
'Fair Uniun, pale Uniun!'
And, from her wondrous weed-hung cave,
   Deep in the green moon-lighted water,
She rose above the whispering wave –
   A demon's awful daughter!
White, white as snow her oozy dress,

**Merlin and Vivien (Henry Ford from *The Book of Romance*
by Andrew Lang)**

White as her face's loveliness,
Supple her boneless limbs as snakes,
And full of radiance, such as breaks
Around the cestus of a star,
And strange as eyes of serpents are
   Her haunting eyes.
What time I cried, 'The fates decree,
That he will grow, who conquers thee,
More young, and beautiful, and wise,
For good, and ill, and high emprize,
   Than all men else that be; –
Wherefore I seek thy spells to break,
O wondrous Lady of the Lake!'

IX

She rose erect, the peerless one,
Fair Uniun, pale Uniun!
She fixed her glassy eyes on mine,

With gaze that swoon'd through soul and
   sense,
And wholly robed in white moonshine,
   In vestal white intense,
She rose before me to the waist,
What time bright silver snakes embraced
Her arms and neck, and lilies white
Throbbed to her sides with veins of light;
The pale moon, trembling overhead,
Slow widen'd like a flower, and shed
   Peace on the place;
And, one by one, peept stars that grew
To silver leaf, and sparkled dew,
Shedding a sweetness strange to trace
Upon the Witch's bloodless face,
   Until I saw, and knew,
The lovely lure I sought to break
In the white Lady of the Lake!

X

Fairer than aught that loves the sun
Was Uniun, pale Uniun!
But, weaving spells and waving arms,
   I gazed upon her unbeguiled,
And gazed, and gazed, and mutter'd charms,
   Till, beauteously, she smiled!
And at the smile, – O wondrous sight! –
Her body gleamed and gathered light;
Next, silent as a fountain springs,
From shining shoulders, golden wings
Uncurl'd, and round about her feet
The water murmured and grew sweet,
   And fair, so fair!
The lady smiled upon me still,
And tranced my fate to tears, until
I, gazing on her, waiting there,
Her gentle eyes, her yellow hair,
   Seemed lost to hope and will;
Then thus in tones like music, spake
That matchless Lady of the Lake:

XI

'Not safely wooed, nor lightly won,
Is Uniun, pale Uniun!
Yet unto those who, by a power
   Greater than mine, are given to me,
I grow in beauty hour by hour,
   And immortality!
Haste, haste thee back to Camelot;
I seek not those who love me not;
Nor, till due time, can mortal gaze
Behold how fair I am, and praise

My matchless beauty at its worth;
And thou, compact of subtle earth,
   Hast yet to learn
How fair I am, what peace I keep
For hearts that ache and eyes that weep,
And how, when humbled, men discern
That mine are eyes more sweet than stern!'
   Whereat a darkness deep
Oppressed my soul, and, as she spake,
Sank the white Lady of the Lake!

XII

O beautiful, and all unwon,
Pale Uniun, pale Uniun!
With wiser wonder in my brain,
   And will as weak as ocean foam,
Stript of my pride, and pale with pain,
   I, Merlin, wander'd home.
But, ever since, in moon and sun,
Fair Uniun, pale Uniun,
Has haunted me from place to place
With the white glory of her face;
And I grow old, grow old, and long
At last to join that white-robed throng,
   Who sweetly sleep,
Watched ever by the peerless one,
Who sweetens sleep when work is done
For still, within her cavern deep,
Where never eye may ope to weep,
   Watches pale Uniun,
Till, at a call, the sleepers wake,
And see the Angel of the Lake!

Part 6

MERLIN IN THE TWENTIETH CENTURY

INTRODUCTION

IN THE TWENTIETH century Merlin has regained his importance as a figure of prophetic and magical status. In particular, modern writers – of fiction, poetry and esoteric commentary – have sought to discover his origins and his continuing influence as a powerful inner being. Thus he is characterized by one of the foremost esotericists of our time, Gareth Knight, as 'a way-shower to a new phase, or epoch, of conscious evolution', while two other writers, Alan Richardson and Geoff Hughes, in their book *Ancient Magics for a New Age* (Llewellyn, 1989) describe in detail the long association of an inner plane being who became a guide to the members of the Stella Matutina, an offshoot of the famous Hermetic Order of the Golden Dawn, originally founded by Macgregor Mathers in 1888. This being became known by the name Merlin and still continues to influence modern-day magicians.

Another writer, the mystic Corinne Heline, calls Merlin 'the Arch-druid of Christ' and says that he 'typifies the individual who enters the Way of Attainment impelled only by an eager thirst for knowledge' (*Mysteries of the Holy Grail*, 1977).

This kind of approach to Merlin has coloured much of the more recent fiction and poetry in which he features, as in the example of the extract from the writing of Michael de Angelo quoted below, as well as in such successful novelizations as Marion Zimmer Bradley's *Mists of Avalon*. Other writers have chosen to look behind the esoteric magus to the old wise teacher, bard and seer of the Celtic peoples, while much of the modern interpretation mingles these and other themes into a great melting-pot of dreams, images and sometimes profound realizations. Just how Merlin will continue to develop in the twenty-first century remains a matter for speculation, but that he will continue to be a powerful and exacting presence is beyond doubt.

MERLIN'S ESPLUMOIR

by John Matthews

IN THE FOLLOWING section John Matthews touches upon two major aspects of Merlin legends, and of tradition in general. The most specific is that of the relationship between Jewish and European legend during the Middle Ages, a relationship exemplified by several motifs and themes within the Merlin texts.

In the *Vita Merlini*, for example, we find themes from Talmudic tradition, and from widespread folktales found as far afield as Northern India. This poses the interesting question of sources for such tales and, as John Matthews observes, exchanges of cultural lore undoubtedly occurred during the Middle Ages. There is no suggestion here of a 'diffusionist' theory, which might imply that Merlin stories travelled from the Far or Middle East, gradually becoming Westernized *en route*: such suggestions are merely a type of crude reductionism with a severely limited linear conception of human development and culture.

What actually happens is far more wonderful and significant than any linear travelling or migratory pattern: similar themes, tales, archetypes and mystical realizations concerning inner truth all share a symbolic language. In simpler terms, people all over the world dream the same dreams, share certain key images and tales, no matter how different their politics, formal religion and local practices or culture may be. This does not imply, by the way, a kind of cosy universalism, for the intense differences between cultures and traditions often outweigh the shared aspects; but as we move into the deeper levels of poetic or spiritual symbolism, we find many shared images.

It is on this level that we find important connections between Merlin, Metatron, Elijah, Enoch and Messianic tradition, not necessarily connected in any way to the orthodox Christian concept of Christ as the Messiah. Indeed, Merlin as a saviour or universal prophetic master, seems to attune more strongly to Jewish mystical tradition, not because of any direct migratory relationship in the tales, but as a curious side-effect of political restrictions imposed by Christianity, which effectively debarred such traditions as active means of spiritual education. In other words, the traditions were always present, but seem in retrospect to relate to other cultures through the enforced absence of certain poetical or sacred themes from state religion.

In most cultures the prophet, sacred ruler, or hidden master, is a recognized figure within spiritual tradition and personal inner development; in medieval Europe, however, writers who preserved ancient traditional themes were obliged to edit carefully material already heavily altered through political religious influence. We are, in short, fortunate that Merlin texts survived at all, as at one time it seemed very likely that Merlin was being set up as a potential 'Antichrist'. . . a terrible negative concept far removed from the primal innocence and beauty of the Child of Light from which he seems to have grown.

The second important aspect brought forward by John Matthews is that of the deeper levels of the 'Hidden Master' tradition; we might call these metaphysical levels, in which we detect implications of the relationship between human awareness and the greater or macrocosmic divine consciousness. Traditions of this sort are enduring and deep, and very different indeed from the trivial notions of superhuman masters that abound in fashionable 'New Age' publications.

There is an important difference between commercialized fictitious personae sold to meet our collective emotional need for reassurance, and the perennial traditions of certain masters or teachers who remain upon inner or conceptual dimensions of consciousness. These beings, found worldwide in mystical practice, are a far cry from cosy helpers or extra-terrestrial last-minute saviours. They are often stern, terrifying and utterly uncompromising in their dealings with mortals, mainly because they too were once human and know our failings only too well.

It has become customary to view the end of Merlin's career in a certain light: as an ageing magician captivated by a young woman. In this scenario Merlin is beguiled into giving away his greatest secrets in return for sexual favours; once the temptress – whose name may be Nimuë, Niniane or Vivienne – has succeeded in extracting this knowledge she at once uses it to imprison her aged lover, sometimes under a great rock, sometimes within a hawthorn bush, sometimes in a glass tower. From here he is said to utter elusive prophecies or gnomic sayings, while in some versions the 'Perron de Merlin', Merlin's Stone, becomes a starting point for adventure, to which those in search of the strange or the mysterious resort, to await events or instruction.

Such is the story which Malory, for instance, gives us in the *Morte d'Arthur*, Book IV, Chap. I.

> Merlin fell in a dotage on the damosel that King Pellinore brought to court, and she was one of the damosels of the lake, called Nimue. But Merlin would let her have no rest, but always he would be with her. And ever she made Merlin good cheer till she learned of him all manner thing that she desired; and he was assotted on her, that he might not be from her. . . And so, soon after, the lady and Merlin departed. . . and always Merlin lay about the lady to have her maidenhead, and she was ever passing weary of him, for she was afeared of him because he was a devil's son, and she could not be rid of him by no means. And so on a time it happed that Merlin showed her in a rock whereat was a great wonder, and wrought by enchantment, that went under a great stone. So by her subtle working she made Merlin to go under that stone to let her wit of the marvels there; but she wrought so there for him that he came never out for all the craft he could do. And so she departed and left Merlin.

Tennyson, four hundred years on, reinforced this in Victorian dress in his poem 'Merlin and Vivien' from *The Idylls of the King*; but there is another version. In this story, which we find in Geoffrey of Monmouth's *Vita Merlini*,[1] the Didot Perceval[2] and various other texts, Merlin has reached a great age, or a particular stage of spiritual development, and decides to retire from the world of his own accord. He is, sometimes, still accompanied by a female companion, though, as in the *Vita*, it is more likely to be his sister than his lover, and the place of retirement may still be a tower, an island or a cave, but these are places of Merlin's own choosing or even construction.

The question is: which of these two versions is the right one, if indeed there is a right one; and which motivation – lust or continued growth – should we believe? To

---

1. *Vita Merlini*, Geoffrey of Monmouth, ed. and trans. J.J. Parry, University of Illinois Studies in Language and Literature, 1925. Edited with commentary *Mystic Life of Merlin*, R.J. Stewart, Arkana, 1986.
2. *Didot Perceval*, trans. D. Skeels. University of Washington Press, 1961.

answer this we have to ask another question: Why should Merlin withdraw from the world? I have already suggested one answer: that he sought further knowledge or the opportunity to grow. Fortunately there are several other figures, though from a different tradition, each of whom shares some of Merlin's attributes as prophet, mystic and seer, and has a specific reason for withdrawing. Consideration of these figures may help to clarify matters.

The figures in question are generally known by the term 'hidden' or 'inner' kings, beings who have responsibility for a particular aspect of tradition or teaching and who continue to administer this even after they have withdrawn from active participation in the events of the world, although they are not actually dead. Among the most notable are Melchizadek, Enoch, Elijah and, I believe, Merlin himself.

Despite their many differences these figures share certain important aspects. They are all mysterious, shadowy beings, who appear at a time of crucial import, and who seem to have neither an orthodox beginning nor end to their lives. Finally, they each withdraw or disappear, leaving conflicting accounts of their actual existence, function or allegiance.

Melchizadek, we may remember, was 'without beginning or end',[3] while Enoch 'walked with God and was not'[4] but beyond this seems to have no point of origin. He is first mentioned, in Jewish traditional sources – significantly as we shall see – as living in a hidden place, from which he watches and records the deeds of mankind and holds occasional converse with God. Later he is represented as a king over men who ruled for more than two hundred years before being summoned by God to rule over the angelic hosts.

To this rather sparse account we can add, from various other sources, that Enoch visited heaven often while still in the flesh, and that he was instructed by the archangel Michael in all things, after which he wrote some 366 books, which may well remind us of the 333 prophetic books of Merlin...

When translated to heaven Enoch had bestowed upon him 'extraordinary wisdom, sagacity, judgement, knowledge, learning, compassion, love, kindness, grace, humility, strength, power, might, splendour, beauty, shapeliness and all other excellent qualities', and received besides 'many thousand blessings from God, and his height and breadth became equal to the height and breadth of the world, and thirty-six wings were attached to his body to the right and to the left, each as large as the world, and three hundred and sixty-five thousand eyes were bestowed upon him, each as brilliant as the sun...'[5] The description continues for several more paragraphs, outlining a truly cosmic figure. At the end it is revealed that Enoch – whose name, not surprisingly perhaps, means 'the enlightened one' – received a new name. As the text puts it:

> A magnificent throne was erected for him beside the gates of the seventh celestial palace, and a herald proclaimed throughout heaven concerning him, who was henceforth to be called Metatron. God declares: 'I have appointed my servant Metatron as prince and chief over all other princes in my realm... whatever angel has a request to refer to me, shall appear before Metatron, and what he will command at my bidding, ye must observe and do, for the Prince of Wisdom and the Prince of Understanding are at his service, and they will reveal unto him the science of the celestials and the

---

3. Hebrews, chap. 7, v. 3.
4. Genesis, chap. 5, v. 24.
5. *The Legends of the Jews*, A. Ginsberg, pp. 138-9.

terrestrials, and knowledge of the present order of the world, and the knowledge of the future order of the world. Furthermore have I made him guardian of the treasures of the palace of heaven, Arabot, and of the treasures of life that are in the highest heavens.'[6]

Enoch has thus become a Lord of Hosts and a guardian of the Treasures of Life in heaven. More interestingly perhaps he is also said to have assumed the position left vacant by the fall of Lucifer.[7] He is thus balancing out the uneven ranks of the angelic host, and perhaps it is not stretching the analogy too far to see here an echo of the place left empty at the Round Table, which will one day be filled by the destined champion of the Grail. I think also that in the description of the revelation of the sciences celestial and terrestrial; the knowledges of present and future, we have another analogy of the knowledge and wisdom of Merlin, derived from within his observatory with its 70 doors and windows.[8]

Many ages after the withdrawl of Enoch another figure appears to represent the mysterious hierarchy of the withdrawn kings. This is Elijah, who even in Biblical sources comes across as a rather cantankerous, argumentative character, not at all above telling God how things ought to be done. The story is told that when the time came for him to ascend to heaven, the Angel of Death was reluctant to admit him. Elijah argued so violently before the gates of heaven that God Himself was forced to intervene and gave permission for a wrestling match between Elijah and the Angel. Elijah was victorious and now sits with Enoch and Melchizadek, like them recording the deeds of mankind.[9] He is also seen as a psychopomp, detailed to stand at the crossroads of Paradise to guide the righteous dead to their appointed place. He is thus, like both Enoch and Merlin, a way-shower, guiding travellers on an inner journey; and, like Enoch, he rules over a portion of Paradise.

Many stories are told of Elijah's travels through the world, and of his many disguises, through which he becomes something of a joker – though always remaining a stern judge of human frailty.[10] Thus he is often to be found travelling the roads with some unsuspecting companion, behaving in an extraordinary manner or laughing unaccountably as one who knows the inner truth of the situation from an unknown source. In this he resembles Merlin closely, since there are several well-attested instances of 'Merlin's laughter', where he has perceived things unseen by others and finds the foolishness of men too funny to restrain his mirth.[11]

Indeed there are so many similarities between Elijah and Merlin that it is very easy to pass from one to the other, especially if one considers one of the most significant accounts of Merlin's end. It is found in the medieval Grail-Romance known as the *Didot Perceval*. Here Merlin declares that God 'did not wish him to show himself to people any longer, yet that he should not be able to die until the end of the world'.[12] To Perceval, he adds: 'I wish to make a lodging outside your palace and dwell there, and I shall prophesy wherever our lord commands me. And all those who see my lodging will name it the *Esplumoir* [or Moulting Cage] of Merlin.'[13]

Now with this word *Esplumoir* we come to the heart of the mystery which connects

6. Ibid. pp. 139-40.
7. Ibid. pp. 137-40.
8. *Vita Merlini* op. cit..
9. Ginsberg op. cit. pp. 137-40.
10. Ibid. p. 139
11. *History of the Kings of Britain*, Geoffrey of Monmouth; Penguin, 1966. Cf. Gaster, M. *Legend of Merlin* (in) *Folk-Lore* II, pp. 407-26, 1905. Also *Mystic Life of Merlin*, R.J. Stewart, chap. 5, 1986.
12. *Didot Perceval*, p. 94.
13. Ibid.

Merlin to the Inner Kings and at the same time provides the reason for his withdrawal.

Much speculation has gone into the meaning of the word.[14] What, after all, is this moulting cage? For a long while it was thought that the term originated from a falcon's cage, and that because Merlin happened to share his name with an actual bird of prey, an elaborate pun was intended. In one sense this was right, since birds moult in order to change, to grow fresh plumage, and Merlin himself under another guise is described as wearing a cloak of feathers and living like a bird in a tree.

However, the real meaning of *Esplumoir* is even more complex, and takes us into some very strange areas. In Celtic tradition we find an episode from the *Voyage of Maelduin*[15] where the voyagers arrive at an island where they see a huge bird renew itself in the waters of a lake. When one of the crew drinks this water he is said never again to be troubled with bad eyesight or toothache, so strong are the properties of the water. The same text adds a Biblical reference for the validity of this episode, from the psalm which says: 'You shall renew yourselves as eagles' and it is to a Biblical, or rather a Judaic, source that we must turn for a further definition of the *Esplumoir*.

In the *Zohar*,[16] one of the most important mystical texts of Judaism, we find a description of paradise which both recalls the earlier passages dealing with Enoch and Elijah, and takes us a step further. In this passage we read of a part of heaven in which is 'a certain hidden place, which no eye has seen but those to whom God show it, and which is called "the Bird's Nest"... within this the Messiah [in Jewish tradition there are many Messiahs, so that Christ is not necessarily meant here] lies ailing... in the fifth hall of Paradise, in the castle of Souls, the Bird's Nest, visited only by Elijah, who comforts him'.[17]

This conjures up a scene which will be well known to students of the Grail. There, in many different texts, we find an old, ailing king, lying in the hall of the Grail castle (which could certainly be termed the Castle of the Soul) visited by Merlin. When we discover that, in a romance almost contemporary to the first known compilation of the texts which became the *Zohar*, the same king is called 'Messias' – a word which could only have come from the Hebrew – the parallel is even greater.[18]

What, then, of the 'Birds Nest'? The text further describes it as a place of prophetic vision:

> The Messiah enters that abode, lifts up his eyes, and beholds the Fathers [Patriarchs] visiting the ruins of God's sanctuary. He perceives mother Rachel with tears upon her face; the Holy One, blessed be He, tries to comfort her, but she refuses to be comforted. Then the Messiah lifts up his voice and weeps and the whole Garden of Eden quakes, and all the righteous saints who are there break out in crying and lamentation with him. When the crying and weeping resound for the second time, the whole firmament above the Garden begins to shake, and the cry echoes from five hundred myriads of supernal hosts, until it reaches the highest throne.[19]

Merlin, also, when he enters his *Esplumoir*, is able to see things that others cannot:

14. Cf. Adolf, H. *The Esplumoir Merlin* (in) *Speculum*, 1946, XXI, pp. 173-93. Also, Neitz, W.A. *The Esplumoir Merlin* (in) *Speculum XVIII*, 1943, pp. 67-79.

15. *Voyage of Maelduine* (in) *The Voyages of St Brendan the Navigator* and *Tales of the Irish Saints* trans. Lady Gregory, Colin Smythe, 1973.

16. *The Zohar*, trans. H Sperting and M. Simon, V, pp. 281ff. and III, pp. 21ff. 1931-4.

17. Ibid. III 22ff.

18. *The Vulgate Cycle of Arthurian Romances*, ed. H.O. Sommer, The Carnegie Institution, vols. I and II, *L'Estoire del Saint Graal*, 1909-16.

19. *Zohar*, III, 22ff.

glimpses of British history just as the Messiah sees glimpses of Jewish history. There is, also, a marked similarity between the apocalyptic descriptions in the *Zohar* and the extraordinary visions of Merlin in both the *Vita Merlini* and the earlier *Prophecies* set out in Latin by Geoffrey of Monmouth in the middle of the twelfth century.

Nor should we be surprised by these points of similarity between Christian and Judaic authorities; the barriers between the two cultures in the Middle Ages were far less severe than is often supposed. It is more than likely that any one of the widely read, much-travelled romance writers could have encountered the tradition embodied in the *Zohar* and elsewhere, and that it became a seed planted in the soil of their own vision.

In Celtic literature also, long recognised as a primary source for the Arthurian mythos, are descriptions of the Otherworld abode of the dead in which both Enoch and Elijah are described as living on a mysterious island until the Day of Judgement; and in an early poem of the bard Taliesin,[20] who also identified himself with Merlin, we find the line: 'I was instructor to Elijah and Enoch.'

Merlin likewise is said to retire to a glass house containing the Thirteen Treasures of Britain – including the Cauldron of Annwn, the Celtic Grail – and this also is on an island. (Indeed, an early nineteenth-century scholar interpreted this in his own partic- ular way, describing 'a museum of rareties in King Arthur's time... which Myrddin ap Morfran, the Caledonian, upon the destruction of that place, carried with him to the house of glass in the isle of Enill or Bardsey... This house of glass, it seems, was the museum where they kept their curiosities to be seen by everybody, but not handled; and it is probable that Myrddin... was the keeper of their museum in that time...!')[21]

Seriously, however, Merlin's *Esplumoir* is here both a treasure house and a place of prophecy, as is the Bird's Nest, and within it, like Enoch and Elijah, Merlin notes down the history of mankind to a clerk named Helyas, whose name is itself a corruption of Elijah, and who writes down all that Merlin recounts from inside his retreat.[22]

Again, in the *Vita Merlini*, we have the description (so ably interpreted by Bob Stewart in his commentary on the book) of Merlin's observatory, to which he with- draws with his sister Ganeida, to study the heavens and the mysteries of creation.[23] Here, the moulting cage is a place of study and learning, a place where, in the magical inner realm built by Merlin himself in another dimension, the prophet and wise man can put together the fragments of his knowledge to make a whole. This is Merlin as Phoenix, and we may remember that in the German *Parzival* romance the Grail is described as a stone having the properties of renewal 'like that from which the phoenix renews itself when it is near to death, and from which it arises again restored'.

Before withdrawing, he was a king, but he rejects earthly sovreignty in order to dis- cuss the meaning of meteorology or the purpose of the stars.

In the Jewish texts already quoted, we have seen that the Bird's Nest is a meeting place between the worlds; within the level of Paradise, or heaven, Enoch and Elijah enter the place where the Messiah sits, viewing the events of Creation. Is there any- thing within the stories of Merlin which further parallels this?

I believe there is. There are several references in Arthurian literature to an early name for Britain being *Clas Merddin*, Merlin's Enclosure, and it is said elsewhere that he built a wall of brass around this island to protect it from invasion or attack.[24] Here, I think, we have the origin or seed-thought of the *Esplumoir*. Along with the references

---

20. *Four Ancient Books of Wales*, ed. and trans. W.F. Skene, Edinburgh, 1868.
21. *Celtic Remains*, Silvan Evans, D. London, 1878.
22. *Prose Lancelot*, ed. and trans. L.A. Paton, George Routledge, 1929.
23. *Vita Merlini* op. cit.
24. *Parzival*, Wolfram von Eschenbach, trans. A.T. Hatto, Penguin, 1980.

'And Touching Breton sands, they disembark'd.' (Gustave Doré, *Vivien and Merlin Disembark*)

to *Clas Merddin* are many more which relate the island of Britain to the magical realm of Faery. In a text relating the adventures of Ogier le Dane, a hero once as famous as Arthur, we find him carried off to Avalon by Morgan le Fay, the great enchantress of the Arthurian legends. The description is interesting:

> The barge on which Ogier was, floated across the sea until it came near the Castle of Loadstone, which is called the Castle of Avalon, which is not far this side of the Terrestrial Paradise, whither were wrapt in a flame of fire Enoch and Elijah, and where was also Morgan le Fay. . . [25]

This is very much the kind of description one gets when the Otherworld is being talked of, and here we also find not only Morgan le Fay but also both Enoch and Elijah.

Again, in the *Vita Merlini*, we find a description of Britain which leaves us in no doubt that the tradition drawn upon here saw this island in a particular light, Britain is:

> foremost and best, producing in its fruitfulness every single thing. For it bears crops which throughout the year give the noble gifts of fragrance to man, and it has woods and glades with honey dripping in them, and lofty mountains and broad green fields, fountains and rivers, fishes and cattle and wild beasts, fruit trees, gems, precious metals, and whatever creative nature is in the habit of furnishing.[26]

This is Avalon as much as it is Britain; Merlin's isle, where adventure begins at the stone that bears his name, and where his voice may be heard upraised in prophetic utterance.

---

25. *Le Roman d'Ogier le Danois*, fourteenth-century prose romance (unpublished).
26. *Vita Merlini* op. cit.

Together with Enoch, Elijah, Melchizadek and many more, Merlin has become a withdrawn or Inner King indeed, one who has chosen to enter an inner kingdom from which he will no longer play a direct role in the affairs of the world, electing instead to mediate events from a deeper level, where the barriers between humanity and the absolute are less defined.

This new house is the real *Esplumoir*, the moulting cage where we loose our ties with the world and move towards another state of being, guided by the withdrawn kings. There are parallels in many other areas of study, including Sufism or the Qabalah. This shifting jigsaw of people and places happens outside time, where different names are given to the same people, manifesting in time and at each junction taking on a new aspect with an ongoing purpose. Thus a late medieval manuscript source wonders that so wise a man as Merlin could have allowed himself to be entrapped by a girl, and speculates as to the real nature of the story. For,

> there are a variety of opinions and talk among the people, for some of them hold that... Merlin was a spirit in human form, who was in that shape from the time of Vortigern until the beginning of King Arthur when he disappeared.
>
> After that, this spirit appeared again in the time of Maelgwn Gwynnedd at which time he was called Taliesin, who is said to be alive yet in a place called Caer Sidia. Then, he appeared a third time in the days of Morfran Frych son of Esyllt, whose son he was said to be, and in this period he was called Merlin the Mad. From that day to this, he is said to be resting in Caer Sidia, whence certain people believe firmly that he will rise up once again *before* Doomsday.[27]

Note that word '*before*'. Merlin is evidently still seen as active from within the sphere of Caer Siddi – which is of course yet another name for the Celtic Otherworld, as well as a place where a famous prisoner, Gwair or Guri or Mabon, once resided.[28]

In the other, parallel version we have discussed, Enoch/Metatron begins as a replacement for Lucifer, righting the balance of power in heaven. He reppears as Melchizadek, initiating a line of priestly kings who lead to Christ, and beyond to the Grail itself. He reappears as Enoch, who becomes Sandalphon, the way-shower, returns yet again as Merlin, who takes the Grail to the Nesting Place, the Bird's Nest, the *Esplumoir*, from where it passes to other hands.

This is all a far cry from the view of a love-sick old fool who allows himself to be tricked into an imprisonment from which he cannot escape. I hope I have shown that Merlin's withdrawal is a willing one, made from choice, to allow him the freedom of spirit necessary to grow and change. This can best be brought about within the chamber of the Grail, which is called by many different names, but had only one identity, like the withdrawn kings.[29] They are the same, yet different, as is the Grail and all it stands for. Merlin is one of those figures who travel through the world for a while, only to withdraw again into the inner realm. This is how he was seen by the medieval writers who knew his story best; I believe it is how he should still be seen.

---

27. P.K. Ford, *The Death of Merlin in the Chronicle of Elis Gruffydd* (in) *Viator* no. 7, pp. 379-90, 1976.
28. *Mabon and the Mysteries of Britain*, C. Matthews, Arkana, 1987.
29. J. Matthews, *Temples of the Grail* (in) *At the Table of the Grail* ed, J. Matthews, Arkana, 1987.

EXTRACTS FROM MERLIN

by Edwin Arlington Robinson

ONE OF THE MOST important of the twentieth-century Arthurian poets is the American Edwin Arlington Robinson (1869–1935), who wrote three long works: *Merlin* (1917), from which the following extract is taken; *Lancelot* (1920); and *Tristram* (1927). All three poems are coloured by an air of pessimism and deal primarily with the dark days at the end of Arthur's rule. *Merlin* opens with an extended meditation by Dagonet, Arthur's fool, and goes on to tell, partly in flashback and partly direct narrative, the story of Merlin and Vivien. But this is a far cry from Tennyson. Here Merlin is no longer a wizard, but rather a brilliant politician, a king-maker in fact; while Vivien is a beautiful, complex woman. The imprisonment of Merlin here is seen as being of his own making. He chooses freely to belong to Vivien and to remain with her. The texture of the verse is dense, and conveys both the thoughts and actions of the characters in a very modern way. Though it is a far cry from the Merlin of tradition, it none the less has considerable power as a narrative. The section included here, from Parts IV and V of the poem, is concerned with Merlin's visit to Broceliande, the forest in which Vivien has her home. Later he opts to return to Arthur's service and remain with him to the end.

     Ten years ago
The King had heard, with unbelieving ears
At first, what Merlin said would be the last
Reiteration of his going down
To find a living grave in Brittany:
'Buried alive I told you I should be,
By love made little and by woman shorn,
Like Samson, of my glory; and the time
Is now at hand. I follow in the morning
Where I am led. I see behind me now
The last of crossways, and I see before me
A straight and final highway to the end
Of all my divination. You are King,
And in your kingdom I am what I was.
Wherever I have warned you, see as far
As I have seen; for I have shown the worst
There is to see. Require no more of me,
For I can be no more than what I was.'
So, on the morrow, the King said farewell;
And he was never more to Merlin's eye
The King than at that hour; for Merlin knew
How much was going out of Arthur's life
With him, as he went southward to the sea.

Over the waves and into Brittany
Went Merlin, to Broceliande. Gay birds
Were singing high to greet him all along

A broad and sanded woodland avenue
That led him on forever, so he thought,
Until at last there was an end of it;
And at the end there was a gate of iron,
Wrought heavily and individiously barred.
He pulled a cord that rang somewhere a bell
Of many echoes, and sat down to rest,
Outside the keeper's house, upon a bench
Of carven stone that might for centuries
Have waited there in silence to receive him.
The birds were singing still; leaves flashed
 and swung
Before him in the sunlight; a soft breeze
Made intermittent whisperings around him
Of love and fate and danger, and faint waves
Of many sweetly-stinging fragile odors
Broke lightly as they touched him; cherry-
 boughs
Above him snowed white petals down upon him,
And under their slow falling Merlin smiled
Contentedly, as one who contemplates
No longer fear, confusion, or regret,
May smile at ruin or at revelation.

A stately fellow with a forest air
Now hailed him from within, with searching
 words

And curious looks, till Merlin's glowing eye
Transfixed him and he flinched: 'My
    compliments
And homage to the lady Vivian.
Say Merlin from King Arthur's Court is here,
A pilgrim and a stranger in appearance,
Though in effect her friend and humble
    servant.
Convey to her my speech as I have said it,
Without abbreviation or delay,
And so deserve my gratitude forever.'
'But Merlin?' the man stammered; 'Merlin?
    Merlin?' –
'One Merlin is enough. I know no other.
Now go you to the lady Vivian
And bring to me her word, for I am weary.'
Still smiling at the cherry-blossoms falling
Down on him and around him in the sunlight,
He waited, never moving, never glancing
This way or that, until his messenger
Came jingling into vision, weighed with keys,
And inly shaken with much wondering
At this great wizard's coming unannounced
And unattended. When the way was open
The stately messenger, now bowing low
In reverence and awe, bade Merlin enter;
And Merlin, having entered, heard the gate
Clang back behind him; and he swore no gate
Like that had ever clanged in Camelot,
Or any other place if not in hell.
'I may be dead; and this good fellow here,
With all his keys,' he thought, 'may be the
    Devil, –
Though I were loath to say so, for the keys
Would make him rather more akin to Peter;
And that's fair reasoning for this fair weather.'

'The lady Vivian says you are most welcome,'
Said now the stately-favored servitor,
'And are to follow me. She said, "Say Merlin –
A pilgrim and a stranger in appearance,
Though in effect my friend and humble
    servant –
Is welcome for himself, and for the sound
Of his great name that echoes everywhere." ' –
'I like you and I like your memory,'
Said Merlin, curiously, 'but not your gate.
Why forge for this elysian wilderness
A thing so vicious with unholy noise?' –
'There's a way out of every wilderness
For those who dare or care enough to find it,'
The guide said: and they moved along together,

Down shaded ways, through open ways with
    hedgerows.
And into shade again more deep than ever,
But edged anon with rays of broken sunshine
In which a fountain, raining crystal music,
Made faery magic of it through green leafage,
Till Merlin's eyes were dim with preparation
For sight now of the lady Vivian.

He saw at first a bit of living green
That might have been a part of all the green
Around the tinkling fountain where she gazed
Upon the circling pool as if her thoughts
Were not so much on Merlin – whose advance
Betrayed through his enormity of hair
The cheeks and eyes of youth – as on the fishes.
But soon she turned and found him, now alone,
And held him while her beauty and her grace
Made passing trash of empires, and his eyes
Told hers of what a splendid emptiness
Her tedious world had been without him in it
Whose love and service were to be her school,
Her triumph, and her history: 'This is Merlin,'
She thought; 'and I shall dream of him no
    more.
And he has come, he thinks, to frighten me
With beards and robes and his immortal fame;
Or is it I who think so? I know not.
I'm frightened, sure enough, but if I show it,
I'll be no more the Vivian for whose love
He tossed away his glory, or the Vivian
Who saw no man alive to make her love him
Till she saw Merlin once in Camelot,
And seeing him, saw no other. In an age
That has no plan for me that I can read
Without him, shall he tell me what I am,
And why I am, I wonder?' While she thought,
And feared the man whom her perverse
    negation
Must overcome somehow to soothe her fancy,
She smiled and welcomed him; and so they
    stood,
Each finding in the other's eyes a gleam
Of what eternity had hidden there.

'Are you always all in green, as you are now?'
Said Merlin, more employed with her
    complexion,
Where blood and olive made wild harmony
With eyes and wayward hair that were too dark
For peace if they were not subordinated;
'If so you are, then so you make yourself

'And then she follow'd Merlin all the way, Ev'n to the wild woods of
Broceliande.' (Gustave Doré, *Vivien and Merlin enter the Woods*)

A danger in a world of many dangers.
If I were young, God knows if I were safe
Concerning you in green, like a slim cedar,
As you are now, to say my life was mine:
Were you to say to me that I should end it,
Longevity for me were jeopardized.
Have you your green on always and all over?'

'Come here, and I will tell you about that,'
Said Vivian, leading Merlin with a laugh
To an arbored seat where they made opposites:
'If you are Merlin – and I know you are,
For I remember you in Camelot, –
You know that I am Vivian, as I am;
And if I go in green, why, let me go so,
And say at once why you have come to me
Cloaked over like a monk, and with a beard
As long as Jeremiah's. I don't like it.
I'll never like a man with hair like that
While I can feed a carp with little frogs.
I'm rather sure to hate you if you keep it,
And when I hate a man I poison him.'

'You've never fed a carp with little frogs,'
Said Merlin; 'I can see it in your eyes.' –

'I might then, if I haven't,' said the lady;
'For I'm a savage, and I love no man
As I have seen him yet. I'm here alone,
With some three hundred others, all of whom
Are ready, I dare say, to die for me;
I'm cruel and I'm cold, and I like snakes;
And some have said my mother was a fairy,
Though I believe it not.'

                              'Why not believe it?'
Said Merlin; 'I believe it. I believe
Also that you divine, as I had wished,
In my surviving ornament of office
A needless imposition on your wits,
If not yet on the scope of your regard.
Even so, you cannot say how old I am,
Or yet how young. I'm willing cheerfully
To fight, left-handed, Hell's three headed
     hound
If you but whistle him up from where he lives;
I'm cheerful and I'm fierce, and I've made
     kings;
And some have said my father was the Devil,
Though I believe it not. Whatever I am,
I have not lived in Time until to-day.'

275

A moment's worth of wisdom there escaped
   him,
But Vivian seized it, and it was not lost.

Embroidering doom with many levities,
Till now the fountain's crystal silver, fading,
Became a splash and a mere chilliness,
They mocked their fate with easy pleasantries
That were too false and small to be forgotten,
And with ingenious insincerities
That had no repetition or revival.
At last the lady Vivian arose,
And with a crying of how late it was
Took Merlin's hand and led him like a child
Along a dusky way between tall cones
Of tight green cedars: 'Am I like one of
   these?
You said I was, though I deny it wholly,' –
'Very,' said Merlin, to his bearded lips
Uplifting her small fingers. – 'O, that hair!'
She moaned, as if in sorrow: 'Must it be?
Must every prophet and important wizard
Be clouded so that nothing but his nose
And eyes, and intimations of his ears,
Are there to make us know him when we see
   him?
Praise heaven I'm not a prophet! Are you
   glad?'

He did not say that he was glad or sorry;
For suddenly came flashing into vision
A thing that was a manor and a castle,
With walls and roofs that had a flaming sky
Behind them, like a sky that he remembered,
And one that had from his rock-sheltered
   haunt
Above the roofs of his forsaken city
Made flame as if all Camelot were on fire.
The glow brought with it a brief memory
Of Arthur as he left him, and the pain
That fought in Arthur's eyes for losing him,
And must have overflowed when he had
   vanished.
But now the eyes that looked hard into his
Were Vivian's, not the King's; and he could
   see,
Or so he thought, a shade of sorrow in them.
She took his two hands: 'You are sad,' she
   said. –
He smiled: 'Your western lights bring
   memories
Of Camelot. We all have memories –

Prophets, and women who are like slim
   cedars;
But you are wrong to say that I am sad.' –
'Would you go back to Camelot?' she asked,
Her fingers tightening. Merlin shook his
   head.
'Then listen while I tell you that I'm glad,'
She purred, as if assured that he would listen:
'At your first warning, much too long ago,
Of this quaint pilgrimage of yours to see
"The fairest and most orgulous of ladies" –
No language for a prophet, I am sure –

Said I, "When this great Merlin comes to me,
My task and avocation for some time
Will be to make him willing, if I can,
To teach and feed me with an ounce of
   wisdom."
For I have eaten to an empty shell,
After a weary feast of observation
Among the glories of a tinsel world
That had for me no glory till you came,
A life that is no life. Would you go back
To Camelot?' – Merlin shook his head again,
And the two smiled together in the sunset.

They moved along in silence to the door,
Where Merlin said: 'Of your three hundred
   here
There is but one I know, and him I favor;
I mean the stately one who shakes the keys
Of that most evil sounding gate of yours,
Which has a clang as if it shut forever.' –
'If there be need, I'll shut the gate myself,'
She said. 'And you like Blaise? Then you shall
   have him.
He was not born to serve, but serve he must,
It seems, and be enamoured of my shadow.
He cherishes the taint of some high folly
That haunts him with a name he cannot know,
And I could fear his wits are paying for it.
Forgive his tongue, and humor it a little.' –
'I knew another one whose name was Blaise,'
He said; and she said lightly, 'Well, what of it?' –
'And he was nigh the learnedest of hermits;
His home was far away from everywhere,
And he was all alone there when he died.' –
'Now be a pleasant Merlin,' Vivian said,
Patting his arm, 'and have no more of that;
For I'll not hear of dead men far away,
Or dead men anywhere this afternoon.
There'll be a trifle in the way of supper

This evening, but the dead shall not have any.
Blaise and this man will tell you all there is
For you to know. Then you'll know
   everything.'
She laughed, and vanished like a humming-
   bird.

[...]

THE sun went down, and the dark after it
Starred Merlin's new abode with many a
   sconced
And many a moving candle, in whose light
The prisoned wizard, mirrored in amazement,
Saw fronting him a stranger, falcon-eyed,
Firm-featured, of a negligible age,
And fair enough to look upon, he fancied,
Though not a warrior born, nor more a
   courtier.
A native humor resting in his long
And solemn jaws now stirred, and Merlin
   smiled
To see himself in purple, touched with gold.
And fledged with snowy lace. – The careful
   Blaise,
Having drawn some time before from Merlin's
   wallet
The sable raiment of a royal scholar,
Had eyed it with a long mistrust and said:
'The lady Vivian would be vexed, I fear,
To meet you vested in these learned weeds
Of gravity and death; for she abhors
Mortality in all its hues and emblems –
Black wear, long argument, and all the cold
And solemn things that appertain to
   graves.' –
And Merlin, listening, to himself had said,
'This fellow has a freedom, yet I like him;'
And then aloud: 'I trust you. Deck me out,
However, with a temperate regard
For what your candid eye may find in me
Of inward coloring. Let them reap my beard,
Moreover, with a sort of reverence,
For I shall never look on it again.
And though your lady frown her face away
To think of me in black, for God's indulgence,
Array me not in scarlet or in yellow.' –
And so it came to pass that Merlin sat
At ease in purple, even though his chin
Reproached him as he pinched it, and seemed
   yet
A little fearful of its nakedness.

He might have sat and scanned himself for
   ever
Had not the careful Blaise, regarding him,
Remarked again that in his proper judgment,
And on the valid word of his attendants,
No more was to be done. 'Then do no more,'
Said Merlin, with a last look at his chin;
'Never do more when there's no more to do,
And you may shun thereby the bitter taste
Of many disillusions and regrets.
God's pity on us that our words have wings
And leave our deeds to crawl so far below them;
For we have all two heights, we men who
   dream,
Whether we lead or follow, rule or serve.' –
'God's pity on us anyhow,' Blaise answered,
'Or most of us. Meanwhile, I have to say,
As long as you are here, and I'm alive,
Your summons will assure the loyalty
Of all my diligence and expedition.
The gong that you hear singing in the distance
Was rung for your attention and your
   presence.' –
'I wonder at this fellow, yet I like him,'
Said Merlin; and he rose to follow him.

The lady Vivian in a fragile sheath
Of crimson, dimmed and veiled ineffably
By the flame-shaken gloom wherein she sat,
And twinkled if she moved, heard Merlin
   coming,
And smiled as if to make herself believe
Her joy was all a triumph; yet her blood
Confessed a tingling of more wonderment
Than all her five and twenty worldly years
Of waiting for this triumph could remember;
And when she knew and felt the slower tread
Of his unseen advance among the shadows
To the small haven of uncertain light
That held her in it as a torch-lit shoal
Might hold a smooth red fish, her listening
   skin
Responded with a creeping underneath it,
And a crinkling that was incident alike
To darkness, love, and mice. When he was
   there,
She looked up at him in a whirl of mirth
And wonder, as in childhood she had gazed
Wide-eyed on royal mountebanks who made
So brief a shift of the impossible
That kings and queens would laugh and shake
   themselves;

Then rising slowly on her little feet,
Like a slim creature lifted, she thrust out
Her two small hands as if to push him back –
Whereon he seized them. 'Go away,' she said;
'I never saw you in my life before.' –
'You say the truth,' he answered; 'when I met
Myself an hour ago, my words were yours.
God made the man you see for you to like,
If possible. If otherwise, turn down
These two prodigious and remorseless
    thumbs
And leave your lions to annihilate him.' –

'I have no other lion than yourself,'
She said; 'and since you cannot eat yourself,
Pray do a lonely woman, who is, you say,
More like a tree than any other thing
In your discrimination, the large honor
Of sharing with her a small kind of supper.' –
'Yes, you are like a tree, – or like a flower;
More like a flower to-night.' He bowed his
    head
And kissed the ten small fingers he was
    holding,
As calmly as if each had been a son;
Although his heart was leaping and his eyes
Had sight for nothing save a swimming
    crimson
Between two glimmering arms. 'More like a
    flower
To-night,' he said, as now he scanned again
The immemorial meaning of her face
And drew it nearer to his eyes. It seemed
A flower of wonder with a crimson stem
Came leaning slowly and regretfully
To meet his will – a flower of change and peril
That had a clinging blossom of warm olive
Half stifled with a tyranny of black,
And held the wayward fragrance of a rose
Made woman by delirious alchemy.
She raised her face and yoked his willing neck
With half her weight; and with hot lips that
    left
The world with only one philosophy
For Merlin or for Anaxagoras,
Called his to meet them and in one long hush
Of capture to surrender and make hers
The last of anything that might remain
Of what was now their beardless wizardry.
Then slowly she began to push herself
Away, and slowly Merlin let her go
As far from him as his outreaching hands

Could hold her fingers while his eyes had all
The beauty of the woodland and the world
Before him in the firelight, like a nymph
Of cities, or a queen a little weary
Of inland stillness and immortal trees.
'Are you to let me go again sometime,'
She said, – 'before I starve to death, I wonder?
If not, I'll have to bite the lion's paws,
And make him roar. He cannot shake his
    mane,
For now the lion has no mane to shake;
The lion hardly knows himself without it,
And thinks he has no face, but there's a lady
Who says he had no face until he lost it.
So there we are. And there's a flute somewhere,
Playing a strange old tune. You know the
    words:
"The Lion and the Lady are both hungry." '

Fatigue and hunger – tempered leisurely
With food that some devout magician's oven
Might after many failures have delivered,
And wine that had for decades in the dark
Of Merlin's grave been slowly quickening,
And with half-heard, dream-weaving interludes
Of distant flutes and viols, made more distant
By far, nostalgic hautboys blown from
    nowhere, –
Were tempered not so leisurely, may be,
With Vivian's inextinguishable eyes
Between two shining silver candlesticks
That lifted each a trembling flame to make
The rest of her a dusky loveliness
Against a bank of shadow. Merlin made,
As well as he was able while he ate,
A fair division of the fealty due
To food and beauty, albeit more times than one
Was he at odds with his urbanity
In honoring too long the grosser viand.
'The best invention in Broceliande
Has not been over-taxed in vain, I see,'
She told him, with her chin propped on her
    fingers
And her eyes flashing blindness into his:
'I put myself out cruelly to please you,
And you, for that, forget almost at once
The name and image of me altogether.
You needn't, for when all is analyzed,
It's only a bird-pie that you are eating.'

'I know not what you call it,' Merlin said;
'Nor more do I forget your name and image,

Though I do eat; and if I did not eat,
Your sending out of ships and caravans
To get whatever 'tis that's in this thing
Would be a sorrow for you all your days;
And my great love, which you have seen by
    now,
Might look to you a lie; and like as not
You'd actuate some sinewed mercenary
To carry me away to God knows where
And seal me in a fearsome hole to starve,
Because I made of this insidious picking
An idle circumstance. My dear fair lady –
And there is not another under heaven
So fair as you are as I see you now –
I cannot look at you too much and eat;
And I must eat, or be untimely ashes,
Whereon the light of your celestial gaze
Would fall, I fear me, for no longer time
Than on the solemn dust of Jeremiah –
Whose beard you likened once, in heathen jest,
To mine that now is no man's.'

                                    'Are you sorry?'
Said Vivian, filling Merlin's empty goblet;
'If you are sorry for the loss of it,
Drink more of this and you may tell me lies
Enough to make me sure that you are glad;
But if your love is what you say it is,
Be never sorry that my love took off
That horrid hair to make your face at last
A human fact. Since I have had your name
To dream of and say over to myself,
The visitations of that awful beard
Have been a terror for my nights and days –
For twenty years. I've seen it like an ocean,
Blown seven ways at once and wrecking ships,
With men and women screaming for their
    lives;
I've seen it woven into shining ladders
That ran up out of sight and so to heaven,
All covered with white ghosts with hanging
    robes
Like folded wings, – and there were millions
    of them,
Climbing, climbing, climbing, all the time;
And all the time that I was watching them
I thought how far above me Merlin was,
And wondered always what his face was like.
But even then, as a child, I knew the day
Would come some time when I should see his
    face
And hear his voice, and have him in my house

Till he should care no more to stay in it,
And go away to found another kingdom.' –
'Not that,' he said; and, sighing, drank more
    wine;
'One kingdom for one Merlin is enough.' –
'One Merlin for one Vivian is enough,'
She said. 'If you care much, remember that;
But the Lord knows how many Vivians
One Merlin's entertaining eye might favor,
Indifferently well and all at once,
If they were all at hand. Praise heaven they're
    not.'

'If they were in the world – praise heaven
    they're not –
And if one Merlin's entertaining eye
Saw two of them, there might be left him then
The sight of no eye to see anything –
Not even the Vivian who is everything,
She being Beauty, Beauty being She,
She being Vivian, and so on for ever.' –
'I'm glad you don't see two of me,' she said;
'For there's a whole world yet for you to eat
And drink and say to me before I know
The sort of creature that you see in me.
I'm withering for a little more attention,
But, being woman, I can wait. These cups
That you see coming are for the last there is
Of what my father gave to kings alone,
And far from always. You are more than kings
To me; therefore I give it all to you,
Imploring you to spare no more of it
Than a small cockle-shell would hold for me
To pledge your love and mine in. Take the rest,
That I may see tonight the end of it.
I'll have no living remnant of the dead
Annoying me until it fades and sours
Of too long cherishing; for Time enjoys
The look that's on our faces when we scowl
On unexpected ruins, and thrift itself
May be a sort of slow unwholesome fire
That eats away to dust the life that feeds it.
You smile, I see, but I said what I said.
One hardly has to live a thousand years
To contemplate a lost economy;
So let us drink it while it's yet alive
And you and I are not untimely ashes.
My last words are your own, and I don't like
    'em.' –
A sudden laughter scatterd from her eyes
A threatening wisdom. He smiled and let her
    laugh,

Then looked into the dark where there was
    nothing:
'There's more in this than I have seen,' he
    thought,
'Though I shall see it.' – 'Drink,' she said
    again;
'There's only this much in the world of it,
And I am near to giving all to you
Because you are so great and I so little.'

With a long-kindling gaze that caught from
    hers
A laughing flame, and with a hand that shook
Like Arthur's kingdom, Merlin slowly raised
A golden cup that for a golden moment
Was twinned in air with hers; and Vivian,
Who smiled at him across their gleaming rims,
From eyes that made a fuel of the night
Surrounding her, shot glory over gold
At Merlin, while their cups touched and his
    trembled.
He drank, not knowing what , nor caring much
For kings who might have cared less for
    themselves,
He thought, had all the darkness and wild light
That fell together to make Vivian
Been there before them then to flower anew
Through sheathing crimson into candle-light
With each new leer of their loose, liquorish
    eyes.
Again he drank, and he cursed every king
Who might have touched her even in her cradle;
For what were kings to such as he, who made
    them
And saw them totter – for the world to see,
And heed, if the world would? He drank again,
And yet again – to make himself assured
No manner of king should have the last of it –
The cup that Vivian filled unfailingly
Until she poured for nothing. 'At the end
Of this incomparable flowing gold,'
She prattled on to Merlin, who observed
Her solemnly, 'I fear there may be specks.' –
He sighed aloud, whereat she laughed at him
And pushed the golden cup a little nearer.
He scanned it with a sad anxiety,

And then her face likewise, and shook his head
As if at her concern for such a matter:
'Specks? What are specks? Are you afraid of
    them?'
He murmured slowly, with a drowsy tongue;

'There are specks everywhere. I fear them not.
If I were king in Camelot, I might
Fear more than specks. But now I fear them not
You are too strange a lady to fear specks.'

He stared a long time at the cup of gold
Before him but he drank no more. There came
Between him and the world a crumbling sky
Of black and crimson, with a crimson cloud
That held a far off town of many towers.
All swayed and shaken, till at last they fell,
And there was nothing but a crimson cloud
That crumbled into nothing, like the sky
That vanished with it, carrying away
The world, the woman, and all memory of them,
Until a slow light of another sky
Made gray an open casement, showing him
Faint shapes of an exotic furniture
That glimmered with a dim magnificence,
And letting in the sound of many birds
That were, as he lay there remembering,
The only occupation of his ears
Until it seemed they shared a fainter sound,
As if a sleeping child with a black head
Beside him drew the breath of innocence.

One shining afternoon around the fountain,
As on the shining day of his arrival,
The sunlight was alive with flying silver
That had for Merlin a more dazzling flash
Than jewels rained in dreams, and a richer
    sound
Than harps, and all the morning stars
    together, –
When jewels and harps and stars and everything
That flashed and sang and was not Vivian,
Seemed less than echoes of her least of words –
For she was coming. Suddenly, somewhere
Behind him, she was coming; that was all
He knew until she came and took his hand
And held it while she talked about the fishes.
When she looked up he thought a softer light
Was in her eyes than once he had found there;
And had there been left yet for dusky women
A beauty that was heretofore not hers,
He told himself he must have seen it then
Before him in the face at which he smiled
And trembled. 'Many men have called me wise,'
He said, 'but you are wiser than all wisdom
If you know what you are.' – 'I don't,' she said;
'I know that you and I are here together;
I know that I have known for twenty years

That life would be almost a constant yawning
Until you came; and now that you are here,
I know that you are not to go away
Until you tell me that I'm hideous;
I know that I like fishes, ferns, and snakes, –
Maybe because I liked them when the world
Was young and you and I were salamanders;
I know, too, a cool place not far from here,
Where there are ferns that are like marching
    men
Who never march away. Come now and see
    them,
And do as they do – never march away.
When they are gone, some others, crisp and
    green,
Will have their place, but never march away.' –
He smoothed her silky fingers, one by one:
'Some other Merlin, also, do you think,
Will have his place – and never march away?' –
Then Vivian laid a finger on his lips
And shook her head at him before she laughed:
'There is no other Merlin than yourself,
And you are never going to be old.'

Oblivious of a world that made of him
A jest, a legend, and a long regret,
And with a more commanding wizardry
Than his to rule a kingdom where the king
Was Love and the queen Vivian, Merlin found
His queen without the blemish of a word
That was more rough than honey from her lips,
Or the first adumbration of a frown
To cloud the night-wild fire that in her eyes ·
Had yet a smoky friendliness of home,
And a foreknowing care for mighty trifles.
'There are miles and miles for you to wander
    in,'
She told him once: 'Your prison yard is large,
And I would rather take my two ears off
And feed them to the fishes in the fountain
Than buzz like an incorrigible bee
For always around yours, and have you hate
The sound of me; for some day then, for certain,
Your philosophic rage would see in me
A bee in earnest, and your hand would smite
My life away. And what would you do then?
I know: for years and years you'd sit alone
Upon my grave, and be the grieving image
Of lean remorse, and suffer miserably;
And often, all day long, you'd only shake
Your celebrated head and all it holds,
Or beat it with your fist the while you groaned

Aloud and went on saying to yourself:
"Never should I have killed her, or believed
She was a bee that buzzed herself to death,
First having made me crazy, had there been
Judicious distance and wise absences
To keep the two of us inquisitive." ' –
'I fear you bow your unoffending head
Before a load that should be mine,' said he;
'If so, you led me on by listening.
You should have shrieked and jumped, and
    then fled yelling;
That's the best way when a man talks too long.
God's pity on me if I love your feet
More now than I could ever love the face
Of any one of all those Vivians
You summoned out of nothing on the night
When I saw towers. I'll wander and amend.' –
At that she flung the noose of her soft arms
Around his neck and kissed him instantly:
'You are the wisest man that ever was,
And I've a prayer to make: May all you say
To Vivian be a part of what you knew
Before the curse of her unquiet head
Was on your shoulder, as you have it now,
To punish you for knowing before knowledge.
You are the only one who sees enough
To make me see how far away I am
From all that I have seen and have not been;
You are the only thing there is alive
Between me as I am and as I was
When Merlin was a dream. You are to listen
When I say now to you that I'm alone.
Like you, I saw too much; and unlike you
I made no kingdom out of what I saw –
Or none save this one here that you must rule,
Believing you are ruled. I see too far
To rule myself. Time's way with you and me
Is our way, in that we are out of Time
And out of tune with Time. We have this place,
And you must hold us in it or we die.
Look at me now and say if what I say
Be folly or not; for my unquiet head
Is no conceit of mine. I had it first
When I was born; and I shall have it with me
Till my unquiet soul is on its way
To be, I hope, where souls are quieter.
So let the first and last activity
Of what you say so often is your love
Be always to remember that our lyres
Are not strung for Today. On you it falls
To keep them in accord here with each other,
For you have wisdom, I have only sight

For distant things – and you. And you are
    Merlin.
Poor wizard! Vivian is your punishment
For making kings of men who are not kings;
And you are mine, by the same reasoning,
For living out of Time and out of tune
With anything but you. No other man
Could make me say so much of what I know
As I say now to you. And you are Merlin!'

She looked up at him till his way was lost
Again in the familiar wilderness
Of night that love made for him in her eyes,
And there he wandered as he said he would;
He wandered also in his prison-yard,
And, when he found her coming after him,
Beguiled her with her own admonishing
And frowned upon her with a fierce reproof
That many a time in the old world outside
Had set the mark of silence on strong men –
Whereat she laughed, not always wholly sure,
Nor always wholly glad, that he who played
So lightly was the wizard of her dreams:
'No matter – if only Merlin keep the world
Away,' she thought. 'Our lyres have many
    strings,
But he must know them all, for he is Merlin.'

And so for years, till ten of them were gone, –
Ten years, ten seasons, or ten flying ages –
Fate made Broceliande a paradise,
By none invaded, until Dagonet,
Like a discordant, awkward bird of doom,
Flew in with Arthur's message. For the King,

In sorrow cleaving to simplicity,
And having in his love a quick remembrance
Of Merlin's old affection for the fellow,
Had for this vain, reluctant enterprise
Appointed him – the knight who made men
    laugh,
And was a fool because he played the fool.

'The King believes today, as in his boyhood,
That I am Fate; and I can do no more
Than show again what in his heart he knows,'
Said Merlin to himself and Vivian:
'This time I go because I made him King,
Thereby to be a mirror for the world;
This time I go, but never after this,
For I can be no more than what I was,
And I can do no more than I have done.'
He took her slowly in his arms and felt
Her body throbbing like a bird against him:
'This time I go; I go because I must.'

And in the morning, when he rode away
With Dagonet and Blaise through the same
    gate
That once had clanged as if to shut for ever,
She had not even asked him not to go;
For it was then that in his lonely gaze
Of helpless love and sad authority
She found the gleam of his imprisoned power
That Fate withheld; and, pitying herself,
She pitied the fond Merlin she had changed,
And saw the Merlin who had changed the
    world.

THE RIDDLES OF MERLIN

by Alfred Noyes

ALFRED NOYES (1880–1958) was a poet, critic and essayist. He is best known for his extraordinary narrative verse epics, which deal with the inner history of Britain. Among the best of these are *Tales From the Mermaid Tavern* (1913) and *Drake* (1906–8), which was serialized in *Blackwoods Magazine* and was as eagerly awaited as a serialized novel. His verse is colourful and lyric, and he manages to capture the essence of a certain kind of pastoral 'Englishness'. *The Riddles of Merlin*, reproduced here, is a poem curiously like those of Ralph Waldo Emerson (see Part 5 above), in which the shade of Merlin is invoked as a source of knowledge and wisdom. Noyes wrote much of his best poetry under the aegis of a kind of nature-spirit whom he named 'shadow of a leaf', who is mentioned in a number of lyric poems and is a major figure in the longer work *Forest of Wild Thyme*.

I

As I was walking
Alone by the sea,
'What is that whisper?'
Said Merlin to me.
'Only,' I answered,
'The sigh of the wave' –
'Oh, no,' replied Merlin,
' 'Tis the grass on your grave.'

As I lay dreaming
In churchyard ground
'Listen,' said Merlin,
'What is that sound?'
'The green grass is growing,'
I answered; but he
Chuckled, *'Oh, no!*
'Tis the sound of the sea.'

As I went homeward
At dusk by the shore,
'What is that crimson?
Said Merlin once more.
'Only the sun,' I said.
'Sinking to rest' –
'Sunset for East,' he said,
'Sunrise for West.'

II

Tell me, Merlin, – It is I
Who call thee, after a thousand Springs –
Tell me by what wizardry
The white foam wakes in whiter wings
Where surf and sea-gulls toss and cry
Like sister-flakes, as they mount and fly,
Flakes that the great sea flings on high,
To kiss each other and die.

Tell me, Merlin, tell me why
These delicate things that feast on flowers,
Red Admiral, brown fritillary,
Sister the flowers, yet sail the sky,
Frail ships that cut their cables, yet still fly
The colours we know them by.

Tell me, Merlin, tell me why,
The sea's chaotic colour grows
Into these rainbow fish whose Tyrian dye
In scales of gold and green reply
To blue-striped mackerel waves, to kelp-brown caves,
And deep-sea blooms of gold and green and rose;
Why colours that the sea at random throws
Were ordered into this living harmony,
This little world, no bigger than the hand,
Gliding over the raw tints whence it came,
This opal-bellied patch of sand,
That floats above the sand, or darts a flame
Through woods of crimson lake, and flowers without a name.
See all their tints around its body strewn
In planetary order. Sun, moon, star,
Are not more constant to their tune
Than those light scales of colour are;
Where each repeats the glory of his neighbour,
In the same pattern, with the same delight,

'At Merlin's feet the wily Vivien lay' (Gustave Doré, *Vivien and Merlin Repose*)

As if, without the artist's labour,
The palette of rich Chaos and old Night
Should spawn a myriad pictures, every line
True to the lost Designer's lost design.

Tell me, Merlin, for what eye
Gathers and grows this cosmic harmony?
Can sea-gulls feed, or fishes brood
On music fit for angels' food?
Did Nescience this delight create
To lure the conger to his mate?
If this be all that Science tells
The narrowest church may peal its bells,
And Merlin work new miracles;
While every dreamer, even as I,
May wonder on, until he die.

MERLIN AND MARK

by Arthur Symons

ARTHUR SYMONS (1865–1945), though born in the nineteenth century, is scarcely a Victorian poet and for this reason his poem is included here rather than in the previous section. A leading light in the Decadent movement, he is also well known as a dramatist and critic. He wrote several Arthurian works, including a verse drama of *Tristan and Iseult* (1917) and several shorter poems. *Merlin and Mark*, included here, is a curious mixture of the Merlin myth with that of Tristan. Merlin also receives his magic powers from a mysterious 'Phoenician', who subsequently disappears.

Yea, I have been in a cavern under the Earth,
Merlin's cavern, where eternally foams the sea,
There where Merlin lived who, but for his birth,
was conceived by no woman's seed: for inevitably
Merlin was made by the inhuman powers a Magician,
He who at Arthur's Court for his Wizardry
was famed: he had his spells from a certain Phoenician
who having given him these, vanished out of his sight.
Here, in his roofed over cavern he was wont to brood
over the world's destinies and his own destiny,
Till at the last the wind and the sea passed into his blood
And always the night was the day and the day was the night,
Initiate always he wove in his fashion spell after spell
For he was evil and cruel and had in his soul some spite:
Serpents rose at his bidding out of the depths of their Well
And they glided and coiled around him and he knew their delight.

There, night after night, Iseult and her Tristram came
She with her fabulous beauty woven in no human passion,
Elemental and pure as the water and the wind and the flame,
He with his nervous beauty and absolute passion,
Lo, on a moonless night there came to him gloomily, Mark,
The wild storms hurled themselves heavenward, there thundered
The wandering sea, and above them the Castle was lost in the darkness stark
On the naked waves; then, the spirits of those two men wondered
This was the life when venal and vital sins were without remission
And on the heads of adulterous loves there was put a price,
The storm surged in Mark's body, the storm of suspicion,
For he knew that the end or the beginning of love turns to some vice.

Merlin devined Mark's thoughts, yet for Mark he had no devotion
All things Merlin devined when with his magic he wrought
Miracles more mysterious than the menacing mysteries of the ocean,
Merlin laughed in his heart, for King Mark had been sold and bought.
Merlin made enter the cavern the blast of the nethermost hell
And he flashed before Mark's vision of a certain infamous tavern
Thereat the great King staggered, for he saw in the Tavern things a man might sell.
Ah, how his vision quailed when Iseult and Tristram shone in the cavern!
And before his vision failed, he saw them awake in one bed.

Then the wrath of the King greatened like the swell of the rising tide,
For the faith he had of Iseult, Iseult had violated,
And he knew that Tristram, with all his passion, had ravished from him his bride.
And that the time had come when one of these had to live
And that if death came to any, death always comes like a foe,
Merlin had vanished, Mark heard the sea wail, and he knew that he had to give
Life to one and death to another; but one seagull knew better, and shouted; 'No!'.

(From *Jezebel Mort, and Other Poems* by Arthur Symons, William Heinemann, London, 1931).

MERLIN AND NIMUË

by R. J. Stewart

IN THE STORY which follows, we are offered a version of the age-old story of
Merlin and Nimuë which, in the hands of the medieval clerics who recounted
much of the Arthurian cycles, became a sour morality tale of an old man besotted
with a young girl. Here, then, is a new telling which may well be the oldest version
of all. But, since all storytellers are well known to be great liars, who can tell?

Some tell that Merlin, with Taliesin the primary chief bard, took the wounded King
Arthur to the Fortunate Isles. There the wise Morgen, skilled in all healing arts,
watched over the Sleeping Lord, keeping him safe for the future. After they had sailed
home, the prophet and the bard, what then? Taliesin founded an academy and spent his

elder years teaching bards how to... well, how to do anything whatsoever, as he knew how to do everything and no one could take him anywhere or drink with him, so he might as well teach. But Merlin went again on his travels, remembering his days as a young man, a wild man, and a mad free man.

It was at about this time that a flock of wandering black birds came over from Ireland, calling themselves saints. These hairy vegetarians stumbled and strutted all over the land, and though some were steered hastily towards Europe, others founded cells and little centres of peace and love and rough wattle-and-daub hermitages in prime sites. Merlin was not filled with affection towards these Irish saints, for they took on the role of druids without knowledge of the law, the role of priests without knowing the Goddess, and the pose of prophets without knowing the power within the land. They preferred drab brown clothing and matted hair, and lived by begging and scrounging, abusing the sacred laws of hospitality. Even more absurdly, they ordered the tribes (who had been feuding since the age of bronze weapons) to love one another and show each other their cheeks, which was, of course, a powerful insult and provocation to war. And all this conflicting and confusing and misdirecting was supposed to originate with their sacrified god, who was simply one of the many sacrificed gods who have passed to and fro since She gave birth to the Worlds.

No, Merlin did not like to see the Irish saints on the hilltops that once been his, in the caves that had once been the home of bears, and most often upon the best river-valley sites that had been unused since Roman times. So he went to the great Caledonian forest, thinking that this could never be a prime site for development, and that the saintly gaggle and their flock would leave it unpecked. He was right, in part, and wrong too, for the first man that he met within the forest was a Culdee saint from Scotland. This one wore a woollen robe that was almost white, had his head shaved in a curious manner, and had washed only last week. He strode along with might and vigour, and in his right hand shook a bell without a clapper, which Merlin thought to be a special blessing.

'How I love the sound of that bell,' said Merlin, as he stooped to take a stone out from between his bare toes.

'Can a man love that which he does not know?' asked the Culdee saint, rhythmically pumping his bell up and down, and never a tinkle or clatter coming out of it.

'Indeed, I love it for itself, especially the unknown, unheard part of it, the mystery of its unringing and the discipline of your silently swinging of it to and fro, to and fro.'

'Do you not think it lacks something? Perhaps... the clapper?' asked the saint, marching along beside Merlin, even though he had been going in the opposite direction when they met. 'Perhaps a fine leaden clapper with a tiny cross cut deeply into it, or even a wooden clapper, though it might split, or one of granite with colours in the grain of it, or, God be praised, one of silver or of gold? Yes, gold would be good, the noble metal that gives tongue so sweetly.'

'I declare,' said Merlin, 'that the clapper which you have is perfect, the most perfect I have ever heard.'

'Ah, but the clapper of my bell is deep in the forest, far away,' replied the saint, deftly juggling the bell from hand to hand, 'hidden in the lair of the brown thief who took it from me.'

'Indeed,' Merlin murmured wisely, 'a sensitive bear or a delicate fox has been drawn by your immaculate spirituality to seek a relic of holiness to preserve for future ages.'

'No, it was a girl. A mere slip of a female girl,' and with this the Culdee crossed himself several times. 'She took it silently in the night, and in the bright morning I rang the bell three times before I realized that the clapper had been stolen.'

Merlin smiled a wise knowing learned mad inspired prophetic sad ecstatic half-smile, for the allusion was not lost upon him. In the bardic schools it was called a Taliesin slip, being a turn of phrase, unknowingly uttered, in which an everyday sexual forthrightness had hidden spiritual undertones. These undertones were detectable and interpreted only by a qualified bard, for the highest of fees.

'And now,' said Merlin to the saint, 'you ring your clapperless bell for your faith. I am astounded by your dedication to that which has been taken from you. Are you sure that you had it in the first place?' With these words he moved into the shadow of a stand of huge trees, ready to vanish before anything else could be said.

'Not so fast, grandad,' shouted the Culdee, grabbing the edge of the prophet's cloak. 'The bell is not clapperless, but absent from its clapper, for which the bell was made, for the clapper was in the world before it. And I ring it entirely and utterly to curse the thief. She called out of the wild rose bush, and put an obligation on the first creature who loved the silent bell, and only in this way can I get the clapper back.'

Merlin stopped, halfway between fight and flight, path and trackless wilderness, stone and thorn tree. He dared not move either way, for this sounded like a serious and obligatory obligation. 'I trust, learned saint, that you will find such a creature, but as for me I hate the sound of all bells, and have come this far to flee them. So, farewell...'

But the saint held fast to the cloak, whispering, 'You clearly said that you loved the silent bell, the earth and sky are my witnesses, the trees are my witnesses, and the stone that you removed from out of your toes. You cannot escape this obligation that I lay upon you: find the clapper that was in the world before the bell was. Bring it back to me by honest or devious ways. There is a blessing on those who serve.' By which he meant that there is a curse on those who do not.

And even as he whispered, the saint made the sign of the cross over Merlin, which no one had ever done before, and splashed him liberally with strong distilled spirits from a little flask that was hanging around his neck. Merlin flinched, licked his lips, and so was utterly trapped by the obligation laid upon him.

As he plunged wildly through the thorn bushes, cloak torn, arms flapping like a crow, eyes goggling in opposite directions, Merlin though he heard the Culdee laugh a deep belly-laugh, not like that of a Christian saint but like a hero or even a god after a great feast. His last coherent thought as he plunged into darkness was, I thought I'd stopped doing this kind of thing years ago.

While Merlin was plunging, a young woman was bathing in a shallow forest pool. First she unbound her black hair, letting it fall to her waist. From out of this mass of hair flowing and twining in all directions she took a number of curious objects. A garland of red and white briar roses came first, which had held her hair up. Next, from the depth of the thick curls, she pulled out a tiny golden pin the shape of a wren. After that a small roll of parchment, tied with a red ribbon, a roll small enough and tight enough to be carried by a starling for as long a distance as there is sea between Ireland and Wales. Last, from the deepest, blackest depths of that thicket of dark hair, she teased out a dark stone, rubbed and rounded into the shape of a tiny pregnant body, with bulging breasts and thighs. This image she placed reverently in the centre of the briar rose garland, to keep it safe from all directions. But the golden wren and the flying scroll she hung by coloured threads upon a branch, where the four winds could turn them as they willed, pivoting each around its unique centre.

Now she lifted her arms and pulled off her ragged shift. Her body was strong and brown, and only slightly moss-green and muddy from splashing through the little streams and over logs and in and out of the marshes and hollows filled with dead leaves and rain. She had built a conical fire stacked with juniper berries and herbs, and into the smoke of this she hung her shift, upon a three-forked staff thrust firmly into the damp earth. Thus naked, her breasts uplifting with the cold air, she jumped into the pool. The pool was not deep, and she was not tall, so she settled happily with the icy water up to her nose, sitting upon the bright sand where the spring bubbled forth, and whispering her blessing through dark lips barely above the light surface. She sighed and settled further, and as her hair floated out over the surface in coils and snakes and spirals and wavings, Merlin fell out of the tangled trees and into the pool.

What happened next? What happened next. . . I hear you say. What *unhappened* was this, though the telling of it is not as strange and true as the unhappening of it. The clouds stopped moving, the sun blinked, the four winds of the world drew a quick breath inwards, and all the animals and birds and fish that were in contact with the earth lifted their feet or bellies or fins entirely off the branches or stones or sand or ground or wherever they were positioned. Fires stood still and ceased to dance, waters paused in their flowing, and all falling things remained in one place, even in mid-fall. Far away in the forest someone stopped ringing a clapperless bell for an instant and closed his eyes tight and screwed up his face in anticipation. And all this for the merest fraction of the delusion of time that it takes for a grey-haired wild-eyed madman to fall out of thorny thickey and get a poke in the eye with a firm young nipple. Otherwise, everything remained the same.

'Unusually dry weather for the time of year,' said Merlin casually.

'Yes,' she agreed, moving the merest fraction out of politeness, 'only four full days of rain this week.'

'And then there were the two and a half half-days of rain.'

'Out of the seven, five and quarter of rain is good.'

'Indeed, unusually good and dry.'

Having observed the rules of politeness, the girl stood up and stepped out of the pool and over to her scented smoky fire. Merlin made himself more comfortable in the freezing water, wriggling down on to the sand and little stones, feeling them press on his thighs. One eye looked up at the cloudy sky through the treetops, while the other looked without blinking at the girl.

'Might one be allowed to ask,' he murmured in Greek, 'what might be the name of a young woman who lives in the forest, bathes in pools and wears rose garlands in her hair?'

'One might be allowed to ask,' she answered in Pictish, 'but might not obtain an answer unless the question was phrased correctly. For example' – and here she showed her youthful impetuosity by switching to local Welsh – 'if she were asked if her name was Gwladys, the answer would be no. If Enid, also no. If Branwen, then not exactly.'

'Aha,' said Merlin in Latin. 'But such a girl, assuming that she existed in the first place, might have a connection, however tenuous, with Branwen, daughter of Llyr?'

'She might,' said the girl in Irish. Merlin swivelled his eyes without moving his head, until one looked at the girl, and the other looked at the tree with the objects hanging from it by red and black threads, moving slowly in the forest winds.

'And if that connection was a tiny scroll,' he murmured in Breton, which was close to Welsh so perhaps he was being lazy, 'would that tiny scroll, between heaven and earth as it is, contain this girl's true name?'

'No, it would not,' she snapped in perfect hieratic Egyptian, 'for her true name is not to be written down in any form of letters, signs or words.'

Merlin blinked, first one eye, then the other. He knew now that her native language was Breton Welsh, and that she had a Pictish mother. The priestesses' tongue of Egypt troubled him slightly, for it was no longer spoken in that land, though one could learn it in the normal way in dreams and visions. He knew also that she honoured the Mother, and that she carried the vengeance of Branwen against all men within her heart. He was sure, though he had no proof, that she was the thief of the clapper. He sighed and waited for her to say something more. While he waited, he inwardly recited an epic tale that can take up to four days in telling, and marvelled at his own impatience in choosing such a short one.

'I propose an exchange,' she said in Saxon, which caused Merlin to fall over into the water. He would have spat at the sound of it, but for his respect for the spirit of the pool.

'Yet you insult me by the language you use to suggest it,' he said, attempting to focus both eyes upon her at once. This he could do only by wagging his head from side to side.

'No insult was intended; I merely had to be sure that you were listening properly.' She had reverted to Welsh, and they both continued to talk in the blessed angelic tongue.

'I propose an exchange thus: you wish to know a maiden's name and I wish to keep it secret. You discover how I may keep my name secret and I will tell it to you.'

Merlin did not pause to think, but spoke with the tongue, the inspired speech, that comes upon prophets and madmen instantly and may not be denied. 'Send your name through time, so that it is not found either in the past or in the present, but will be found in the future when the world is ready for it.'

'Indeed, indeed, just as the Sleeping Lord is waiting in time to return from the Fortunate Isles. And a shame that is, for I have the only thing will heal him.'

Merlin gasped and goggled and could hardly breathe. He leapt out of the pool and sloshed his way over to the fire, reaching out for her.

'What is it? Where is it?' he croaked, forgetting all the rules of the game. But she slipped out of his cold, wet hands, and plunged into her dress, hanging as it was from the three-pronged staff. She snatched up the little black stone figurine, and waved it over her head, then held it close to her breasts.

'It is this image of the Mother, from the dawn of time, when our ancestors walked as equals with the people of the *sidh* and as companions with the birds and beasts and fish. And without this no wounded man can be cured, even if he be the king himself. And I reclaimed it from a thief, who had taken it to be the clapper of the bell.'

Merlin sat down for a moment upon the fire of scented twigs and berries, then leapt up again with his robe and cloak smoking and steaming at the same time. This was the very object that he was obliged to retrieve, yet it surely did not belong in the saintly bell. It was the very object that he had to retrieve, yet he himself needed it for the healing of the king, which meant the healing of the land through time. He could neither meet the obligation nor cheat it. Whatever he did would be wrong.

'I will make this bargain with you,' he said, and his eyes came into full focus as his clarity of mind returned. 'I will take your name through time with me, and promise to guard it. In return you will give me the Mother stone, and in return for that I will take it too, with your name, through time, where no saints shall steal it, and where it will be hidden, ready to come to the Sleeping Lord when it is time for him to awaken.'

'Done,' she said, and with complete trust handed him the little black stone figure of the Goddess from the dawn of time, when all beings in the world were equal and walked together in joy and peace. Merlin blinked for an instant, for as he took the figure in his hands, a flurry of images seemed to blow like leaves past his eyes. The last one was of huge red-haired man with stag's antlers upon his head, wearing a flaming cloak all fire within and green leaves without, spinning around and around, and turn-ing himself into the image of Christian saint, laughing all the while.

Merlin nodded at this, and walked around the clearing, around the pool three times. On the third circuit, he came to something that he had not seen on the first two, though surely it had been there all the while. It was a great rock, seamed with white quartz, greater than the size of man. He laid his forehead against, then one ear, listen-ing. He put the little Goddess into one of the many pockets in his robe and cast off his cloak. Then, leaping into the rock, he passed his hands over it, and it quivered.

'This will do,' he said, and passed his hands through it. When his arms were deep in the stone, up to the shoulders, and half of his face was gone in, and his knees, and feet, she came over and stood close to him. Then he was in the stone completely, and merged with it, and no one passing by would know he was there, except that they might see the shape of an old man in the folds and shadows of the rock. Then she pressed her dark lips to where his ear might be in the rock, and her warm, moist breath passed into it, as she whispered, 'My name is Nimuë.'

THE TINTAGEL VISION OF THE CELTIC PRIESTHOOD

by Michael de Angelo

MICHAEL de ANGELO'S extraordinary visionary novel *Cry Myrddin: The Coming of Age of Merlin* (Gododdin Publishing, 1979) seems to us to represent one of the finest twentieth-century versions of the Merlin myth. It is steeped in the Celtic traditions from which the figure of the great bard and magician emerged, and it offers a deeply moving account of the forces which shaped him. Yet, it remains virtually unknown, save to a handful of people who obtained one of the limited issues of the book published in Seattle, America, in 1979. We have been unable to discover anything about the author, who remains as mysterious as the subject of his book. Our attempts to contact him also proved fruitless and the extract from his novel is published here as a tribute to his work, which we very much hope he will one day see for himself.

On the high cliffs of the wooded coast, the sky rises from beyond the sea's horizon, climbs layered clouds to expand overhead. The wind is shining in golden red that the white gulls sail upon in their search. And they scream, the same scream that ancient seafarers heard when ending their journeys in swollen eyes and parched mouths. The trees hold the high ground; their branches stir, telling of the many wanderers who have passed below, ignorant of life in forms not human. The thin fog very distant marks the water's edge. The green of the evergreens, the blue-gray of the sky, the white-gray, the wind whipping the waves, a rushing forth, din of cannon battering cliffs.

The sea returns ever, ancient mirror of man's beholding. The tide rises, calling all back, its waiting body, its voice upon the land.

Birds circle, fly upwards. Hundreds rise in an ascending spiral of wings beating, silent. They are distant, flying into where the sky is blue and silken.

To the east, the hills green and yellow and orange, colors softened in veils of mist.

To the north, now at last he could see it, a mile down the coastline. Tintagel Head. An immense spur of rock and earth, brown cliffs rising hundreds of feet from the sea, and upward to steep grassy slopes, to a small plateau. But for a narrow bridge of rock holding it to the mainland, it was an island.

Gorlois had been wise in sending him here. For it was here that the Celtic priesthood dwelled, isolated from the outer world for hundreds of years. Only in recent times had they begun to accept a few infrequent visitors. Now he would learn for himself what secret might lie hidden here. And he was in need of others on the way. Here he might find a month's sanctuary, or a few hours companionship.

He rode the last stretch of coastline leading to the rock bridge. He dismounted and tethered his horse to a shrub. A narrow path bounded by cliffs on either side led to the gate, two huge oaken doors set with cross-pieces of iron, held in a high arched wall of stone. He knocked.

There was sound behind the gate, but no answer. He knocked again.

'Who goes there?' It was a voice that seemed unfamiliar in its role.

'It is I, Prince Merlin.'

'We have no need of princes here.'

'Gorlois has sent me.'

'Gorlois? On what errand?'

'None. I come of my own choosing.'

'Then we are not obliged to allow you entrance.'

'Allow me by your faith.'

'What of your faith?'

Merlin hesitated. 'I worship God in all men.'

The gatekeeper was silent for a moment. 'And where is your service given, Prince Merlin?'

'Wherever it is needed.'

'In war or in peace?'

'I have told you.'

'Where have you taken your teaching?'

'From where the wind carries me, and in the valley of Llwyn Cerrig Bach.'

The door was unlatched and opened. 'Your work is well known here, and well respected.'

'Then do you so love your own work that you would ask me these many questions?'

'I had to be sure it was you.'

Merlin caught what seemed to be a playful glimmer in the old man's eyes. The answer had not satisfied him, but already the man had turned and begun to climb a narrow winding staircase of stone that led to the plateau above. Merlin followed.

Once on the plateau he could see ten or fifteen buildings spread over a few acres of fields. Their walls were flat stones piled thirty or forty high. In each wall a narrow peaked arch had been cut for a window. The roofs were of stone and sod. Near the center of the cluster, he could see a well. And beyond, in the outer field, the dark brown soil of a garden was visible.

'Where is everyone?' Merlin was somewhat confused.

The old man turned to him and looked into his eyes.

'Everyone?'

'The others. Are there not others?'

'Oh yes, there are, others,' he answered, speaking the last word with some amusement.

'Well?'

'I would not be too anxious about meeting them if I were you. They are not a very talkative group. In fact, they are bound by a vow of silence.'

'And you?'

'I am not of their order.'

'Then why are you here?'

'Questions, questions. I am here of course for the same reason you are.'

Merlin witheld his next question for a moment. This old man reminded him of someone. Was it possible that ... 'You have known Ioin?'

The old man smiled to himself, then hesitated, as though searching his memory. 'Let us discuss that another time.'

'How is it that you are accepted by these priests?'

'Now that is a story as long as time itself. But I will tell you a little of it. You see, there are many different callings within one vision; we recognize another working in harmony whatever the outer appearance of his life or endeavours.'

'What is this vision you speak of?'

'Come, we will eat now.' He began to walk so quickly toward a large rectangular building that Merlin had to run a few paces to catch up with him. At the doorway, they ducked low to enter.

It was dim inside, and it took a moment for his eyes to adjust to the light. As his vision grew sharper, he saw thirty robed men sitting at long wooden tables and benches, eating quietly in the glow of six candles. They stopped and looked up. The old man addressed them.

'Brothers, Prince Merlin has come.'

There was not a word, but the slightest nodding of heads, and a glimmer of recognition and joy in their eyes, and perhaps a trace of sadness. Merlin felt a sudden stirring in his own heart, as though he now shared with each man a common depth of love and life and labor.

Two bowls of broth and black bread awaited them on the table. They sat down. His mind quieted.

His bowl was wooden, roughly carved, with a handle that had a loop of thin rope tied through it. The spoon was the same. The steam from his broth swirled and rose upward. He took his spoon in his right hand and stirred it slowly. Carrots, turnips, and melde leaves, their colors soft in the candlelight. Their aroma was rich and fragrant, like the dark soil from which they had come. He lifted a spoonful to his mouth, and sipped it, drawing a breath of air through his nose as he savored it on his tongue. The water of the broth tasted of sunlight. He chewed the vegetables slowly, and swallowed. And he felt nourished as the food became one with his body.

And all around him as well, the others were not unmindful of their partaking. Whatever their work was here, he could see it was now in their eyes. This food was taken in service to that love and labor.

One by one they finished and began to leave. He followed them outside. At a water-filled basin cut in a boulder, each man stopped to wash his bowl and spoon, before tying them to the rope around his waist.

They walked toward the western edge of the island. The sun was near setting, in layers of pastel purple and red. A slight wind blew in from the ocean, damp and salty. Near a stone and sod hut, a huge fire was burning. The men disrobed before it, entering into that hut and four others like it.

Merlin joined them in the last hut. They sat down cross-legged, on woolen mats spread over the ground. Inside it was completely dark, no windows and a low roof. Someone entered with a bucket full of red glowing rocks, and emptied them into a pit dug in the center of the hut. The air filled with their dim red light, and grew warm. A branch of sage was laid over them. It began to smoke slightly, filling the hut with its pungent aroma, while the air grew hotter beneath the low roof.

More rocks from the fire were emptied into the pit. Beads of sweat began to form on his forehead. The dry heat stung his nostrils and throat. A bowl of water was poured slowly onto the rocks, exploding into hissing and steaming. He took a deep breath; the steam pierced his lungs. The heat of the rocks burned on his shins as he tried to protect them with his hands. More water, the hut filled with steam.

In many voices, a low wail began. With their hands they slapped their legs, chests, arms in a slow rhythm. The wail became a chant, moving freely, syllables transforming, merging into one sound. The slapping grew harder, deeper, flesh unfeeling in the steam. The chanting faster. More water, steam, hissing, rocks still red and glowing in the darkness. Breathing deep, deeper, more deeply than he had ever known. One breathing, the wailing louder, finding overtones. Water poured, steam, the air on fire, lungs burning, sweat pouring, and the chant began to slow. Their bodies became still. The rocks grew dark, then completely black.

The door flung open, and they escaped into the cool night, plunging one after another into a waist-high pool of water. Cold. Instantly surrounding him, a gasp. His body shook. He jumped out onto the ground, and drew a long deep breath.

His body heat returned from within, filling his chest and limbs with a warm fiery glow. The earth at his feet was cold. Overhead, the sky had turned black, filled with thousands of brilliant points of light. The steam rose from his skin. The ocean waves crashed far below. The wind gusted. The limbs of an evergreen danced, twisting and swirling, heaven above, earth below, alive, alive. Light in his eyes, the wind on his body, the soil at his feet, this breath his very first, this moment its own revelation. Heaven above, earth below, and his body the very altar of their communion. And the flesh, was good, and it was strong.

They began donning their robes, moving forth to form a circle around the fire. The wind shook the branches while the silence grew louder, the stars brighter, and the earth stronger. The light descended. It passed amongst them, whirling around and around the circle, filling the ground itself with its life. His head grew faint; he almost fell. Then it was over.

The men returned to their sleeping huts. Merlin was shown a pile of straw. He lay down, and slept.

> In a small boat with her, he approached the dark shore. The boat grounded on the rocks. They began wading in the waves.
>
> Twilight comes the archer. She is all powerful. With one swift arrow both their hearts are pierced, and they fall beside each other on the shoreline, with the waves washing over their bodies.
>
> But still they breathe; their wounds are gone. At last they have reached the land. Lying on their backs, moonlight on their upturned faces. The archer is not evil. Wind at twilight sailing ever on.

The priest of the last night-watch awoke them before dawn. In the moonlight, Merlin could see a thin trail of mist moving through the open window. The sound of the surf was strong, but distant. The smell of the air was saltier than before. They pulled their long wool robes over themselves, and walked the trail that led to the center of their small settlement, to the well.

Each took a cup of water, drank it slowly, then walked over to the grass and sat facing east. For a long time they were silent.

At last the night began to depart; the stars grew dim. The sky turned silver, then red, then orange. The gulls flew low overhead. The sun began to rise over the hilly plain, a clear yellow orb. When its complete circle was visible, they entered into the chapel, a hut of flat piled stones.

The eldest took his place behind the altar. The others knelt on stone benches. On the altar were two lit candles, and a book. The priest opened it, and began to read. Dust stirred slowly in the sun's rays coming through the windows.

'Sa tus bhi an Briathar ann, agus bhi an Briathar in einecht le Dia, agus ba e Dia an Briathar. Is e a bhi ann i dtus ama in eineacht le Dia; is trisdean a cruthaiodh gach ni agus ina eagmais-sean nior cruthaiodh aon ni da ndearnadh. Is ann a bhi an bheatha, agus ba i an bheatha solas an chine dhaonna. Bion an solas ag soilsiu sa dorchadas, agus nil bua ag an dorchadas air.'

'In the Beginning was the Word, and the Word was with God, and the Word was God. The same was in the Beginning with God. All things were made by Him; and without Him was not anything made that was made. In Him was life, and the life was the light of men. And the light shineth in darkness, and the darkness comprehended it not.'

He continued the sermon in the ancient tongue. When the service was complete, each man went to take up his labor for the day. Merlin was left alone, standing before the chapel door. He decided to wander around the perimeter of the plateau. He walked until he came to a grassy slope. He lay down on the grass to watch the clouds' creations overhead.

Surely there must be more, he thought. But perhaps those secrets are not as easily given out. For now, I have nowhere else to go, so I will remain, and listen.

The hours passed. He explored more of the settlement. In the afternoon he sat in meditation, watching the sun begin its slow descent toward the horizon. At sunset, he returned again to the eating place, to find the gatekeeper awaiting him at the doorway.

'Prince Merlin,' he said, 'if you will let your hunger pass, we will speak more.'

'Very well.'

'Come, then.'

Merlin followed him to a small hut. They entered it and sat down on the wooden floor near one corner. The old man lit a candle and held it up between them so that he could see Merlin's face.

'You do not know who I am, do you?'

'No.'

'I am Melchar.' He stopped to see if this drew forth a response from Merlin. Seeing it did not, he continued. 'Oh well, I thought Ioin might have told you.'

'Then you do know Ioin?'

'Oh yes, Ioin was my teacher as well.'

'Does he still live in the hills, Melchar?'

'Now that is a question not easily answered. But it was indeed a great fortune that he allowed you to come to him, made possible by his grace alone, and his knowledge of the realms.'

'I do not understand.'

'I would not venture to explain it further. But it is a great omen.'

'He is still alive?'

'He is not where any of us could easily find him.'

'I could find him.'

'You know not what you say.'

'Is he dead then?' Merlin was becoming upset.

'You forget his teaching.'

'What teaching do you – '

'Some last words perhaps ... "That boundaries of the living and the dead are not as commonly seen ..." 'Melchar smiled softly, opening his eyes wide.

'What! How can you know this?' He looked into Melchar's eyes, hoping to find the answer.

Melchar put his hand over Merlin's heart. 'Some day, young brother, all this will be given over to your understanding. But for now, there is more. Do I have your trust?'

Merlin shook his head, still very much bewildered.

'Merlin, you were raised a Christian?'

'Yes.'

'And hold to the teachings of that faith?'

'I abide by his teaching, and not by what words other men would make his.'

'You speak of the Christ?'

'Call him what you will.'

'He was the Son of God.'

'And so we are all. By his own words, he said, "You are Gods".'

'What of his words, "I am the Way, the Light, and the Truth"?'

'He spoke true. God is the voice and vision of our own true Self.'

'Few would understand it so.'

'I fear you are right, Melchar.'

'We are not all strong; we hold to the image of one man who was not unfaithful to the spirit within him.'

'And so are unfaithful to our own spirit.'

'Not always. The ways of the power are unfathomable. In time it brings all within its realm, but in many different ways.'

'Why worship the man, and not the spirit?'

'How many can worship what does not have human form? The spirit's realm is often frightening to traverse, and one takes comfort in the guidance of a human voice.'

'I find my kinship in the kingdom of the star-lit night.'

'Do not be so harsh, Merlin. This is a land of leaders. The people need a figure of loyalty and devotion, one who upholds the new faith.'

'A man who lived four centuries ago cannot unite the clans, or halt the barbarian invasion.'

'Perhaps not, but his spirit embodied in a warrior of near equal greatness, a warrior king –'

'You speak not of Uther or Ambrosius, for I fear they are not but Romans in their hearts.'

'I speak not of them.' He stopped for a moment. The silence grew heavy. 'I speak not of them, but of one who will come after them.'

'Then who?'

'He is yet to be born.'

'It is a distant hope then. The Saxon threat is upon the tribes. Their way of life is already near crumbling.'

'No, it is far more than a hope. For this sanctuary has stood for four centuries, and for four centuries the vision has grown. Now the time of waiting grows short, and the time of fulfillment is at hand.'

'Then your prayers have been for this warrior?'

'More than prayers. Meditations, studies, chants. For four hundred years Tintagel has been inhabited with but one purpose, and every hour of every day has been dedicated to the forging of this one vision, unbeknownst to the generations of kings that have passed.'

Merlin was silent for a moment. 'Why do you tell me all this, Melchar?'

'There is one thing that is certain, Merlin, you have been within the circle before, and you will yet be with us when you leave.'

'You think me part of this work?'

Melchar drew a breath and nodded. 'Let me tell you of a passage from our sacred books. Sometime after the massacre at Anglesey, near the turn of the first century, a high Druid made a prophesy. It was this: When the great city falls, and the island weakens, the falcon will come from the north. And the lords of war will join with him to create the unseen foundation of a nation that will become the strongest in all the world, and nowhere will its flag be unknown.'

'It is a great prophesy.'

'And the answer to your question.'

'How so?'

'Very simple. Llwyn Cerrig Bach, to the north. Merlin, the smallest of our native falcons.'

'You do not mean –'

'Yes, I do, Merlin.'

'Can it be so,' Merlin whispered, his breath suddenly holding high in his chest, and his eyes growing wet with some new and unknown emotion.

'Merlin,' Melchar continued, 'you are yet young, but soon it may seem the weight of the world is upon you. Try to remember that you are not alone.'

Merlin nodded, speaking to himself. 'He who having once put his hand to the plow, looks back, is not worthy of the harvest.'

For a long time neither of them spoke.

Finally Merlin addressed Melchar as if in a trance. 'And what of the warrior king?'

'The falcon roams far and high over the land. Use the power that has been granted you. The seed of a nation is in your hand.'

'And by what name do you call the coming one?'

'Arthur, the bear.'

'Arturus, a noble name. I too will pray for the coming of the bear.'

'Only remember, Merlin, our dreams are not endless, nor all powerful. That is why in this life there can be only one dream, and the heart, the mind, and the will must all be consumed in this one fire.'

'I know it too well.'

'Go with Him, then.'

'And with you always.'

Merlin left through the narrow door, crouching so as not to strike his head. His heart and mind now filled with a great new excitement, and a great new fear. Had destiny so marked him? Would he be worthy of his calling? He wandered out into the open fields beneath the stars.

Whose voices are these? Are they truly mine, not descended from the star's haven, but born of my own vision and work? What now approaches so near? I am alive. It could not be otherwise. I am here to fulfill what now lies before me. And the danger can no longer stalk me. I am free. It is given. It will be so. I am born of this moment, no other. And father to more ahead. I hold the stars in my hand, no longer lost. I am born again from the ashes of my own body. Communion! The night sings. It roars.

The stillness is on my tongue. I swallow the silence. Rain, heaven's precious gift. Now I see what lies ahead. Praise the darkness, first worship, dark of earth, dark of woman, dark of mother womb.

Live the beginning. Live the end. We are held in the embrace, the one embrace of all holding, for it is over uncharted seas that the wind blows strongest!

But wait. Have I not gone forth in faith before? And found only bitterness waiting? What purifying fire have I not now come to despise, even as it exalts me? What trial that has not stolen my hope? And yet, so far have I come on this path of sorrows that all else forsakes me; to turn away from this doorway leaves me with nothing.

My shadow lies flat on the stone. Will it be only I that ever knows it, or will it leave the sound of its passing forever etched in a shaping of wind that will speak for all time to those who have ears to hear?

Wind, you are my guardian, and my confessor. Darkness, you are my most faithful companion. And I know, beyond the touched, beyond the world, there is a place, there is a place. Night spirit invade! Night spirit invade! Night spirit invade!

His hands opened, fingers spread, shot upward on upstretched arms. Fire! He stood like a spire of rock. The light rose up within him, in a fire that devoured the gates of past and future. And all life and creation was before him, and all was his.

He stood on the highest part of the sloping fields, the clouds in great moonlit towers above him, as the wind began to stir, to sweep, to rage and explode. Fire! The gateway to the kingdom.

And he knew he must leave this very moment. He strode into the empty hut where he had left his belongings, then rushed out of the gate. It was deserted, but leaning across the oak doors was a freshly carved staff. Its head was the head of a dragon, its foot, a dragon foot. Melchar's gift. He took it and let himself out through the gate.

'Farewell, Melchar, I will return again to Tintagel.' His spirit was uplifted; his pace was smooth and strong. He walked through the night, through the dawn, and by midday he knew his destination.

An uneven conical hill appeared seemingly from nowhere to rise more than six hundred feet above the flat plain. Its lower portions were shrouded in trails of mist, but its summit was clearly visible, a high grass-covered mound a few hundred yards square.

He did not know what power it was that drew him there, but he walked the entire afternoon, and late into the evening to reach it. Now it was nearing midnight. The sky was clear and black, but the stars were hidden from him by the low fog. He began the climb. The way was not difficult, but he was weary, and as he rose higher he was exposed to the cold blasts of wind. He walked upward, the summit receding before him. At last he reached the top. He walked slowly around the few hundred yards of its perimeter. Below, the smaller hills on the horizon pushed upward like islands through the sea of fog that spread for miles in all directions. Above, the stars were shining clear. He grew silent within, and sought guidance. It was his own voice that came forth.

As in any room there is a place of power where one must stand, so on any country-side there is a hill that rises above the rest, and in any nation, there is a countryside that holds the keys to the kingdom. This then will be my first gift to you, Arturus, young bear – an island of power where you may find right dominion over the empire, and sacred communion with the stars.

Above all mortal pathways, mounted only in deep worship, here will be an island inviolate of the veiling mists. By night, it will ride above, a lake of moonlight in the clouds, where the shadows of all things to be will find haven, and be given succor. Here you will find your beginning, and perhaps, your end.

MABON, THE CELTIC DIVINE CHILD

by Caitlín Matthews

IN THE FOLLOWING piece Caitlín Matthews discusses themes which are dealt with in greater detail in her two-volume study of the Mabinogion: *Mabon and the Mysteries of Britain* (Arkana, 1987) and *Arthur and the Sovereignty of Britain* (Arkana, 1989). In the same year Geoffrey Ashe, writing in the first *Book of Merlin* (Blandford Press, 1987) identified Merlin, Mabon and the primal god of Britain with one another. There would seem also to be many shared elements in both Geoffrey of Monmouth's *Vita Merlini* (see above) and the shamanistic or totem animal themes in Celtic legends that may relate to the divine child Mabon, as a type of Celtic Apollo. We might add also to this one aspect of the controversial work of professor Barry Fell, who claims that inscriptions to 'Mabo-Mabon' written in *ogham* script upon stone have been discovered at ancient sites on the east coast of America (*America BC*, Pocket Books, New York, 1976).

Is it possible that Mabon was in fact a major pre-Christian deity, the Celtic Child of Light, and that his cult was extensively developed through Europe, and perhaps found even across the Atlantic, due to the presence of Celtic settlers? It seems unlikely, even if the American evidence is finally accepted, that we shall ever know the true status of Mabon, for his legend bears all the negative signs of having been heavily edited or perhaps at one time banned, for religious propagandist reasons.

Yet enough remains to suggest the nature of Mabon and his primal tale. Mabon relates to the youthful Merlin who prophesied before King Vortigern, and in archetypical symbolic terms Mabon, young Merlin, and the child Apollo are virtually identical. Once again, we are dealing with resonances of a primal prophetic and religious tradition, and with various figures representing that tradition within specific cultures or periods of time. William Blake took up this prophetic theme, recreating in his own symbolic language the primal imagery of the powers of the land, and the transformation of awareness that is possible when humans and land become attuned properly to one another.

Of the many archetypes in Celtic mythology, one of the most intriguing and evasive is that of Mabon, the Celtic Divine Child. In *Mabon and the Mysteries of Britain*,[1] I have identified many of the characters within the Mabinogion who manifest the Mabon

---

1. Mabon and the Mysteries of Britain, C. Matthews, Arkana, 1987.

archetype, but here I would like to range more widely and examine the evidence from a broader basis.

The core of Mabon's identity and function is embedded deeply in Celtic and Arthurian tradition and was obviously well known to earlier oral tradition, if the fragmentation of his archetype is anything to go by. Traces of his story appear in folk tradition and medieval romance. In the aptly named Breton text, the *Roman du Silence*,[2] there is a reference to two minstrels performing the *lai Mabon*, attesting to an extant medieval story. Unfortunately, the minstrels are not permitted to give us any verses in this text. Similarly a manuscript of the Shrewsbury School[3] speaks of a *lai* entitled *Rey Mabun* but is as taciturn as the *Roman du Silence*. It is almost as though Mabon's story was so well known and ubiquitous that it is tacitly assumed the story bore no further repetition.

How a British Celtic archetype became the subject of a Breton *lai* is perhaps something we will never be able to trace with any exactitude. Where literary tradition takes over from oral tradition, written evidence runs out and we turn to archaeological back-up. Mabon is the local name of the Romano-British deity, Maponus, to whom many dedications have been found in Northern Britain, especially along Hadrian's Wall and the area of the Solway Firth.[4] The characteristics of the British deity in the centuries before Rome may only be guessed at, but he certainly equated, in the Roman mind, with aspects of Apollo and Orpheus.[5] It is possible, though there is little evidence for this, that Maponus was the focus of a minor mystery cult among his Romano-British devotees. Closely associated with Maponus was the cult of the Matres, the Triple Mothers: a fact which should not surprise us, since Mabon is universally called Mabon, son of Modron – Son, son of Mother. The twin cults of Modron and Mabon were undoubtedly ancient before their Classical overlay, and it is this primal tradition which we shall attempt to reconstruct.

The names Mabon and Modron are really titles, not personal names. They are remnants of a mystery tradition where these titles were applied to great divine archetypes, in much the same way Demeter and Kore in Greek tradition have no personal appellation but are known as Mother and Maiden. This custom pertained in Celtic countries where heroes and chieftains swore a variation on this carefully phrased oath: 'I swear by the gods which my tribe swears by'. Such a formula obviated the use of a name. This caution sprang from the reverent custom of concealing the deity's name from the irreverent or uninitiated. Even today, the devout speak of 'Our Lord' and 'Our Lady' rather than the more familiar Jesus and Mary. It is possible that in the pre-Roman era one might have wandered the length and breadth of Britain swearing 'by the Son and his Mother' without any loss of understanding, each tribe holding a Mother and Son in reverence. Indeed one might so swear today without any blasphemous intention.

It is this central premise that we must bear in mind that the titles, Mabon and Modron, are applicable to various youths and their mothers, though certainly not arbitrarily and without warrant. This game of substitution can be played only with a select set of mythic pieces which bear traces of the original archetypes.

The earliest textual reference to the myth of Mabon appears in *Culhwch and Olwen*, one of the many stories appearing in a medieval compilation called the *Mabinogion*.[6] In

---

2. Roman du Silence, L. Thorpe in Nottingham Medieval Studies V, II. 2761-5, 1961.
3. Shrewsbury School MS vii, fol. 200.
4. Pagan Celtic Britain, A. Ross, Routledge & Kegan Paul, 1967.
5. A Traveller's Guide to Celtic Britain, A. Ross, Routledge & Kegan Paul, 1985.
6. The Mabinogion trans. Lady C. Guest, Ballantyne Press, 1910.

this story, Culhwch falls in love with a giant's daughter, Olwen, but in order to win her he is set 39 impossible tasks by Olwen's father, Yspaddaden. Chief among these tasks is the finding of Mabon. Culhwch is one of the oldest stories of the *Mabinogion*, stemming from an oral tradition which has its roots in the period immediately following that of the Dark-Age Arthur, *c.*537 AD. It embodies traces of ancient often lost stories once prominent in proto-Celtic tradition. The story teller gives a version of Mabon's story which betrays the manner in which a once-potent myth can be smoothed into folk-tale.

When Culhwch asks for information about Mabon he is told that the child was taken from between his mother and the wall when he was three nights old and that no one knows where he is now, nor indeed whether he is alive or dead. Mabon has departed from the memories of mankind, but the memories of animals prove more retentive, and it is to the animal kingdom that Culhwch directs his search. With him on this quest is Gwrhyr, an interpretor of animal's speech. They start with the blackbird.

The blackbird has not heard of Mabon, though she has pecked an iron anvil down to its wooden base, and she passes them on to the stag of the plains. He remembers a single sapling which grew to be a mighty tree, but even that has withered. He sends them on to the owl of the wood who has seen the triple growth and uprooting of the forest, but has never heard of Mabon. She passes them on to the eagle who has pecked the stars from the heights of a mountain until it is only a few feet high. He has never heard of Mabon, but has rumour of something via a salmon with whom he once battled. The salmon has never heard of Mabon but has been troubled by a crying from the walls of Caer Loyw (Gloucester). The heroes mount on the salmon's back and are led to the walls where they ask the mystery question: 'Oh who is it that there laments within a house of stone?'[6]

They receive the answer: 'It is Mabon, born of Modron's womb, within these walls alone.' Mabon is then brought out on Cai's back and liberated to help Culhwch fulfil the rest of his impossible tasks which will qualify him to marry Olwen.

In this story Mabon is very much a subsidiary character: a famous archetype which the story teller has inserted into the narrative in order to give Culhwch his place among the older heroes. Much the same happens in later medieval romance, where Arthur occasionally makes a guest appearance in order to give the story authenticity within the Matter of Britain.

Nevertheless, the story teller has preserved many elements of Celtic belief and practice. The long search through the agency of animals is closely associated with the transformatory sequence which most Celtic poets boast of having undergone. The poets Amergin[7] of Ireland and Taliesin[8] of Britain both claim to have inhabited various shapes. This must not be taken to mean a literal shape-shifting, any more than it necessarily implies a reincarnational memory.[9] More precisely, these poets speak of an initiatory sequence of realisation which every initiate of the bardic mysteries undergoes. In that moment of revelation, a complex web of imagery is presented in one vision. Like Celtic knotwork, everything in this vision is connected, leading to further interpretation. It may be the work of a lifetime to comprehend this sequence, which is really a visionary glyph of knowledge.

Forming a chain back to the beginning of time, the animals of Mabon's search each

---

7. Ancient Irish Tales, T.P. Cross and C.H. Slover, Figgis, 1936.
8. Mabinogion *op. cit.*
9. The story of Tuan mac Carill and Fintan, famous reincarnated Irish sages, reveal a similar pattern. Cf. C. and J. Matthews, The Encyclopedia of Celtic Wisdom, Element Books, 1994.

represent a species of knowledge and a non-linear age of time. Encoded both within these beasts and in the story of Mabon's finding is an inner history, an encyclopedia of information and a direct experience of the worlds – both human and otherwordly. This chain of information is borne out from an evolutionary point of view, where each species of animals is part of life's history, each bearing some part of the genetic pattern of creation.

This, then, is the major source for Mabon's extant myth. We find other traces in the Welsh *Triads*,[10] the mnemonic verses which encapsulate sets of knowledge. Triad 52 speaks of Mabon as being one of three famous prisoners.[11] Both the *Mabinogion* and the *Triads* preserve the most persistent part of Mabon's mythos – that he is imprisoned and released. Both these texts are the last remaining links with the tradition of Mabon as a native deity rather than the literary character which he later becomes. They retain his numinous power though neither is as informative as we would like them to be. Taking these texts alone, the paucity of evidence does not help us reconstruct, in even partial fashion, the lost myth of Mabon.

We are fortunate that the Mabon archetype found a vehicle of transmission which showed no signs of abating its progress: Arthurian legend. Any character lodged in the tales which comprise the Matter of Britain has been gifted with the kind of immortality associated with the ancient gods and heroes of British tradition. But what of Mabon? Is it possible to reconstruct something of his original mythos with any certainty? It is certain that the full power of Mabon's archetype has been lost to us, but it is likely that a once-potent god-form such as the Wondrous Child might have left notable traces.

As Alwyn and Brinley Rees have stated in *Celtic Heritage*: 'traditional tales used to be transmitted by a priestly order in the Celtic lands, and diverse blessings accrued to those who heard them related'.[12] It is in such traditional stories that the Matter of Britain found its roots. The myth of Mabon, perhaps once widespread, a story to be related as part of a seasonal ritual during the winter months, became merely the story of Mabon in later times. I write 'merely'. but the hero-cycles which are told of semi-mortals like CuChullain, Fionn and others proved memorable in both oral and literary tradition. May we legitimately posit the existence of Mabon's archetype through a series of linked hero-stories?

The repertoire of a professional Celtic story teller including the learning of some 350 stories in which individual heroes appeared in definable story-cycles. Thus the story teller could relate the following tales about the hero's life: his conception, his youthful exploits, his adventures, his wooing of a maiden, his otherwordly voyaging, his hostings and raids; and finally, his woeful imprisonment, vision and lamentable death.[13] I propose to reconstruct here a similar hero-cycle applicable to Mabon's archetype, by juxtaposing stories of other heroes who share in some part of the Mabon mythos, or which they have inherited in the process of oral transmission. Such is the wealth of material scattered throughout both Celtic and Arthurian texts that such an experiment is possible. If Mabon represents x, the unknown factor, in this mythic equation, we must set something to work in his place and see what manner of revelation is given.

We are able to tell one story of Mabon's conception, or *compert*, as the Irish story-lists define it. For a Divine Child like Mabon we would expect to know of at least one otherworldly parent, and this is the case:

---

10. *Trioedd Ynys Prydein* trans. Rachel Bronwich, University of Wales Press, 1961.
11. *Ibid.*
12. *Celtic Heritage*, Alwyn and Brinley Rees, Thames and Hudson, 1961.
13. These are all species of stories which recur in the professional Irish story-lists. They are known, respectively, in Irish as: *compert, macgimartha, echtra, tochmarc, immram, slugard, rain, indarba, fis* and *aided*.

In Denbighshire there is a parish which is called Llanferres, and there is a Rhyd y Gyfartha (Ford of Barking). In the old days, the hounds of the countryside used to come together to the side of that ford to bark, and nobody dared to go to find out what was there until Urien Rheged came. And when he came to the side of the ford he saw nothing there except a woman washing. And then the hounds ceased barking, and Urien seized the woman and had his will of her; and then she said: 'God's blessing on the feet which brought thee here.' 'Why?' 'Because I have been fated to wash here until I should conceive a son by a Christian. And I am the daughter to the King of Annwn, and come thou here at the end of the year and then thou shalt receive the boy.' And so he came and he received there a boy and a girl; this is Owein, son of Urien, and Morfydd, daughter of Urien.[14]

This Welsh story was preserved in oral tradition until the sixteenth century, and we may be sure that it tells the story of Mabon's conception, except, of course, that the story is told of Owain ap Urien, an historical character of the sixth century who was incorporated in Arthurian legend as Owain or Yvain, Arthur's nephew or cousin, according to some versions.

The fact that Owain's mother identifies herself here as a daughter of the King of Annwn is very significant, since a triad[15] speaks of the parentage of Owain and Morfudd from Urien and *Modron, daughter of Afallach*. Both the folk story and the triad obviously refer to the same tradition. Now, in Arthurian tradition, the wife of Urien is Morgan, Arthur's half-sister;[16] and Morgan is, in the earliest references,[17] the guardian of the realm of Avalon – Afallach being the original king of that paradisal island. Morgan is thus acting here in the role of Modron, and Owain in the role of Mabon.

Mabon's conception represents an intersection of linear time by paradisal dimension, for he is the child of earthly and otherworldly parents. Their meeting is the meeting of worlds, peoples, cultures brought into sudden alignment, and the divine child is born to mediate this set of encounters. The appearance of such a child, innocent and full of otherworldly knowledge, is the signal for a focalisation of opposing powers. All that does not wish to change, all that wishes to maintain the existing order and impose its will upon the world, gathers itself against Mabon, whose very existence represents a threat.

It is not possible to reconstruct a full hero-cycle for Mabon. Of his *indarba* or imprisonment we have already heard in the *Mabinogion*, noting that this is the most prominent feature of his mythos. That the *indarba* should occur so early in a hero's career is quite extraordinary, for the implication in *Culhwch* is that Mabon was stolen from his mother when he was a baby, though by the time of his liberation, he is grown to be a mighty hunter, capable of besting the fiercesome boar, Twrch Trwyth. This latter exploit represents Mabon's youthful deeds or *macgnimartha*; but perhaps Mabon's imprisonment is really of another order?

---

14. *Trioedd Ynys Prydein op. cit.* p. 459. It is perhaps significant to note that the greeting which Urien receives from Afallach's daughter is the same as the five-fold blessing found in some native British pagan rituals. A corrupt form of this blessing was collected in the Cheshire district:

Bledsian we thyn fote that habben brung thee in this weges [ways].
Bledsian we thyn cneo [knee] that sceol cneolin until that sacren awltar.
Bledsian we thyn wame; withuten swilyke we willen nat by.
Bledsian we thyn breost forman in belte and in strang [beauty and strength].
Bledsian we thyn lippa that sceol spricka that sacren nama.

15. *Trioedd Ynys Prydein op. cit.* p. 185, Triad 70.
16. *Le Morte d'Arthur*, Sir Thomas Malory, University Books, 1961.
17. *Vita Merlini* ed. and trans. J.J. Parry, University of Illinois Press, 1925. See also 38.

Within Celto-Arthurian tradition there are many instances of children being abducted, usually by otherworldly powers or in order to gain a special training. It is among stories of this kind that we can most authoratively see the half-covered trail of the Wondrous Youth, Mabon. There are two famous child abductions which bear obvious parallels with his myth, and a still more famous third: the abductions of Pryderi and Lancelot, and the obscure childhood of Arthur himself.

We learn that the abduction of Pryderi from his mother, Rhiannon, is caused by the enmity of Gwawl, an underworld noble who was once affianced to Rhiannon until Pwyll came to claim her. Gwawl was tricked into giving up his destined bride and humiliated by being put into a miraculous food-providing bag and beaten with sticks. For these blows he returns vengeance in one crushing attack: the abduction of Pryderi. It is not known how or where Pryderi is taken in the story; but, simultaneously, a British nobleman, Teyrnon, discovers that his own favourite mare has foaled. In previous years her foal had been stolen, and this night he keeps watch, for it is May-Eve, the time when the otherworldly powers are most free to operate. He sees a gigantic claw come through the stable window to steal the foal and strikes at it. The foal is dropped and Teyrnon rushes outside to pursue the attacker. Finding nothing there, he returns to discover a newly born child in his stable alongside the foal. He keeps the boy and names him Gwri Golden-Hair.

The boy is, of course, Pryderi. He is raised by Teyrnon and his wife while Rhiannon silently suffers the ignominy of standing at the horse block where she must tell her story to every visitor, offering to bear each into the hall on her back: her punishment for having eaten her own child, for so she stands accused. Gwri is, however, recognised and brought back to his parents and Rhiannon is released from her punishment. Her son is acclaimed by her with the saying: 'My anxiety is over.' And so he is named, losing his secret childhood name, Gwri, and becoming Pryderi or 'anxiety' instead.[18]

I have dealt with the many ramifications of this story in *Mabon*,[19] where the obvious comparisons between Mabon and Pryderi are paralleled. Here we note that Pryderi's 'imprisonment' is really a fostering. He is cared for by an earthly, astute guardian who raises him and gives him a name to protect him from the otherworldly powers which threaten his existence. Pryderi is not abducted and imprisoned by his family's enemy, Gwawl at this point, although this does happen in a later story when Pryderi is a man.[20]

Rhiannon is clearly shown to be a type of Modron in this story which best preserves the Passion of Modron. Like the unnamed mother of Urien's children, Rhiannon is likewise the daughter of a King of an otherworldly realm, Annwn, the Underworld. She is likewise fated to marry a mortal man and bear a famous son. The symbolic attributes of Modron are distinct in Celtic tradition: she often bears twins, she is associated with the Underworld, and is often represented by horses, dogs and blackbirds or ravens. She suffers the loss of her child and undergoes a passion in this period similar to that of Demeter for Persephone, abducted into the realm of Hades,[21] or makes a lengthy search for her son, like the Blessed Virgin who loses her Son in the temple.[22] Great burdens are set upon the shoulders of Modron: those who lift them are the helpers and companions of the Great Mother, and they have their place in the freeing of Mabon from his prison.

18. In most of the examples cited as archetypes of Mabon in this chapter, the hero, when a child, has a secret name which is replaced when he becomes adult; this usually happens at a juncture when he accomplishes his youthful exploits.
19. C. Matthews, *op. cit.* chapters 2, 4 and 9.
20. *Manawyddan, Son of Llyr* in *Mabinogion* op cit.
21. *The Homeric Hymns* trans. Apostos N. Athanassakis, Johns Hopkins University Press, 1976.
22. St Luke chap. 2 vv. 41-52.

The suffering mother is again a feature of Lancelot's own abduction. Indeed, the beginning of Lancelot's story is called 'The Tale of the Queen of Many Sorrows', where it tells of Lancelot's father, Ban on Benoic, who dies suddenly from the shock of seeing his castle burned by his enemies. His wife, Elaine, leaves Lancelot – still a babe in arms – on the ground and rushes to assist her stricken husband, only to turn back and see her son being embraced by a maiden who takes him away with her. She is none other than the Lady of the Lake. She takes him with her to her lake-domain where he is kept safe from attack by his family's enemies. The Lady does not name him, but calls him 'the Fair Foundling' or 'the Rich Orphan'. She raises him to be a knight and later arms and names him herself. He is then sent back into the world to avenge his father and restore the lands which had been stolen by his enemies.[23]

If we follow an earlier story of Lancelot's abduction, *Lanzelet*,[24] a twelfth-century text which undoubtedly drew on Celtic traditions absent from the *Prose Lancelot*, we find that Lancelot is taken into the Otherworld for the sole purpose of releasing the Lake-Lady's son from enchantment. This son is called Mabuz, and he has been cursed with cowardice by an evil magician called Iweret. Lanzelet is raised by the Lake Lady to become an accomplished warrior – a late example of the Celtic tradition whereby boys were trained in war skills by women-warriors.[25] The Lake-Lady likewise arms and eventually names Lanzelet, although he remains nameless until he has accomplished her will, which is to kill the magician who cursed her son.

In this story, Lanzelet is almost a substitue for Mabuz. Mabuz himself is unable to move freely on his own behalf, for he is destined to live a strange existence within the Castle of Death – a prison in which he is trapped by the curse and a prison likewise for all knights who stray within its walls, for it renders them cowardly also. He is unable to make free use of his lands, realms analogous to the Lands of the Living in Celtic tradition,[26] for these are held by Iweret. When Lanzelet is released from his fostering, a fully trained knight, he starts to accomplish all that Mabuz would have done, had he been free. He kills Iweret and wins back Mabuz's lands, but for Mabuz there is no ultimate release, for his curse cannot be lifted. It is so that Mabuz's lands are awarded to Lanzelet who also marries Iweret's daughter. In this story, Lanzelet is clearly Mabuz's active 'twin' or substitute – they are, after all, foster-brothers. The author of the story has not fully comprehended the ancient tradition of Mabon's imprisonment but knows sufficient of the story to incorporate it in some manner. It is as though 'Mabon's prison' instead of being the 'place of Mabon's imprisonment' has become 'the prison administered by Mabuz'. Lanzelet accomplishes the *macgimartha* or *slugard* of the Mabon-cycle in this story.

What of the third abduction of which we spoke? Mabon is closely associated with Arthur, who, according to *Triad 52*, undergoes a mysterious imprisonment:

> And one (Prisoner) who was more exalted than the three of them was three nights in prison in Caer Oeth and Anoeth, and three nights imprisoned by Gwen Pendragon, and three nights in an enchanted prison under the Stone of Echymeint. This Exalted Prisoner was Arthur. And it was the same lad who released him from each of these three prisons – Goreu, son of Custennin, his cousin.[27]

---

23. *Sir Lancelot of the Lake*, L.A. Paton, George Routledge and Co., 1929.
24. *Lanzelet*, Ulrich von Zatzikhoven, K.G.T. Webster, Columbia University Press, 1951.
25. *Warriors of Arthur*, J. Matthews and B. Stewart, Blandford Press, 1987.
26. His lands are called the Fair Forest and are described in terms familiar to anyone who had read accounts of *Tir mBeo* as the terrestrial paradise.
27. *Trioedd Yns Prydein, op. cit.*, p. 140. In *Culhwch and Olwen* in the *Mabinogion op. cit.* there is a rare reference to Arthur's imprisonment when Glewlwyd, his porter, lists this as one of many adventures he has undergone with his king.

These references are encapsulations of stories which are lost to tradition, but which were clearly associated once with the disappearance and freeing of Mabon in Celtic imagination. There is a later tradition in which Arthur is 'lost'. He is conceived on Ygraine by Uther, who visits her in the shape of her husband, Gorlois: a transformation which is effected by Merlin, so that Uther is effectually a daemon or incubus.[28] Arthur is taken away after his birth by Merlin in order to be fostered by Sir Ector,[29] although his fostering in the land of Faery is spoken of by Layamon.[30] Arthur is thus hidden at the time of greatest danger to himself, during the interregnum between Uther's death and his own revelation as the rightful king who can draw the Sword from the Stone. The early part of Arthur's life parallels the Mabon archetype, but what of its latter end? Arthur is destined to weld Britain into a single country within himself as overlord. Nearly all his attempts to live a personal life are failures: he is at his strongest when he serves his country, who we can see as Sovereignty, the Goddess of the land, who represents Logres or Britain.[31] He does not die, precisely, but is wounded and borne away into Avalon to be healed by Morgen.[32]

Both the abductions of Lancelot and Arthur are really fosterings, times of withdrawal and preparation for great exploits. From these and the other examples of our Mabon archetypes we can see some part of the pattern coming clear. The manifestations of Mabon's archetype betray distinct features: the child is born of a mortal and an other-worldly parent. He is lost or abducted shortly after birth – usually because he is a threat to the established order, or because he is in danger from enemies. He is raised secretly, usually in an otherworldly environment, where he learns deep wisdom and the skills for his destined task. He is released from his obscurity or prison by a character bearing characteristics similar to or more mature than himself[33] and is so enabled to start a life-cycle which proves to be redemptive, not personal. At the end of his life he does not die, but is withdrawn into a state of spiritual life.

We will see the latter part of this pattern more clearly from one of the closest exemplars of the Mabon archetype – Merlin. Merlin is born of a virgin and a daemon.[34] As Merlin Emrys, he is abducted by Vortigern's men, who are seeking for a suitable sacrifice to help sustain Vortigern's tower, which keeps tumbling down. This tower is a figure of the state of Britain – in collapse under an unlawful, bloody and treacherous king. The perfect sacrifice, say Vortigern's druids, should be a boy whose father is unknown.[35] Merlin Emrys fits this description perfectly. However, since he is a type of Mabon, there is more to him than first appears. He is the innocent child who can refute philosophers and make clear the state of the country. He reveals the true cause of the tower's collapse as being the two dragons which are imprisoned under its foundations. He reveals to Vortigern the true state of Britain both now and in the future in a series of brilliant prophecies.[36] Here we see revealed another part of Mabon's cycle, his *fís* or vision, wherein his inner knowledge of creation reveals itself to men.

Merlin Emrys prophesies and then helps establish the reign of the Pendragons: first-

---

28. The daemon or incubus is of course a real otherworldly being, but Uther's assumption of another shape enables the conception of Arthur, who may be said to have an earthly mother and an otherworldly father.
29. *op cit.*, Malory, Book I, chap. 3.
30. *Arthurian Chronicles*, Wace and Layamon, trans. E. Mason, p. 177, Dent, 1962.
31. I have dealt with Arthur's relationship to Sovereignty in the second of my two-volume study of the *Mabinogion: Arthur and the Sovereignty of Britain - Goddess and Tradition in the Mabinogion*, Arkana, 1989.
32. *Vita Merlini op. cit.* (See also 38)
33. This part of Mabon's cycle I have identified as the Succession of the Pendragons cf. C. Matthews (1987).
34. Wace and Layamon, *op. cit.* p. 145.
35. C. Matthews (1989). In my commentary on *Lludd and Llefelys* I have shown the many parallels of this sacrificial role.
36. *The Prophetic Vision of Merlin*, R.J. Stewart, Arkana, 1986.

ly Uther, and then Arthur. He is really their forerunner. This is significant in relation to Mabon, since an early Welsh poem[37] speaks of Mabon as 'the servant of Uther Pendragon': a single reference which helps us link Merlin's function as prophet with Mabon's own lost function as releaser and enabler.

We note that Merlin does not have a personal life. His function is to serve Britain and to act as prophet and adviser to kings. When his task is done, he is withdrawn to the realm of his unknown father, the Otherworld. Geoffrey of Monmouth speaks of his house with many doors and windows through which he can observe the heavens.[38] Merlin does not die, but voluntarily retires from the realm of men into his Otherworldly abode from which he can still remain in contact with Logres and from where certain people, sensitive to Merlin's role, can faintly hear the 'the cri du Merlin'.[39]

Merlin's withdrawal from the world, like Mabon's imprisonment, has not always been perfectly understood by the later Arthurian romancers who have spoken of his entrapment by Nimue, Vivienne or the Lady of the Lake.[40] Merlin's spiritual maturity is mistaken for senile infatuation, so that they tell of his revealing the method by which he can be trapped in his crystal tower, under his rock or in his thorn tree – those later representations of his place of retirement – to sinuous and treacherous damsels. These stories merely reveal the deterioration of the tradition. For in later stories Mabon similarly undergoes a diminution where, in Chrétien's *Erec*,[41] he becomes Mabonograin, a giant warrior, trapped within an enchanted garden where he is enslaved to a faery mistress whose domain he defends against all comers.

Both Merlin and Mabon's later commentators may stray from tradition, but they yet manage to retain aspects of older fragments which do not come down to us in any other way. From Merlin's story and from related tradition we can establish the archetypical Mabon death story or *aided* which appears nowhere else: the withdrawal of Merlin to his *esplumoir*.[42] Although there is one further example from late Arthurian tradition which has possibly inherited a vital part of Mabon's archetype: the Character of Galahad.

The Arthurian tradition is exceedingly persistent. Whatever has been honoured, reverenced or sained by holy custom remains embedded within the Matter of Britain, becoming mythologically subsumed in the variant texts. Their unravelling is the work of many scholars. We have seen how Mabon's archetype did not totally fade from the tradition but appeared in strange guises. It should come as no surprise to find that it resides in the highest flowering of the Arthurian legends – the Quest for the Grail.

The original Grail winner is Peredur or Perceval;[43] in him we find many broad traces of Mabon's archetype, as I have shown in my study of the *Mabinogion*. Galahad appears much later in the French texts and has always seemed to me to be a foreign usurper of Peredur's role. However, Galahad inherits not only the characteristics of Mabon but also those of Lancelot, his father, who, as Arthur's best knight, is directly descended from the Celtic original 'freer of the cauldron', Llwych Lleminawg.[44]

Galahad is conceived by Elaine, the daughter of the Grail guardian, Pelles, at whose behest and with the connivance of Dame Brisen, she appears to Lancelot in the shape of

37. *The Romance of Arthur*, ed. J.J. Wilhelm, and L.Z. Gross, p. 19, Garland Pub. Inc. 1984.
38. *The Mystic Life of Merlin*, R.J. Stewart, Arkana, 1986.
39. *Merlin*, ed. H.E. Wheatley, Early English Texts Soc., p. 692. 1869.
40 *Studies in the Fairy Mythology of Arthurian Romance*, L.A. Paton, Burt Franklin, 1960.
41. *Arthurian Romances*, Chrétien de Troyes, D.D.R. Owen, Dent, 1987.
42. Cf. John Matthews' essay, *Merlin's Esplumoir*, in this volume.
43. *Mabinogion op. cit.* and Chrétien de Troyes *op. cit.*
44. *op. cit.*, C. Matthews, (1987), pp. 107-8, 156.

Guinevere, the only woman Lancelot desires.[45] In this mysteriously un-Christian conception of the most Christian knight, we see the ancient archetypal pattern emerging. Elaine, like Uther in Arthur's conception, acts the part of fantasy-being, a succuba. Her son, Galahad, is brought up surrounded by women in a monastery, just as Lancelot is raised by the totally female population of the Lake-Lady. He is brought to court by a holy man after his obscure youth and undertakes the quest for the Grail. What most people consider to be Galahad's worst features – his seeming priggishness and ultra-holiness – are revealed to be the simplicity and innocence of a man living a redemptive, not a personal life. His one function – the reason why he was born – is to reveal the potentialities of the spirit and release them, in the shape of the Grail. When this is achieved, he is withdrawn from the earthly sphere at Sarras, the Grail city, where his companions seem to see him die; but we must look upon his death as upon Merlin's withdrawal to another mode of life. Like Merlin, who is aided by his sister, Ganieda, to withdraw into his last retreat,[46] so Galahad is enabled to make this transition through the mediation of the holy maiden, Dindraine;[47] as indeed Arthur is enabled to pass into Avalon through the mediation of Morgen.[48]

Here we see Modron's part in Mabon's hero-cycle; in whatever guise she takes, Modron appears at both the beginning and the end of his cycle. For Mabon is a servant of Sovereignty, of the Goddess of the Land. His service is to the land, a redemptive, not a personal life. He represents the truth and justice of the Goddess, his mother, from whom he comes and to whom he returns. He is, in fact, Sovereignty's son, when he appears as Mabon the Divine Child. His enemies always strive to imprison or sacrifice him because he is incorruptible, pure and discerning, but the truth remains that he cannot be overcome unless he voluntarily commits himself into the hands of his enemies.

We have traced Mabon's infolding life and career from conception to withdrawal; what is his true purpose within our native mythology?

Mabon stands at the nexus of a three fold tradition. As a Celtic deity he is the joy of the Otherworld, the God of Youth and Delight. As a proto-Christian archetype, he is a Liberator of the Light, the Long-expected One who redeems the world. In non-religious, Arthurian tradition – which inherits elements of the two former ones – Mabon appears again as the perfect knight, conceived strangely, destined to free the waters of the wasteland and bring the Grail into manifestation through his offices.

The reason why Mabon cannot be found by one person's effort, nor from the testimony of one animal, is that he cannot be known by one single part of creation; he is the sum of creation. He is the Child of the Dawn, the First Born of the Mother. It is his task to harp creation into existence and to be the Shepherd of the orders of creations – birds, beasts and fish all answer to him. He exists from the beginning and can be found – in archetypal terms – within the terrestrial paradise. His mythos explicates this in other terms – he is known to be imprisoned, hidden or lost, just as our own innocence is lost. Whoever finds Mabon finds the primal source of truth and integrity. His mother, Modron, is the land, the goddess who guards the gates of death and living. An exchange takes place between them which is at the heart of native mysteries.[49]

---

45. Malory, Book XI, chap. 2. I have examined the role of the dream-woman or succuba from her roots in the Sovereignty figures of Celtic tradition in *Arthur and the Sovereignty of Britain op. cit.*
46. *Vita Merlini op. cit.* and 38.
47. *Quest of the Holy Grail*, trans. P. Matarasso, Penguin, 1969.
48. *Vita Merlini op. cit.* and 38.
49. *Op. cit.* C. Matthews (1987), pp. 177-86.

King Arthur asks the Lady of the Lake for the sword Excalibur (Walter Crane)

Modron, for the sake of the land, permits Mabon to become lost to her. She enables his birth into the earthly realms by lying with a mortal man; in this way Mabon has dual divine and human citizenship. He is brought up secretly and taught all the skills which he will need. He forgets his origins but he remembers these at his initiation into manhood, when he enters the totemic tree of time where linear time is intersected by the otherworldly dimension. At this point he is given his earthly name, although he never ceases to be a Mabon. His mother watches over his career and either in person, or in the guise of messengers, encourages and helps him to fulfil his mission, which is to reconstruct the primal patterns of peace which exist endlessly in paradise but which are lost in the earthly realms.

The accomplishment of this pattern takes many forms: Mabon may appear as a warrior, hunting down whatever is corrupt; or as a poet-seer whose prophetic utterances show pathways through confusion; or as a sacrificial king, who brings justic to a war-torn land. He does not live a personal but a redemptive life. He upholds the honour of his mother in the persons of other women who represent her in the earthly realms, priestesses who mediate her influence and power; he is also a guardian of his mother's rights where she functions as Sovereignty – the Goddess of the Land – by wielding justice, truth and discernment in the administration of the land. He may act as the forerunner or adviser of a king. He is not permitted to perform rites of healing in his own right or for his own benefit, although he may enable others to do so. His part is to establish the patterns of peace, but others have to wield them. When these patterns are established, he must withdraw from the earthly realms and return to the paradisal Otherworld, where he is restored to his first condition, as the Son of Modron, the keeper of creation.

This archetypal pattern of Mabon's inner function has been drawn only from native sources and traditions, but it is not hard to see why the essential core of Christianity grafted so easily onto the existing mythos of the British Isles. There is almost no join, for the two traditions – Celtic, or proto-Celtic mythos and Christian mythos – flow together in an organic way. Ways of worship may change, but stories never.

The cycle of Mabon does not have to be forced to parallel that of Christ: they are the same mythic pattern. A seventh-century Irish poem attests to an intrinsic understanding of the Mabon archetype where it speaks of the Blessed Trinity as:

> Threefold God, three noble united Persons,
> Wonderful sole King of Heaven, infant, holy warrior.[50]

The horn which releases Mabon from his long imprisonment is blowing to assemble all peoples to a meeting place outside time to discover that the mediations of *all* traditions are valid, that they grow out of one another and will continue to do so.

The purpose of Mabon for our own time is the same as for all times: truth, justice and discernment are the heritage of all peoples; these are the means of healing the wounds of our earth and the pathways by which we may restore our lost innocence.

MERLIN IN MODERN FICTION AND CINEMA
by John Matthews

THE TRIVIALIZING OF Merlin in modern entertainment conceals a remarkable truth; he is as coherent in good fiction as in legend, despite the seeming paradox of his incoherency! When we see Merlin in cartoon form, as a comedy sketch in a TV panel game or in more ambitious attempts at trivialization such as the ill-fated Broadway musical, we see the work of people who have made no attempt to understand him, merely to use his name for superficial ends. Yet whenever an author has tried to reach an understanding of or with Merlin, certain coherent elements always appear.

This does not imply that the coherence is in the mind of the author, nor that there is some 'master plan' instructing our imaginative works about Merlin, but there is no doubt that authors who make serious attempts at describing Merlin, even in science fiction form, tap into a set of images of enduring quality. Curiously, these images are not all drawn from the Merlin root material in early Celtic sources, nor from the Arthurian literature of the Middle Ages.

What are these images, and how do they relate to one another? A short summary would perhaps be as follows.

---

50. *Irish Origin Legends and Genealogy*, Donnchadh Ó Corráin, in *History and Heroic Tale: A Symposium*, ed. T. Nyberg, Odense University Press, 1985.

Merlin has three aspects: the bright youth; the mad prophet and shaman; the wise elder. All three are concerned with the interaction of spiritual and magical powers, with a strong emphasis upon a relationship with the land, the environment and particularly the land of Britain.

Behind the aspects is a god-form. This deep and powerful image is given emphasis in the works of John Cowper Powys and C.S. Lewis, though it also appears in many other approaches to Merlin, both published and private. This god-form guides or aids humanity through the triple expression described.

Thus Merlin, born of a mortal maiden and an otherworld spirit according to the chronicles, acts as the mediator for deep powers manifesting through the land into human consciousness. His threefold appearance is initially that of the lifetime of any person; youth, adulthood, maturity, but into each of these aspects is channelled the most potent dynamic power, imagery and mystery of each life phase.

As a youth, he is the eternal child, of spiritual purity; as a mature man he is the wild fervent power of magic or transforming consciousness; as an elder he is the epitome of wisdom, learning, transcendant knowledge and, of course, experience. In fictional works unconnected to one another, this coherence out of diversity is apparent; and occasionally the deep ancient god-form appears, the non-human power behind the semi-human Merlin. This power may also take a number of shapes, but what is remarkable is that authors of quite different style, cultural background and quality of work may be imaginatively aware of its existence.

There is no chronicle source for Merlin as a god or titanic power, only a few hints in early Welsh poetry. Later romances and chronicles were divided between the magician of Arthur's court and the increasingly orthodox image of a diabolical being – though there is no mention of Merlin linked to Arthur in the early sources, and certainly no question of evil. A *daemon* is not the same as a *demon*. The first is a guiding and instructing spirit (such as inspired Socrates) well known in classical allusions and cosmology, while the second is the product of Judaeo-Christian propaganda and subtle editing. Yet this confusion has brought modern writers into contact with the image that is at the foundation of the figure of Merlin. . . a mysterious primal god or tutelary being.

In primal cultures, the wise man or *shaman* (to use an increasingly popular term which should perhaps be limited to its Siberian cultural origins) acts as the vehicle for spiritual power, which may manifest itself in derivative forms, such as spirits or totem animals, or may occur in its own right, albeit filtered through human consciousness. Both of these elements of mediation or priesthood, known in all cultures and religions worldwide, are present in the Melin legends. In the *Vita Merlini* of Geoffrey of Monmouth, shamanistic Celtic and spiritual religious elements are intentionally fused together, with Merlin growing through his wild prophetic fervour towards a spiritual retirement in an astrological observatory in the woods. Geoffrey was clearly aware that the aspects or faces of Merlin need not be contradictory, but are highly energized presentations of changes and modes of consciousness shared by all men and women.

The other significant element dealt with at length by Geoffrey is that of sexuality or polarity. The entire *Vita* is an adventure reaching from the personality to the universe, and guided at all stages by sexual or polarized relationships. These are catalysed by the figure of Ganieda (Merlin's sister) who is very similar to Minerva or the Celtic Briggidda; a number of other women also appear in the role of pleasant or vengeful lovers, and of course as the famous priestess and shape-changer Morgen, who cares for the wounded King Arthur in the Fortunate Isle.

Sexuality is naturally a central subject for writers of fiction; although after the perverted post-medieval role ascribed to woman in Malory, and to a much greater extent in Tennyson, it is sometimes difficult to grasp the essence of Merlin's relationship to women.

As all of the examples cited deal in varying ways with the theme of sexuality or polarity, we should examine briefly how this theme connects to the primal myths of universal creation, for this is where the key to Merlin and woman may be found. (The following is merely a summary of a subject which demands a separate study in its own right.)

Merlin's love of women, sometimes moralized into a sexual weakness, is a reflection of his otherworldly father's love for his mother. This in turn relates to one of the most ancient mythical themes, and like all Merlinic lore is intimately concerned with both environment and the spiritual intimations found in all religions, magic and mysticism. Traditionally, spirits of a certain order 'between the moon and the Earth' are said to advise men and women, hear their prayers and convey them to divinity, and to join in love with mortal women.

This theme is merely a microcosmic or lesser reflection of a great religious motif; it finds its epitome in the Virgin Birth, known in many religions but refined and featured in Christianity. In short, divinity joins with humanity. In pagan religions, this was part of the procreation and fertility of the earth, while in Christianity it has become tidied up by successive schools of scholarship and moralizing Church fathers who wished to cut their congregation off from other cults.

Gnostic worshippers, fusing pagan and early Christian wisdom, knew full well that the appearance of Christ within the world was a sexual matter, and the mystical adoration of the Saviour in later writings, prayers and meditative practices leaves us in no doubt as to the potentially sexual quality of otherworldly inspiration. This does not imply, and never has implied, a physical or gross element to such spiritual realizations; merely that, if they are to be true, they must be true on all levels.

In the Old Testament and many other mythical books or tales, we have the famous legend of angels who copulated with mortal women, breeding a race of giants upon earth. Once again, this, like later variants of the Merlin legend, has become corrupted into a wilful misrepresentation of sexuality; it is really a myth reflecting certain stages of the relationship between humanity and divinity. In orthodox Christian religion, it is God's love of the World that causes Christ to be sent as a Saviour.

The fall of Lucifer into the earth, the love of angels for mortal women, the impregnation of a virgin, the relationship between humankind and the land, and the love of God for Humankind, are all woven together inextricably. . . for they are part of the polarity pattern of existence. We could define this pattern in mythical and religious terms, as above, or in psychological jargon, or in the formulae of science, but whatever words we choose to use the truth is undeniable; the mysteries of life are mysteries of polarity. For us, polarity is usually sexual in the most individual or personalized sense, but for otherworldly beings (be they daemons on one level or Divinity upon another) the personal reflection is absent, and sexuality partakes of a transcendant metaphysical quality, while including physical manifestation.

Thus the various sexual convolutions of Merlin in modern fiction are not merely misunderstandings or corruptions of the source material (in which the sexual weakness, sin, evil or grossly sensual elements are not to be found) but are explorations of a universal theme expressed through the mediating figure of Merlin.

Finally, this section suggests, subtly, something rather remarkable about fiction that deals with Merlin. We opened this introduction with criticism of the trend towards trivializing myth in modern entertainment, a trend that is by no means confined to the figure of Merlin. Even quite outrageous and perhaps poorly written treatments of Merlin in almost any context can carry within them the primal mythic elements that contribute to the protean figure of the prophet, magician and wise man. What, we may ask, is the difference? Why do some treatments of Merlin fail utterly and even inspire revulsion, while others, poor as they may be, speak truth?

> Because I am dark and always shall be, let my book be dark and mysterious in those places where I will not show myself.

This passage, from a medieval text about Merlin, makes a good point from which to begin this brief exploration, because it exactly describes what has happened. In no two versions is Merlin ever the same – even allowing for the idiosyncrasies of the various authors who have written about him, the divergence is so great that it would be difficult to imagine that it was the same character were it not for certain basic common factors which, ultimately, seem to reveal the figure at the heart of this constellation of disguises.

Merlin has remained 'dark and mysterious' despite everything. Yet somehow, none of those who have chosen to write about him have been able to resist asking the question: who – or what – is he? Their answers have been as diverse as they possibly could be, picturing Merlin as god or jester, as prophet, wiseman and sage; as an old lover caught in the silken wiles of his young pupil; as an alien being, brought to earth on cosmic business; as a wondrous child or an Atlantean priest; as a servant of many gods or of one Goddess; as a charlatan and a liar and a madman. But always, between the disguises, we glimpse another face, that of a grey-clad pilgrim and wanderer, sent here long ago to guide and guard the destiny of kings and of men – a majestic mage steering the barque of the island that has been named after him: Clas Merdin – Merlin's Enclosure, or, in Kipling's words:

> Merlin's isle of Gramarie
> where you and I will fare.

We perhaps know Merlin best in his most familiar guise – as the wise and foresighted wizard who stands behind Arthur in the early days of his reign and who acts as adviser and councillor to the young king until he himself is ensnared by a beautiful young woman who becomes his apprentice. Modern fictional versions of this basic tale do exist, but it is at some less familiar aspects that I wish to look here, in the belief that an examination of the many facets of Merlin's character which they portray, will throw some light on the *real* Merlin, the enchanter in hiding.

ATLANTEAN ORIGINS

The span of his years is certainly immense; possibly, like Melchizedek, 'without beginning or end.' Surprisingly, few writers of this or any age have looked for his beginnings. It is in the writings of the esotericist Dion Fortune (1890–1946) that we first find mention of Merlin as an Atlantean priest who fled from the destruction of the lost continent, bearing with him the princess Igraine, destined to become the mother of Arthur.

Though Dion Fortune wrote no novel of Merlin himelf, this idea has surfaced in two recent books of very different quality: *The Mists of Avalon* (1982) by Marion Zimmer Bradley, and *Merlin and the Dragons of Atlantis* (1983) by Rita and Tim Hildebrandt. In the latter, Merlin is a scientist from Lemuria, a land adjacent to Atlantis and far older. It has adopted more peaceful and mystical ways than those of its more powerful neighbours, who now seek to perfect a race of genetically-engineered dragons to protect their vast cities and great domains. Merlin's thirst for knowledge brings him to join those working on the project, but when it is successful and the dragons are subsequently taken over by evil forces, he helps to destroy them, bringing about also the premature fall of Atlantis and the destruction of all that he loves. But Merlin himself does not die; he places himself in an induced state of hibernation from which he will wake to bring about the realization of a new dream, the creation of a new Atlantean state within the world of the Arthurian heroes. Then, we are told:

> he found his child and taught him well. The child grew with wisdom and knowledge into manhood. Thus for a brief second in history Merlin saw Arthur have his Camelot.
>
> (p.105)

Dragons of Atlantis represents an effort to show Merlin as a transcendent figure, able to operate over vast distances of time, through the use of knowledge no longer current in our world. Atlantis is merely the latest image of the Otherworldly realm from which Merlin has always been recognized as coming, while the image of Merlin himself is much as we would expect him to be portrayed in our time: as a scientist rather than as a wizard or seer; as someone imbued with endless curiosity about the nature of creation and its foremost offspring: mankind.

Marion Bradley's book is both well written and imaginatively satisfying, though, for her, Merlin is a title borne by many rather than a name belonging to any one figure. Here, as in numerous recent versions of the story, the setting is post-Roman Britain, in which Merlin acts as an agent of those who seek to unite the shattered country into an unshakable force under the banner of Arthur. But already, before that dream is even begun, a deeper split exists – a religious division between Christianity and those who follow the way of the Goddess of Earth. Bradley's interpretation seems to say more about the current spiritual divide between orthodox religion and eco-pagan groups than about any actual spiritual divisions existing in post-Roman culture. Nevertheless, her personal colouring of events gives the book its vigour and also allows her Merlin to voice a genuine observation:

> There are now two Britains... their world under their One God and the Christ; and beside it and behind it, the world where the Great Mother still rules, the world where the Old People have chosen to live and worship.
>
> (p. 15)

Igraine, soon to be the mother of the young king, remembers an earlier time, an earlier incarnation. In a waking vision, she stands on Salisbury Plain and watches the fiery sun rise over the great stone circle – and beyond,

> To the West, where stood the lost lands of Lyonesse and Ys and the great isle of Atlas-Alamesios, or Atlantis, the forgotten kingdom of the sea. There, indeed, had been the great fire, there the mountain had blown apart, and in a single night, a hundred thousand men and women and little children had perished.

'But the Priests knew' said a voice at her side. 'For the past hundred years, they have been building their star temple here on the plains, so that they might not lose count of the tracking of the seasons... These people here, they know nothing of such things, but they know we are wise, priests and priestesses from over the sea, and they will build for us, as they did before'...

(p. 63)

The speaker is Uther, who shares Igraine's reincarnational memories. From their love is soon to issue the young Arthur who with Merlin's aid will try to build a new and perfect expression of Human endeavour. Here, we may see Merlin as representing the latest of a line of priests descended from the long-ago escapees of the doomed land, who have carried the seeded memories of the past within them until it can be brought once again into manifestation.

In a different way this is the aim of Merlin in Andre Norton's *Merlin's Mirror* (1975), where the image is a creation of a race of alien beings known as the Sky Lords, who in the infancy of the world leave behind them a hidden computer installation pro- grammed to begin its work many thousands of years later, by the creation of heroes and leaders who will raise the race of men to their own height. There is an implication also that the Sky Lords will themselves have perished by this time, perhaps as a result of a long struggle with an opposing force called 'the Dark Ones'. These are not intrinsically evil, it seems, but are opposed to the actions of the Sky Lords and their aim to hasten the development of humanity.

In this science fiction version of the story, Merlin is created by means of the artificial insemination of a British woman who sees only a computer-generated image of a beau- tiful golden man – an ingenious twist to the story of Merlin's birth in Geoffrey of Monthouth's twelfth century *Historia*. But, just as Merlin represents the Sky Lords, so are the Dark Ones represented by Nimue, and the ancient destiny of the King, his wiz- ard, and the priestess who brings about their downfall, is here played out in images drawn from the cosmic world of the science fiction novel. In the end, Merlin, who has read all the future in his computer-operated 'mirror', sees that his dream of a united land under the figure of Arthur, is doomed to fail, and he retires, like the Merlin of the Hildebrandt novel, into a self-induced sleep to await a more auspicious time when he may try again.

In Susan Cooper's *Dark is Rising* sequence (1965–79) we are afforded a glimpse of Merlin once again in immortal guise, as a combatant against thⁿ powers of evil. To the world at large he is known as Dr Merriman Lyon, a professor of Arthurian studies and an archaeologist – two roles we may well imagine Merlin adopting in a twentieth-cen- tury setting. In reality, however, he is one of an immortal race known simply as 'the Old Ones', whose endless task it is to combat the ancient forces of the Dark. This is more openly dualistic than either Andre Norton or C.S. Lewis, but as in both of these writers, and in the work of the Hildebrandts there are echoes of Merlin's Atlantean ori- gins. Once again his task is to guide the steps of human protagonists – here a group of children – rather than directly intervene in the age-old war of Light and Dark. As in his guidance of the young Arthur in the original romances, this role is one which requires him to adopt many faces and forms, becoming elusive and secret and unfathomable in order to perform his task.

MERLIN'S PRIMARY TASK

We have seen already that Merlin is often shown to be a priest or councillor of kings, who comes from a far-off land where civilization, or knowledge, may be more advanced than in the rest of the world. We can be sure as well that he is possesed of occult or prophetic knowledge, and we can extend our understanding of his role or function further by turning to another Merlin-type figure, who does not bear his name but who occupies a position in almost every way the same as that taken by Merlin. The relevant passage goes thus:

> Warm and eager was his spirit... opposing the fire that devuors and wastes with the fire that kindles and succours in wan hope and distress; but his joy, and his swift wrath, were veiled in garments grey as ash, so that only those who knew him well glimpsed the flame that was within. Merry he could be and kindly to the young and simple, and yet quick at times to sharp speech and the rebuking of folly; but he was not proud, and sought neither power nor praise, and thus far and wide he was beloved among all those that were not themselves proud. Mostly he journied unwearyingly on foot, leaning on a staff; and so he was called among men of the North Gandalf, the 'Elf of the Wand'.
>
> J.R.R. Tolkien: *Unfinished Tales* pp. 390–1

Gandalf, of course, in Tolkien's mythology, is one of the Istari, emissaries of the Valar, great angelic forces who watch over the world and mediate between God and creation. This is completely in line with the primary task allotted to Merlin in the majority of the stories about him – to guide and shepherd the destinies of men. It is in this guise that we encounter him again and again, both in the medieval stories, and in the writings of modern authors – books as varied and far apart in scope as John Cowper Powys's *Porius* (1951), Mary Stewart's Merlin trilogy (1970–79), Peter Vansittart's *Lancelot* (1978) and Linda Halderman's fantasy *The Lastborn of Elvinwood* (1980).

The Merlin of Porius, is half-man and half-god, a huge, slow earth-man, smelling of mould and green things. His work is devoted to the return upon earth of a new Golden Age, the age of Saturn/Cronos, of which god he sees himself as a true atavar. Descriptions of him abound in Powys' extraordinary book. Here is just one:

> Myrddin Wyllt was dressed in his long black mantle; and at the place where his great beard reached the level of his navel, it was tied with the usual gold thread whose tassels hung down to his knees. His head was bare, and his long fingers at the end of his long arms were making slow majestic movements as if writing upon the interior darkness of the tent... But it soon occurred to Porius that what the man was doing lent itself to another and quite different interpretation; namely, that instead of inscribing things on the air he was *tracing out things* that had already been written upon it!
>
> (p. 405)

Powys's Myrddin Wyllt (or the Wild) is linked specifically with an ancient race of aboriginal giants, the very children of Cronos it seems, of whom the last remnant live out their days in the fastness of Welsh mountains. In Linda Halderman's book, Merlin is again associated with the destiny of a race of huge people – though here they have remained hidden, and have dwindled, becoming in time a smaller race, the denizens of Faery, who have no love for he whom they call 'the Old One', blaming his actions in a dim and distant time for their own present state. Their traditions tell how once their giant ancestors

> ... dwelt in the mountains to the north mostly, herding and farming and minding their own business. He, the Old One, lived alone in the south. What he is and where he came from, I cannot say. Perhaps your legend of him being the offspring of a demon has

some truth in it. I don't pretend to know. We call ourselves the First Folk, because it is our belief that our gigantic ancestors were the first people to live on this island. Yet they called him the Old One [even then].

(p. 136)

The present day heroes, seeking to enlist his aid in the matter of two changelings, find the Old One living in semi-retirement in a cottage in the depths of the English countryside. On their way to visit him they discuss his history – the story of him being the son of the devil, and of his entrapment by Nimue:

Ah yes, Nimue... A naive ruse, but one that worked. It was the end of what he calls his political phase... Arthur turned out to be a bitter disappointment, more interested in holding bloody tournaments than in planting gardens, [Merlin's great love]... and unnaturally preoccupied with his wife's activities... Arthur is one of the main reasons he's down on the Celts... he decided to retire. Arthur refused to let him go, so he paid Nimue to invent the cave story and slipped off to live in blissful solitude...

(p. 64)

Here we have a glimpse of a lighter side of Merlin's nature, yet he is still a difficult and even a dangerous character, who can be both chancy and unreliable in his dealings with humanity. Peter Vansittart, in his novel of Lancelot, paints an even more oblique portrait. Here, Merlin is generally referred to as 'He' – a mark of respect and caution towards the Old One, whom one should never address by name unless invited to do so. 'He' seems, at first glance, an unprepossessing character:

Despite the familiar dirt caking his ears, beard, bare feet, the sacklike gown under gaudy robes, he repelled me less, his hierophantic mendacities more lively than the dismal hush that passed for entertainment with Artorius. Last year his hand motions had induced a snowfall when least required, his explanations being acceptable as minor poetry by anyone without scholarship or sensitivity. He had also acquired an adroit method of inclining his head so that a shadow of a bird or animal was reflected on the wall behind him.

(p. 144)

Merlin is brought back to life – literally since he is summoned from his grave by Ceneu, the current King of the Britons, to assist in the last desperate attempt to stem the tide of the invading Saxons – in Nikolai Tolstoy's *The Coming of the King: the First Book of Merlin* (1988). This is the first in a projected trilogy, though a second volume is yet to appear at the time of writing – and follows on from Tolstoy's excellent study *The Quest for Merlin* which appeared in 1985.

The Coming of the King is an immensely long and discursive book, frequently interrupting the flow of the narrative for long digressions on matters of siege warfare or for huge set pieces such as the feast of Maelgwyn Gwynedd, in which devils and daemons are conjured up to join in the baroque festivities. The setting of the book is Northern Britain two generations after the departing of Arthur, and consists in part of Myrddin's (Tolstoy opts for the more ancient figure and the traditional spelling) rambling memoirs, in which he recalls not only the time of Arthur but mythological time as well. He is conflated somewhat with the figure of Taliesin, which gives Tolstoy an excuse to retell the powerful myth of the shape-shifting bard, and to lead the way into the depths of Annwn itself. For this is not just a tale of historical characters and events – it is a vast spiritual tract, an allegory as densely allusive as Spenser or Bunyon.

Tolstoy is primarily a historian and Celticist, and the immense structure of his learning, which is intended to support the book, only succeeds in hampering the story – almost drowning it in details which leave the reader alternatively gasping or reaching for a Welsh dictionary. The figure of Myrddin which emerges is, however, probably the closest anyone has got since Geoffrey of Monmouth to the real figure: immemorially ancient, powerful and merging almost with the land itself. In this Tolstoy is closest to J. Cowper Powys and C.S. Lewis in his delineation of the character of the old mage.

> It seemed to King Ceneu and his companions that there arose from the centre of the *gorsedd* a man greater far in stature then the men of their own time. His clothes were but the undressed skins of beasts, his hair thin and grey and flowing, and his aspect paler, emaciated, wild. He lacked his left eye, which was but a puckered, sightless socket. His gaze seemed to portend both pain and anger. . .
>
> (p. 18)

This telling is bardic, drawing upon the *Mabinogion*, and the old poems of Myrddin and Gwenddydd [see above, Part 1] to fuel a powerful and extraordinary archetype.

Stephen Lawhead, in his trilogy *The Pendragon Cycle* (1988–89) again harks back to Atlantis and develops the theme farther than ever before, establishing an Atlantean community, ruled over by King Avallach and his son Prince Taliesin, within the land of Celtic Britain. The second volume of the trilogy *Merlin* (1988) concentrates on the figure of Merlin himself, Avallach's grandson and thus the inheritor of the Atlantean bloodline. He recalls listening to 'sad stories of Lost Atlantis' as he walks with Avallach 'The Fisher King' in the gardens of Ynys Wittrin (Glastonbury).

The book follows the outlines of the *Vita Merlini* in its general shape and structure, though developing the character and story of Merlin far beyond the scope of the medieval tale. Here Merlin is both King of Dyfed and a reluctant seer, whose pain and passion in the wilderness is set forth in all its stark reality. The story is told in the first person, and at the very opening of the book Merlin recalls the various ways in which he has been recognized:

> Emrys is the name I have won among men and it is my own. Emrys, Immortal... Emrys, Divine. . . Emrys Wledig, king and prophet to his people. Ambrosius it is to the Latin speakers, and Embries to the people of Souther Britain and Lloegres. . . . But Myrddin Emrys am I to the Cymry of the hill-bound fastness of the west.
>
> (p. 15)

His long life, including years of wandering in the wilds of the hills, are chronicled, as are his love for Ganieda, his association with Ambrosius, Uther and finally Arthur himself. Lawhead's long and intricately woven chronicle places Merlin squarely centre stage, and links him both to the dim and distant realm of Atlantis and to the founding of the great Arthurian kingdom which is so much his own work. Of all the recent portrayals of Merlin it is perhaps the best and certainly the most moving.

THE PROPHET

Merlin's prophetic gifts are so much a part of his character that they almost seem to pass unnoticed at times, though it is by this means that he is enabled, primarily, to bring about the shaping of the destiny of others. Mary Stewart, in her trilogy of books about Merlin (*The Crystal Cave*, *The Hollow Hills* and *The Last Enchantment*) makes these powers central.

In the first volume, Merlin discovers his ability to 'see' future events; but his visions are the product of fits brought on by staring into a pattern of crystals, rather than by inner or magical contact, and throughout the remainder of the book and those which follow it, ingenious solutions are found for many of the more mysterious aspects of Merlin's life. Thus we read nothing of his magic, only of his technical skills, which enable him to position the 'Hele Stone' of Stonehenge at its present site, rather than (as in the medieval stories) raising the whole monument or causing it to fly through the air or float across the Irish Sea.

This portrait of Merlin succeeds in flattening out the character in an effort to explain it – psychological motivation accounting for most of his life – though he remains a prime mover in the setting up of a stable kingdom under the enlightened rule of Arthur.

The third volume of the trilogy recounts the relationship with Nimue – almost the only attempt to tell his story fully since Tennyson debased it to Victorian drawing-room melodrama in his *Merlin and Vivian* of 1890. In Mary Stewart's version, with Arthur established as king over all of Britain, Merlin retires to the wilderness. There, attacked by a subtle poison administered to him by Morgause, he is nursed back to health by a youth named Ninian, who of course turns out to be a girl, Niniane, or Nimue:

> The dim-seen figure in the mist, [seemed] so like the lost boy, that I had greeted her and put the words 'boy' and 'Ninian' into her head before she could even speak. Told her I was Merlin: offered her the gift of my power and magic, gifts that another girl – the witch Morgause – had tried in vain to prise from me, but which I had hastened eagerly to lay at this stranger's feet.
>
> (p. 365)

THE LOVER

Thereafter, the story follows the more familiar track. Nimue becomes Merlin's – pupil until in the end, his powers begin to fade and she takes over the role of guardian of Arthur's realm. Finally, Merlin himself withdraws, promising to return. His end is left uncertain.

The only other significant treatment of Merlin as a lover, is in a book by the American author, James Branch Cabell. Cabell is something of an oddity amongst those who have dealt with Arthurian themes in fiction in that he sets his book, *Something About Eve* (1935), within the framework of a huge invented universe of chivalry and the erotic, spanning vast areas of time and space. In a chapter entitled 'The Chivalry of Merlin', the old wizard is summoned, along with King Solomon and Odysseus, to give an account of himself before he passes 'into the realms of Antan' (Cabell's name for the Otherworld), to discover the true meaning of his life:

> 'I was Merlin Ambrosius. This wisdom that I had was more than human. . . but I served heaven with it. . . ' And then Merlin told about the child Nimue who was the daughter of the goddess Daina, and of how old, wearied, overlearned Merlin had come. . . [to love her]. Then Merlin told to Nimue, because she pouted so adoringly, the secret of building a tower which is not made of stone, or timber, or iron, and is so strong that it may never be felled while this world endures. And Nimue, the moment he had fallen asleep with his head in her lap, spoke very softly the old rune. . .
>
> (p. 190)

And Merlin confesses that he was happy for a long time while in his tower, until he saw his 'toys', the men and women of the Arthurian age, begin to break each other and to become filled with hate and lust and barbarity. But even then he lingers on, happy with his child love and the peace of his tower – only now does he seek enlightenment in the Otherworld, where perhaps he may find reasons for the failure of his dream ...

For, whatever Merlin's end, whatever his origins, he never ceases to be concerned with this world and the people who live in it. His function within what we may call the 'inner history' of Britain varies hardly at all from Geoffrey of Monmouth to Mary Stewart. As the prime mover in the setting up of Arthur's kingdom, and of the Round Table; and as prophet, guardian and sometime tutelary spirit of Britain, he remains true.

Thus, in Parke Godwin's *Firelord* (1980), when he assumes another guise, that of the Wonder-Child, it is to offer Arthur some cursory advice:

> The boy was seated on a flat rock... He looked maddingly familiar with his shock of blond, curly hair and blue eyes glistening with secret excitement: things to do and tomorrows that couldn't be caught up fast enough. He *shimmered* all over, he made me tingle with the energy that came from him...
>
> (pp. 5-6)

Here, Merlin is, in some sense, Arthur's own inner self, able to show him a vision of the future, of the great king and warrior whose presence draws the very utmost effort from the men who follow him – the man that Arthur is to become, driven by the Merlin within:

> Deep in me, Artos stirs.
> Stay away, I tell him. Go back to sleep.
> But Artos wakes... opens his eyes inside me. 'It's time' he says.
> Time for what?
> 'I know what Merlin wanted to teach me,' whispers Artos in my soul.
> 'To be a king over men. To know what they are and the price of knowledge.'
>
> (p. 84)

THE TEACHER

Merlin's function is indeed often to teach – though he may choose to do so in some curious ways. In T.H. White's *The Sword in the Stone* (1938) he teaches by example, turning Arthur into animal, fish or bird. So that, from his encounter with a great pike that lives beneath the walls of his foster-father's castle, he learns that power for its own sake leads nowhere; while from a position high above the earth, Arthur as a bird discovers that boundaries are an illusion fought over without reason. And of course, all that he learns stands him in good stead when he comes to draw the famous sword from the stone – the act that will make him King:

> All round the churchyard there were hundreds of old friends. They rose over the church wall all together, like Punch and Judy ghosts of remembered days, and there were otters and nightingales and vulgar crows and hares and serpents and falcons and fishes and goats and dogs and dainty unicorns and newts and solitary wasps and goat-moth caterpillars and cockindrills and volcanoes and mighty trees and patient stones. They loomed round the church walls, the lovers and helpers of the Wart [Arthur] and they all spoke solemnly in turn...
>
> (pp. 279–80)

Nor is it surprising that Merlin should choose this method of teaching. His earliest incarnation was as the Wild Herdsmen, the Lord of the Beasts, and even the trees and stones obey his call.

But it is as tutor and guide to the young king that we know him best, and as such he appears again and again in modern retellings. Catherine Christian in her excellent *The Sword and the Flame* (1982) has him arranging for Arthur to acquire his second, more famous sword, Excalibur. But in a variation from the more traditional episode, where he receives it from the Lady of the Lake, here Merlin assists in its forging by an ancient Smith God, from a lump of meteorite:

> It is now (says Merlin). Listen, Old One, the stream sings for it. The fire-spirits call for it. Fetch the King-sword here, to the anvil, and finish its forging, while the power of the Dragon and the power of the Merlin are together in this place to give you strength.
>
> (p. 52)

That the shaping of King or sword may extend beyond a single lifetime is shown in those versions of the story where Merlin or Arthur come again, after a long sleep, in Avalon or the Hawthorn Tower, to continue the work left unfinished at the end of the Arthurian Age. In the final part of C.S Lewis' science fiction trilogy (*That Hideous Strength* [1945]), Merlin is awakened by the striving of the forces of good and evil – here represented by Ransom, Lewis' space voyager, and a totalitarian group seeking control over the earth. Here, somewhat as in Powys's version, Merlin is seen as almost a god – a force as old as time itself; a massive, primitive power virtually without limit. When he and Ransom first meet there follows a marvellous riddling exchange in which each tests the knowledge of the other. When Ransom has successfully answered a whole string of questions, Merlin asks another which he deems even harder: where is Arthur's Ring?

> 'The Ring of the King,' said Ransom, 'is on Arthur's finger where he sits in the House of Kings in the cup-shaped land of Abhalljin, beyond the seas of Lur in Peralandra. [Lewis' name for Venus.] For Arthur did not die; but Our Lord took him to be in the body until the end of time. . . with Enoch and Elias and Moses and Melchisedec the King. Melchisedec is he in whose hall the steep-stoned ring sparkles on the finger of the Pendragon.'
>
> (p. 337)

Ransom is thereafter revealed as Arthur's successor, the new Pendragon, to whom Merlin once again pledges his service, and whom he aids in the final overthrow of the modern day forces of evil. References to Numinor (sic) and the 'Far West' in this book confirm the identification of Merlin with Gandalf in Tolkien's *Lord of the Rings*.

REINCARNATION

The theme of the recurring acts of Merlin and Arthur is taken up again by the science fiction writer Tim Powers in *The Drawing of the Dark* (1977). Here, Merlin is the guardian of the Wounded Grail King, who is kept alive, by a curious twist of the old story, not through the daily descent of a dove bearing a wafer in its beak, but by a yearly draught of a unique elixir – Hertzwestern Beer! Merlin, the owner of the inn where this mysterious drink is brewed, recalls the latest incarnation of Arthur in the shape of a seventeenth-century Irish mercenary named Brian Duffy, to help him protect the elixir against an ancient and implacable enemy. The substance of the book is concerned with

Duffy's adventures and with his unwillingness to allow memories of himself as Arthur to come to the surface. But throughout the old story the figure of the old magus moves subtly. He is old, here, an undying figure who seems eternally destined to pit himself against the enemies of light

In this guise also, he reappears in a children's book, *Merlin's Magic*, by Helen Clare (1953). Here Merlin calls upon figures as diverse as Walter Raleigh, Morgan-le-Fay, Francis Drake and the Greek god Mercury to aid him in frustrating an invasion of Robot-people who, because they lack the essential human function of the imagination, seek to steal it from mankind. Were they successful, Merlin implies, he himself, as well as Arthur and the other great figures, once mortal but now transformed into mythic archetypes, would all fade. The resulting loss to humanity would, of course, be almost without equal, and it is up to the great wizard to save the day again!

THE TRICKSTER

Despite Powys's version, which comes near to it, we lack a truly shamanistic novel of Merlin. However, Merlin the trickster is not unrepresented. Apart from Linda Halderman's book there are two others: Robert Nye's *Merlin* (1978), and to a lesser extent, Thomas Berger's *Arthur Rex* (1979), which both deal with this strange, untoward side of the magus' nature.

Berger is closest in many respects to Malory's version, though his book is a comic masterpiece shot through with gleams of the high fantasy of the original Arthuriad. In a scene near the beginning of the book, two knights seek out Merlin at an enchanted fountain in the forest:

> And both the knight and the horses, being sore thirsty, drank from the crystal water of the spring (into which one could see forever because there was no bottom) and by the time they had soaked their parched throats the men had been transformed into green frogs and the horses into spotted hounds.
>
> Now in despair and confusion the knights clambered with webbed feet from the steel armour which had fallen around them as they diminished in size, and the horses howled in dismay.
>
> 'None may drink of my water without my leave,' said a voice, and looking aloft the frogs saw it was the raven that spake.
>
> Then the glossy black bird flapped his wings twice and before their bulging eyes he was transformed into a man with a long white beard and wearing the raiment of a wizard, which is to say a long gown, a tall hat in the shape of a cone, both dark as the sky at midnight with here and there twinking stars and a horned moon. And the next instant Merlin (for it was he) caused both knights and horses to return to their proper forms and only then did he laugh most merrily.
>
> (p. 3)

Nye, on the other hand, aiming for a comedy of Eros, plumbs the depths of Merlin's character, as very few writers have managed to do. I make no secret of the fact that this is almost my favourite portrait of Merlin. It is funny, irreverent and profound, and underneath its scatalogical humour and endless word-play, there is a deeply researched picture which draws upon nearly all the many disguises of Merlin to reveal him, at last, as a strangely sorrowful creature, mourning for the even more sorrowful creatures over whom he has been given care.

From within the crystal cave of his retirement, Merlin views past, present and future with a jaundiced eye. He describes himself as:

Merlin Ambrosius. Merlin Sylvester.
Merlin the magician. Merlin the witch.
The wisest man at the court of King Arthur,
and the greatest fool. Well, shall we say the only *adult*
[...]
My mother was a virgin.
My father was the devil.

(p. 3)

For Nye, this is the crux of the matter – Merlin partakes of *both* natures – human and non-human, good and evil, god and devil. Within him are the legions of hell and the armies of heaven. He is the battleground and the object of conquest and defence: ourselves – humanity. It is part of the subtle alchemy of Nye's book that he is able to show up the black side of human nature – as well as its silly side: all libido and bluster – and yet give a sense of the triumph of man over his own shortcomings. Merlin is the *deus ex machina* who stands ready to intervene, who laughs and plays the fool but who, underneath, *cares* for his children.

It is virtually impossible to get a proper feeling of Nye's book from a quotation – you have to read it all. Here are just two short extracts from the beginning and end of *Book 3*:

The boyhood of Arthur. The madness of Merlin.
    Look.
    A golden-haired boy running through a deep golden pool of sunlight falling into the trees in the deepest deep of the wild green wood.
    Arthur running through the golden and the green.
    His golden hair. His green tunic.
    'Sometimes you seem mad, or a fool, or a boy like me.'
                              [...]
I teach him. Merlin teaches Arthur.
    To KNOW
    To DARE
    To WILL
    To KEEP SILENT.
    Arthur is not a good pupil...

(p. 150–2)

And at the end:

They bare away Arthur no man knows where.
(Unwise the thought: a grave for Arthur.)
The first queen has the face of the Virgin Vivien.
The second queen has the face of the Lady Igrayne.
The third queen has the face of the King's half-sister, Queen Morgan le Fay.
    Now without a sail, without oars, the draped barge passed out from the shore.
It is black upon the waters, and then gold.
Little pig, listen.
The wind in the reeds.
The laughter of Merlin!

(p. 211)

There are echoes here of Malory, Geoffrey of Monmouth, old Welsh poetry, and even of Tennyson.

DEFINITIVE PORTRAITS

No one book has yet appeared which attempts to deal with all the aspects of Merlin's character, and perhaps there could be no such book. Robert Nye comes closest in my opinion, and there is the recent collection of stories by Jane Yolen, published under the title *Merlin's Booke* (1986), which has great diversity, but lacks the coherence of a novel. Only one recent product of imaginative thinking seems to me to illustrate all the faces of Merlin, making it, for me, the definitive portrait to date.

I said imaginative portrait, because it is not a book. But I make no apology for including it here, because in every other way it fits the notion of a fictional retelling. I refer to the film *Excalibur* (1983), directed and co-written by John Boorman and Rospo Pallenburg. At one time the intention was to call this film *Merlin* and it is the figure of the mage that dominates the action. Here we encounter him in each of his major aspects. As controller of destinies, he engineers the birth of Arthur, the giving of the magical sword, the shaping of the Round Table, and the quest for the Grail. But he is not of human blood and follows the old ways, which, as he tells his pupil Morgana, 'are numberèd'; and, as he tells Arthur later, he is already fading: 'My time is almost over. The days of men are here to stay.' Like Gandalf, when his work is done, he must depart into the West to become 'a dream to some, a nightmare to others.' Throughout the shifting patterns of the film, Merlin emerges, from Nicol Williamson's portrayal, as tetchy, loving, ingenious, amused, surprised. Possessed of god-like powers, vision and cunning, he is all of the Merlins in one. Finally, he is as baffling as ever, escaping before us like smoke, blown across the blood-soaked field of Camlaan. Yet, it is in that dark ending that Merlin reveals himself most clearly. Let Parke Godwin's *Firelord* say it for me. In this scene Arthur is dying – or fading, however one wishes to see it. Merlin appears, as a boy again, juggling with brightly coloured balls:

> The coloured balls soared higher, four of them now, five, six. The shimmering boy balanced and timed their flight so skilfully that they moved in a smooth circle like the sun. 'Don't they shine, Arthur? Shaped from the finest tomorrows. Not an easy job, you know. Another dreamer to be born in the same old place: where's he's needed'.
>
> He was my genius, this juggler, always the more impressive part of me. Or was I merely a facet of him, designed to lead and care for men?
>
> (p. 364)

This is why Merlin will never be forgotten, why he keeps returning, under the guise of such diverse characters as Mr Spock in the television series *Star Trek*, or as Obi Wan Kenobi in the *Star Wars* saga. Even in novels like Lawrence Durrell's *The Revolt of Aphrodite* (1974) or Walker Percy's *Lancelot* (1979) we may detect the figure of the old mage, looming up against the backdrop of contemporary dreams or board-room politics.

Merlin cannot fade. He is too much a part of us all, too deeply rooted in our hearts and minds and souls. He is as much the Spirit of Britain as Arthur, and it would be hard to imagine one without the other.

In the collection of stories by Jane Yolen, Merlin's story is brought up to date in a most intriguing way. The story is set in the near future, when a group of reporters have been summoned to a news-conference at which it is revealed that Merlin's tomb has been discovered beneath Glastonbury Tor, and that along with the ancient wizard's mummified body is a strange box, which is to be opened by the Prince of Wales under the eyes of the world's press. Each of them sees something different, but one of Celtic origin, McNeil, see more than any – though what, he dare not say:

> Could he tell them that at the moment the box had opened, the ceiling and walls of the meeting room had dropped away? That they were all suddenly standing within a circle of corinthian pillars under a clear night sky. That as he watched, behind the pillars one by one the stars had begun to fall. Could he tell them? Or more to the point – would they believe?
> 'Light,' he said. 'I saw light. And darkness coming on.'. . . Merlin had been known as a prophet, a soothsayer, equal to or better than Nostradamus. But the words of seers have always admitted to a certain ambiguity. . .
> 'My darlings', he said, 'I have a sudden and overwhelming thirst. I want to make a toast to the earth under me and the sky above me. A toast to the arch-mage and what he has left us. A salute to Merlin: ave magister. Will you come?'

Among the new generation of writers who have added significantly to the Arthurian mythos is Charles de Lint, a Canadian who writes like an angel and whose perceptions of the darkly wooded world of the Celts runs as deep as any previous writer. In his novel *Moonheart* (1989) he introduced the figure of Taliesin into modern day Canada. In the sequel *Spiritwalk* (1992), a section appears called 'Merlin Dreams in the Mondream Wood'. This is almost a separate piece of writing from the rest, though it opens up themes which are further explored throughout the remainder of the book. In it one of the characters, Sara Kendell, comes to live in the Tamson House, a kind of gateway between the worlds where figures from the Otherworld enter and depart at will. Here, in the garden of the house, she encounters a mysterious being:

> In the heart of the garden stood a tree.
> In the heart of the tree lived an old man who wore the shape of a red-haired boy with crackernut eyes that seemed as bright as salmon tails glinting up the water.
> His was a riddling wisdom, older by far than the ancient oak that houses his body. The green sap was his blood and leaves grew in his hair. In the winter he slept. In the spring, the moon harped a windsong against his antler tines as the oak's boughs stretched its green buds to wake. In the summer, the air was thick with the droning of bees and the scent of wildflowers that grew in stormy profusion where the fat brown bole became root.
> And in the autumn, when the tree loosed its bounty to the ground below, there were hazlenuts lying in among the acorns.
> The secrets of a Green Man.

(p. 6)

This Merlin is old, older perhaps than any of the others we have considered. He is both Arthur's Merlin and Geoffrey's Merlin and something else as well – the Old Earth Man, the Green One, the Walker in the Woods who had been on this earth for as long as the earth itself has been. De Lint's contribution, though slight in volume, is as significant of the way we regard Merlin as any other writer in this age or the past.

Thus we may see that as we get further from the time of Merlin, we seem to curve back upon our road to a time even earlier, when Merlin is almost a god, and when the elements which were to go into the creation of the character, were first stirring in the hearts and minds of the primal storytellers.

MERLIN, KING BLADUD AND THE WHEEL OF LIFE

by R.J. Stewart

IN THIS FINAL section R.J. Stewart looks in detail at some of the many complex symbolic and cosmologic references within the Merlin myths, and specifically within the writings of Merlin's 'biographer' Geoffrey of Monmouth. In addition, he links the themes of Merlin's prophecies and his magical life in the wilderness to the story of Bladud, the mysterious founder of the city of Bath, in whose story he finds many points of similarity with the life of the mage. Taken in conjuction with the extracts from the *Vita Merlini* included in Part 2 of this collection, it makes a striking coda to the rich and varied material we have gathered in this place. Much more remains, of course, to be said and written about the ever-changing, yet strangely constant, figure of Merlin.

Bladud king of Britain had Logres and Albany. He made a university and a study at Stamford, and a flame and his Temple at Bath his city, which university dured to the coming of Saint Augustine, and the Bishop of Rome interdited it for heresies that fell among the Saxons and Britons together mixed.

> . . . In Caer Bladim he made a temple right
> And set a flamyne theirein to gouerne
> And afterwards a Fetherham he dight
> And sett To fly with wings, as he could best discerene,
> Aboue the ayre nothying hym to werne
> He flyed on high to the temple Apolyne
> And there brake his neck, for al his great doctrine!
>
> *Hardynge's Chronicle*, 1543

A certain monk of Malmesbury, Eilmer by name, had in his youth hazarded an attempt of singular temerity. He had contrived to fasten wings to his hands and feet, in order that, looking upon the fable as true, he might fly like Daedalus, and collecting the air on the summit of a tower, had flown for more than the distance of a furlong; but a gitated by the violence of the wind and the current of the air as well as by the consciousness of his rash attempt, he fell and broke his legs and was lame ever after. He used to relate as the cause of his failure his fogetting to provide himself with a tail.

William of Malmesbury, Gesta Pontificum, 1125

INTRODUCTION

I wish to state at the very beginning of this essay that it is not confined to 'solar mythology' or 'shamanism'. For nineteenth- and twentieth- century interpreters of myth and legend – either anthropological or psychological – solar or seasonal mythology became a great catch-all system, a type of non-explanatory reductionism which labelled material without giving relative understanding. In the latter part of the twentieth century shamanism is used in a similar manner, often being applied (like glue or wallpaper) to subjects and traditions that probably have no connection with shamanism whatsoever.

I shall be making a number of comparisons between Merlin, the less well known figure of King Bladud, and that ancient cyclical pattern and symbol best summarized by the term 'the Wheel of Life'. The comparisons will certainly include solar mythology and primal magical/religious practices similar to Siberian shamanism; but neither of these fascinating subjects are proposed as the origin or explanation for the material compared.

My main argument is that Geoffrey of Monmouth synethesised and developed certain harmonic themes from Celtic tradition, probably from druidic tradition, and certainly from oral tradition. There is nothing startlingly original in this suggestion, as scholars have been making similar proposals since the nineteenth century and a considerable array of research and publication concerning Celtic studies in general now exists. I am of the opinion, however, that certain aspects of the symbolism employed by Geoffrey in his works, particularly in the *Vita Merlini*, show a mystical and magical psychology which is by no means confined to medieval Christian orthodoxy. The general opinion on the matter is that Geoffrey employed his considerable imagination and skill to develop obscure traditional themes which he himself may not have understood.

We may set the question of Geoffrey's personal understanding on one side for the present, as it does not directly affect the matter in hand; his imagination is abundantly evident, but there are so many eminently practical developments of magical psychology in the *Vita* that it cannot be merely a sustained flight of whimsy based upon extensive reading and misunderstanding. I suspect, but cannot offer proof, that Geoffrey may have understood more than modern scholars give him credit for; this essay will show some of the myriad connectives within his work that are revealed by careful examination.

The magical psychology of the *Vita Merlini* has been examined in my book *The Mystic Life of Merlin*; there is no need to repeat this as evidence in our present context. I propose to concentrate in detail upon the curious relationship between Merlin and King Bladud, and their location upon the ubiquitous Wheel of Life, a pattern used throughout the *Vita* by Geoffrey of Monmouth. The reader does not need to be familiar with the total *Vita*, as any relevant sources and contexts will be given wherever necessary.

My inspiration for this comparison comes from the more recent work of another prolific Geoffrey (Ashe) who, during his talk at the 1986 Merlin Conference, published in *The Book of Merlin*, enabled me to bridge two areas of study which I had already published but had not attempted to fuse together. Back in 1980 I had examined King Bladud as part of my research for *Waters of The Gap*, a book on the Romano-Celtic mythology of Aquae Sulis, Bath. Subsequently I had published two books on Merlin, based upon the *Prophecies* and the *Vita* by Geoffrey of Monmouth. King Bladud appears in the *History of the Kings of Britain* in which the *Prophecies* are encapsulated, and in a short but important passage in the *Vita Merlini* itself. It was Geoffrey Ashe's view of Merlin as a possible title deriving from an ancient British god, similar to Apollo, that convinced me to merge the two areas of research. For Bladud, as I already knew, was also a title rather than a name, and was also associated with Apollo. Could there be some connection between Merlin and Bladud? Would Geoffrey of Monmouth or his bardic sources have been aware of this connection? Did the figure of Bladud reveal any further insights into Merlin? These were the questions that were uppermost in my mind at the time of writing.

The Wheel of Life

To reach any understanding of ancient lore, be it mythical, magical or seasonal, we must first realize that it has a strong tendency towards cyclical patterns. However, the cycles are not closed circles or 'complete systems'; such closures are the restrictive fantasies of materialism or narcissistic intellect. We must look, instead, for open-ended patterns or spirals based solely upon various levels of natural experience. 'Experience' ranges from simple seasonal observations to highly refined stellar maps and analogues; it also encompasses a perennial insight into imagination, human consciousness, and the cycles of polarity that exist both individually and communally in terms of human energy and interaction.

We should not necessarily expect to find ancient lore in forms easily accessible to the modern intellect, as much of it derives from cultures with a communication basis very different from that of our own; the difference is noticeable particularly in matters of the visual imagination and oral collective tradition. While collective, often extensive, memory formed the foundation of culture worldwide, it has a decreasing role in modern mechanized or electronic societies. In this sense our consciousness is rapidly devolving and losing both ability and content; such is the price that we pay collectively for advances in *exteriorizing* knowledge and information. The argument is complex and probably insoluble through debate or discussion – only change through time will define the gains or losses.

One of the reasons, often unstated, for the enormous early popularity of Arthurian material is that its sources (such as Geoffrey of Monmouth) formed a signficant bridge between oral collective imaginative tradition and the written form. If we are to recover the roots of lore relating to Merlin, we must cross such bridges, recover whatever lies on the other side, and reformulate it in modern terms. Perhaps Geoffrey in his own time and culture did exactly this.

When we examine old tales, myths, magical or psychological expositions and similar source material, we should consider them in the light of cyclical patterns inherent to pre-materialist worldviews. But we should not use such patterns as definitive or restrictive tools for rule-of-thumb interpretation or reduction. With this major consideration

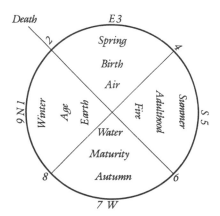

The Wheel of Life: The Elements, The Seasons and Nine Transformations

in mind, we can examine the Wheel of Life, which is a central symbol in the legend of Merlin, and is later to be found in literature, expanded from oral magical and mystical traditions. Expressions of the Wheel of Life range from cosmic and apocalyptic vision to the construction of the Arthurian Round Table.

One of the most profound expositions of the Wheel is Geoffrey of Monmouth's *Vita Merlini*, written in elegant Latin verse in about 1150. This text incorporates many Celtic traditional elements fused with classical mythology, cosmology, cosmography and natural history. The *Vita* also develops a refined system of elemental psychology, defining sterotypes and archetypes of human personality, and showing relationships and interactions between various types. But it is not limited to personality by any means, for the human subjects, described as various characters within a rambling bio-graphy of Merlin, are clearly linked to god and goddess forms which are sometimes named explicitly or at other times merely described in functional terms.

The human adventures and relationships which are placed upon the Wheel of Life are shown to be reflections of a macrocosmic pattern that runs holistically (or perhaps we might say holographically) through a series of worlds attuned to a primal fourfold cycle, described in this extract from the *Vita Merlini*:

> Meanwhile Taliesin had come to see Merlin the prophet who had sent for him to find out what wind or rainstorm was coming up, for both together were drawing near and the clouds were thickening. He drew the following illustrations under the guidance of Minerva his associate.
>
> 'Out of nothing the Creator of the world produced four elements that they might be the prior cause as well as the material for creating all things when they were joined together in harmony: the heaven which He adorned with stars and which stands on high and embraces everything like the shell surrounding a nut; then He made the air, fit for forming sounds, through the medium of which day and night present the stars; the sea which girds the land in four circles, and with its mighty refluence so strikes the air as to generate the winds which are said to be four in number. As a foundation He placed the earth, standing by its own strength and not lightly moved, which is divided into five parts, whereof the middle one is not habitable because of the heat and the two furthest are shunned because of their cold. To the last two He gave a moderate temperature and these are inhabited by men and birds and herds of wild beasts. He added clouds to the sky so that they might furnish sudden showers to make the fruits of the trees and of the ground grow with their gentle sprinkling. With the help of the sun these are filled like water skins from the rivers by a hidden law, and then, rising through the upper air, they pour out the water they have taken up, driven by the force of the winds. From them come rainstorms, snow, and round hail when the cold damp wind breathes out its blasts which, penetrating the clouds, drive out the streams just as they make them. Each of the winds takes to itself a nature of its own from its proximity to the zone where it is born. Beyond the firmament in which He fixed the shining stars He placed the ethereal heaven and gave it as a habitation to troops of angels whom the worthy contemplation and marvellous sweetness of God refresh throughout the ages. This also He adorned with stars and the shining sun, laying down the law, by which the star should run within fixed limits through the part of heaven entrusted to it. He afterwards placed beneath this the airy heavens, shining with the lunar body, which throughout their high places abound in troops of spirits who sympathize or rejoice with us as things go well or ill. They are accustomed to carry the prayers of men through the air and to beseech God to have mercy on them, and to bring back intimations of God's will, either in dreams or by voice or by other signs, through doing

which they become wise. The space below the moon abounds in daemons, who are skilled to cheat and deceive and tempt us; often they assume a body made of air and appear to us and many things often follow. They even hold intercourse with women and make them pregnant, generating in an unholy manner. So therefore He made the heavens to be inhabited by three orders of spirits that each one might look out for something and renew the world from the renewed seed of things.'

Vita Merlini, trans. J. J. Parry

From the Four Original Powers, which are expressions of the consciousness of divinity, the *Vita* eventually defines Four Seasons upon the planet Earth. This seasonal and Elemental system is the basis for Merlin's adventures. He experiences hardship at Winter alone and mad in the wildwood; he remembers love at Spring in his encounter with Guendoloena, a Celtic Flower Maiden similar perhaps to Blodeuwedd in the *Mabinogion*;[1] he undergoes a test of strength at Summer, where he contests wills with a powerful king (his brother-in-law Rhydderch) and is the subject of a ritual drama culminating in the Threefold Death, a sacrificial theme central to Celtic myth and religion.[2] In the Autumn he learns to balance his energies and begins to benefit from the fruits of his experience, guided by his sister Ganieda. In the development of the *Vita* Merlin travels around the Wheel more than once. . . and sometimes there are vast encyclopedic educational digressions.

The Wheel of Life, therefore, is connected to Merlin on a number of levels; defined in the *Vita* as follows: Stellar/Solar/Lunar/Natural or Earth. His adventures are attuned to the Seasons, but also incorporate the Elements within his own nature. His madness and fervour is due to an imbalance of Elements, an excess of certain energies, and is finally restored by a curative spring which gushes up from beneath the earth. Significantly, this miracle occurs just as Merlin has learned the pattern of the cosmos; he cannot be whole until he has some comprehension of a transcendent reality.

While he was speaking thus the servants hurried and announced to him that a new fountain had broken out at the foot of the mountains and was pouring out pure waters which were running through all the hollow valley and swirling through the fields as they slipped along. Both therefore quickly rose to see the new fountain, and having seen it Merlin sat down again on the grass and praised the spot and the flowing waters, and marvelled that they had come out of the ground in such a fashion. Soon afterwards, becoming thirsty, he leaned down to the stream and drank freely and bathed his temples in its waves, so that the water passed through the passages of his bowels and stomach, settling the vapors within him, and at once he regained his reason and knew himself, and all his madness departed and the sense which had long remained torpid in him revived, and he remained what he had once been – sane and intact with his reason restored. Therefore, praising God, he turned his face toward the stars and uttered devout words of praise. 'O King, through whom the order of the starry heavens exists, through whom the sea and the land with its pleasing grass give forth and nourish their offspring and with their profuse fertility give frequent aid to mankind, through whom sense has returned and the error of my mind has vanished! I was carried away from myself and like a spirit I knew the acts of past peoples and predicted the future. Then since I knew the secrets of things and the flight of birds and the wandering motions of the stars and the gliding of the fishes, all this vexed me and

1 *The Mabinogion* trans. Jeffrey Gantz, Penguin, 1976. Blodeuwedd is found in the story of 'Math Son of Mathonwy'.
2 *The Mystic Life of Merlin*, R. J. Stewart, Routledge and Kegan Paul, 1986.

denied a natural rest to my human mind by a severe law. Now I have come to myself and I seem to be moved with a vigor such as was wont to animate my limbs. Therefore, highest father, ought I to be obedient to thee, that I may show forth thy most worthy praise from a worthy heart, always joyfully making joyful offerings. For twice thy generous hand has benefitted me alone, in giving me the gift of this new foundation out of the green grass. For now I have the water which hitherto I lacked, and by drinking of it my brains have been made whole.'

Vita Merlini, trans. J. J. Parry

The Wheel expresses cosmology, solar mythology and the passage of the Seasons, while the mad Merlin expresses primal nature practices and magic relating to animals, prevision, inspiration, feats of strength and Otherworld encounters. These aspects of solar mythology and of practices similar to shamanism are but two connected parts of a much greater whole. The Wheel is clearly defined upon a number of levels, and Merlin undergoes a series of encounters and transformations which eventually lead him towards an advanced spiritual maturity in which nature-magic is consciously outgrown.

Table of Transformations Found in the *Vita Merlini*

1) Grief or guilt	North	Earth
2) Compassion	North-East	
3) Disorientation	East	Air
4) Sexual liberation	South-East	
5) Pre-vision	South	Fire
6) Cosmic vision	South-West	
7) Curative transformation	West	Water
8) Liberation from inner powers	North-West	
9) Spiritual contemplation	North	Spirit

Merlin undergoes nine transformations of his consciousness while spiralling around the Wheel of Life. In some cases there may be more than one full circle between each transformation; the positions upon the Quarters and cross-Quarters of the Wheel of Life are idealized locations relating to the Four Elements. In the extended drama of the *Vita* Merlin encounters transformative situations and personal relationships, in which the Elements or Quarters of the Wheel are channelled through certain individuals or adventures.[3]

MERLIN, MABON AND TIME

One of the themes stated by Geoffrey in the *Vita*, and found in his earlier Merlin book, the *Prophecies*, is that Merlin is a figure who encompasses time. In human terms this is resolved through the conclusion of the *Vita*, in which Merlin has travelled around all levels of the Wheel of Life (which is a spiral) until he has witnessed all things:

There stands in the wood an oak, rugged and full of years, so worn by the passage of devouring time that its sap fails and it rots through. I saw this tree when it began to

---

3 *Vita Merlini*, trans. B. Clarke, University of Wales, 1973. For a modern analysis of the magical psychology see note 2 above, and *Living Magical Arts*, R. J. Stewart, Blandford Press, 1987.

grow, and I saw the falling of the acorn from which it sprang, while a woodpecker perched and watched on the branch above. I have watched the acorn grow unaided observing every detail.

Vita Merlini

Merlin retires to spiritual contemplation in his black cloak, the ideal figure of the Hermit.

In the *History of the Kings of Britain*,[4] however, which includes the *Prophecies*, Merlin is a youth endowed with supernatural origins and startling prophetic powers which reach to the end of time in a dramatic apocalyptic outer vision. In short, his inner abilities fly far beyond his apparent outer age and form; the transcendent power is resolved in the *Vita* by making the Hermit typical of the first-and-last man who has experienced all things. Thus Geoffrey combines the youthful Merlin with the mad Merlin (a mature man) and the aged hermit Merlin. The Three Faces may appear separately or fused into one trans-temporal being. Although scholars frequently show this conflation to be literary, and speculate upon Geoffrey's own understanding of traditional Merlin legends, there is no problem in terms of mythical symbolism or magical and psychological insight. Geoffrey, regardless of any possible literary confusion over Welsh and Scottish legends, has the imagery right.

As has been suggested... in my own *Mystic Life of Merlin* there are connections between Merlin, Mabon the divine child of the ancient Celts, and the image of Apollo who was a god both of the Sun and the Underworld.[5] Geoffrey of Monmouth may well have been aware of these connections; he maintains the tradition of a prophetic youth, and employs certain images which are also found in the *Mabinogion* connected to Mabon.[6] The removal of the child from his mother, which is central to the Mabon myth, is repeated in the early life of Merlin in the *History*. During the mysterious hunt for Mabon, found in the long tale of *Culhwch and Olwen*,[7] a number of totem animals are encountered in a sequence using imagery reminiscent of the *Vita*, in which Merlin is associated with wolf, stag, goat and other creatures. In *Culhwch* these beasts clearly state the theme of great age, each creature representing an older race than the preceding one. Only the oldest of them all, the Salmon of Llyn Llyw, knows where the divine child is imprisoned.

In this sequence we may see echoes of the ageing of Merlin, and in both the *Vita* and in *Culhwch* the symbolism of an oak tree is employed.

The Stag said: When I first came hither there was a plain all around me without any trees but for one oak sapling which grew up to be an oak with a hundred branches. And that oak has since perished, so that nothing now remains of it but a withered stump...

Culhwch and Olwen

Merlin is closely related to the Stag in the *Vita*, as he leads a herd of stag and goats, acting as Lord of the Animals, an important figure in Celtic myth.

---

4 *Historia Regum Britanniae*, Geoffrey of Monmouth. Translators include: J. A. Giles, 1844; L. Thorpe, Penguin, 1966.

5 *Apollo* appears in classical mythology as the god of poetry, music, and prophecy; the patron of physicians, shepherds, and the founder of cities. All males suddenly taken from the world by death were said to be struck by the arrows of Apollo. His original home is sometimes said to be Hyperborea, or even the land of Britain, where he is celebrated by song, dance, and the music of the lyre. He is associated with the serpent python, which he slew while just a babe, and with the seat of prophecy at the oracular site of Delphi, in which a priestess presided over a mysterious underground source of inspiration. His symbols and animals are the bow, quiver, plectrum, serpent, shepherd's crook, swan, tripod, and laurel.

6 *Mabon and the Mysteries of Britain*, C. Matthews, Routledge and Kegan Paul, 1986.

7 See note 1 above.

So he spoke and went about all the woods and groves and collected a herd of stags in a single line, and the deer and she-goats likewise, and he himself mounted a stag. And when day dawned he came quickly, driving the line before him to the place where Guendoloena was to be married. When he arrived he forced the stags to stand patiently outside the gates while he cried aloud, 'Guendoloena! Guendoloena! Come! Your presents are looking for you!' Guendoloena therefore came quickly, smiling and marvelling that the man was riding on the stag and that it obeyed him, and that he could get together so large a number of animals and drive them before him just as a shepherd does the sheep that he is in the habit of driving to the pastures.

The bridegroom stood watching from a lofty window and marvelling at the rider on his seat, and he laughed. But when the prophet saw him and understood who he was, at once he wrenched the horns from the stag he was riding and shook them and threw them at the man and completely smashed his head in, and killed him and drove out his life into the air.

Vita Merlini

The *Mabinogion*, as we know them, were set out two hundred years after Geoffrey, but are certainly based upon oral traditions of much earlier date. It seems likely that both the *Vita* and the theme of Mabon in *Culhwch* are based upon an oral tradition. While we cannot restore this oral tradition fully, it appears to be based upon the following elements:

1) A divine child taken from his proper place
2) A sequence of animals and birds encompassing all time and knowledge
3) The recovery of the child and his restoration to his rightful place

These three elements are developed at great length in both the *Prophecies* and the *Vita*, with the additional change of the youthful Merlin into first a mature and then an aged person, representing spiritual development in human terms.

Geoffrey's Merlin, therefore, incorporates the essence of the lost Mabon cycle with added material showing how this cycle manifests itself in human experience. Once again, we find that the spiralling pattern of myth cannot be confined by simplistic explanations; it manifests itself through a series of conceptual and physical levels. A faint echo of Mabon or of Apollonian themes may be found in the *Vita*, where the mad Merlin is soothed by a Messenger playing upon the *crwth* or lyre. In the story this Messenger is crucial to Merlin's return from winter madness: music enables the Prophet to return to civilization.

The Messenger heard the prophet lamenting, and broke into his lament with cadence played upon the cither (*Crwth* or lyre) that he had brought to charm and soften madness. Making plaintive sounds with his fingers striking the strings in order, he lay hidden and sang in a low voice. . . [here the Messenger sings of Merlin's wife Guendoloena, comparing her to goddesses, stars, and flowers]
. . . The Messenger sang thus to his plaintive lyre, and with music soothed the ears of the prophet that he might become more gentle and rejoice with the singer. Quickly Merlin rose and addressed the young man pleasantly, begging him to touch the strings once more and sing his song again. . . thus little by little was Merlin compelled to put aside his madness captivated by the sweetness of the instrument.

Vita Merlini

A number of connections are recognized between Maponus (Mabon), Apollo, the lyre, and the island of Britain, from both legend and inscription.

Whatever source or sources Geoffrey drew upon, the connections between Merlin and Mabon were somehow defined, possibly taken from a long exposition of mystical, magical and psychological transformation in the form of a dramatic epic. This is certainly the overall design of the *Vita Merlini*, which has additional material from sources contemporary to Geoffrey, in which medieval knowledge of the natural world was listed, drawing upon many classical sources but elaborated by other influences.

It is possible, though unproven, that Geoffrey's audience was familiar with popular tales and songs echoed by themes in the more sophisticated *Vita*, *History* and *Prophecies*. By the twelfth century such material as remained from ancient religious or mythical traditions was in the possession of bards or itinerant entertainers; the enduring oral tradition was upheld in a diffuse form far removed from any concept of formal druidic learning or coherent Mystery instruction. In this last context Geoffrey is particularly important, for he combined diffuse elements from mystical/magical tradition into the exposition of the *Vita*, just as he had previously combined diffuse elements from history or pseudo-history within the *History of the Kings of Britain*.

KING BLADUD

Geoffrey employs another curious and overtly magical person in both the *History* and the *Vita*: King Bladud.

> After Hudibras came his son Baldudus (Bladud) who reigned for twenty years and built the city of Caerbadus now called Bath. In it he built warm baths for the curing of diseases. He made Minerva the deity of these baths and in her Temple placed inexhaustible fires; these never burned down or turned to ashes but when they began to fail became balls of stone. Bladud was a man of great ingenuity who taught necromancy throughout Britain, continually doing wonderful deeds. Finally he made himself wings to fly through the upper air, but he fell on the Temple of Apollo in New Troy, his body being broken into many pieces.
>
> *History of the Kings of Britain*, trans. Aaron Thompson

Geoffrey uses the name Bladud in more than one context in the *History*, and a significant reference linking the theme of Bladud/Apollo with that of Mabon/Apollo is found in the character Blegabred or Bladud Gabred (*History*, 3, 19): 'This prince, for songs and skill in all musical instruments excelled all musicians that had come before him, so he seemed worthy of the title of The God of The Minstrels'.

We can see from the above that a number of themes and symbolic elements are shared by both Merlin and Bladud. Before proceeding with comparisons, we should summarize the attributes of King Bladud:

1) He is a prince or king
2) He practices necromancy or magic
3) He is associated with healing springs
4) He is associated with the goddess Minerva
5) He flies through the air
6) He crash-lands upon the Temple of Apollo
7) He may be associated with music, bards, or minstrels ('joculatores')

We should add to this initial list the fact that Bladud has a specific location within the

Land of Britain; the hot springs of Aquae Sulis, Bath, in the south west of England.[8] This emphasis upon location is not mere coincidence, for both Merlin and Bladud have specific places in which they reflect the function of an ancient divinity; at the same time both have a non-localized identity or archetypal nature. We shall explore this subject further as we proceed.

Geoffrey, together with his chronicle source for Bladud, is further supported by a local folk tradition from the Bath area, and the hard evidence of the archaeological finds in the Romano-Celtic temple of Sulis Minerva. Before briefly considering the archaeological material, we should examine the folk tale. Here is the complete story of the pigs that lead Bladud: as told by Robert Pierce M.D., in 1713:

> Bladud, eldest son of *Lud-Hudibras*, (then King of *Britain* and eighth from *Brute*) having spent eleven years at *Athens* in the Study of the Liberal Arts and Sciences (that City being in those Days the chief Academy), not only of *Greece*, but of this part of the World also) came home a *leper*, whither from that hotter Climate he had conversed in, or from ill Diet, or Infection, it doth not appear, those unletter'd times giving down little or no Account of things (though of greater moment) then transacted; but a *leper* he was, and for that reason shut up, that he might not infect others. He, impatient of this Confinement, chose rather a mean Liberty than a Royal Restraint, and contrived his Escape in Disguise, and went very remote from his Father's Court, and into an untravell'd part of the Country, and offers his Service in any common Imployment; thinking it (probably) likelier to be undiscover'd under such mean Circumstances than greater. He was entertain'd in Service as Swainswicke (a small Village, two Miles from this City) his Business (amongst other things) was to take Care of the Pigs, which he was to drive from place to place, for their Advantage in Feeding upon Beachmasts, Acorns, and Haws &c. the Hills thereabouts then abounding with such Trees, tho' now few, of the two first, remain. Yet there is a Hill, close upon the *South* Part of this City, that still retains the name of *Beachen Cliff*, tho' there is scarcely a Beach-Tree left upon it.
>
> He thus driving his Swine from place to place, observ'd some of the Herd, in very cold Weather, to go down from the Side of the Hill into an *Alder-moore*, and thence return, cover'd with black Mud. Being a Thinking Person, he was very solicitous to find out the reason why the Pigs that wallow in the Mire in the Summer, to cool themselves, should do the same in Winter; he observ'd them farther, and following them down, he at length perceiv'd a Steam and Smoak to arise from the place where the Swine wallow'd. He makes a way to it, and found it to be warm; and this satisfied him that for the Benefit of this Heat the Pigs resorted thither.
>
> He being a *Virtuoso*, made farther Observation; that whereas those filthy Creatures, by their foul Feeding, and nasty Lying, are subject to Scabs, and foul Scurfs, and Eruptions on their Skin, some of his Herd that were so, after a while, became whole and smooth, by their often wallowing in this Mud.
>
> Upon this he considers with himself why he should not receive the same Benefit by the same Means; he trys it, and succeeded in it; and when he found himself cured of his *Leprosie*, declares who he was; his Master was not apt to believe him, at first, but at length did, and went with him to Court, where he (after a while) was owned to be the King's Son, and after his Father's Death succeeded him in the Government, and built this City, and made these *Baths*.

Several elements in this tale are connected with both Merlin and Mabon:

---

8 *The Waters of the Gap*, B. Stewart, Bath City Publications, 1981.
The British King Who Tried to Fly, H. C. Levis, 1919. Reprinted 1973, Bath.

1) Bladud is a royal person exiled or displaced from his rightful land
2) Totem animals lead him to the therapeutic springs
3) He is cured by magical water
4) He claims his true inheritance.

Bladud's totem animal is the pig, which features strongly in the Mabinogi of *Culwch and Olwen* as a powerful Underworld beast; in a Welsh poem of early date, we find Merlin addressing a pig as his totem companion, though in the *Vita* he is also associated with both the wolf and the stag.[9]

Before comparing Bladud and Merlin further, and defining the areas of symbolism that they share, one interesting detail should be considered: Bladud is not a name but a title. The name 'Vlatos' appears on Belgic coins struck shortly after Caesar's conquest of Gaul. The image upon the coin is a male Celtic head, with tiny wings sprouting from a neck torque, the symbol of royalty. It is a Gaulish king or tribal leader, bearing symbolic wings and royal insignia, who is likely to have been a leader of mercenary troops under Roman rule. The world 'Vlatos' is quite a close rendering of the Celtic pronunciation of 'Bladud' which is likely to have been literally *Vlathus* or *Vlathuth*.

The period between our medieval chronicle of the flying Celtic king and the Belgic coin bearing the words 'Vlatos Atefla' and a winged male head is considerable; but we have another winged torque bearing a head of a major significance which partly bridges the gap. In the late eighteenth century a remarkable male Celtic head was excavated from the silt that covered the ruins of the temple of Sulis Minerva. Popularly and inaccurately known as the 'Gorgon's Head' this image is the apotropaic guardian of the Romano-Celtic Temple. He has long flowing hair and moustaches, a fierce challenging look, and is given a position of prominence upon a pediment showing a star above and the sea and various underworld creatures below him. Significantly, he sprouts a pair of wings from either side of his head, and carries serpents twisted into a design reminiscent (though this is not possible to prove) of a neck torque.

This wholly Celtic figure, placed upon the 1st century pediment of a Romano-Celtic temple, seems to fly through the air and see all. He soars above the underworld (shown by an owl and another uncertain creature); furthermore he is supported by two classical Victories, and surrounded by an oak wreath...this indicates that he is associated with the theme of the Victorious Sun, a cult that would have been familiar to both Roman and Celt in different forms. Could this figure be the image preserved in the chronicle descriptions of King Bladud?

Also associated with the temple of Aquae Sulis is a carving of Apollo playing a harp (now built into the church tower at Compton Dando, Somerset). Geoffrey equates Bladud and Apollo. while a number of classical references associate Apollo with British folk religion...

BLADUD AND GUARDIANSHIP

It is interesting that Bladud, a figure of distinctly druidic and solar attributes, was the father of King Leir, whose name is connected with that of Llyr, an ancient sea-god. Leir was buried, according to Geoffrey, in an underground chamber beneath the River Soar, dedicated to the God Janus. Janus is the guardian of doors and gateways in classical mythology, and has two, or sometimes four, faces; he appears in the apocalyptic vision of the *Prophecies*, where he guards the gateways of creation under the control of the

---

9 *The Apple Tree*...

goddess Ariadne (The Weaver). It seems that a theme of guardianship is connected to Bladud's kingship, just as it is connected to Merlin's function as prophet.[10]

In the *Vita Merlini* Bladud appears as guardian of springs and wells, with his consort Queen Aileron (whose name may be derived from the French word for *wings*). The theme of springs and wells leads onto islands, and finally to the Fortunate Isle where the wounded Arthur is taken by Merlin and Taliesin.

> Of all islands Britain is said to be the best, producing in its fruitfulness every single thing... it has foundations of health giving hot waters which nourish the sick and give pleasing baths, which quickly cure people. These baths were established by Bladud when he held the sceptre of the kingdom, and he gave them the name of his consort queen Aileron... [*here a long list of islands follows*] The island of apples, which men call The Fortunate Isle, gets its name from the fact that it produces all crops of itself; the fields have no needs of the plough or of farmers and all cultivation is lacking except what nature herself provides... thither after the battle of Camlan we [*Merlin and the bard Taliesin*] took the wounded Arthur, guided by Barinthus who knew well the ways of sea and stars...

In the cosmology and cosmography of the *Vita Merlini*, the island of Britain occupies a sacred or symbolically central location, within which we find King Bladud acting as guardian of the therapeutic springs; we are then told of a series of increasingly fabulous islands culminating in the Fortunate Isles, ruled over by the priestess or enchantress Morgen and her nine shape-changing flying sisters. Bladud once again, as in the *History*, has the role of linking human and non-human realms, or nature and the Otherworld. In Celtic myth, the gates to the Otherworld or underworld were found in wells, springs, or holes in the ground.[11] The curious figure of Barintus, pronounced Barinthus, a guide or supernatural ferryman, carries Merlin and Taliesin with the wounded Arthur, to the Fortunate Isles.

The remainder of this legend is not directly relevant to our present analysis of Merlin and Bladud, but the figure of Barintus bears some relationship to the lineage of Bladud and other divine king-guardians of the land of Britain...a genealogical table reveals some interesting connections.

THE LINEAGE OF KING BLADUD AND
THE GUARDIANS OF BRITAIN

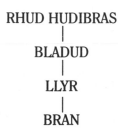

RHUD HUDIBRAS
|
BLADUD
|
LLYR
|
BRAN

---

10 *Janus* appears in Roman mythology as the deity who presides over all beginnings and endings, hence our derivation of the month January. The first hour of each day was dedicated to Janus, whose title is Father; his festival was the Roman New Year's Day, and he was traditionally said to have been in Italy before the appearance of any other gods. Images of Janus show a figure bearing a sceptre and a key seated upon a glittering throne. He has two faces, youthful and aged, light and dark, looking ahead and behind. Some images of Janus have four faces, one for each Quarter of the World; he is also known as the god of the cross-roads. All doors or passages are under the guardianship of Janus, and his primal nature is further supported by the tradition that he was co-ruler with Saturn of the lost Golden Age.

11 *The Under World Initiation*, R. J. Stewart, Aquarian Press, 1985.

Rhuth or Rhud Hudibras, father of King Bladud

His name contains the element *Rud* or *Ruth*, implying the Welsh word *rhod* or Wheel. The wheel is connected to flight through the Irish druid Mog Ruith (meaning 'Son of the Wheel') who flew through the air wearing a feathered cloak. The sun was known as the *Roth Fail* or wheel of light. The term is found again in the Mabinogi which features Arianrhod (silver wheel), a thinly disguised Celtic goddess whom later interpreters have equated with the wheeling stars or with specific constellations.[12] She may also be related to the Ariadne, or weaver-goddess, whom Geoffrey describes during the apocalyptic vision of the *Prophecies of Merlin*; a goddess who dissolves the cosmos, and is further related to a Gate-keeping or guardian figure who stands before her portals; this guardian is called Janus in the *Prophecies*.

Arianrhod, silver wheel, is the mother of Lleu in the Mabinogion; Lleu means *bright* or *shining*. Like Merlin in the *Vita* he marries a Flower Maiden, and is associated with the sacrificial Threefold Death. Either Geoffrey and his bardic sources have borrowed freely from the source-tale known to us in the Mabinogi of *Math son of Mathonwy* to colour the tale of Merlin, or, as seems more likely, Merlin and Lleu share certain attributes relating to a Celtic solar deity and the ritual sacrifice whereby the land is renewed.[13]

Rhud Hudibras is linked to a prophetic Eagle, which uttered verses while he was building the walls of Shaftesbury.

Bladud, son of Rhud Hudibras

Bladud is also associated with the wheel of the sun, in the legend of his illness, regeneration, and flight. His name may mean *bright-dark*, and he acts as the patron of the healing thermal springs under the goddess Minerva. He is also associated with necromancy and the employment of a magical or inexhaustible fire in honour of the goddess. Bladud has the pig as his totem animal.

Llyr, the son of Bladud

Llyr is related to the ancient sea god, Llyr, or *Manannan ma Lir* in the Irish sagas. He is connected with the horse as a totem animal, in the form of sea horses or waves. The name 'Lir' literally means 'sea'. In the *History*, we find that Geoffrey has attached a legend in which a Temple of Janus is dedicated to Llyr or Lear, situated under the river Soar. This theme of guardianship and an underwater or underworld location is central to the Celtic pagan religion.[14]

Bran (and Branwen), the children of Llyr

Bran is a gigantic figure who is able to wade the Irish Sea. Called Bran the Blessed, he carries the minstrels and musicians upon his back, and acts as a bridge for his army to march across. (*Branwen daughter of Llyr*, Mabinogion.) In the latter part of this legend, Bran has his head cut off, and set as a national guardian in the White Hill, now the location of the Tower of London. He fulfilled the role of guardian against invasion until, according to the Welsh Triads,[15] Arthur dug up the head out of misplaced duty or pride.

---

12 *The White Goddess*, R. Graves, Faber and Faber, 1961.
The Prophetic Vision of Merlin, R. J. Stewart, Routledge and Kegan Paul, 1986.
13 See notes 1 and 2 above.
14 *Historia*, ii, 14: 'She buried her father (Leir) in a certain underground chamber which she had dug beneath the river Soar, downstream from the town of Leicester. This chamber was dedicated to the god of two faces, Janus. When the feast day of the god came around, all the craftsmen in the town used to perform there the first act of labour in whatever enterprise they were planning to undertake during the coming year.'
15 *The Welsh Triads*, R. Bromwich, University of Wales, 1961.

Thus in Bran we have the lineage of Bladud, the sea, musicians, guardianship, and the sacred or magical head. The totem animal of Bran is the raven ('Bran' means 'raven').

ARTHUR AND BARINTHUS

The legend of King Arthur being cured in the Fortunate Isle by the priestess and shape-changer Morgen is perhaps the most revealing element in this web of connections; for the wounded king is carried to the magical realm of regeneration by a seer (Merlin), a bard (Taliesin), and a mysterious ferryman... Barintus. It seems likely that Barintus is a loosely disguised member of the lineage of divine kings or guardians listed above and is, in fact, a sea deity similar to Llyr. Thus the healing of Arthur, another guardian king, is linked to a visionary cosmography in which King Bladud presides over healing springs, while Morgen presides over the Otherworld. Both are flying druidic characters, connected to Celtic deities. Furthermore Barintus exhibits all the evidence of being of the same lineage as Bladud. It seems that Geoffrey or his bardic source is tapping into an ancient tradition dealing with the magical guardians or sacred kingship of the land of Britain, and its close relationship to a divinity of both sea and sun.

BLADUD AND MERLIN

By the twelfth century, we find Geoffrey of Monmouth combining native Welsh or Breton names and terms with Norman French and Latin; his books abound with curious names, puns, and allusions. The Celtic language sources for Geoffrey's characters have been commented upon by various scholars, but there is still a great area of research untouched.

In our present context, however, it is the use of the name Bladud (in varying forms) that is important. When we analyse the name, the legend, and the archaeological evidence, several remarkable connections are obvious. We have already considered Bladud's legend, his connection to the Romano-Celtic temple of Sulis Minerva, and his further appearance as guardian or patron of the therapeutic springs in the *Vita Merlini*. We have also touched upon the curious connection between Bladud, Llyr, Bran and the role of divine king or guardian, equated in Geoffrey's Latinized text with the ancient deity Janus, guardian of all doors, turnings, crossroads, and gateways.

If we regard Bladud as a Celtic (Welsh or Breton) name, it suggests a further connection between the various elements described above. Bladud may be derived from two root words; *bel bal* or *bla* meaning Bright, and *dud* or *dydd*, meaning dark. If Bladud or Beldud or Baldudus is one of the many names in Geoffrey's work with either intentional or traditional Celtic language origins, it seems to mean *Bright-Dark* which fits in with the career of the legendary king who flies through the air like the sun, crash lands upon the temple of Apollo, god of the sun and Under World, and is dashed to pieces.

If he is partly related to the sun and the seasons, though this is by no means his sole mythical or magical explanation, the name *Bladud* reinforces the cyclical pattern; displacement, exile, disease; curative powers from beneath the earth; setting up a temple and an eternal flame; practising necromancy and flying through the air; being dashed to pieces on the Temple of Apollo. The cyclical events turn from dark to light and back to darkness; but, even so, this seasonal magical/psychological pattern is not the entire picture.

We noted above the connection between the lineage of Bladud, the role of Guardianship, and the God Janus who appears in both the *History* and the *Prophecies* firstly in connection with King Llyr and an underground temple, and secondly with the apocalyptic vision and a mysterious goddess called Ariadne who unravels the solar system. If we accept that the Welsh or Breton suggestion of Bladud's name as a god-term or functional description is correct, he is a type of Janus figure.

In this curious role, Bladud functions on three spiralling levels of the Wheel of Life:

1) *Personal*. His career as exiled prince, cured and restored, ruling king, and final reaching beyond the earth into flight.

2) *Seasonal*. A cycle from Winter to Spring (exile and illness to cure) on to Summer (kingship, eternal flame) and Autumn (teaching the fruits of his wisdom throughout the land) and finally a new cycle in which he flies, like the sun, to land upon the Temple of Apollo.

3) *Universal* or cosmic. A primal role of combining light and dark, acting as guardian of gates and doorways ranging from therapeutic springs to the cosmic function of creation and dissolution.

CONNECTIONS AND COMPARISONS

The connections between Merlin and Bladud are sufficient for us to compare the two figures directly:

Both partake of the 'lost child' motif: Bladud in his exile and Merlin (of magical origin) taken from his mother by King Vortigern.
Both partake of a seasonal cyclical life adventure.
Both are involved in a ritualized or mythic death motif.
Both are connected to arts of prophecy, magic, and druidic practices.
Both are linked with totem animals: the pig (shared by both figures) and the deer.
Both have links with the fragmentary Mabon cycle found in Welsh legend
Both are concerned with springs and therapy in individual ways.
Both are kings or princes.
Both are connected with the passing of King Arthur into the Fortunate Isle.

There are, however, a number of features unique to each character, and these are not interchangeable or derived from each other:

Merlin: Is connected to specific prophecies and utterances.
Has a developed human career in the *Vita* and *History*.
Does not fly through the air.
Is not associated with a specific temple site, though there are indications that he has ancient connections with both Maridunum and Stonehenge. It may be significant that Stonehenge is often suggested as the temple of Hyperborean Apollo found in classical references.

Bladud: Is in many respects a more ancient or primal figure, and is nearer to a god-form than Merlin.
Is said to have contracted leprosy, an incurable disease of a wasting nature, but is not associated with madness, grief or suffering.
Is associated directly with the goddess Minerva (or Sulis/Minerva in archaeological evidence of Aquae Sulis).
Is cured by following a totem animal to hot springs.
Teaches magic and necromancy throughout the land (which Merlin, contrary to modern opinion, does not do in the early sources – he is limited to prophetic

utterances, and in the Vita to profound magical and spiritual transformations within himself).

Is not associated with stellar lore, as Merlin certainly is.[16]

It seems from all of the above that Bladud is an expression of a very primal and enduring god-form, connected to the sun and the seasons, but with a deeper role as the god who fuses Light and Dark, the god of the Gates or Crossroads. Merlin, however, is a prophet inspired by the powers which Bladud represents; and both are connected to a goddess similar to Brigidda and Minerva, sharing many of the attributes of druidism.

While both characters have localized expressions, Merlin at Maridunum/Carmarthen, and Bladud at Bath/Aquae Sulis, they are not limited to these sites. Merlin appears in connection with various locations in Scotland, and may share with Bladud the classical connection of Stonehenge (built by Merlin) and Apollo (whose temple was the site of Bladud's fall from the sky).

Bladud is further connected with legends of flight which are found throughout the western world, the most famous of which is the classical Greek myth of Icarus, who flew too close to the sun and thus had his wings destroyed. A similar tale is related of the Gnostic Simon Magus who attempted to fly by magic, and of the Irish druid MacRhoth whose name simply means 'Son of the Wheel'. The legend is certainly not limited to Bladud alone, but he is a major expression of it according to the evidence of the substantial temple of Sulis Minerva, which is associated with him in British tradition.

We must remember that when Geoffrey wrote about Bladud, drawing upon earlier traditions and perhaps the third century writings of Solinus, the temple of Sulis Minerva was lost under the accumulated soil and mud of several centuries. It was not re-discovered until the eighteenth and nineteenth centuries, vindicating the traditions attached to King Bladud and his worship of Minerva, set out by Geoffrey and confirming local folklore.

There may be a further connection between Bladud and the River Avon, which loops around Aquae Sulis, suggesting that his mythical role as a flying deity is perhaps more complex than its localized manifestion at Bath. The site of Malmesbury Abbey, also upon the Rover Avon, was first established in about 635 by a Celtic Irish monk, Maidulph. According to a chronicle written by a Malmesbury monk (*Eulogy of History*, Rolls Series No 9, Vol 1, p. 224) the site was called Caer Bladon at this period. A charter of 675 also states that the site was 'near the river Bladon'.

Bladon, or Bladim, is also the ancient name for Bath, and Caer Bladon or Caer Bladim are names commonly associated with Aquae Sulis and King Bladud in the medieval chronicles. The connection is strengthened by a witty tale recounted by William of Malmesbury in which a monk, one Guilmerius, tried to fly from Malmesbury Abbey tower with artificial wings and crash landed. Is the monastic chronicler here mocking a folk-tale or local legend, similar to that found in the other Caer Bladim further down the River Avon?

CELTIC PRIMAL TRADITIONS

In order to demonstrate the connections between Merlin, Mabon, and Bladud, we should summarize the foundations of British Celtic primal religion, magic, and tradition.[17] These foundational subjects at the roots of Celtic religion are revealed by legend,

---

16 See notes 2 and 12 [Stewart] for Merlin and stellar lore.
17 *Pagan Celtic Britain*, A. Ross, Cardinal, 1974.

early literature, folklore, classical sources, and archaeology. Although authorities are often uncertain as to the connections between the various subjects or elements of primal tradition in Britain (and in other Celtic regions of Europe) there is little doubt about the basic units or themes described in our list. Nor is there uncertainty over the essential fusion of these themes; they are undoubtedly connected in a harmonic or cyclical pattern which persisted from the earliest, even prehistoric, times, reaching well into the nineteenth and twentieth centuries in attenuated forms as folklore. The figures of Merlin and Bladud give us some positive clues to the connections between these foundational elements.

RELIGIOUS ELEMENTS
Prophecy
Prophecy includes prevision, second sight, and possession of divine inspiration.

Ancestor Worship
This includes concepts of genealogical magical inheritance, similar, but not identical, to modern definitions of genetics. Thus the essence or spirit of a king, hero, or other person may appear through successive individuals who are descendants. Ancestor worship includes practices which were termed 'necromancy' in the medieval chronicles: a primal religion in which the spirits of the ancestors played a central role in human daily life. This theme is found throughout the ancient world, and is also the foundation of the Greek/Roman religion. All life springs from a mysterious Under World where energies are regenerated and ancestral spirits reside.

The Sacred Head
The head was held in special reverence by the Celts. It was used as an object of worship in primitive times, and later appeared in cult practices associated with stone heads, masks, sacred skulls and similar objects. Magical skulls were preserved for centuries in Gaelic speaking regions, and were still employed for therapeutic purposes as late as the nineteenth and early twentieth centuries.[18] The magical head also appears in a number of folktales, and in the important Mabinogi of *Branwen daughter of Llyr*, in which the head of Bran 'king' or 'leader' acts as a guardian power defending his company against all grief and suffering, and subsequently as a guardian against the invasion of Britain.

Seasons, Stars and Cycles
The relationship between the seasons and the stellar patterns was central to early cultures. In Celtic legend we have many references to Seasonal patterns, supported by archaeological evidence from the Romano-Celtic period or earlier. It is clear from early sources, ranging from Julius Caesar[19] through to medieval chronicles and tales, that one of the major arts of the druids involved cosmic science; we are not certain of the form that this took, though it seems likely to have been a fusion of stellar, seasonal, and elemental, and was ultimately a reincarnational theory. We also have archaeological evidence such as the Coligny calendar, and the much debated alignments of stone monuments from prehistoric times and cultures preceding the Celts.[20]

---

18 *The Folklore of the Scottish Highlands*, A. Ross, Batsford Press, 1976.
19 *The Conquest of Gaul*, Julius Caesar, trans. S. A. Handford, Penguin, 1951.
20 *The Stars and the Stones* M. Brennan, Thames and Hudson, 1983.
The Stone Circles of the British Isles, A. Burl, Yale University, 1976.
Megalithic Sites in Britain, A. Thom, Oxford, 1967.

Underworld and Otherworld

A firm concept of another world or series of worlds (connected to Ancestor worship) is found in all Celtic lore. This realm may be under the earth, or across the sea. The Under World is the realm of the powers of life and death in unity, and holds certain magical objects of regenerative power, such as a Cauldron of Immortality. Entrance to the Under World or Otherworld is usually through water, lakes, springs, or wells. These subterranean gates were held in such reverence that, prior to the Roman invasions, vast hoards of offerings were laid up by the Celts in lakes or springs. There is also some evidence that wells or deep shafts were dug solely for religious purposes.

Goddess and Heroes

Primal Celtic religion orbited around a goddess figure. It would be too simplistic to say that the culture or faith of the early Celts was entirely matriarchal, but there is no doubt that the most potent and often terrifying divine images were female. Detailed analysis of goddess forms in early literature and from archaeological evidence suggest a triple aspected goddess, though in many cases she appears only in a single role, or sometimes in a multiple role involving six or nine personae. We may summarize this triplicity as:

1) Maiden, sister, virgin; inspired of human cultural development
2) Lover, partner, fertile power; inspirer of sexuality and procreation
3) Destroyer; mother of life and death, patroness of prophecy

The first aspect of the goddess is typified by Briggidda, a major Celtic goddess later modified into the Celtic Saint Brigit or Bride. She is equated frequently with Athena and Minerva, sharing many attributes and functions. This goddess plays an important role in the story of Merlin, Bladud and, of course, of classical heroes and sacred kings.

The second aspect of the goddess is typified by Venus, in Celtic legend Blodeuwedd, or Merlin's wife Guendoloena, both sensuous flower maidens. In early Irish tradition the shape-changing role of the goddess is well defined, but by the time of the medieval tales and chronicles drawn from tradition, the aspects tend to separate.

In the *Vita Merlini* the Flower Maiden, despite her alluring and otherworldly beauty, is rejected by Merlin as he grows beyond sexual attraction towards spiritual maturity. This is rather different from a superficial rejection of sexuality, and really shows the soul or spirit moving from one aspect of the Goddess towards another. Significantly it is Merlin's sister Ganieda who plays the role of Minerva, or educator and enabling feminine power, in the *Vita Merlini*.

The third aspect is typified by the Morrigan, a goddess of life and death, and by the mysterious Faery Queen who inspired prophecy and prevision in later Celtic traditions. In the *Vita Merlini* a strange shape-changing figure called *Morgen* rules a magical island where King Arthur is carried to be cured of his wounds.

This goddess of life, death, regeneration, is also found as the Apple Woman in the *Vita*, a vengeful character who distributes poisoned fruit beneath a greenwood tree. The fruit, like that of the Fairy Queen and her magical Tree in the ballad of *Thomas Rhymer*,[21] brings madness to mere mortals. The fearful triplicity is also found in the *Prophecies* where a goddess transforms the Three Springs of Life, Desire and Death which rise up from the centre of the land.

---

21 See note 11 above for analysis of *Thomas Rhymer*.

Totem Animals or Beasts

A complex enduring relationship between animals, humans and the environment is found in Celtic symbolism. This extends from overt symbols such as zoomorphic decorations through to profound magical interactions. In such interactions, beasts stand for spiritual qualities or for specific energies. Typical examples are the relationship of the crow with the goddess of death and life (the Morrigan), or of the Under World pig found in the Mabinogion, or in connection with King Bladud as we saw above.

It seems likely from the use of animals in tradition, such as the sequence of animals and birds in *Culhwch and Olwen* which leads progressively to the discovery of the lost child Mabon, that a very active system of animal symbolism relating to the human psyche and to magical arts was fundamental to Celtic culture. Merlin is found addressing a pig in an early Welsh poem, while in the *Vita Merlini* he has a wolf as a companion in the wildwood, and later becomes the leader of a herd of deer and she goats, while riding upon a stag. Certain powers of nature were, and still are, vested in specific animals, typified through their innate characteristics. Gods, goddesses, heroes and clans all had totem (typical and traditionally maintained) animals or birds. This system is still preserved today in an attenuated form in modern heraldry, and some of the primal aspects of totemism have undergone a popularized and frequently confused revival in modern pseudo-paganism.

Springs, Wells and Therapy

These are closely related to the Under World or Otherworld concepts outlined above. Therapeutic wells and springs are well known in the modern twentieth-century Celtic cultures, where they are often associated with Catholic saints or the Virgin, as orthodox religion replaces the earlier pagan images. It is significant in this context that both Merlin and Bladud have intimate connections with water sources. Merlin gains his prophetic vision by discovering a hidden spring holding two dragons (in Geoffrey's *History*). The sequence shows a clear insight into the relationship between natural sources (springs, wells, underground caverns) and human prophetic powers. Geoffrey is drawing upon an earlier Celtic tradition, which he repeats in the *Prophecies* with a vision of the Goddess of the Land and Three Fountains.

In the *Vita Merlini* a discourse on the pattern of the cosmos leads on to a description of the microcosm of Earth and the four winds and seas. This in turn leads to the subject of the island of Britain, and on to certain mysterious lands which include the Fortunate Island, clearly an Otherworld location. One of the purposes of this vast discourse is to reveal that there are many healing springs, lakes and pools in the world. Thus the scene is set for Merlin's final cure from madness, by the providence of a spring which suddenly appears from deep beneath the ground.

King Bladud, as we have seen, is cured of leprosy by bathing in the thermal springs found flowing at Bath, and becomes a patron of the springs, of therapy, and a worshipper of the goddess Minerva. The little-known Celtic goddess Sul or Sulis is conflated with Minerva in the Romano-Celtic temple on the site. Her name means eye, gap, or orifice, and she is literally the power of the gap through which the waters flow. We find this portal symbolism of a goddess in the apocalyptic vision of the *Prophecies*.

To summarize, we may suggest that springs and water sources are the gates to the Under World; that they are associated with a goddess, and are further associated with a *guardian*, who is usually male. This imagery may extend to a univeral vision, as in the Prophecies, or may be entirely localized, as at Aquae Sulis.

Mysterious or Virgin Birth

Certain heroes and gods have a mysterious birth; in our present context we may cite Merlin, born of a virgin and spirit or daemon, Mabon born but stolen away, and Apollo, the classical Greek equivalent.

Mysterious Death or Sacrifice

The theme of sacrificial death permeates ancient cultures, and has been dealt with at great length by many scholars. The relationship between death, life, the Underworld and rebirth played a significant role in Celtic culture, and is found in many legends which relate to our present theme. In the Mabinogion, *Lleu* undergoes a curious ritualized death which is known generally as the Threefold or Triple Death. The same ritualized death sequence is connected to the Scottish prophet Lailoken, who is identical with the figure of Merlin in many ways.

In the *Vita* this death is laid upon a sacrificial youth, who seems to stand for all mankind, and not directly upon Merlin. We find once again, that pursuit of a totem beast, the stag, plays an important part of the tale, as the youth dies while hunting.

King Bladud, however, flies through the air, like the sun, and crash lands upon the Temple of Apollo. This seems to be a reference or echo of solar and seasonal symbolism; his being dashed to pieces is reminiscent of a widespread myth in which a solar or saviour figure is dismembered to fructify the land. In both the Merlin and the Bladud tales, therefore, there is a theme of death which is connected to other mythical and magical sacrificial matters.

CONCLUSIONS AND DEVELOPMENTS

From all of the foregoing, we may list the following conclusions:

1) There is a connection between kingship and guardianship in British tradition deriving from primal Celtic belief. This connection appears in the twelfth century attached to the figure of Merlin.

2) In literary developments from Geoffrey of Monmouth through to the present day, the hereditary magical role of the king is increasingly attached to the prophet or magician in a manner that is not present in the earliest sources. Originally, we may infer, there was a working relationship between the prophet (symbolized by Merlin) and the king (symbolized by Vortigern or Arthur). The most primal figure that fuses the druidic and regal functions is that of King Bladud, who may indeed derive from a cultural period in which seer/druid/god were at one time identical.

3) For the modern student the sequence of imagery should be reversed as follows:

Arthur	High King
Merlin	Prophet
Bladud	God King

We may develop this theme by adding the linear personae such as Rhud Hudibras or Leir, who connect to Bladud, or the lineage of Arthur. In all cases, it is the figure of Merlin who combines the human and divine realms in one individual, due to his mysterious parentage, which is both mortal and immortal.

Arthur is born of mortal parents acting out a mysterious conception rite (the father in disguise), while the lineage of Bladud is clearly that of immortal or divine beings; Merlin, traditionally said to be born of a human virgin and a daemon or spirit, bridges the two realms.

But none of the foregoing is of any value without the root concept of a feminine power, the goddess of the land. She is explicitly present in early Irish legends, but later modified to the important pseudo-classical Minerva found in the works of Geoffrey. A number of other primal goddess forms are found connected to Merlin: Ariadne, a weaving goddess; an unnamed figure who encompasses the Land of Britain and transforms the Three Springs of Life, Desire and Death; and the mysterious Apple Woman who controls the poisoned fruit of prophetic madness.

To these feminine images may be added personae in the *Vita*, who have the dual role of human character and divine archetype: Merlin's sister Ganieda who is a powerful enabling figure steering Merlin's passage around the Wheel of Life; and Merlin's wife or sexual counterpart Guendoloena who has all the attributes of a Celtic Flower or Nature goddess. The first of these two equates to Minerva/Briggidda, while the second equates to Venus/Blodeuwedd.

We must always be aware that imagery and connectives such as those ascribed to Merlin, Bladud, and the Wheel of Life are not merely literary detective work. They are the foundations of a magical transformative tradition which is intimately connected to the environment. The value of such a tradition is not merely one of ancient lore, but has a potential for modern application. Such application may be either crudely political in terms of environmental activism, or more potent and pervasive in terms of individual meditation and inner rebirth.

The modern tendency of turning Merlin into a 'New Age' cosmic stereotype of a wise elder is extremely enervating and misleading; it suggests the ultimate end of the tale without any of the means, methods, or motivations whereby such an end may be brought into human experience. If we examine, even superficially, the source material for Merlin, which ranges from Scottish legends dealing with the prophet Lailoken to the medieval developments of Geoffrey of Monmouth, it is quite clear that he has a strong human element; the pseudo-mysterious spiritualized Elder is certainly not Merlin, whoever else he may be.

It is in this last context that the Wheel of Life is so vitally important to our understanding; only one aspect of Merlin, or one turn of the Wheel, corresponds to the wise elder. This one aspect must be balanced by the spiralling sequence of aspects and adventures under the inspiration of the Goddess, mediated through the archetype of the divine seer-king.

FURTHER READING

Listed here are ancient and classic texts, works of criticism, modern novels and plays. It is intended only as a guide to the vast literature on the figure of Merlin.

TEXTS

We have included here all the major versions of the Merlin story. There are others, in Dutch, German, Portuguese and Spanish. These are omitted on the grounds that they are mainly for a more specialist readership who will seek them out for themselves.

De Borron, Robert: *Merlin*, ed. A. Micha, Geneva: Librarie Droz, 1979.

Geoffrey of Monmouth: *The Life of Merlin (Vita Merlini)* ed. and trans. Basil Clarke, Cardiff: University of Wales Press, 1973.

Geoffrey of Monmouth: *History of the Kings of Britain*, trans. Lewis Thorpe, Harmondsworth: Penguin Books, 1965.

Heywood, Thomas: *The Life of Merlin*, Carmarthen: J. Evans, 1812.

Le Prophecies de Merlin, ed. L. A. Paton, London: Oxford University Press, 1927.

Lilly, John: *England's Prophetical Merline*, London: John Partridge, 1644.

Lilly, John: *Merlinus Anglicus Junior: The English Merlin Revised*, London, 1644.

Lovelich, Henry: *Merlin* (3 vols), London: Oxford University Press, 1904-32.

Malory, Sir Thomas: *Works* (3 vols), ed. Eugene Vinaver, Oxford: Oxford University Press, 1971.

Merlin, or The Early History of King Arthur (4 vols), ed. H. B. Wheatley, London: Kegan Paul, Trench, Trubner, 1865-99.

Merlin: Roman en Prose du XIII Siecle (2 vols), ed. Gaston Paris & J. Ulrich, Paris: Société des Anciens Textes Français, 1886.

Of Arthour and Merlin (2 vols), ed. O. D. Macrae-Gibson, London: Oxford University Press, 1973, 1979.

Prophetia Merlini of Geoffrey of Monmouth: A Fifteenth Century English Commentary, ed. C. D. Eckhardt, Cambridge, Connecticut: Medieval Academy of America, 1983.

Roman de Merlin, ed. H. O. Sommer, London: Ballantyne, Hanson, 1894.

Rowley, William and William Shakespeare: *The Birth of Merlin*, with additional chapters by R. J. Stewart, Denise Coffey and Roy Hudd.

Skene, W. F., ed. and trans.: *The Four Ancient Books of Wales*, Edinburgh, 1868.

Theobald, Lewis: *Merlin, or the Devil of Stonehenge*, London: John Watts, 1734.

CRITICAL WORKS

This is a selection only of the vast literature concerning Merlin. Many of these books themselves contain extensive bibliographies, listing many more studies.

Adkins, Nelson F.: 'Emerson and the Bardic Tradition' *Publications of the Modern Language Association*, 1948.

Adolf, Helen: 'The Esplumoir Merlin: A Study of its Caballistic Sources' *Speculum* 21, 1946.

Blackburn, W.: 'Spencer's Merlin' *Renaissance & Reformation* 4, 1980.

Colton, J.: 'Merlin's Cave & Queen Caroline' *18th Century Studies* 10, 1976.

Davis, Courtney: *King Arthur's Return*, London: Blandford, 1995.

Gollnick, James, ed.: *Comparative Studies in Merlin from the Vedas to C. G. Jung*, Lewiston, New York: Edwin Mellen, 1990.

Goodrich, Peter, ed.: *The Romance of Merlin*, New York and London, Garland Publishing, 1990.

Harding, Carol E.: *Merlin & Legendary Romance*, New York: Garland, 1988.

Jarman, A. O. H.: *The Legend of Merlin*, Cardiff: University of Wales Press, 1970.

MacDonald, Aileen: *The Figure of Merlin in Thirteenth Century French Romance*, Lewiston, New York: Edwin Mellen, 1990.

Markale, Jean: *Merlin l'enchanteur*, Paris: Retz, 1981.

Matthews, Caitlín: *Mabon and the Mysteries of Britain,* London: Arkana, 1987.

Matthews, Caitlín: *Arthur and the Sovereignty of Britain*, London: Arkana, 1989.

Matthews, John: *King Arthur and the Grail Quest*, Blandford, 1994.

Matthews, John: *The Unknown Arthur*, Blandford, 1995.

Matthews, John and Stewart, R. J.: *Warriors of Arthur*, Blandford, 1987.

Paton, L. A.: 'Merlin and Ganeida', *Publications of the Modern Language Association* 18, 1903.

Rich, Deike & Ean Begg: *On the Trail of Merlin*, London: Aquarian Press, 1991.

Stein, Walter Johannes: *The Death of Merlin*, Edinburgh: Floris Books, 1984.

Stewart, R. J., ed.: *The Book of Merlin: Insights From the Merlin Conference*, Poole, Dorset: Blandford, 1987.

Stewart, R. J. and Matthews, John: *Legendary Britain*, Blandford, 1988.

Stewart, R. J., ed.: *Merlin and Woman: The Book of the 2nd Merlin Conference*, London: Blandford, 1988.

Stewart, R. J.: *The Merlin Tarot* (illustrated by Miranda Gray), London: Aquarian Press, 1988.

Stewart, R. J.: *The Mystic Life of Merlin*, London: Arkana, 1986.

Stewart, R. J.: *The Prophetic Life of Merlin*, London: Arkana, 1986.

Stewart, R. J.: *The Way of Merlin*, London: Aquarian Press, 1991.

Tolstoy, Nikolai: *The Quest For Merlin*, London: Hamish Hamilton, 1985.

Contemporary Works

Countless modern Arthurian novels, plays and poems exist, and have been widely discussed, listed and catalogued. The list below is therefore only partial, and contains only those works which we feel are the best and which offer a comprehensive range of the materials available.

Berger, Thomas: *Arthur Rex*, New York: Dell, 1985.

Binyon, Lawrence: *The Madness of Merlin*, London: Macmillan, 1947.

Fry, Christopher: *Thor, With Angels*, London: Oxford University Press, 1949.

Furst, Clyde B.: *Merlin*, New York: Updike: 1930.

Hill, Geoffrey: 'Merlin' in *For the Unfallen*, London: Routledge, 1959.

Hildebrandt, Rita and Tim: *Merlin and the Dragons of Atlantis*, New York: Bobbs-Merrill, 1983.

Lawhead, Stephen: *Taliesin*, Oxford: Lion Books, 1988.

Lawhead, Stephen: *Merlin*, Oxford: Lion Books, 1988.

Lawhead, Stephen: *Arthur*, Oxford: Lion Books, 1989.

Lewis, C. S.: *That Hideous Strength*, London: Bodley Head, 1945.

Morland, Harold: 'The Matter of Britain', London: Graal Publications, 1984.

Matthews, John: 'The Story of Grisandole' in *The Round Table* 4: 1 & 2, 1987.

Muir, Edwin: 'Merlin' in *Collected Poems*, London: Faber, 1952.

Munn, H. Warner: *Merlin's Godson*, New York: Ballantine, 1976.

Newman, Robert: *Merlin's Mistake*, London: Hutchinson, 1970.

Norton, Andre: *Merlin's Mirror*, New York: Daw, 1975.

Nye, Robert: *Merlin*, London: Hamish Hamilton, 1983.

Powys, John Cowper: *Porius*, London: Macdonald, 1951.

Saberhagen, Fred: *Dominion*, New York: Tor, 1982.

Stewart, Mary: *The Crystal Cave*, London: Hodder, 1970.

Stewart, Mary: *The Hollow Hills*, London: Hodder, 1973.

Stewart, Mary: *The Last Enchantment*, London: Hodder, 1979.

Tolstoy, Nikolai: *The Coming of the King*, London: Bantam, 1985.

Trevor, Meriol: *Merlin's Ring*, London: Collins, 1957.

Yolen, Jane: *Merlin's Book*, New York: Ace, 1986.

White, Terence Hanbury: *The Once & Future King*, London: Collins, 1958.

White, Terence Hanbury: *The Book of Merlin*, London: Collins, 1978.

Wilbur, Richard: 'Merlin Enthralled' in *Poems 1943-1956*, London: Faber & Faber, 1957.

Williams, Charles: *Arthurian Poems*, The Boydell Press, 1991

INDEX

This brief thematic index is intended as a general guide to some of the themes and aspects of Merlin found in the book.